Beautiful Souls

The Awakening:

Beautiful Souls - Part IV

by

Hal Eisenberg

Some names and identifying details have been changed to protect the privacy of individuals.

Copyright © 2024 by Hal S. Eisenberg. United States. All rights reserved.

Creative Consultant and Edited by Allison Teicher-Fahrbach

No part of this book may be reproduced by any means without the prior written permission of the author, except for brief passages quoted in reviews.

Cover Illustration Copyright © 2024 by Fatima Farrukh
The author may be contacted at eisenbergleadership@gmail.com

ISBN: 9798300567019

Library of Congress Control Number:

Printed in the United States of America

First Edition

10 9 8 7 6 5 4 3 2 1

100% of the proceeds of Beautiful Souls will go to the mission, vision, and programs of Windows of Opportunity, Inc. (www.eisenbergacademy.org/wooinc) and The Passion Centre, Inc. (www.thepassioncentre.com)

Windows of Opportunity has built and implemented the world's first and most comprehensive education system for raising 21st Century leaders and engineering a society that is going to support them.

Windows of Opportunity's vision is that the world becomes one healthy community through higher consciousness education. The systemic approach promotes healthy communication to encourage trust-based relationships, which supports acceptance of each other and reduces fear to create an expressive, open society. This leads to people connecting to and expanding their souls through a higher love consciousness, which helps people live optimal lives and supports others to do so as well.

The Passion Centre is a collective of amazing people finding and activating people's passions, building dreams, and creating optimized humans. **The Passion Centre** acts like a Passion Incubator; we help people from all walks and stages in life understand their PASSION and turn it into ACTION to move the world forward in a positive way.

Each of us has a dream in our heart that the world needs. There are gifts that lay dormant, and passions that are unexplored. At **The Passion Centre**, we believe people's dreams, gifts, and passions are the world's greatest hidden economic and social resource. To that end we have made it our mission to help you find your gifts, activate your passion, and build that dream that you have inside of you. It's only when we focus on that place do we truly service the world.

Dedication

There is an energy behind this finale that I have only come to know as a higher love consciousness.

Dedicated to the soul who lifted me, carried me, mentored me, loved me, cried with me, celebrated with me, and continues to inspire me with every breath I take.

Queen Elizabeth II once said, "History is not made by those who did nothing." For those leaders, movers, and shakers before my time who inspired me, as well as the beautiful souls in my life making history every day through their acts of love and compassion. You are my heroes.

Namaste times infinity.

Contents

Dedication... vii
Acknowledgements x
Prologue 5
Part IV: The Awakening 8
   Chapter 1: The One that Got Away 10
   Chapter 2: Higher Consciousness..22
   Chapter 3: Refuse to Sink………………………………………51
   Chapter 4: Keep the Faith… 116
   Chapter 5: Always Just Another Day 134
   Chapter 6: This House is Not For Sale............................218
   Chapter 7: Carpe Diem... 248
   Chapter 8: You Gave Me Her 280
   Chapter 9: Home… 324
   Chapter10: Beautiful Souls… 440
   Chapter10.5: Between Faith and Destiny….........................468
   Chapter 11: Epilogue 474

About the Author..483
About the Windows of Opportunity 486
About The Passion Centre 488
Fatima Frk- Illustrator bio 490

Acknowledgements

In the original "War and Peace" version of this book, my acknowledgments extended to 20 pages. I was a bit overzealous and wanted to ensure everyone felt my love and appreciation. Perhaps that version will be an extra on the audible release of the Beautiful Souls series. For the sake of time and space, we are going to keep the acknowledgements short and sweet!

Scott - You are the greatest miracle and blessing anyone can ask for. Your birth into this universe gave me direction and an infinite amount of blessings. You saved me. The day you were born, the world changed colors, my eyes opened up, and you were a quintessential piece of my awakening. I love you dearly.

Vittoria - My gratitude is endless for the quiet encouragement, deep spiritual kinship, love, friendship, sustenance, and lifelines you provided during my journey. You never get the credit you deserve and you never ask for it. I cannot count how many times your tireless support had my back on those days I needed picking up. There are no words to truly express who you are and what you bring to the table in this crazy vision of mine! I love you dearly.

Allison - Nobody truly knows this - but this series would not have happened without you. Your ability to edit and process endless hours with me on what I wanted to say truly deserves sainthood. Your friendship goes far beyond the boundaries of what we call "COSTUSA", and is truly priceless. From the early church days of post-its on the wall to figure out this story to 6 A.M. phone calls when I had a spark of inspiration, you were always there to help me process these downloads. I am blessed that you have gifted me with all your talents and shared this journey with me. I love you dearly!

Kira - There are friendships, there are relationships, and then there are "soul" ships, and that is what we have. No words on this page can express the depths we have traveled in life and conversation. Your light and energy connected to my soul in a way that transformed and elevated me to heights unimaginable. Your guidance has been priceless, and I cannot express in words the energetic blessing it has been to be a part of your world. I love you dearly!

Leslie - Thank you for holding space for our souls to reunite and blessing me with your infinite compassion. I am eternally grateful!

Aunt Barbara – There are simply no words to express what it meant to be found by you. You never gave up on loving me even when all odds were against you. That is a value that will be **ingrained** in me for all of eternity. I sense you with me always, and I know you are my guardian angel, my bridge over troubled water. You are my unsung hero.

Morena – Thank you. I love you. May we all find the "Morena" in our souls.

The S.P.A.R.K. family (Sparkies) – You were the real deal… and real deals never die. Sparks can begin fires, and your fire is going to spread for generations to come. Thank you for creating the roots for an optimal approach to education **transformation**.

The WOO family (Woosters), and the thousands of names that put my vision, my dreams, and myself on the map - There are close to 600,000 souls to date that have found, and built their dreams within this vision, and provide me with the feeling of fireworks within my heart. There is nothing I have ever loved more than seeing each of you spread your wings, become leaders in your own right, and follow your passion into action, creation, and impact despite the odds. You are each my reason for being, and the consistent smile in my soul.

Regina – It feels like a lifetime ago when we sat on that cold floor in the studio kitchen, and you taught me what it was to have a dream and never give up. You planted the seeds of possibility and was there the day WOO sprouted. Thank you for being a rock star in my life, both literally and metaphorically. Your commitment to my souls' work, our band Outlet, and your endless unconditional acceptance and support is a blessing beyond what words could ever capture.

Timmy, Paul, Dave, Louie, Diane, Alex, Kasia, Kenny, Jane, Cheryl, Melinda, Nicole, Antonio, and Veronica – Thank you for being the embodiment of friendship, a symbol of hope, and my teachers throughout this journey. God Bless You. I love you with all my heart.

Every other soul whose path has crossed with mine – We all have a story behind the story, and it has been my greatest honor that our stories have shared some pages. Never give up. Always refuse to sink. And never stop dreaming big dreams. Keep the Faith!

This is not a story of rags to riches, but rather from lost to found.

"Remember that everything is one.
There's a beating in my chest from the sound of the drum.
We are warriors, peacekeepers of the land.
Stewards of the earth here to carry out a plan.
If everyone's connected, then reach out and take my hand.
The time has come and now we got to choose to make a stand.

- J Brave

Prologue

Patience is something that does not always come naturally, and yet when we let go and let the universe support us in its own way, we tend to find our way in return.

That's the funny thing about my story: I realize now that when I let go and just let certain things be, life became more fluid. As with the locks on the Erie Canal, my journey forward could not continue until the time was just right. If I had moved differently or rushed certain situations, I would have run aground, and my ship would take longer to sail forward.

When we have a foundation beneath us, we can move with purposeful force, intentional impact, and a means of understanding ourselves better.

Think about it for a second; when you are swimming in the water, you are able to go further when you push off of a wall or a solid surface.

I needed to build that solid surface in order to propel myself forward. I had to experience everything I did within my life in order to make it to where I am today.

We have the innate ability to conquer challenges that come our way and asking for support is often something we must do in order to be able to go with the flow.

Life sneaks up on you when you least expect it, however there can be so much more happening behind the scenes of the cinematic feature that is your character and your essence. Everything that makes you who you are, is being meticulously created in this universe, even when we least expect it.

If that sounds crazy to you, I understand that. Know that even in my most idealistic state of mind, I could have never fathomed what my life would become.

Each and every day that passes, I think about everything that happened within my life and brought me to where I am today.

With each event I process through, I am in awe of how one slight change may have prevented me from becoming who I am today. One little slip may have forced me to slide into something that would not have served my soul's true intentions.

Trust the process, trust in what this world has in store for you, and most importantly, trust in yourself.

Sometimes I wish I was this accepting of my life from the start.

I could only imagine where I could have been if I had been more open to experiencing life in all of its forms from the beginning.

However, I will never know if one little slip may have brought me into a deeper, darker world.

I guess I will never know.

All I know is that faith is something that is incredibly important to have; faith within ourselves, our experiences, and the world can create so many possibilities within our lifetime.

These are all truths that are self-evident to me now.

∞ ∞ ∞ ∞ ∞ ∞ ∞ ∞

All I knew at the time was that Faith was the answer to every prayer I had ever had.

She was the sun, and I was the moon, and oftentimes those roles changed. At times, we were contrastive opposites on a journey towards finding our respective selves. We were both yearning to find the most divine form of love ever known to the human world, yet we were clashing in more ways than could be imagined.

Sometimes love is composed of hugs and kisses, sometimes love is waking up next to someone who you helped bring into this world, and sometimes love is fighting for each other day after day.

Still, something was not adding up. Something was preventing us from being together at that time, and I wish I realized that sooner.

Faith's love tore me apart.

Her absence and fading presence made me feel that my affection was not worthy to anyone.

The manner in which she desolated me moment after moment, day after day, and night after night forced me into such dark places. Though in reality, I know that I allowed all of that to happen at the time.

I was preventing myself from seeing the truth, and though I am constantly venturing on this path of self-acceptance, I wonder if I have ever truly forgiven myself for what happened during Faith's appearances and disappearances.

Part IV: The Awakening

CHAPTER 1

The One that Got Away
~

"And these were our words. Our words were our songs. Our songs are our prayers. These prayers keep me strong, and I still believe."

- Bon Jovi, American Rock Band, Sayreville, New Jersey

Faith's absence left a gaping hole in what once was a broken, yet finally actualized, soul. I figured that maybe love was never going to find me. I assumed that maybe I was never meant to be in a relationship. Maybe, I surmised, I would always dance to the tune of being forever alone in my own skin.

Essentially, life was uncertain and I was on the verge of moving forward without a partner by my side.

For once in my life, that actually seemed okay.

A lot of people from Windows still didn't think I should give up so easily. Though they were not pushing me towards Faith, they were encouraging me to keep the faith. They told me that I should not give up and should keep looking.

Bryan would even chime in on what I should do.

"Dad," he would always begin with an endearing tone. "Why are you doing this to yourself?"

'What?' I would try playing stupid to deflect my emotions, but I could not shake the truth from my shoulders.

"Dad, you care about everyone else and you always look out for everyone," Bryan paused. "Who looks out for you?"

I didn't know the answer.

I mean, Morena had helped me through so much this far, but Morena was not close to the "power couple" image I had brewing in my head.

My soul was yearning for someone who could be my equal. I ached for someone who could complete me in every essence of the notion.

I found myself wandering the sanctuary day after day and night after night.

The stained-glass windows were drastically different at night, though the spiritual energy still lingered within the confines of the walls.

My prayers began to grace the walls of the church once again, as I searched my soul for what I should do.

I had been walking around with a heavy heart since losing Faith. It had been about six months of sorrow at this point, but with the New Year starting shortly, this sense of a "new beginning" did not fill my heart with hope.

I wondered: 'Will I ever have a good year? Will my life ever make sense?'

The One that Got Away

I sensed in my soul that I would not have been able to connect with God and develop my spirituality, if it were not for the love I felt with Faith.

Still, that notion needed to be swept to the side if I intended to find my purpose in life.

I needed hope. I needed strength. I needed answers. I needed-

At that moment a resounding thud from the far end of the room spooked me: someone was walking into the church.

Footsteps made their way up to the sanctuary as a voice crept around the corner.

It was Eve.

"What are you doing here so late?" She seemed stunned to see me there.

'Oh,' I dried my eyes. 'I was just, I was just praying.'

"Oh, okay." She looked at me blankly for a moment.

I sat in one of the pews and rested my chin on the one in front of me.

"Well, I will leave you to it." Eve retreated into the darkness as I heard her start rummaging through papers in the church's office.

The energy, the attraction, and the spiritual connection between Faith and I were so strong for so many years. I could sit and argue for hours that it was the ultimate love.

Why did things unfold the way they did?

What was I missing?

Was I ever really sure of anything?

I guess, in some way, it was supposed to happen that way.

There was something much bigger going on there and we were both being prepared for it.

She may not have been ready to face her demons, and I knew that I was also struggling, but it looked like there was no need for a partner in my life.

To trust someone again and bare my soul to the universe, well, that woman would have to be beyond special. There would have to be an overwhelming number of signs and unwavering strength from the universe in order to be with someone else.

I knew, somewhere deep inside, that Faith would return.

She always did before, but that time she was just taking longer than usual.

I had to pray. I had to process.

The door to the church slammed shut, and I could tell that once again I was alone with my thoughts. Eve left and it was just me, myself, the spirits, and the angels around me.

I felt the Circle of Angels there with me, although it appeared that I could not see their physical presence.

I felt blessed to have the sanctuary all to myself. The energy in the room spoke to my soul in ways that could never be articulated.

It was quite possible that Faith and I were really this incredible love story, and this was part of that love story.

Maybe whomever she chose to date would be a part of her development. Maybe what she went through as a child contributed to the woman she is today. Maybe seeing my life and experiencing it through her soul, and in return not being able to handle who we were, was part of our cohesive development.

Maybe, I figured, that is what relationships are all about: being a venue to learn about your own soul.

It sure did feel like a lesson was brewing in the strength of being alone. I did want to spend the rest of my life with her, but whatever will be will be.

If what we were going through then would help us maintain a solid foundation in the future, I figured, then we needed to be apart in order to grow. Our relationship would embody every essence of the word "faith."

There needed to be clarity. There needed to be a certain level of guidance.

As D.B. Harrop, a famous author, once said: "Have a big enough heart to love unconditionally, and a broad enough mind to embrace the differences that make each of us unique."

That being said, it is important to share your story and passions with the world. We are all on this road through life. We have all of these tremendous thoughts and feelings inside.

Why not get them out in the most beautiful and expressive ways possible?

Why not go for it? Well, whatever "it" is anyway.

∞ ∞ ∞ ∞ ∞ ∞ ∞ ∞

The One that Got Away

It had been quite a journey: a search for love, a discovery of faith, and a tale of finding yourself.

I have learned a lot of tough lessons, but I feel my soul has grown from it. Emotionally, I had been dragged through the mud and felt absolutely desolated at times, yet these experiences have molded me.

Every conversation matters. Every person I have encountered matters, and in hindsight, I realize I did not treat everyone in my life fairly, including myself.

I found myself pondering more questions while in my resolute and self-inflicted solitude: Where do our life stories come from? Who makes up your story?

Each person who has walked through my life contributed to my story, but can other people say the same?

I do not believe that the universe provides accidents. Relationships, whether good or bad, can waltz into our lives and create an avenue to learn something deeply about ourselves.

Moments, and people who grace each of our moments, all create a story of rare blessings. Sometimes we are able to see these blessings, while other times we shut these blessings out for we do not relish in all that they can become.

That is what happened between me and Alessandra.

∞ ∞ ∞ ∞ ∞ ∞ ∞ ∞

I believed life was all about love, and that love is an incredible energy. I think we attract people into our own lives when we emit similar energy, and like all things in life, energy changes from time to time. Sometimes you are in alignment with a person, and sometimes you just aren't.

I devoutly believe that is what happened between Alessandra and I.

When I was at an event that one of the after-school programs was running, a woman with flowing chestnut hair approached me. She was short in stature, but you could tell she had a big heart just from her approach.

"Hey, I was told to come to you, you're Scott, right?" The woman was perky and appeared to be excited.

'Yeah,' I kept fiddling with some paperwork. 'I'm Scott.'

"I'm Alessandra, I'm one of the volunteers here today."

'Okay, well, just sit tight and I'll let you know what we need.'

I did not mean to be curt. I did not intend upon Alessandra walking into my life, especially when and how she did.

Alessandra was watching me out of the corner of her eyes and twirling her hair around her finger. I was unsure of what to make of her, but I knew that she was watching me.

I looked up from the clipboard and asked if she was okay, but she just responded with a faint "Mm hmm" and continued watching me.

"Scott," one of the kids motioned for me to walk over to him. "That woman is totally flirting with you, do something, man."

I smiled and rubbed the back of my neck. 'No, she is not.'

"Yeah, man, she is. Go back there and ask her out."

'No,' I whispered and pulled him aside. 'I'm not dating anymore.'

"I know," the kid said. "So, ask her out."

I rolled my eyes and turned to head back over to the table, but she was directly behind me.

"Go on," she muttered. "Ask me out."

What was happening? Who was this woman?

Again, more questions flooded my head.

Alessandra sat and told me all about her passion for bands like Bon Jovi and Def Leppard, which was certainly up my alley, however I was filled with such trepidation about letting her in. She managed to slip her phone number into my pocket, and I sat in the sanctuary with the piece of paper in my hand, wondering if I should take a leap of faith.

I called Morena on my way to the church, and she somehow managed to make it there before I even left the event. When I arrived, Morena was patiently waiting on the steps outside of the church.

'I don't know what it is,' I looked over at Morena as I fiddled with the keys to the door. 'She seems like she is crazy about me.'

"Well, with all of your *endearing* qualities, it does not seem like a surprise." Morena tucked her hands in the back pockets of her jeans and followed me into the sanctuary.

I took my usual seat in the pews and began to pray.

'Can I emotionally handle this, Morena?'

The One that Got Away

Without skipping a beat, she moved closer to me: "Are you asking me, or are you asking your soul?"

Instantly, I grew defensive.

'I just asked you, Morena, did you not hear me?'

"Well," she did not return my unpleasant tone. "Ask yourself first. Then ask the world. Be comfortable in your own skin before you rush into getting hasty with someone else."

'I am not getting *hasty*,' I quipped at her.

She looked at me with her eyebrows raised.

"Okay," Morena plopped down a few pews away from me and began to run her fingers across the wood.

It was in those moments that I chose to take the leap of faith.

Within seconds, Alessandra's phone number was in my hands and I was calling her.

"Are you sure about that?" Morena chirped.

I paid no attention to her and continued to dial the number.

Alessandra seemed so happy to hear from me, and I was surprised that she seemed thrilled to actually hear from me.

We ended up scheduling a date together, for she had won Def Leppard tickets in some sort of MTV Unplugged contest.

In the days that followed, the two of us ended up on television since we were seated in the second row of the exclusive concert.

Occasionally during the concert, she would look over at me and smile. I thought it was creepy, but little did I know at the time, she was savoring our moments together.

At least I would like to think that was what she was doing.

Our mutual love for music led us to a Def Leppard concert at Coney Island in the baseball stadium there.

After the show, we had so much fun that neither of us wanted to go home. She was laughing and touching my arm repeatedly, which signified that she seemed quite interested in me.

Security guards kicked us off of the field after the end of the show, so we began to walk around the stadium until someone found us and told us to exit through a random door on the side. The two of us had no clue where we were, but the next thing we knew, we were staring down the members of Def Leppard.

Beautiful Souls

The two of us met the entire band and started to talk to them as if they were not celebrities. Rick Allen, the drummer of Def Leppard, began to chat with me about how his wife was from Queens. Alessandra and I tried containing our excitement, but you could tell she was in awe of the entire band.

Rick Allen and I began to talk about his charity agency, and I told them about Windows of Opportunity's Rock Your Heart Out music empowerment program. We spoke about how I would love his company and Windows to work together, he told me who to contact at his company, and at the next concert in their tour, Alessandra and I were able to get backstage again to talk about all of this.

Alessandra and I stood in Rick Allen's dressing room as the three of us spoke about his accident. As a kid, I was reading about how Rick Allen lost his arm in the newspapers, however I was actually getting a chance to hear about the story from his own lips.

To say it was an exhilarating feeling to be in the presence of one of your drumming heroes is an absolute understatement.

Despite losing his arm, Rick Allen continued to drum. Though he spoke about the pain, the struggles he dealt with, and overcoming his adversity, one message stood out in my mind: it is literally possible to overcome anything.

The heart and human spirit can create absolutely anything.

∞ ∞ ∞ ∞ ∞ ∞ ∞ ∞

Alessandra's fun and free nature helped me see myself in a different light, though I was not cognizant of how I was actually treating her. The way she adored me could be seen for miles, though I was still reserved and struggling to live within the confines of each of our special moments.

When we went to see Bon Jovi in New York City, she almost got stuck in the subway car door. The two of us laughed for hours, and the moment reminded me of that last day I spent with my Aunt Barbara.

Once we got to the concert, something drew me to the giant American flag in front of us that stretched out across the first ten rows.

The first song Bon Jovi performed, "Undivided," somehow tugged on my heartstrings. I did not know what it meant at the time, but I felt fully present in that moment.

The One that Got Away

I knew I would never forget that moment or that day. It would live in my soul for all of eternity.

Though we had been dating for months, every time I looked over at Alessandra, I did not feel what I felt with Faith.

It seemed as if Alessandra's love and companionship was a cheap version of the soul-enriching love I had with Faith.

Maybe that was my problem: I was too busy comparing Alessandra to Faith, that I didn't cherish her for who she was.

Alessandra tried to love me, but I was so sealed off from who she was at the time. The two of us had a beautiful picnic in the park once, and Alessandra even tried to set up a few surprises for my birthday. Though she knew I hated the day and everything it meant to me, she still tried to make me happy with a cake and my favorite snacks.

She desperately tried to be whom I needed, and she was perfect in every essence of the word, but I was not ready.

I blew it.

∞ ∞ ∞ ∞ ∞ ∞ ∞ ∞

Alessandra showed up at my after-school jobs quite often and slowly grew to hate the work I did. She was very jealous that I spent so much time with the kids, while I left her to fend for herself regularly.

She would show up, her jeans wrapping around her curves ever so slight, tapping her long fingernails against the doors and windows where I was teaching, pleading to know when I would be leaving work.

It got to the point where I wouldn't pick up her calls anymore.

Then it got worse:

She began sleeping very late, she started to call at all hours of the night, and she would cry when I would not give her attention.

To this day, I panic when it comes to balancing everything in my life.

I want to give people all of my love and attention, but it is hard to do that and to maintain my health at the same time.

The mounting stress swallowed every inch of our relationship.

Then she gave me an ultimatum: "Scott, it's all or nothing."

Those words stung my mind and continued to crush my soul.

Did I love her? I think so.

Did I show her? No.

I chose "Nothing."

She cried and left gifts at my mother's house in College Point, though I continued to ignore her and disregard her emotions.

Then, one day months later when I started to feel really sick, I started having heart problems. I figured I could fill the void of my loneliness by calling her and asking to be friends with benefits, but she slammed the phone down in my ear.

Alessandra was an awesome and perfect woman, but I did not appreciate her for all of who she was.

In hindsight, she was probably the most fun and exhilarating person who I dated, and when I say dated, I mean that I never did seem to fall into an "I love you" stage with her.

I was too naive at the time and too close-minded to see what she meant to me.

I will always regret how I treated her, and I hope that she realizes how much of an impact she had on my soul.

In a different time and in a different place, I am sure we would have worked, but I was too stupid to realize that.

The two of us were made for each other, or at least I think that is what could have been if I actually gave her love a chance, but I know I screwed up our love.

We had this odd story that proves how alike we were, though I am unsure if we were ever truly in alignment: the two of us would name squirrels that climbed around outside of our windows. When we were kids, we found solace and peace in nature.

It is unfortunate that our compassion could not transcend into a healthy relationship.

As the lyrics to "Blaze of Glory" from Bon Jovi flowed through my ears, I could not help but think about the perpetual impact that I was leaving on Alessandra's heart:

"You ask about my conscience
And I offer you my soul
You ask if I'll grow to be a wise man
Well I ask if I'll grow old

The One that Got Away

> *You ask me if I've known love*
> *And what it's like to sing songs in the rain*
> *Well, I've seen love come*
> *And I've seen it shot down*
> *I've seen it die in vain*
> *Shot down in a blaze of glory*
> *Take me now but know the truth..."*

I realized that I would always love Alessandra and that she would always hold a special place in my heart. She was the perfect girl, but the timing was definitely off. I do not know the damage I inflicted on Alessandra, but if she could see these words right now, I would apologize profusely.

I don't know what ever became of her story, though I am sure that she lived every moment of her life to the fullest, regardless of who was in her life.

In the sanctuary, I found myself praying and speaking to anyone who would listen again. Though I was very closed-off in the relationship I had with Alessandra, I still felt immense pain once I finally shut her out.

"Why don't you just speak to her one-on-one?" Morena stood at the edge of the pew, waiting for a response.

The words shot from my mouth like daggers ripping further into my soul.

'Why do you always have to start an argument, Morena?' spewed mercilessly from my lips, forcing the tears to the edges of my eyelids.

Morena sat in absolute silence. She pulled her sleeves down to hide the superficial scars that burned into her patiently distraught frame.

Everything she did was in slow motion: her eyelids turning downward before she cast her eyes towards the left, her pupils growing in size as she exhaled the pain, her slender sniffles hiding between the naturalistic breaths that expelled from her body. She was wholeheartedly broken to her core, yet she was resisting the urge to let the pieces go. She clung to them with such might, almost hoping that her existence would not be defined by another man's ignorance and misunderstanding.

Morena was brilliance and beauty wrapped into one, but the whole world casts a demeaning eye on a woman with passion and fervor coursing through her veins. Yet, something in her yelped.

It was a sign. It was a voice.

It was a resilient heart and a growing soul.

'Morena, what have you done to grow your soul today,' I quizzically awaited a response.

Clearing her throat almost instinctively, she glanced up and met my eyes: "What?"

'What have you done for yourself?'

"Scott, I…" she begged her soul to find the words she so truly needed to say, "I… I have never heard that question before. No one has ever asked, well, no… no one has ever asked me that."

A grin crept up, wrinkling her pristine cheek. Her tears melted away. Years of pain faded in between the breaths that escaped into the air.

Morena and I glared at each other for a moment. My hair fluttered in the wind as hers whipped around her line of sight. We kept walking through the trails of Alley Pond with purpose: growing our own souls through the small steps we would take. I told her she did not have to answer the question. I told her she could think about it. Still, an inquisitive side to her nature peeped between her drying eyes.

"Scott, let me ask you the same thing: what have you done to grow your own soul?" She wrapped her body around the billowing winds, catching a flighted sense to her aura in the process.

Her eyes glowed and her entire spirit took to the skies. At that moment, I had realized no one had asked me that, ever. Not a single person. Not a single lover from the past, spiritual or not. All it took to open my eyes was another broken, shattered soul… whose scars dove further than the depths of the ocean.

And there we stood, grinning like idiots in the woods, realizing that we both needed to wake up.

And dawn was on the horizon.

CHAPTER 2

Higher Consciousness

"Maybe there's a God above, but all I've ever learned from love was how to shoot somebody who outdrew ya. And it's not a cry that you hear at night, it's not somebody who's seen the light, It's a cold and it's a broken Hallelujah"

- Jeff Buckley, American singer, songwriter, guitarist, Anaheim, California

Beautiful Souls

Life changes when you realize that you should truly appreciate everything you have. Absolutely everything can change in the blink of an eye: your relationships, your health, and your mental well being… the list goes on and on.

Why is it that we have to lose what we have in order to genuinely realize what could have been?

I am not just talking about Alessandra, Faith, Elyza, Gemma, or any of my relationships. There is a bigger picture manifesting here, and I was blind to everything as I was living my life.

I was clinging to hope as a sort of hope-a-holic. Is that even such a thing? If so, that sounds utterly pathetic. I do not want to fix the world. I want to expand it. I want people to find their light and what they are made of. We need to shift systems, not change them. Life has to be translated from a disempowering mindset to an empowering one. So many systems need revamping.

Education is key because it springboards society into so many other systems. We have to start there.

I was scared though. I wondered, 'How do I give up fear?'

I always wanted to please everyone and that stopped us from growing as a company. The world was demanding my kindness and my soul, but I created that space. It brought me to ask: How do I stop it? I didn't want to stop helping people.

How could I balance it?

I couldn't let anything stop me. I couldn't let people mess with me. I couldn't let my heart be messed with.

I was scared to be alone.

How could I be what the universe intended me to be while dealing with what I had to deal with in everyday life?

How do you emerge from being just a raindrop in the ocean to being an entire wave?

I had lived my life in the reflection of all that I knew I could be: Standing in the shadows of a towering deity that exists solely in the eyes of the fallen, and a shattered existence wallowing in the puddles of self-pity and faltering righteousness.

I stood before people not as I knew I could be, but as a faint portrait of a masterpiece: a faded canvas scrapped long before the artist could ever paint his imagination onto the hearts of many and souls of few.

Maybe this was my fate.
Maybe this was the existence that was predetermined for me.
Maybe this was how the light burns out.

∞ ∞ ∞ ∞ ∞ ∞ ∞ ∞

In the shadow of my overwhelming depression, not many people seemed to remember I even existed.

It was interesting, since I worry so much about the feelings of others; I figured that my phone would be ringing off of the hook.

Though it wasn't.

In the end though, I know I will always care about people even if they do not care for me.

At the time, I probably didn't even have spare time to let things like that bother me at all. Life is way too short and I am getting a taste of that fear as I grow older.

If I did not awaken my soul and appreciate the small blessings, such as the people who loved me and go above and beyond for me, then my entire story would have ceased long before it needed to. There were still people in my life who tried to help me dig out of the funk I was in.

Morena would call occasionally, but I kept sending her to voicemail. Part of me worried about disappointing her or not being able to express myself to her.

As pellets of rain dripped down my skin, it felt that my memories were springing forward with such a violent force. It was as if the angels were saying, "Do you see the lessons? Do you realize your full potential? Are you hearing our messages?"

Through strife and struggle, I was blind to the ambition and growth circling around me. I was succumbing to the loss I was naturally accustomed to.

I lost my apartment in Bayside when the landlord passed away. He was an elderly man who was kindly renting out a basement apartment to me. Though it was illegal, it was small and it was a place where I could rest my head at night.

With my finances spinning out of control, because every penny I made was being funneled directly into Windows of Opportunity and its programs, I was homeless again.

Beautiful Souls

I moved my things into the attic of the Queens Community Church and slept in my Monte Carlo. Though the car was no place to call home, it was cozy and often warm.

It was supposed to be temporary, but I was not able to dig myself out of the financial turmoil I was already in. Money flowed right out of my pockets and into my programs' accounts. Students were succeeding while I was silently suffering, and I was okay with that.

My long nights of working in the church's office led me to pass out on the table, which eventually led to countless nights sleeping on the floor of Queens Community Church.

To try to maintain some semblance of hygiene, I kept a ratty old towel with me and washed up in the sink. I joined a local gym to shower each day, but I swallowed every ounce of pride I had left in order to keep moving forward.

I was surviving, not living, at this point.

I kept wondering: Did I forgive everything that happened with the lawsuit? Is that what was holding me back? I knew I had to forgive if I am to heal. My career was almost crushed, but things turned out okay, I made it through. However, I felt I lost my edge.

Life was different than it was before. I didn't feel good about it, I needed to commit to myself to feel better about everything, but I did not know how. I thought I was okay. Then all of that stuff happened with Faith. Then Alessandra.

I felt like people judged me silently.

How could I let go of this pain?

I was hurt and I was allowing that to be my primary focus. I was frustrated. I was too distraught. I needed to breathe.

It is okay to make mistakes. I know that now and I have made many. Vision without technique is blindness. I had to keep building on what I knew. I needed to follow my soul and the messages I was getting from the universe.

The world was occurring to me through the lens I had on, so I had to remember to change those lenses from time to time, or be open to the lens of other views, which led me to the fact that I needed to be open to changing my perspective.

That was the hardest part. I had to put myself in the places that gave me the most potential. I needed to work in a school or schools that allowed me to build and explore different concepts.

Higher Consciousness

I needed patience, planning, and perseverance. I had to value the person I worked with, as much as the work I did within a system that had to be created to support both simultaneously.

I knew if I could figure out how to connect with my passion, it would bring me to a deeper place of empowerment. I had to learn to reframe every challenge and problem into an opportunity and a blessing.

I had to stop telling myself I was wrong for my thoughts and my feelings.

∞ ∞ ∞ ∞ ∞ ∞ ∞ ∞

For months, I caught myself dreading the fact that I had to leave work. I was preoccupied with work and inspiring youth during the day; however, I hid away in the catacombs and attic of a building I hoped could one day house countless youth programs.

One night in the midst of the summer, I was sweating profusely in the church attic. The air was oppressive and stale, and I could not tell if I was struggling to breathe due to the atmospheric pressure or the weight of my own choices.

Somehow, I managed to fall asleep, only to wake up to a faint "Hello" drifting throughout the sanctuary.

I gathered my things hurriedly and began to dart down the stairs as quietly as possible. Though as I made my way down the steps, I was met with two panicked eyes staring back into my own.

"Scott, for heaven's sake, it is just you," Paul smiled.

'Sorry to startle you, I was just getting some work done.'

Paul glanced at the clothes and various toiletries in my hands.

"I see," He sounded skeptical.

'Yeah, so I will just be on my way.'

As I passed him, he gripped my arm.

"How late were you here, son?"

'I-' I didn't know what to say.

"It is 5:30 in the morning now. Were you here all night?"

Again, I did not know what to say. I finally got caught, and I didn't have any answers for him.

Paul softened his glance and put his hand on my back.

Beautiful Souls

"Son," he motioned to the pews in the sanctuary. The two of us found a place on the pew to the right of the doors. "You are not in trouble."

'Okay,' I quivered slightly. I was not sure what he was going to say next.

"I want you to know that Queens Community Church is your home. *We* are your home. I never want you to feel as if you can't spend time here." In a way, I think he sensed I was homeless and in need of a place to lay my head.

After those moments, we chatted for a bit about the next adventure for Windows of Opportunity, and he discussed how he was so proud that I was a part of the community.

"You truly do put the unity in opportunity, Scott," Paul joked.

I helped him set up the sanctuary for some sort of morning event they were having in a few hours, then I was on my way.

I sensed that Paul always knew about the sacrifices I was making on behalf of youth and Windows of Opportunity, yet he never wanted to say anything. I did, however, usually come "home" at night to a cool or warm attic depending on the season, which meant that he must have turned on the air conditioning or heat in the church before he left for the night. I didn't want pity, for that does not help. A helpful space needs to be empowering, and Paul helped give me that space.

His soul knew that I was in need of some silent compassion, and he happily snuck in a few acts of kindness when he could. We all have gifts and a purpose. We all have something to deliver in this world, no matter how big or how small. Each moment in our life acts as a chance to express what we are capable of doing.

This was a commitment of an entirely different kind. This was not a job. This was integrity. This was not a display of morals.

This was my human spirit showing up.

I was going to do what I said I was going to do. I was going to deliver some sort of plan. I was going to make sure I am always aligned with my principles. I was going to speak up for what I stand for. I was going to get support from the universe. I knew that the right team would come. I told myself I would shift the education system and other systems connected to it. I would manifest change in society. I would stick to my guns. The universe is a world of enrollment and it had enrolled me to shift the education system.

Higher Consciousness

I felt that in my soul.

Still, I wondered, how do I create a platform for change while allowing my soul to continue to emerge?

We must empower souls.

I pondered: How do we access other people's power and my own power simultaneously?

What do I stand for?

What do people stand for?

Is that where they find their power?

I would look at myself in the crusted-over church mirror and ask: 'Do you walk the talk or just spout out thoughts?'

I think I did a little bit of both, but I needed to make a stand to forge ahead.

Why was I scared of my own voice? Perhaps because I was always told I was wrong or not made to feel good enough?

I got so upset because I knew deep down my intentions were true, but I did not know how to keep feeling my inherent power. I did not know if anyone would listen to my voice, though hypocritically I taught everyone to have their own.

I needed to go within and listen.

People ridiculed me, including myself. I did not know how to stop listening. When people ridicule me, can I recognize the issues that come up in myself? If people can do this on a larger and less-demeaning scale, then we can overcome and lift ourselves to new heights.

I knew I was not a bad person, though the ghosts of my past made me think I was.

I always fell short. Was that my intended legacy?

Sometimes, I am my own worst enemy.

On those silent July days when the sanctuary was slightly illuminated by the rising sun, I would find myself pacing the pews and talking about my ambitions.

I wanted to be the shift, the devout answer; I wanted the universe to create through my existence.

I had pages and pages of goals for WOO. Among them was the expansion of programs, creating a movement, raising money, running events and conferences, and being in more schools and getting in front of thousands of youth to inspire them.

I saw it clearly at the time and I didn't at the same time. I needed a new lens to see what I wanted to transcend. I did not want to be part of the problem. I did not want the problem to be my identity. I wanted to be the expansion of that thought.

I was so tired. Could I do it all?

There are two different types of tired: tired as in the idea that I am mentally exhausted and weary, and the other idea is the idea of being so tired that I need to let go of the fight. I did not want to let go of the fight when I had not made it to the battlefield yet. Then again, was there a battlefield, or was it just a figment of my imagination pushing me to see something else?

A truly open mind is the rarest thing on this planet. That is the mind I wanted. I wanted to defy logic and break the boundaries that society saw as the norms. This is in leadership, communication, and in love.

I wanted the abnormal as normal. Within that field of comprehension rests the truth of the soul.

What woke me up on the hardest days of my life to do the work that I do?

It was my vision for humanity and the search for a love I knew had to be out there, but I couldn't believe if it was true or not.

Is there such a thing as blind faith or should it be faith with inquiry? Should we continue to go deeper and search for more answers?

I wondered how do I incorporate that into my programs?

My programs are great, but this Project Evolve venture made me feel like there was more. I was linked to the concept and I was building it out, but there was another level here to reach for but I couldn't figure it out yet.

I wondered: Is the relationship between whatever you see: God, the divine, the universe, Allah, at a level of higher consciousness? There could be if you open your mind up and connect in that manner.

If I did not take action at that point, then was I condoning this broken system permeating society? If anything is possible, then nothing is impossible. Right? Or was I fooling myself? I had spent months on this.

I hardly saw the light of day except to see my clients and run my programs.

Nobody saw how depressed I was, for I merely lied and wore a mask.

Higher Consciousness

I was lost. I needed help. I needed a deeper spiritual type of help. I wanted to be there for humanity. I had all these ideas laid out in hundreds of pages and books in front of me in the church.

I had been in there for months just obsessing on building this dream.

I wanted to move beyond my story. I was co-existing with the pain and the loss of my Aunt and every relationship after that.

How do I stop the pain? How do I finish my silent grieving? I kept picking at the scab on my heart, which could not seem to heal.

My life had become my project.

I wanted to break the boundaries of my life and what society settles for. It would be a bigger crime to know you can change a system and not even try... I implored upon the universe: Can you bring me the right support and people to help me?

In the midst of this series of questions that fluttered through my core, I did not realize that the subtle noises behind me were that of another human being.

She stood there in the shadows of the stained-glass windows, just watching me ruminate and create images before my very existence.

"You don't pick up my calls anymore, why?" I turned and saw her.

Morena's hair was shorter, her frame taller, and her voice more confident.

'Oh hey,' I was slightly caught off guard again.

"Hello Scott." She crossed her arms and made her way up the aisle.

The two of us sat on the altar and she began thumbing through all of my notebooks. It was almost as if months had not passed since the last time we saw each other or spoke.

'What are you doing here?' I looked at her quizzically.

"You have vision, you have ideas, and you are hiding from the world. I see it, Scott." She did not sound angry, rather she sounded determined.

I motioned to the papers before me: 'I am leadership. I embody faith. I represent an idea... or are they just masks that I wish were real. I have to stand in my power and allow people to stand in their power. This is Windows of Opportunity.'

Morena looked on in silence, just allowing her eyes to graze over everything.

"There are stories behind every story," She finally said.

'How does that play into this vision and into what I want to inspire on this planet?'

The two of us sat there, mainly in silence, reading through pages and pages of notes I had sprawled out across the floor. A piece of paper with a single quote flew from one of the pages:

> "The work which is most likely to become our most durable monument, and to convey some knowledge of us to the most remote posterity, is a work of bare utility; not a shrine, not a fortress, not a palace, but a bridge."
> - Donald Langmead

At that moment, I needed that message. I thought to myself what other messages would spring forth from this seemingly perpetual darkness I was entrenched in.

Time would have to fill in the rest of that tale.

∞ ∞ ∞ ∞ ∞ ∞ ∞ ∞

When I woke up the next morning in the attic of the church, I was alone. The floor was cold, which was a nice juxtaposition to the intense humidity floating through the air. I rolled over in my own puddle of sweat, only to find a quote resting on a scrap of paper:

> "Until one is committed there is hesitancy, the chance to draw back, always ineffectiveness. Concerning all acts of initiative and creation there is one elementary truth the ignorance of which kills countless ideas and splendid plans: that the moment one definitely commits oneself, then Providence moves too." -
> W.H. Murray, The Scottish Himalayan Experience

It really made me think about how long I had spent wallowing in a sea of questions, yet I was devoid of pursuing answers.

I had so much potential, though I found myself trapped in expectations and a fractured reality. The skills, gifts, and talents I had ran rampant through my veins, though my heart was not beating in tune with any of those aspects.

Something told me that I desperately needed a change of scenery: it had been years since the lawsuit was over, yet I felt like its shadow was clinging to my body.

Grace, the woman who I met at United Global Shift in Toronto not long before the brunt of the lawsuit came to its ultimate conclusion, called hoping to chat with me. As the two of us spoke and caught up, she told me to come visit her in Canada. She told me she was living at a place called the Sunshine Coast and that I was welcome to come stay by her as long as I would like.

Those fateful words, "All you have to do is pay for your flight up here, I'll take care of the rest," were what drew me in.

I wanted a sign from the universe, and here it was: a new adventure was placed before me.

I wasn't sure what to expect and went into this whole idea of Grace's without any expectations.

I was so exhausted from the whirlwind of events that took place over the past few months. Between the internal pressures and external stressors plaguing my soul, I figured I had no time to bask in the anxiety I was feeling.

Had I really sat down and thought about it, I would have let my past heartbreaks stop me from wiggling in this experience that was about to happen.

However, there are no coincidences, and I am learning that rapidly. Faith was gone, Alessandra was becoming a fleeting memory, and I had to heal from the shattered situations I was a part of. There is a certain oddity that exists in running from the situation I was in, but maybe God was giving me this moment in order to fully embrace the closure I so desperately needed.

Within a week, my flight was booked, Morena was tasked with watching over Windows of Opportunity, and my mind was set on growing. The type of growth I expected, however, was holistically unknown to me.

After months of running on fear and adrenaline, I ended up passing out on the plane to Canada. It was a detox from society of sorts, for the Sunshine Coast would prove to be a rather isolated region.

∞ ∞ ∞ ∞ ∞ ∞ ∞ ∞

Beautiful Souls

As my feet hit the runway in Vancouver, butterflies spread throughout my stomach. I was so nervous and I didn't really know why.

Once I walked out of the customs area and saw her, Grace's gentle embrace made me feel as if everything would be okay. I wanted to see where she was from and where her incredible spirit came from. The two of us walked around and began to engage in philosophical conversations about life. Grace happily obliged to act as a tour guide, and it was nice to be a visitor of sorts for once.

The two of us ate at a quaint French restaurant, where the aromas of fresh bread and exquisite cuisine flooded the air. It was an elegant change of pace from eating leftover Chinese food from a Styrofoam tray in a church attic.

As the night came to a close on our first day venturing around Vancouver, Grace informed me that I would be staying with a friend of hers during my trip. She explained that a family member of hers would be staying at her house, and her close friend had a spare guest room where I could stay.

At first, I was nervous. I travelled all the way to another country, another coast, and another time zone, and the only familiar face I knew would be a few blocks from where I would be staying.

When the two of us walked up to her friend's house, I saw a series of windchimes swaying in the patient atmosphere. There were faint melodies from the soft metallic clanking, which seemed to wrap around the house that ushered me towards the front door. Grace's high heels clicked against the wooden planks on the porch.

"You coming?" She said, turning to meet my wandering eyes.

'Yeah,' I practically skipped up the steps to this whimsical house.

I took a deep breath as she knocked on the door, for I felt anxious about meeting her friends.

A short-statured man appeared before me, his gray hair askew and his sweater slightly covered in crumbs of some sort.

"Oh dear, Grace," he began to brush himself off. "I am so sorry, I fell asleep on the couch. Please, come in." He stepped aside and allowed both of us to pass.

Grace gave him a big hug as she walked past; it seemed that they were very good pals who were thrilled to see one another.

Higher Consciousness

I looked around his brightly colored living room, which was dimly lit by candles and faint lamps. The man extended his hand and placed his hand on the side of my right arm:

"I'm Sam, welcome to our home," he grinned.

'Our?' I asked quizzically.

"My wife, Hannah, will be home shortly. She is out delivering some goodies to our neighbors," Sam took a seat on the couch and motioned for Grace and I to do the same.

I was skeptical for a moment, but his mannerisms and his spirit were rather open.

"I do not know what Grace has told you," he began to sip from a teacup to his left. "But I am a medium."

'Oh, no,' I was unsure of what to say. 'Grace didn't give me too much information.'

"That's okay," Sam spoke softly. "It gives us a chance to have a more enriching conversation about our souls."

Our souls; it was the way he said it that struck me with a certain sense of nostalgia mixed with serenity. The three of us began to talk about New York City and my life in, as Sam called it, such an urban paradise.

The entire evening was incredibly spiritual, and he even started to talk about how my aunt was my guardian angel.

A general warmth rushed over my soul, for I knew it was the truth.

When a woman with blonde and white streaks in her hair entered through the front door, the energy shifted in the room. It felt as if all of the plants adorning the walls turned to greet her.

"Hello, you must be Scott," the woman dropped her bags on the floor and rushed right over to me. "I'm Hannah."

The woman didn't hesitate a moment, she just threw her arms around me and embraced me. It was as if she sensed the pain within my soul.

The four of us engaged in such lovely conversations about growth and empowerment until Grace fell sound asleep on the couch. She curled into me as if my warm body had a gravitational force over her exhausted frame.

Sam threw a blanket over her and told me to just turn off the lamp beside me before going to bed for the night.

I took a stroll over to the window as Grace's faint breathing lulled my heartbeat into a sense of belonging. The moon glistened as its light struck

Beautiful Souls

the water. For once, I felt that I could have a good night's sleep despite the continuous chirping of wind chimes that swayed outside the open window.

My shoes made a muffled clunking noise on the floor, and that was the last thing I remember hearing before my head hit the pillow and I passed out.

∞ ∞ ∞ ∞ ∞ ∞ ∞ ∞

The next morning, I woke up to the smell of blueberry pancakes drifting into the room. Hannah was hunched over a frying pan in the kitchen pushing a metal spatula around to scrape all of the batter from the edges of the Teflon.

"Good morning, how are you?" Hannah didn't even look up from the pan, it was almost as if she sensed my presence.

'Hi,' I groggily made my way over to her and sat on a stool next to the counter.

Hannah plopped the plate in front of me as the scent of pancakes rose to meet my exhausted face.

"Eat," she grinned. "Grace woke up earlier and she said she'll be right back… but first, breakfast."

Hannah edged the plate towards me again.

Though I met Sam and Hannah just the night before, I felt as if they had been a calming presence in my life for years.

After nibbling on the delicious pancakes, Grace re-entered the house and greeted me with a genuine smile. Within minutes, the two of us were out and about on a walking tour of Gibsons, another coastal town filled with smiling faces.

We waltzed through the streets and down to the beach. The two of us eventually ended up eating lunch at a pleasant local seafood place called Smitty's, where lobster and fried clams were fresh and bountiful.

Once we ate, the two of us walked down to the boardwalk where we saw an inscription before us in chalk. It said, "Before I die, I want to…" and people were lining up to respond to the statement with chalk.

Grace wrote three words in front of her toes: "Change the world."

I didn't even hesitate when she passed me the chalk. I wrote, "Make a real difference in our world with a great team around me."

Higher Consciousness

Hours later, Grace dropped me off at Sam and Hannah's house and explained that she had to visit with her current houseguests. Without missing a beat, Hannah wrapped her arm around mine and said that I could go to dinner with her, Sam, and Hannah's younger sister.

They didn't really know me, yet they treated me like family. It was pure unconditional love.

The third day I was there, I woke up to Hannah and Sam leading a peaceful meditation just beyond their back porch. A few neighbors of theirs were sitting with their legs folded in the lush greenery that sat in the middle of their backyard. I looked on with my curiosity peaked, only to be brought into the circle as Sam motioned for me to join them.

That afternoon, Grace and I sat in on a prayer circle experience that Sam and Hannah were hosting. It was unreal. I felt the positive vibrancy in the words from the souls in the circle, as about twenty-five of us sat around. My mind wandered into a deep trance until I saw a white light, the sunrise, and doves fluttering above my head.

Sam later explained to me that it may have been Jesus giving me a blessing, and that the dove was a symbol of inner peace. I loved the energy and spirit emulating from this entire experience.

Maybe this is what I needed to recenter my soul in the context of this universe.

Though I felt myself missing Faith dearly, I tried to control my tears.

Hannah must have sensed my deep sadness, as she pressed a reassuring hand on my shoulder.

"It's okay to let go," Hannah whispered.

'I know,' the tears began streaming down my face. 'I did, and that is why I am crying.'

∞ ∞ ∞ ∞ ∞ ∞ ∞ ∞

The next day as Grace apologized to me for having to leave; I told her that it was totally okay. I had not booked a flight back to the United States, nor did I know how long I was going to stay, but Hannah and Sam assured me I could stay as long as I wanted.

I loved the energy there and something told me not to leave as of yet.

Sam walked me down to the beach, where plenty of people from the town were resting on the sand. As the two of us left our footprints in the sand, he pointed out the Inuk, or Indian sacred rocks, where I would eventually have spiritual, soul-searching conversations about who I was while sitting around the rocks.

People were waving at us and calling out our names: it was your typical small town feel, where almost everyone knew each other's names. Though I was just there for a few days at this point, people were greeting me by my name.

We ended up going kayaking on the Pacific Ocean, and I could swear I was living out the scenes from *The Notebook*.

People looked on as we navigated through the water and made our way towards what was beyond the land we were encircled in.

As we passed the last bit of land we could see, I looked out at the sheer expansiveness of the ocean. The sight of the calm waters and the deep midnight blue ripples beyond Canada made me realize that there is an entire world beyond the horizon. We may not always see what is beyond our shores, but life exists past our perception.

I had to remind myself that.

In the few days I was here, I was learning more about myself, my power, and who I truly am despite being so far from, "home." It was something about the majestic beauty of Canada that seemed to recenter my soul.

Growth is genuinely incredible.

"Hey," Sam shouted as he was drifting through the water.

'Hey,' I smiled back at him.

"Scott, it is okay to struggle," he began. "Just don't live in that struggle for too long."

It was almost as if he could feel the pain leaving my body and floating away.

"Trust the process, just trust the process." Sam turned his kayak around and I could hear the plastic sloshing in the water. I turned my kayak as well and we ventured back to the shore.

The two of us were silent as we retreated to the dock. I spent every moment embracing the sound of the water and the warm sun beaming on my face. Sam began talking to me as we paddled back, but he told me that I should listen and not reply right away.

"Patience," he muttered softly.

We spoke about my Circle of Angels, my Aunt Barbara, and all of the light that encompassed my soul. He encouraged me to love myself and support myself, as the angels were attempting to do the same.

"Your soul is so full of light," Sam's eyes glistened as the sun glazed across them. We spoke about my evolution of faith and love, and how true, divine love was out there.

'Divine love?' I perked up.

"Listen to the water, not the words," he recommended.

Sam seemed to close his eyes and let the water just guide him. He continued to discuss the enlightenment I was about to embark upon and the blessings I would receive shortly.

I had studied a lot of different schools of thought at this point, but divine love was new to me.

As we approached the dock, the two of us were greeted with an eloquent view of Robert's Creek. I could see elaborate swirls and rock formations as we stood on the wooden planks. The swirls spoke to me in a manner that was spiritually awakening. It was as if the universe was trying to talk to me, but I was unaware of what it was saying at the time. Before we stepped onto the kayaks, I don't think I truly appreciated the symbols, swirls, and intricacies before, but I had a new appreciation for them.

It was almost as if I had to travel beyond the beautiful scenery, then return in order to truly cherish what was before me. The vivid colors were soothing to my soul, and I could feel my soul spiraling between the swirls and the spaces between them.

When Sam and I returned to his humble home, we spoke more about divine love. He explained that it was a school of thought as opposed to a religion. The entire concept seemed philosophical and spiritual in nature.

Though Hannah was cooking something enticing in the kitchen, she even chimed in on the conversation: "We have the ability to love one another, to feel one another, to provide for one another, and genuinely raise the bar of our life's true purpose."

I heard each of the words flowing from her mouth, and for once there were a series of statements I could genuinely resonate with.

My mind was exhausted, and though I spoke with God and my angels often, I am not sure I was fully connected to them. I was lost. The pain in

Beautiful Souls

my heart radiated to other parts of my body, and I tended to lose myself in the midst of what is and what could be.

I sensed I had a spiritual calling to visit this place.

So many people rely on me for emotional support and comfort, yet what happens when I am holistically unaligned with what I so truly want and need in this universe?

I was suffering. I was in the depths of an intense spiritual pain.

I was in desperate need of salvation.

Has God put me through this as a preparation for what is to come on this next journey?

∞ ∞ ∞ ∞ ∞ ∞ ∞ ∞

The lyrics to "More than Words" by Extreme fluttered through my head:

> *"Saying I love you*
> *Is not the words*
> *I want to hear from you*
> *It's not that I want you*
> *Not to say, but if you only knew*
> *How easy it would be to show me how you feel*
> *More than words is all you have to do to make it real*
> *Then you wouldn't have to say that you love me*
> *'Cause I'd already know."*

Love exists beyond words. The song anchors me to a time when I was leaving a hardware store with Faith, who seemed like she was about to become my girlfriend at that time, and we sang the words to that song in unison.

It seemed like an intense bonding of love. It seemed like an expression of love.

Yet time said otherwise.

"Be patient" hung at the tip of my tongue, almost as if Sam was inside my head and ushering me to a certain train of thoughts.

Though I felt that I was utterly derailed from ever finding love.

My ego was interrupting the bigger picture here.

I woke to another beautiful morning on the Sunshine Coast feeling disconnected; yet rested. What was happening to me?

Everything within my core felt as if it were on fire. I was nervous, nauseous, but I felt that I was at peace for a change.

Hannah was standing in the kitchen watching me flicker my eyelids open.

"You have a special angel assigned to you, her presence is strong," She was looking directly at me.

'Oh, thank you,' I was unsure of what else to say.

Why do I have an angel? Who is my angel? Why was I so special?

Moments later, Sam motioned for me to join him on the porch, to which I automatically drifted towards him.

"Your life will be very different in four years' time," he spoke softly again. It was almost as if he whispered his thoughts into the universe, hoping they would soon come true.

He liked to drop insightful comments in my direction, but somehow, they were a window to my soul.

'Maybe in four years I would be married' was the first thought that popped in my head.

Sam must have known what I was thinking, for he just smiled and averted his glance to the water.

I had slept well, but Faith's memory and "More Than Words" lingered in the forefront of my mind.

Sam invited me to join in a prayer with a number of visitors they were having, to which I happily obliged. Something magical was happening.

Suddenly, I felt filled with love.

Hours later, I found myself, Sam, and three other people walking around in the Soames Woods. I loved walking in nature and having talks about spirituality. It felt natural and quintessential to the growth of my soul.

It became obvious: I had to take care of my soul and build a strong foundation for my emotions before I let my mind crumble.

Divine love, this new school of thought, was the way.

While walking on the trails, I felt as if the trees were parting to let us travel through the landscape.

When we emerged from the woods, more people came to join us in a prayer. The faces of strangers suddenly felt like family, though in an altered sense. We were bonded by mutual thought, not by blood, which represented how devoutly we were committed to growth.

It had always been my soul's mission to help people and raise the spirits of those around me, though I never knew what that looked like until Elyza helped me hone my passion for helping youth.

The experiences I was a part of on the Sunshine Coast were a holistic representation of spiritual growth. Divine Love was a school of thought I was being exposed to, and I was an eager student.

I soon found out that Divine Love was not something automatic, nor was it guaranteed when a person passed from this life to the next.

Apparently, as we pray for our Father's love, we help our loved ones in the next realm. As a result, we then help grow our souls and those around us.

I was blessed to learn this knowledge from such enlightened people. There was no exchange of funds or membership; the only currency that was required was being open-minded.

It is a true community.

∞ ∞ ∞ ∞ ∞ ∞ ∞ ∞

Upon getting out of the shower the next morning, I felt more refreshed than usual. My showers in New York had been quite scattered during the past few months, and I could feel the difference between sloshing a ratty sponge in the sink of the church versus the cool, calming waters of Canada rushing down my spine.

My skin and hair felt different, but no one seemed to notice or comment on it.

I tend to think that most people are not cognizant of their surroundings. At this point, I all but lost track of the time I had spent here so far, but Sam and Hannah continued to welcome my presence in their home.

I had been an active participant while here, but I was taking everything in and absorbing the energy here at the same time.

Back in New York, I was balancing the relationship between Windows of Opportunity, the Queens Community Church, and myself. Oftentimes, this balance did not suffice for my soul or my innate sense of self, for everything happening around me seemed more important than what was going on in my own head.

At this point in my journey, I realized that the small arguments I would have with people in New York were inundated with negative energy and detrimental spirits that encompassed many.

I am sure that upon first glance, this whole experience and school of thought seem to be inundated with hocus pocus, but this is all far beyond that.

Divine Love is a series of questions and thoughts that augment upon each other to create a better sense of our respective souls.

How do we truly give our souls more space to explore developmental thoughts and notions?

How do we become more positive, more loving, and strengthen our souls to overcome difficult situations and live a higher form of existence?

We need a communal place to speak and express ourselves.

Step one of any journey should be to love ourselves. Though I did love who I was, it took me many years to comprehend that I am more than my circumstances.

The past is just a series of moments that surmount to strength.

Though I realized that I deeply regret a lot of what I had caused or experienced in life, I discovered that everything was building to help me become a better man.

I continued to listen to Sam, Hannah, and the community they were building there. With every prayer or soul-searching activity we did, Sam encouraged us to create questions we would ask God. Though we were limited to just five questions, my mind succumbed to my usual inquisitive nature.

My mind was racing.

I began to think about what God would intend for me and my life. How would my personal growth flourish in contrast to the souls around me? Are prayer circles and lightworkers the answer? Can a small group of people impact the world on a large scale?

Does change exist?

Can I be strong enough for this world?

"Scott," Sam murmured. "Just five questions, son."

Beautiful Souls

I had not realized I shut my eyes for what must have been about thirty minutes, so that my thoughts could stir up a series of questions.

The impact of that day is something I would not soon forget. It was a powerful and spiritually deep day that I still process in my mind.

There we were, about twenty different souls, overlooking scenic mountains and the calm waters nearby.

Within my mind I kept asking questions, though I discovered that in order to develop my soul, I had to strip away the ego deep inside of me.

I sensed the shift in energy that my soul was experiencing.

I sensed my Aunt Barbara was with me.

∞ ∞ ∞ ∞ ∞ ∞ ∞ ∞

In the days that followed, Sam spoke about how our planet was in trouble and that our work truly matters.

As I expressed my opinions within the group, I found that seemingly total strangers wanted to hear my story.

While sharing an abbreviated version of what I had endured, most people were stunned or leaning into my discussion; it was almost as if I suddenly became a centre of light.

Maybe I was a beacon of hope.

As I spoke about my past relationships, Sam gripped his fingers around his knees and glared into my eyes.

"Scott, you will find love soon," he sounded solemn, but very reassuring.

Afterwards, I walked around for what seemed like hours. His words rumbled in my mind as an avalanche of unanswered questions. Who was he talking about? Was there truth behind his words?

∞ ∞ ∞ ∞ ∞ ∞ ∞ ∞

Something was bothering me and I was not sure what unbalanced my soul. I figured maybe New York was not the place for me. Maybe I had a life in Canada. Maybe I was just lost.

I wondered, 'Will I ever find my way home?'

∞ ∞ ∞ ∞ ∞ ∞ ∞ ∞

Higher Consciousness

Sam and Hannah continued to lead prayer circles and discuss the innate gifts each soul has within.

I could tell, as we all sat in silence, that something shifted in the depths of my core.

It was time to return to New York.

I booked my flight for the following morning, and promised to keep in touch with Sam, Hannah, and the community on the Sunshine Coast.

On my last day of my trip, there were plenty of moments filled with gratitude, tears, and transformative conversations.

As I made a final walk to the beach by Robert's Creek, I watched the waves ebb and flow. It reminded me of the last line of F. Scott Fitzgerald's *The Great Gatsby*: *"And so we beat on, boats against the current, borne back ceaselessly into the past."* Though in that current state of mind, I knew history was not going to repeat itself.

Sam and Hannah made a delicious breakfast for me and I was on my way to New York.

∞ ∞ ∞ ∞ ∞ ∞ ∞ ∞

Tears filled my eyes as I gazed upon the buildings of New York City from within the airplane. It was mid-August at this point, and I had been in Canada for about three weeks. My heart was heavy, but I knew I had a mission to work towards.

I slammed my eyes shut and hoped for the best: 'Angels,' I wept. 'Please be with me.'

That first night back, it was hard to sleep at the church again. The cold floor showed no mercy towards my soul. Nothing felt right. I was easily slipping back into the daily routine I once had, though deep within I knew that everything was changing. Rearranging my schedule to benefit my new health and higher consciousness-based lifestyle would be a difficult transition period, but I desperately needed it. I know that if I maintain my prayer and meditation practices, I would be able to handle the work and life I was leading.

I felt good.

If I eased into this sort of new transition in my life, everything would be powerful and smooth.

Beautiful Souls

There are spirits and angels working with me, and I felt a sort of cloak of protection reigning over my soul.

I have to keep the faith.

Although I missed being in Canada, and the positivity that embraced me when I was there, I knew that I would return there one day.

The relationship I have with myself trumps any relationship that I was a part of in the past. Until someone extraordinary crosses my path, I refuse to let my soul express itself in a romantic way ever again.

'I am worth it,' lingered on my lips.

As August dwindled down, I packed my schedule with so many counseling appointments and business meetings. Morena was handling the paperwork from the back end of Windows of Opportunity, and the two of us continued to meet and talk about life and my newfound education related to spirituality.

She was very receptive to everything I learned. Morena even seemed genuinely interested in prayer circles, lightworkers, and the entire divine love movement. In a sense, I always knew that Morena was part of a higher school of thought; I just did not realize what she was capable of discussing until we finally dove deep into the recesses of my soul.

As the two of us walked the usual paths of Alley Pond Park in the sweltering heat, Morena looked me in the eye and said her favorite catchphrase: "Maybe what you are searching for is not what you are looking for."

'What does that even mean?' I snapped at her.

Her eyes looked sullen as she turned away from me.

"One day, you will realize it."

'One day?'

"One. Day."

When the two of us made our way to the end of the trail, I discovered Sam and Hannah had emailed me a message. The two of them said that Sam received a powerful message about me. In their respective elaborate way, the two of them were certain that I would soon meet a girl at a school who would be the one for me.

Who would have the audacity to assume this?

At that point, I swore off relationships. I did not want to be seen as so weak and lonely that I would just pursue anyone or toss my fragile heart around.

My heart was permanently removed from my sleeve, and I was keeping it that way. I don't quite understand my feelings sometimes, but the law of attraction and my own soul's growth were worth it.

I was steadfast in acknowledging I would not find love within a school building, especially since I was usually working for after school programs and with youth.

August came to a close with a wealth of knowledge at the tip of my brow: I had to grow Windows of Opportunity's reach, and I was excited to continue running after school programs at different locations.

Despite being surrounded by the usual New York mayhem, things were going well.

∞ ∞ ∞ ∞ ∞ ∞ ∞ ∞

I received a call from Bryan, who had just settled into a new dorm room for his upcoming year at Stony Brook. When his grandfather, Gemma's dad, passed away, he decided to leave his car to Bryan. Though we were grateful for this and thankful for the love that still existed within our family, Matheson men do not seem to have such good luck with cars.

It turned out that Bryan accidentally drove the car into the brick wall of a deli. Fortunately, no one was injured, but the car needed quite a lot of repairs.

As I sat in the autobody shop watching the mechanics work on the car, I began thinking about my parents. Though I had a very strained relationship with them as a kid, I thought it was about time I officially buried the hatchet and released the pain I endured from my soul.

I love my parents. I do forgive them for everything I went through. Forgiveness is not about excusing the act. Forgiveness is a gift for the soul: it gave me the permission to move forward towards a solid, healthy place in my life.

I let go of the pain knowing that in the experiences they granted me, they reacted from their own innate pain. They had a limited comprehension of love and the way they displayed it.

There was a limited comprehension of unconditional love. Yet in my mature and wiser years, I developed an understanding of loving humanity.

I do not hold them responsible for the moments we experienced together.

I loved my parents very much, and this moment, where I watched Bryan's car transforming before my eyes, I discovered that love for a child manifests in many ways.

However, youth need the most optimal experience possible.

I only hope to give Bryan the love and support he deserves.

While I was still sitting there, I rested my head against the back wall and let my mind drift to a safe haven.

As my phone rang, I picked it up instinctively and without thinking of who it could be.

It just so happened that it was a former elementary school friend of mine, who I kept in touch with on and off throughout the years. She told me that her school's principal was looking for a social worker to run a series of after school leadership programs, and that I should come in right away for the interview.

The next day, I found myself sitting in the empty halls of Lincoln Memorial High School. All I knew about the school was that it could be a place where I could expand my leadership programs on a larger scale.

Lincoln Memorial was doing some sort of education initiative called Social Emotional Learning, which seemed right up my alley. Still, I was not sure if I wanted to stop working for the other schools I was a part of. After all, I had been with those schools for years.

Then a familiar voice emerged from the principal's office. She gazed at my long blonde locks, seemingly unfazed by my black jeans and dark gray t-shirt.

"Hey, I recognize you," she started.

I turned and looked at her. She did look familiar, but I was working with so many people at this point, I did not know where I knew her from.

I rose and shook her hand.

"I'm Shirley," she smiled and I felt the energy in my soul shift.

'Hi, it's nice to meet you,' I grinned back at her, thinking that maybe this was the start of a new chapter in my life and Windows of Opportunity's legacy.

"I remember you," she shouted joyfully. "You broke up the fight at Musicapalooza years ago… my son was the drummer of the band."

Then it hit me: I did know her. I did remember who she was.

Higher Consciousness

The two of us spoke for a few minutes, catching up about what happened since that fateful night, and she blurted out the two words that I never thought would be uttered to me in a school system ever again: "You're hired!"

Without hesitation, I apologized to her and said that I was not interested in being an employee, only in expanding WOO. I would be more than happy to provide her with programs created by Windows of Opportunity. Her face dropped instantly as desperation filled her eyes.

After everything that happened with the lawsuit, I made a personal vow to myself never to work as an individual school employee ever again. Yet here I was, standing in the office of a school principal, being offered a job.

"Please," Shirley begged. "I promise that we are a good school."

I saw those eyes before: the glance of someone ambitious who just wants to make a difference in the world.

"You can trust us." Her words stuck out in my mind.

Everything deep within me felt as if I could not go against the maltreatment the system brought to me years ago. Still, I was slowly becoming the man who was working past misunderstanding and misjudgment.

Something deep within me called upon me to take a chance.

She appeared passionate about shifting the system… if she was willing to take a chance on me, and carte blanche on creating something to impact youth in an extremely positive way, what was I waiting for?

The voice within me begged that I take a chance on her.

A brief pause stood between us as I chose to take a leap of faith.

'Ok,' I smiled at her. 'You have a deal. You can have me and Windows of Opportunity.'

She thanked me profusely and the partnership between Social Emotional Learning and Windows of Opportunity began.

In the few days that stood between beginning to work at Lincoln Memorial High School and letting go of the pain within, I was told I needed to take a student safety seminar that was mandated by the state. That Sunday, I walked into the room eager to learn about how to help students from the state's perspective, and I directly shook hands with fate.

My former supervisor, the woman who launched the lawsuit against me, was the woman running the seminar.

Beautiful Souls

Though I was shaking and my heart was pulsating from my chest, I knew this was God's way of testing my strength and faith. Sam's wisdom, "Patience," came to the forefront of my mind.

She recognized me and greeted me warmly, but we did not talk much. I did not tell her where I was going to be working, though I knew that she could figure it out if she wanted.

Spirituality and positivity are muscles. I had been trying to work it out but I struggled deep inside. I wanted to create possibilities.

You can't learn to swim unless you are in the water so I had to jump in and be in action… Lincoln Memorial High could be the best place to take that first step towards something bigger. The day I could forgive without condoning an act against me is the day I would get my life back, for leaders inherently get the job done.

I needed to jump off a cliff, metaphorically speaking, and build my wings on the way down. I knew I had a higher purpose. I was not going to figure it all out in hiding.

The world is numb. What comes from the heart goes to the heart. The world is just putting bandages on issues. We had to go bigger for real change to occur. My license did not make me an expert. A license is just a part of a social system, just like a degree. My experience and my soul gave me the strength to move forward… so forward is where I intended to go.

∞ ∞ ∞ ∞ ∞ ∞ ∞ ∞

On my first day of work at Lincoln Memorial High School, I washed my body in the church's sink with that ratty old sponge. Remnants of a mysterious dream were floating through my head as I prepared myself for whatever was to come next.

I glanced in the mirror, the water droplets cascading from my freshly-shaven face, and watched my eyes brighten with the possibility of something powerful ahead of me.

'If I am going to rock the boat,' I watched my face ease in the mirror. 'Will you sway with me?'

I stand for the fact that youth can change the world: "For youth by youth" had been Windows of Opportunity's mantra for as long as it has been in existence. Youth can make a real difference, and have a powerful positive voice. I stand for programs that are innovative and impactful, filled with empowerment and possibility.

Possibility is the seed we are planting, and watering it with platforms of opportunity.

As I pulled up to the school, I took a deep breath and turned off my car. When the key slid from the ignition, I felt my fear fade away.

This was not just another day... This was the first day of whatever would come next.

CHAPTER 3

Refuse to Sink

*"If she runs away she fears she won't be followed...
What could be the worse than leaving something behind"*

- Vanessa Carlton, American musician, singer, songwriter, Milford, Pennsylvania

New beginnings come with their faint scent of resolute hope. As situations present themselves before our very eyes, we find that our experiences have tainted an unwavering part of who we are: our respective souls. We may transform and transcend as time progresses, but nothing truly prepares us for the next chapter. Nothing knocks on our door and says, "Hey, the next part of your life is beginning now."

We just ebb and flow with the tides, floating in the infinitesimal abyss that lingers between who we once were and what we will become. It is a beautiful feeling: embracing the new piece of our puzzle, while recognizing that all of the pieces before us had to be earned along our respective journeys.

Morena's voice persisted from within the depths of my mind: "Make each day count."

For once, I was not counting the seconds on a clock or counting on a relationship to manifest before me. I was making a conscious effort to count on my innate longing to do good in this world…

As it always should have been.

There is a balance that exists between all the light we cannot see and our true soul emerging from the ashes. The plight of miscommunication remains fervent when we do not, even for one moment, stop to look at our surroundings. When we choose to cast aside logic and reason, and replace it with the lies of false supposed prophets, we throw our dignity through the dirt as well as our soul.

Mud and hate should not cast a shadow on who we are and all our souls wish to grow into.

We should not and will not forget those who brought us to where we are today. We must carry the legacy and torch of those whose physical entities perished long before their goals were fulfilled. We must blaze a trail with enough tenacity to say, "You do not scare me and you do not own me."

We must encourage the lost and lonely to find their wholesome, consummate power through the energy they put forth into this world. We must light a candle in honor of those who cannot see through the darkness.

We must thrive through ashes. We must dust the pain off and grow.

We must heal ourselves and heal the world.

Refuse to Sink

For one day, and I knew this to be an evident and eventual truth, I was worthy of love.

I just never knew what kind of love, until I found my perpetual equal.

I am rushing too far ahead with the story though, for there is a lot that happened between then and now.

∞ ∞ ∞ ∞ ∞ ∞ ∞ ∞

As the sun climbed over the high school, I watched the gargoyles look sternly upon the landscape. Their eyes were downcast in a way that could strike fear in even the sternest individuals.

When I entered the school, although this was not my first time in the building, I felt as if everything shifted. The world tilted on its axis for a moment and caught me off-balance: This was my new workplace.

Though I would just be working part time after school here, the principal, Shirley, insisted that I meet with the entire staff so that I could feel like part of the blossoming family they were developing there.

I happily obliged, but within my first few minutes there, I realized that I did not know where to go.

Shirley, clad in a crisp jet-black suit, made her way into the hallway and rested her eyes on me: "Scott, I am so happy you are here!"

She sprung forth from the conversation she was engaged in, and made her way over to me instinctively.

"What's new," she put her arm around me as if we were old pals just catching up.

'Nothing,' I smiled, trying to hide the silent anxiety sifting through my soul.

"I forgot," she snapped her fingers. "I have to show you your new office."

'New office?' My puzzled expression caught her off guard.

"Yeah," Shirley grinned as if she were slightly confused. "You have an office here."

An office. My *own* office. It was a pleasant surprise, to say the least.

Never in my life did I instantly get offered a space to call my own. Though I had some semblance of ownership over past places and areas, Shirley had granted me the capacity to express myself within the confines of a school.

It was something I did not expect, though it welcomed a plethora of unrequited feelings.

As the two of us walked through the brightly painted hallways adorned with positive messages and images, it felt like I was finally in a high school that was meant for me. When the two of us traveled downstairs and unlocked the door, the dim sunlight cut through the room and rested at my feet. There was a wooden desk, a leather couch, and chairs that reminded me of my old office in my other high school.

Images of the International Beer Club hanging out in the hallways of Jamaica High School danced through my head.

I wondered what Tommy was doing. I wondered what Danielle would have been doing if she had not joined my Circle of Angels. I pondered what my life would have become if I had a Social Worker running programs for youth when I was a student.

I was hopeful that the same guidance counselor who helped me had been helping students for years.

My middle school teacher, who took my friend and I to dinner, came to mind. Where was she now? What happened to all of the souls in my life who shaped my perspective of high school?

Many of the moments from my elementary, middle, and high school years were fading into the sunset, but that did not mean I was not cognizant of their impact on my soul.

"Well," Shirley stood there eagerly waiting for me to say something.

A seemingly long pause hung in the air as I slowly spun around the center of the office.

'It's perfect.' I did not know what else to say. This school felt holistically different from my previous school, and I did not think it was as oppressive of a situation as my own high school experience.

Shirley smiled again, "I'll let you explore in here for a bit. Our staff meeting is in the library in 30 minutes."

The door edged shut behind her as I became acquainted with the energy in the room. It was different. It was unique.

It could have been my home.

After sitting on the couch for what felt like hours, I made my way towards the school's library. Sam's comments seemed to be coming true.

I was in a better place, a clearer space, and somewhere that was genuinely different from where I once was.

There were faces strewn about the library, some seemed familiar with one another, but it seemed like there were a lot of young, brand new teachers.

Shirley was standing at the front of the room, shuffling papers behind a podium, motioning for me to take a seat at one of the tables.

I found a spot near two women who appeared to be meeting for the first time. They seemed friendly enough, and I figured that if the three of us were new to the staff, we would form some sort of conversation based on where we came from and how we got here.

The woman on the left, who was closest to me, seemed to be nervous about her first day on the job. Though she carried herself confidently, the woman kept playing with her fingers and twirling her hair. It is truly amazing how you can discern a person's nervous tendencies if you pay close enough attention.

The woman on her right, who kept pushing her glasses towards the bridge of her nose, was perched with one leg tucked under the other. It was almost as if the leg folded underneath her was keeping her from teetering over and into the woman next to me.

As Shirley began her welcome speech, she explained how a number of new staff members, myself included, would be joining the school this year. After a few moments of giving some basic information about the school, she told all of us to turn to each other, introduce ourselves, and talk about the strangest thing we had on our minds.

The two women and I looked at each other and smiled coyly. I was unsure of what to say and how to start a conversation between the three of us, but I figured that I would take a stab at it.

'Has anyone ever heard of Anna Kendrick?'

The two women looked at me, wide-eyed.

"What?" The woman on my left stopped twirling her hair. The other sat quietly with a blank look on her face.

'So, I was watching this movie called *Pitch Perfect 2* a few months ago, and I saw this actress Anna Kendrick,' the women continued to look at me. 'I know that people always say they are *in love* with a famous person, but I would *love* to meet her. Seriously, I am a huge fan of hers.'

The women giggled and did not know what to say.

I continued: 'The moment I found out there was another *Pitch Perfect* movie; I knew I had to watch it. I don't know what it is, but she seems to have captivated me.'

"Well," the woman on my left began twirling her caramel hair again. "What would you do if you ever met the *one-and-only* Anna Kendrick?"

I was unsure of how to answer, but the three of us started laughing.

"I'm Emma," the woman who was twirling her hair extended her hand.

The woman next to her grinned and shyly extended her hand as well, "I'm Joy."

The three of us continued our conversation, and I shrunk into my new office rather quickly. This dynamic was something I was not accustomed to. Here I was, sitting with a bunch of teachers, nonchalantly talking about my interest in Anna Kendrick and *Pitch Perfect*.

What was wrong with me?

Why was I hooked on talking about love or relationships, though I was set on never getting into another relationship again?

I heard a knock on my office door, believing that Shirley was coming to speak to me about what type of timeline I had to implement my programs.

Emma crept into the doorway with a coy grin on her face. She seemed like she had some sort of purpose for coming into the room, but I was unaware what she would want.

"Hey," she looked at me as if she knew me my whole life.

'Hey, what's up?'

"Um…" it seemed that she was trying to find a lucid explanation for coming into the room. "I was going to ask if you needed to borrow, like, cleaning wipes, or… something."

'No,' I picked up the antibacterial wipes that Shirley left in my room. 'I have enough, thank you.'

"Oh," she seemed disappointed. "Okay."

'Hey,' I caught her attention as she was trying to leave the room. 'Sorry for rambling about Anna Kendrick before.'

"Oh," she began twirling her hair again. "The first day of anything is awkward, right?"

I laughed, 'Yeah, right.'

An awkward pause cut between us.

"Do you mind if I get your phone number?" Emma held her cellphone towards me. "The principal said that you are the Social Worker, and that you would be working part time with us."

'Yeah, sure.' I snatched the phone from her hand and began typing my cell number in.

"I mean," she began searching for words. "If you aren't here and I have a question, I'd want to ask you right away. I can't wait to help the kids."

'Is that why you wanted to be a teacher?'

"For the kids, yeah."

'That's awesome, what are you going to be teaching?'

"Social Studies," she gulped.

'That's good,' I flashed her a smile. 'Every child needs a good teacher, and it seems like you're going to do great.'

"Thanks," she turned bright red and shot her eyes towards the floor.

'You are welcome.' I handed the phone back to her, which she grabbed quickly.

"I appreciate it." She did not know what else to say, and neither did I, so she began turning away.

'Uh,' I tried to think of something cordial to say. 'Good luck with your first day of school tomorrow.'

"Thanks," she eyeballed the couch and my bare walls. "I can't wait to see how you decorate this space."

I looked around at the walls.

'Oh, yeah,' I chuckled. 'I didn't even think of how I was going to decorate.'

"Sorry, I don't mean to be rude," she spoke more confidently now. "I like to paint."

'Really?' I swiveled my chair so my body was facing her. 'What do you paint?'

"Mainly landscapes and stuff, nothing crazy," she tilted her head and shrugged.

'That's really cool,' I was running out of things to say to her, but something seemed to be keeping her in the room.

We locked eyes for a moment, and I could see specks of mocha in her chocolate brown irises.

'You have a story,' I said to her. 'I don't know what it is, but I can tell something exists behind those eyes.'

She blushed again and started moving towards the door.

"I look forward to working with you," she lingered in the doorway for a moment before letting it slam behind her.

Our exchange was odd, but I figured that it was just another example of how I interact with people who are looking for my expertise and insight, without actually getting to know me.

Once the day was over, I retreated to my silver Monte Carlo and drove back to the damp church attic.

∞ ∞ ∞ ∞ ∞ ∞ ∞ ∞

If I were ever to fully explain or express my innate pain and agony, I feel that I would fill a river with my tears. How do you articulately express to someone how much agony your soul is in? How do you fathom expressing your inner voice to another human being? How do you tell someone you are suffering, when you don't even know precisely what you are dealing with?

When does it become clear that you need to reach out for help, even when it appears that no one is listening?

How do you know if someone is listening?

Is there anyone out there who could truly hear me?

Is there anything that would provide salvation to the torment I deal with regularly?

How devoutly tortured is my soul?

When will this suffering cease to be?

When will I stop clawing at the possibility to merely survive each day, and truly get a chance to live?

I had nobody and I had never felt so alone.

There was something wrong with me.

Nothing had been the same since the day I lost Faith.

I had the celestial kingdom at my beck and call.

I had a deeper relationship and faith with God than ever before.

Anna Kendrick seemed so far out of reach, but has characteristics that seemed perfect.

I was sitting in the attic of a church on a Tuesday night bored out of my mind and so very alone.

That is why I stayed busy. I hated that feeling. It was dingy there. The darkness succumbed to the broken crevices of my soul. I was trying to play "home." It was embarrassing.

I put myself in a spiritual refuge. I was closer to a sense of a spiritual vibration like never before, and yet it felt pathetic.

I had to clean myself in a church sink, wash my hair with a plastic cup, and regularly give myself a sponge bath.

Those were the nights that reminded me how sad my life really was.

Faith turned her back on me and loved a guy who said he would never commit to her. She still chose him over me and opted to add salt to the wound. She threw our "friendship" and our relationship away.

The only people I had were people who needed me and sucked as much out of me as possible, which I didn't actually mind because I cared about them deeply. It was God's work I was trying to carry out. At least I mattered in that respect.

Sometimes something inside of me said not to go on… but I could never do that. I still had to persevere.

The faint chime and flickering light from my cell phone made me realize that it had just been a few hours since I left work. Another day would prevail over this one, and maybe I would get some clarity regarding my life, my future, and any prosperity that would conjure up the next puzzle piece to my journey.

When I glanced at the screen, a new number had texted me a few words, which made me chuckle:

"Hi, It's Anna Kendrick."

I looked through my phone and found the letter I wrote to Anna Kendrick the first time I saw her in *Pitch Perfect 2*, but never sent, because I did not want her to think I was one of those lunatics that chase celebrities:

Dear Anna,

Don't worry… Let me start by saying I am not a crazy insane fan and I am sure the chances of you actually reading this is probably zero to none, but if possible, I am hoping the universe pulls on your heart strings, and raises

Beautiful Souls

your curiosity enough to read this through… My name is Scott and I am the CEO and Founder of a NY based non-profit agency called Windows of Opportunity.

I do a lot of work in education and have a huge dream of reforming the education system. I am all about giving youth a voice, and a sense of purpose, belonging, and passion to make a difference in the world. I have created many leadership programs and have reached 250,000 youth to date through these programs. Many say I am successful, but I feel like I have not begun to scratch the surface of my potential. Anyways, I feel compelled to write to you and share this story with you. I've been so swamped in my own non-profit agency and mission to impact the world that I guess to be honest, and I'm embarrassed to say, I just discovered who you are today.

I have been pushing an event that supports a youth message that "we are all beautiful" and I needed a break from going out there, speaking to sponsors, helping people, and going full force on these projects. I just came from a big sponsorship meeting and I was mentally exhausted. I could not focus at all.

So I decided to go to the movies, which is often what I will do when I am feeling drained and just want to escape. There was nothing really playing and I was with one of my program directors. She turned to me and said we should see Pitch Perfect 2. My first reaction was "Isn't that some teenie bopper movie or some slapstick comedy?" She laughed at me and said, "You didn't see the first Pitch Perfect?"

Obviously not.

Anyhow, she pushed and pushed and I decided to see that movie against my better wishes. Fast forward, with a huge tub of popcorn on my lap, the second you came on the screen, like I'm sure many men and boys in the world probably feel, I was completely taken in by your energy. Or, at least your character's energy. Not seeing the first one or any of your movies I leaned over and asked my director "Who is that?" She whispered back, "Anna Kendrick." I replied, "Wtf is an Anna Kendrick?"

Shaking her head at me in shame, she was like, "I can't with you." Of course, the rest of the movie I was glued to your energy, and I love music. Being a drummer, and loving all styles of music, I really appreciated your talent, as well as the rest of the cast. I'm a spiritual guy and felt like there was more to who you were on that screen.

Refuse to Sink

At first, I was joking around after the movie about how beautiful you were, how the universe was going to make sure we meet, and where the hell have I been that I never heard of you. When I left the movies, I turned around to my program director and said I would do anything to meet you, but I'm sure she's nothing like her character Becca in the movie. When we went back into the church, we did a tremendous amount of work. Later on in the evening I decided to go on YouTube and look up your name. I saw some interviews with you and was completely taken in by how genuine, natural, and real you seem. Apparently, many people feel this way about you, and are instantly attracted to that aura, even if they do not have the emotional maturity to express it. I told my program director I was going to meet you and we were going to become true real friends, and maybe perhaps you would even be interested in the youth that I help and the mission I have in the world. She thought I was crazy and I said based on my spirituality and my faith, I am sure that anything in this world is possible. I explained to her that "stars" are people too, who all have a story and happen to (in most cases) be blessed to do what they love to do... and if I can feel the energy of somebody's personality, then why not try to reach out and strike up a real friendship?

I felt like if anyone would be real enough to handle media and life the way you do (and I can't imagine how difficult it must be at times) that you may be willing to actually sit down with me and see what I'm about. Crazier things have happened in this world and how do you know if you don't ask? I would love the opportunity to speak with you or meet with you about the work I do, and learn more about who you are. I attached my website and information about my vision and you can Google my name and see that I'm not totally insane and that it would be safe to contact me. I now put this long shot into the hands of the universe and I look forward to a possible friendship in the future.

All the best,

Scott

I never sent this letter because I figured I would rather trust the universe. Besides, so many people must contact her. I stood by the affirmation that if it's meant to be, it will happen.

Beautiful Souls

I am a rare genuine soul who would love to meet another rare genuine soul. I once almost went to a book signing that she was appearing at, but I chose the youth program that needed me to present that day. I took that as a sign as it was not the proper time or place.

I guess you never truly know where life will take you; that's probably the most realistic and honest summary about my entire life.

Regardless, this text was clearly someone's effort to be funny.

It was Emma's effort to come up with a witty first text.

I texted her back after I let my mind wander, and the two of us struck up a conversation about trivial things. At least her text was a welcomed distraction from the musty church.

Before I knew it, I had fallen asleep with my phone laced between my fingers. I did not remember passing out, but I knew that I was exhausted and my mind probably ushered in some semblance of a dream-like state while I was texting with Emma.

∞ ∞ ∞ ∞ ∞ ∞ ∞ ∞

In the days that followed, I started to meet the students at Lincoln Memorial High School and started to implement the programs that Windows of Opportunity had to offer. It was a refreshing new start.

With Shirley as both my principal and boss, it was nice to have some freedom to help youth become empowered and finally advocate for themselves.

Emma would always stay after school, watching the kids communicate with one another, and often tried to refer students to me through text messages and little notes she would leave for me.

Her presence was interesting. I could tell she seemed to be flirting with me quite frequently, but I did not want to assume anything. After all, Faith was the last person I truly loved or cared for, and since my soul was shredded by her actions; I could not fathom getting hurt again.

'Never again,' I promised myself.

Then one day, during one of the after-school programs, I was talking to the kids about things that they seemed to fear the most.

Emma sat there, her feet tucked underneath her and a smile adorned across her face, helping me counsel the kids. I even asked her what her fears were, and though she blushed and tried to shy away from responding, I sensed she wanted to spill everything to me right then and there.

The next morning, there was a notecard that was slid under my door: The white envelope simply said:

"To feed your dying hunger of my fears."

The inside read as follows:

Scott,

Don't go all social worker analytical on this but I have some general fears: I am TERRIFIED of drowning. I'm a terrible swimmer. One summer I just jumped in the pool and almost inhaled all the water. I suddenly had to hold my nose. WTF. Once after that I was swimming under water and someone jumped right on a float I was under. I thought that was my moment to drown. I also don't like that you can't see underneath you in ocean water so I never just dive in. I'm slowly taking small risks when we go on the boat and I have to jump in the water to pull the anchor to shore.

I am double terrified of riding a horse. When I was 6 we were camping and I was with my cousins and siblings around horses and I don't know what spooked them but they ran, I fell, and got stepped on in the back by one. My aunt found me and I cried A LOT! I've tried since, two times, getting on a horse. I totally broke down and full-blown cried both times.

I am scared I won't be a mom. Idk why. I can't picture myself old, so Idk. If I can't see raising older kids, like will that mean something will happen to me. Or if it is more I won't be in the era of time where I'd have kids like no longer here on Earth. It is scary. I try not to think about it.

Brings me to dreams of being shot in the back. I have NEVER told anyone but I am constantly scared to death looking over my shoulder.

Recently I have been having fears of divorce. Not linked to just my recent ex, but since I started with my college boyfriend years ago. Maybe 3ish years now. It has been a fear on radar.

Love, Emma

Beautiful Souls

Love. Emma.

The fact that she signed the card with "Love, Emma," scared me. I was not sure what to think.

Who was this woman?

Was Sam right when he said I would meet someone?

No, he couldn't be.

How could he have known?

I felt my stomach churning and turning over and over again.

The nausea brewing in my stomach felt like it was about to burst at any moment.

Emma seemed to be persistent when it came to pursuing me, but what if I was just imagining everything?

I paced the floor of the sanctuary nightly again.

Morena came over to chat with me about relationships and my future in general.

She sat in the middle of one of the pews, gazing up at the stained-glass window undergoing a metamorphosis in the waning sunset.

"So, what exactly are you worried about?" She did not avert her eyes from the image she was glaring at.

'It's Emma,' I started. 'She seems like she is something else. There is something about her. She seems like she could be the one.'

"You've had many *ones* over the years, Scott," she sounded monotone at this point. "What makes you think that she is *the one*?"

I stopped wandering around. 'Are you being condescending?'

"No," she said matter of factly. Morena caught my glance, "I just don't want you to have your heart shattered into bits again."

'So you think that she is not the answer?'

"What exactly is the question here, Scott?"

I didn't know. Maybe she was right: how could I find someone so soon after Faith? Was this God's way of tempting my strength?

'Emma is pursuing me; do I just give in to her?'

"Giving in implies that she is some sort of momentary element you are forcing yourself into."

'She isn't.'

Morena rose and walked up to me, "What makes you believe that?"

Again, I didn't know.

She dragged her right pointer finger over my heart in the motion of a cross. "What have you done to protect your soul from any more pain?"

'I don't know.' I moved away from her.

"You crumbled when Faith left, because you made her a part of your foundation. However, you have to be your *own* strength, Scott."

I pivoted and met Morena's eyes.

'I don't know how to let someone in without caving to their every whim. I love with all of my heart.' Tears began welling in my eyes. 'That's all I ever really knew.'

I could see Morena smiling and looking at me with a sense of pride in her eyes.

"You know what you have been through, now you just have to commit yourself to a new mindset."

'How?'

Morena rested her hands on my shoulders, "Only you can answer that."

Emma's texts kept coming in nightly. We would talk about leadership skills for the kids and spoke briefly about her story.

It was clear that Emma was immersed in a wealth of pain: she would talk about how love was complicated for her, and that she loved with her whole heart just like I did.

After the kids would filter out of my office for the night, Emma would hang around and talk with me. I found myself comfortable in her company, to the point where we would talk just about anything and find a way to see the silver lining in every and anything that happened in our respective lives.

A still silence hung in my office as the falling leaves brushed against the window.

'Isn't it weird?' I tried to break up the quiet moment in the room. 'The leaves change into such beautiful colors as they drift from the trees.'

"Well," she started awkwardly. "It is mid-October."

'Yeah.'

Again, there was a resolute silence in the air.

"As a painter, I find that certain colors hold more value in a situation," she shot me an alluring glance.

'Oh,' I wasn't sure what to say.

"If burgundy is the color of love what is the color of this connection we have?"

Emma had looked deep into my eyes and began to move closer to me. I had only known her a few weeks but I could feel my soul shivering.

"I can tell you have a story to tell," she said mockingly, almost echoing what I said to her not long ago. There was a hint of flirtation in her voice.

I smiled at her and said, 'Take a seat then, and I will tell you.'

Emma sat down on the leather couch, and I began to tell her about my car accident. With each word that left from my lips, she appeared to hang on every single syllable.

In the days that followed, I found myself writing in journals, *our journals*, to mutually discuss our stories.

I have always been amazed by the fact that every single thing I have read has been made up of the same 26 letters, but just arranged differently. Every time the letters are weaved together, emotions burst from them like lava from a volcano. The words combined seep into my soul, grasp it, and speak to it. The words speak to me as if I were learning a new language: slowly, yet patiently.

Each time I read what she writes about me and how she sees me; peace reverberates through my entire body. The words crash into my skin and latch onto my soul with such a pristine gentleness. The cracks of my soul become filled with her thoughts and her ramblings, and she didn't even notice how much she had struck me.

She didn't realize how much she had changed me.

I was at the mercy of how she rotated her wrist, with her fingers firmly grasped along the pen, and brushing my story onto the page. My life was her masterpiece and her artwork; yet somehow through writing about my life and my experiences, she faded behind the words and raised me onto a pedestal.

She ambitiously floated in my shadow and glanced at me with such wonder, almost like a child on Christmas morning. She told me that my presence was a gift, but I was afraid that if she continued to pull the wrapping paper layer by layer, she would realize that this gift, my soul, had been damaged for a long time. Still, knowing her, she would pull out glue, tape, bandages, and whatever else she carried with her and would whisper, "It's okay, I can help you fix it."

Refuse to Sink

∞ ∞ ∞ ∞ ∞ ∞ ∞ ∞

'Morena, I think this may actually be real,' I muttered to her as I paced past her in the sanctuary.

"Then if you think it is real, it is real," She smiled at me and I felt the weight of my past slowly edging off of my shoulders.

'How do I know if she is or is not the one unless I go for it?'

"Go for what?"

'Ask her out, I don't know.'

"You," Morena chuckled. "You are actually going to ask her out?"

'Yes,' I yelped. I think she may really like me; maybe it is more than that.

"Then," Morena patted me on the shoulder with her fingers catching slightly in my cotton shirt. "Go find out your truth."

I had to. I just had to.

It was about time I started living, not just surviving.

During this time, Faith also chose to re-appear in my life. She texted me, and asked if the two of us could get together. I figured that with this new chapter of my life starting to open up, I would try to reconcile the loose ends of the relationship that broke my heart into pieces.

If she had contacted me any other night but October 24, 2015, I would not have been able to meet with her.

I figured: 'Is this the universe lining up, or am I just overanalyzing everything?'

In usual fashion, and reminiscent of days far in the past, Faith asked to go to a cultural restaurant. It was only when I was with her that I would try new things and experience life differently.

We met at the Peruvian restaurant not far from the church, and spent the next two to three hours just talking, sharing, and laughing, as if we had not missed a beat. We talked about our break up and mutually apologized to one another.

When I brought up the other guy she was seeing, Faith began to cry.

Instinctively, I grabbed her hand, but I knew that I was not going to make the same mistake. Though my feelings for her were still there, and I mean, how could they not be considering all we had gone through over the years, I knew my life was on a different path.

The way she expressed herself and her beauty were exquisite, but despite how much she missed me, and how much I did miss her, I knew that there was a lot of our story that was greatly rooted in absolute pain.

I did not want to suffer anymore.

I knew, from just a few moments of looking into Faith's eyes, that Emma had potential.

Upon driving Faith home, we gave each other a hug that was real and powerful. She wanted a father figure in her kids' life and she was confident in sharing that with me.

Still, God put Emma in my life, and though she constantly brought up her ex that she seemed to have left permanently, I was interested in her.

Something in Emma's soul ignited a fire within me. It felt so real.

Faith re-entering my life made no sense at all, but I figured that there had to be a story behind the story there.

The next morning when I woke up, I participated in my ritualistic tendencies before work. I twiddled with my hair nervously all throughout counseling sessions with the students at Lincoln Memorial.

I knew Emma would be gracing my presence shortly after the kids' departure, so I puttered around the office cleaning up what I could.

When she finally walked in the door, she was wearing black heels that clicked slightly as she entered the room.

The second I laid my eyes on her, and from that moment on, I knew my destiny had been fulfilled.

Emma handed me the journal, ready for me to read the beautiful words she wrote down for my eyes only, and our hands brushed against one another's.

Without hesitation, the two of us felt something in that touch.

As our eyes shut slowly and our lips grazed each other's, I discovered that there was a part of my soul that could still love.

Upon stepping back and meeting her gaze, she looked different than she had before. I had never realized how deep her eyes were. Like roses, her cheeks were in full bloom.

From the moment our lips met, I had not stopped thinking of her. In seconds, four to be exact, two worlds collided, but did not crash. Two walks of life found the same path for a change. It was magical, but only because for once it just seemed so natural.

A small part of ourselves became vulnerable, and for a moment we said everything we ever wanted to say without using words. The sensation is something that can never be duplicated or recreated.

A flicker of light from a singular burned down candle in the darkness of the night.

The oil in a lantern that had not been discovered for years.

A life preserver thrown in the exact moment I fell overboard.

A strong bandage that managed to miraculously connect the fibers of a shattered heart.

A sign that there is an ounce of hope left in the world, as long as you realize that what you are searching for isn't always what you are looking for.

Emma was an absolute pain in the ass, but for some reason, which I didn't know, she listened to me. She listened to me on a level I could never fathom nor comprehend. She flew into my life like a wrecking ball, but rather than plow down every fiber of my being, she rested her pale hand on my heaving frame and softly whispered, "It'll all be okay."

Then suddenly, it was. Just like that, just because she uttered those four words.

∞ ∞ ∞ ∞ ∞ ∞ ∞ ∞

As November rolled around, I found myself eagerly waking up at 5:15 each morning in order to read a text message from Emma. Each day, we would take turns writing in one of our countless journals about whatever was on our minds.

Her words were slowly softening the hardened shell that had melted around my soul. It was as if she was sent to me because the universe wanted me to finally experience true love.

Love. There I was, I had just met her, and suddenly I was proclaiming my love for her.

Each day was more magical than the next and in a way I could never have imagined or expected. The past two weeks brought me to new heights, and it was her soul that granted my soul the wings to fly again. I could finally push past the limits of a difficult story and soar to new expressions. It was the reigniting of an ember that supposedly burned out long ago.

Like waves crashing slowly and gently against the rocks of some random shore under a cool, summer's night, the peaceful desire and yearning for true love never gets old… specifically with her.

I saw her in every girl's eyes, she was in the fresh air that I inhaled each brisk night, and her presence existed in all of the spiritual moments the universe bestowed upon me.

Her essence was all around me.

We continued to chat regularly, which led to late nights and early mornings inundated with what we perceived to be true love blossoming in the late fall air.

After one night of running a leadership program at the school, one of the students did not seem to want to go home. Emma sat in the room and watched me counsel the student one-on-one.

In the moments that passed, I felt all of my energy focusing on the student, and I almost forgot that Emma was perched upon a chair and embracing the scene unfolding before her.

I forgot what I told this student and over the years I realized that the advice I gave students seemed to seep out of my mouth without hesitation. Yet in all of those moments, I felt as if the words that I spoke were not from my soul, rather they were from a place of higher consciousness.

Students and those around me would listen intently, and I could tell when the advice I was giving them reached a special part of their soul. At that moment, with Emma watching me and embracing every word I spoke, I was petrified to know what was going through her mind. All I knew was that she was listening, and it was in a way that transcended any semblance of focus that anyone had ever bestowed upon me.

Once the student left and we were alone together, Emma smiled modestly and stood up.

"Would you mind walking me to my car?" Emma blinked repeatedly and grasped at her bag, which almost slipped off of her shoulder.

'Yeah, of course,' I said.

"Thanks."

The two of us walked in silence until we reached the employee lot. She kept kneading her hair as we moved forward in the night, and I could see the twinkle in her eyes shine almost as bright as the stars above.

When we got to her car, she paused for a moment by the door handle and sighed deeply.

'Are you okay?' I was genuinely concerned at this point.

"Yeah," she let out another exasperated sigh.

'You don't sound like you are okay,' I moved against her car and stood perpendicular to her.

We stood in silence, as she seemed to keep taking deep breaths to calm herself down. I didn't understand what Emma was doing at the moment, but time was about to set our story on a different path.

The cool evening descended upon us, which led her to toss her bags in her car, shift her eyes towards me, and as her car door slammed shut, she asked if we could go sit in my car.

'Sure,' I responded. I was getting quite cold as well, but I did not know what Emma intended in those fateful moments.

Little did I know, this conversation was about to define our mutual path into whatever was coming next.

As the two of us leapt in my Monte Carlo and the engine began to purr slightly, I caught tears welling in her eyes.

'What's wrong?'

"Nothing, nothing."

Emma pulled her sleeves over the palms of her hands and looked me in the eyes.

"How do you do it?" Her voice started to crack.

'Do what?'

"You have been through so much, and you keep going, how?"

I reached out my hand towards hers and intertwined our fingers.

'Because I always try to keep the faith.'

"I refuse to sink," Emma said confidently.

Her words cut through me like fragile glass.

'What?' She caught me slightly off guard. I always assured myself that I *refused to sink* and, after years upon years of whispering this mantra to myself, those words managed to escape the lips of another human being.

What were the odds?

"I refuse to sink, it is something I have always believed in," she began. "I really like anchors: the imagery they depict, the symbolism, they are truly beautiful. They remind me to stay anchored to who I am."

Her description was beautiful, and suddenly anchors became one of my favorite symbols, too. Well, of course the infinity sign is tethered to my soul in many ways, but the anchor became a holistically unique part of who I am.

We spoke for a bit about anchors and infinity signs, until the conversation came to an awkward standstill.

"I-" her voice was strained again. "I'm sorry."

'Why are you apologizing?' I whispered.

"I don't want to-," she began tearing up again. "I don't want to be the one who breaks your heart."

'Emma,' I drew her in closer to me. 'You could never break my heart.'

Her tears dripped onto my leather jacket and rolled down into my lap.

"I think I love you," she murmured into my chest.

Emma glanced up and met my gaze.

'I love you, too.'

She kissed me in a way that was indescribable, and our first night where our bodies physically coalesced into one commenced. The touch of her skin felt so natural, but I found myself clumsily moving around her while trying to savor the moment.

The two of us danced within the confines of the car as if we were unsure of how long the moment would last. With each tumultuous twist, I found myself yearning for our skin to touch for longer periods of time.

From that sudden passionate encounter, and from the connection I felt from just existing in her presence, I could tell our connection was a bond that would not break.

The windows began to fog and her passionate moans became more fervent. As my gentle kisses edged along every one of her curves, I could feel her writhing in the heat of the moment, as our connection grew deeper and deeper.

I slid my hand between her legs and she pulled me closer to her. My fingers moved slowly, but with devout purpose, which sent her into a frenzy of pleasurable commentary.

As the moments flashed before our eyes, I realized that this situation would manifest itself over and over again throughout the weeks that followed. Frankly, I was delicately satisfied by watching her pleased face melt in the heat of our passionate embrace.

It made me feel that despite my earlier incidents with Gemma, and situations with Starr while I was in Texas, I did have the capability of pleasing someone and in such a physical manner.

Though I was still wrought with nerves, the two of us smiled at one another when we finally collapsed on the folded-down seats of my car. As Emma rolled towards me with a breathy, "Hey" dripping along with the beads of sweat on her supple skin, I savored our first intimate moment.

'Was that what you wanted?' I was genuinely curious how long she was holding that in. Did she want this to happen?

Emma reached out and brushed the fingers on her right hand along my face.

"You can do that to me *any* time," the wide grin spread between her cheeks.

I felt that her heart was eternally woven into the fabric of my soul's tapestry.

Our first moment was not perfect, but it was ours.

And that is exactly what I wanted it to be: ours.

∞ ∞ ∞ ∞ ∞ ∞ ∞ ∞

Eventually our rendezvous led us to new heights. When I came into work, I could feel her watching me walk down the hallway to my office after school. It got to the point where she would send me flirtatious text messages about a special skirt or heels she wore just in my honor.

Sheepishly, I always replied that I could not wait to take whatever she was wearing off of her later that night.

Though it could be mistaken that the physical love we explored together was what held us together for so long, it was much more than that.

We were ensnared in a passionate embrace whenever others were not around, but our conversations were what drew me into loving her more than I could imagine.

Day by day, I realized that we are caught in the balance of a deep-rooted connection and comfortable space. We are sewn into the seams of alignment and individualism. Yet with each turn of the needle and thread, we simultaneously become cohesive independent souls on their respective and collaborative journeys.

Beautiful Souls

By themselves, a needle and thread are useful in their own right, but when they are together, absolute magic is created. Two souls weave through one another to create a symbiotic medium: a synthesis of the perfect notes being played in undeniable harmony. Time weaves its own legacy through the experiences we create in developing our own reality. It feels like just yesterday you were standing next to me, us talking about the gift that is the future that could be created.

Though we have the perfect pitch, it was clear we had two different songs that played in our lives. My beat does not match your march, yet somehow it all works... even if it just comes in bursts or a little bit of time here and there.

Regardless of anything that happens in life, I came to the realization that communication is key: you can sing and I can drum and though we are vastly different, we need each other to create beautiful music.

Until the day comes where you learn to play your instruments in tandem with another's innate ability to create sweet music: you play your melody, and I'll play mine.

Thoughts like those drifted through my mind as I watched her move through the school merely glaring at my presence, and I quickly acknowledged that she would hide our relationship from the world... at the time, I just did not understand why.

Then I went away to Canada for the weekend.

∞ ∞ ∞ ∞ ∞ ∞ ∞ ∞

I always had that innate fear that I would hear "Goodbye to Romance" again, and see the girl of my dreams in the arms of another man. Each time I left for too long, even just a few days, I would sense a shift in my relationships when I returned to whatever I considered home.

Still, you can't shatter something that is already broken into fractions of whatever it once was. I pray that those who try understanding that when someone looks into a fire and smiles, they're not someone who you should dare mess with.

Standing in front of the mirror, I saw a panicked version of myself that brought me back to my childhood.

'I would say that I could see pain and suffering in your eyes, but you won't even look at me anymore,' my voice cracked as tears rolled down my cheeks.

'No,' I told myself. 'This is not middle school or high school anymore.'

I don't believe in the existence of hell in terms of the mythological story we conjure up as human beings. The concept exists in the torments of our minds and as a result of the pain we experience.

Losing Emma at the time could be the closest thing to the fiery, eternal damnation of hell that existed in the confines of my mind.

It would be a manifestation of the ultimate pain.

The thing about a six-hour flight to the Sunshine Coast is that it leaves you with plenty of time to ruminate about whatever is on your mind. Emma spent weeks before Thanksgiving acting sweet and spiritual, but something was missing. I felt I was not privy to every inch of her story, though I saw how gorgeous she was in the pages of our countless journals.

The two of us concealed our strong feelings for each other in a series of brick red, leather bound journals we called "The Vault." We wrote back and forth with the intent to express ourselves without inhibitions. Her letters stung an intricate part of my soul, for I knew that she was always hiding a part of who she was from the outside world:

Scott,

I feel like these pages are going to be finished before you know it! Today was a bad itching day for me. I have like... itch "hot spots." Today my inner thighs are beat red and I cannot stop. Other hotspots are my shins and my armpits. Ekkkk, I cannot believe I just said that! I am so embarrassed!

Why is it so easy to speak to you? That makes me nervous.

I truly, honestly was in so much physical pain from the scratching I did there that they were burning all day. I couldn't put them down to rest against my body. I should have seriously called out of work. You know I felt badly about our afternoon and I did not realize until you first said it that maybe I wasn't ready for it. Maybe I'm not ready for any of this. I cannot handle my emotions around you and I need to back off and hide at times. I scratched Monday night, so maybe, this is all stress related and it was in the back of my head?

Beautiful Souls

I'm really not sure.

Consciously, that was not my reason, but subconsciously you could have been right. Any hunches about why I cannot stop scratching my thighs today? This is all so confusing. Ew, My handwriting up top looks different than the body. That annoys me. I texted you a few minutes ago "surprise" because you thought we were done for the night. Right now, I am sitting in bed with two dogs curled into tight balls huddled against the sheets. I have the drop-down attic stairs in my room that something must've bent because it's slightly cracked open and my room is an icebox. I still need to pack for this upcoming weekend but figured I would write you first. Also, sidenote, I always want to ask how your day went but you have a job with a lot of confidentiality and I never want to come across prying and putting you in an uncomfortable place.

As much as I do make you tell me some things, I hope you know they are all safe with me. As much as some of it is interesting to hear, I want you to be able to tell me as a release off of your chest. I feel like you carry so much weight. But like you said we are a team and I think that's how we function best. I was hoping I would hear from you before bed and my phone just beeped. Let's see what you said!

Emma

I do wonder what was going through her mind at the time.

Though I wholeheartedly thought I belonged to her, Emma was caught between a promise she made to herself and an expectation she never thought would appear.

The thought of sleeping next to Emma and being in her arms kept me tethered to New York, although Sam, Hannah, and their neighbors on the Sunshine Coast were calling upon me to delve deeper into the concept of higher consciousness love.

Upon texting Emma, and waiting for her to respond, I felt a tinge of Audrey's situation fluttering through my mind. Would I return to find Emma in the arms of another? Would I be ensnared in another situation where I lost the love I hoped I could have?

When she would finally reply later that evening, she was frigid and distant.

In one of our letters, Emma and I had talked about marriage. We talked about kids. I conjured up images of a Cinderella story romance permeating our journey.

There I sat, in the middle of the most beautiful place on this Earth, with my head in my hands and fearful of what was going through Emma's head. Our conversations went from deep and exhilarating, to glaring at my phone and wondering when she would text back.

She had to still love me… she had to…

Though we were thousands of miles apart, her voice on the other end of the phone assured me that we were, indeed, still in love.

"Scott," she broke out into innocent tears. "I love you. It will always be us."

'I know. I love you too.'

She had to be the one. She needed to be my one, special love. I felt it in my bones and in my soul.

During my flight back to New York, my mind was racing as I thought of the perfect thing to say to Emma when I saw her.

Would I walk in, wrap my arms around her, and profess my undying love for her?

Would she fall into my chest and cuddle with me throughout the night?

Regardless, she said it would always be us. That's how it would be.

∞ ∞ ∞ ∞ ∞ ∞ ∞ ∞

Upon my return, I watched the rain cascade down the basement window to my office. It had been hours since my feet touched the ground in New York, yet something seemed horribly wrong.

Emma was at work, but dodging my presence and text messages.

I feared the worst, but then again it was Emma I was dealing with.

She loved me. She said it countless times. Our words and shared moments had to mean something.

Together was our favorite place to be.

After I finished counseling students for the night, she stood in my doorway and let the phrase "We need to talk" jab daggers into my chest.

The two of us walked in silence to the parking lot, where just days prior we were ensnared in a seemingly loving embrace.

Her energy was holistically unaligned with mine. I could not pinpoint exactly why I felt the two of us needed to re-connect on many levels, but there was something in her eyes that was not there before… a certain lingering sensation. Emma appeared to have a yearning feeling to speak her mind, though each time the thought would materialize in her head, her lips would push her words further into the pit of her stomach.

As the rain washed over our conversation, I felt a stoic cleansing of my soul and spirit in one fatal swoop. When the two of us approached her car, I saw her take a deep breath and shift her gaze from mine.

'What's wrong?' I placed my hand on her shoulder, and she ripped away from me instantaneously.

"Nothing," yet I heard the tears mingling with her voice.

'Please,' I moved towards her again. This time she did not turn away.

Our lips were just seconds away from one another's, yet neither of us moved closer to soothing our souls.

"I'm confused," she whispered into the unsettling physical space between us.

'About what?'

"About us." Emma motioned towards both of us and stepped back.

The rain grew more rampant and pulled her mascara further down the edges of her face. Even with the water washing over us, she was still as beautiful as ever.

We were the epicenter of an image from a romance novel, though the scene was about to transform into a tragedy.

"It's my ex," the long pause she took between her thoughts sent my soul into a frenzy. My heart rate skyrocketed far above the clouds as her voice shook.

"It…" she trailed off for a moment, almost as if she was reminiscing about better days in an effort to keep herself from breaking down. "It's Greg; he wants to propose to me. He misses me and I think I miss him too."

Her words shot through my soul.

I was shattered. My mind diverged from my body as I felt everything in my system start to shut down.

It was "Goodbye to Romance."

The rain began pouring down as she wept and got into her car.

I could not help but cry at the sight of her leaving. Was this for good? Was our story coming to an end just as soon as it had begun?

The hollowed sensation in my soul rang throughout the empty parking lot as she drove off and left me standing there alone. I learned that tears

Refuse to Sink

and blinding rainstorms go together so well: once the raindrops mix with teardrops, all of the pain appears to wash away.

She shattered every piece of wholesomeness I had left in my body.

That upcoming Thanksgiving weekend, Greg would whisk her away and hinted he was going to propose once and for all. Months ago, before we met, she gave him a ring and said, "I will leave it in your hands."

She signed away her heart before I had a chance to even meet her, though her soul was screaming, "I didn't know it was you I was waiting for."

I watched the raindrops roll down my front windshield as my heavy heart rested against the driver's seat of my car.

"Goodbye to romance,
Goodbye to friends and to you
Goodbye to all the past
I guess we'll meet, we'll meet in the end."

There was a shift occurring within me that was both spiritual and devastating in nature.

I needed her like I needed oxygen to survive, but now I had to breathe on my own. She was getting her fairytale ending and I was met with another roadblock.

Why me?

Just… Why me?

∞ ∞ ∞ ∞ ∞ ∞ ∞ ∞

I was never into following the rules, or abiding by standards or labels and whatnot. Still, I felt that Emma and I were a couple. Everything seemed so real and powerful, yet the moment she said that her ex was back, I could not handle it.

Emma had her heart set on keeping our relationship a secret at Lincoln Memorial High School, for she figured that no one would accept us. She always said that our reputations and careers came first. I understood that.

Still, I felt empty inside.

It made me feel as if she truly didn't want me.

I came so far and I was beginning to see just how far I could go. After longing for that "power couple" relationship for what seemed like my entire life, Emma appeared to be the other half of me.

I began to wonder why God put me in such a powerful situation, especially when he was going to pull her away from me.

Would God be mad at me if I got on my hands and knees and begged for her to come back?

Would God get mad?

Would I still be able to move forward if I didn't have Emma coexisting with me?

Why else would God send her to me?

It was Emma who appeared to be the equivalent to any definition of happiness in my soul. Our souls are constantly being developed whether we realize it or not, yet God had to have a complete and consummate love for us whether we wanted more of it or not.

In the process of all of this, Eve would send me text messages about the church and what needed to be done there. She tried to start an argument with me, though the senseless drama paled in comparison to what I was dealing with when it came to Emma.

I felt safe within the walls of the church, and I felt even safer with Emma by my side.

She was the best person who could walk into my life, yet it seemed that she was running from me. Our connection was a matter of balance, and I needed to re-evaluate what it meant having her in my life.

During one of my nightly meltdowns at the church while Emma had fallen off of the radar, Morena came to help me process what was going on.

As I paced the sanctuary floors, leaving a murmured creak from the floorboards below, I felt my body heaving with each repulsive tear that dropped from my eyes.

Morena sat there, humming a melody I didn't really recognize, occasionally pausing to take a deep, long breath.

'What are you doing?' With my voice cracking, I sat beside her.

"Everytime I hum the melody to 'You are my Sunshine,' I always take an extra pause between certain lines."

'Why?' I sat back. 'And why are you humming *that* song?'

"We all need a bit of sunshine sometimes." Morena smiled at me.

Refuse to Sink

'So why all the pauses?' I wiped my tears.

"It's called a caesura," she continued to hum.

'A cesarean?'

"No, silly, it is a timely pause," she started. "It is kinda like a strategic silence."

'Okay,' I remarked.

"Maybe you and Emma need this strategic silence to find out who you are."

I heard her. I understood her and suddenly, everything made sense.

∞ ∞ ∞ ∞ ∞ ∞ ∞ ∞

As a creature of habit, I spent Thanksgiving weekend soulfully alone. I watched the dust in the sanctuary settle with a sort of delicate curiosity. As the rock band Kansas said, *"Are we but dust in the wind?"*

As Outlet and I met for band practice, I felt my drumming was distant. My soul was elsewhere and all I wanted was her in my arms. I wanted Emma beside me. Elyza asked me if I was okay, and though my emotions were jumbled and I desperately needed to confess my love for Emma, all I could muster up was, 'I'm fine.'

Fine drowning in my own sorrows, I guess.

In the days that followed, Emma returned from her short trip with Greg and made her way back down to my office.

"Hey," she mumbled as she walked in the room.

'Hey.' I gripped the bottoms of my sleeves and crossed my legs at my ankles.

We looked at one another for a moment until she finally spoke: "I missed you."

Emma rushed forward and kissed me on the lips. I wasn't sure how to respond, but her touch felt so right.

The two of us sat down and just started talking. Although I still felt she was holding back, she confessed that she did truly, madly, and deeply care about me.

"Like I said," Emma grasped my hand. "It will always be us."

And so that's how things were: we were "us" again.

Our afternoon meetings at Kissena Park in Queens and early morning text messages continued on. We would delve deeper into what made

Beautiful Souls

each other's souls grow and expand in ways neither of us ever thought were imaginable.

Together, we were a force to be reckoned with. Individually, we were becoming professionals with a penchant for helping youth achieve their goals.

Every moment we spent together was a journey filled with love, excitement, and a devout yearning for whatever would come next.

∞ ∞ ∞ ∞ ∞ ∞ ∞ ∞

Though Emma did consider herself to be spiritual, once I went to a spiritual guide to help me sort through my feelings for her, she did not want to know what the guide said. Morena, on the other hand, encouraged me to read what this spiritual guide told me out loud.

As Morena said, "Speak what you wish for into the universe, you do not know who is listening."

I read the transcript of what was told to me to Morena.

The notes read as follows:

'You must tell Emma what you want.

She needs that. If you are not honest with her, she will turn away. It is a lot for you Scott to say you love yourself, but if you honestly show that, Emma will come around and choose you. Yes, she has not told you yet but she is going to be struggling over a choice.

You are being too patient. If you show her less patience, then you will get more from her. The issue from your soul is you do not want to pressure her.

God has brought you both together for a reason and wishes you to be together.

Your Aunt is here and approves with her but has a warning. She may have to take a step with another soul first so that she can get her power back. She knows that you do not understand that at this time but you will in the future. Emma is very interested in taking the next step with you but is also very scared.

If you are less patient, she will love herself more. If you give in easy, she will get comfortable and not make the moves in her best interest.

Emma has to face her fears.

She will be receiving an offer that will be hard for her to say no to in order to have a better life with you Scott. Emma is scared and needs to work with her inner anger and fears to finish something karmic. This is something karmic with another soul, another relationship in her life.

She has to get angry at that soul, but in many ways is not able to get to the root of that. This relationship has something to do with what she is angry with. She is turning a blind eye based on fear. This relationship is acting a certain way towards her.

This is freewill.

Emma can be another way but she may choose to be a certain way with him. This is up to her. This relationship is invading her boundaries but she must see that. Emma loves you Scott for the new boundaries and borders you have created for her. You let her be her and this is something she deeply desires and fears judgment on. Emma's spirit matches your spirit when you hold this space of truth for her, and this is the energy and connection you feel. This can easily turn though. You are both creating what humans call "falling in love" but at this time you are both too scared to admit it.

What is going on here is divinely driven.

Stop being scared, Scott. Emma will love you more when she discovers the truth about your past. Your whole past. Emma sees the world as a mathematical equation. If you do not give her all the factors, her equation will compute the wrong answer, but she will not know it is the wrong answer. This will be up to you, Scott, to present to her.

If you present the right equation, Emma will feel more confident in you as a couple. If you present the wrong equation, you risk losing her forever, and her never knowing the genuine truth of your soul.

Let this be your warning.

Your past Scott will allow her inner light to shine more. In knowing your whole story, she will know that after all was said and done you chose her. If freewill doesn't bring you to this loving conclusion there will be darkness for many years, and then hope again.

This will be a big fear for you to face Scott. This will be tough. Let your love for Emma guide you to the right choices. The word "competition" keeps coming up. Emma feels she will not have to compete. She has a difficult time with the fear in her mind, and she has not learned to come from her soul yet. She does know that your love for her is pure; she just cannot comprehend why.

Beautiful Souls

More is coming and she will feel more engaged with you as the months unfurl. Communication is key. If you share with her this reading, her soul will smile.

Emma likes when you make her smile, Scott. Even when she tries to hide it.

Emma really cares about you a lot. God brought her to you based on the law of attraction. We angels are answering your prayers. The masculine side of you attracted her. Fathering patterns brought Emma to you.

Emma helps you to learn how to love yourself more.

This is your journey.

This other relationship that will challenge you makes you feel alone and disconnected from your God force. You do not need to be jealous of any other soul.

If she does not choose you, this is okay.

Your journey shall continue.

You will always have to work on yourself. Growth is endless. You do not need to fear the outcome. There is no time limit.

Emma will take all the time she needs to work on this karmic necessity and will realize in her own time, not human time, that she still has the option to choose you. This can be weeks, months, and maybe years.

Your choices may change by the time she realizes, but this cannot be seen at this time. Freewill impacts many infinite possibilities.

Yet, no matter what, the love shall remain. Maybe silent, but constantly true, and rarely rearing its head. Your being is allowing the space for Emma to love herself more, but if you push too hard she will be forced to face herself too fast and will leave you.

She must be empowered to go at her own pace.

Something is coming up about her father. There is something about the way he pushes into her life. Her brothers are not going to like you at first. You are a threat to the family balance. They will give you a hard time. Emma knows this. She is a fish out of water there and often feels trapped. Emma does not want you to know yet or she has not faced it yet, however, she loves her family very much. Family is an important value to her.

You have jealousy in your heart Scott. This will be your downfall if you do not resolve. We must look at this. It has to do with loving yourself. There is a lot of love there with Emma. I know this scares you as well. Emma and yourself are very well suited in the male/female balance. There is love here. The angels approve of this relationship.

Refuse to Sink

Your jealousy Scott has to do with your masculine pattern issues. Your father figure was not good. The imprint from your dad is causing your jealousy. The answers to resolve this will be in your alone time and what you choose to do with it.

Prayer and meditation are important.

Emma and you will have balance and be together according to the angels, but this may take some time. They are saying this is a message from God… "in time" is the important phrase to focus on. Do not act according to this knowledge and reading. You are to both be yourselves and follow your own path and guidance.

This is the journey.

When and if this is meant to be, the unfolding of this union will help you each to grow individually as you go through this experience. There is a magnetic and physical attraction between Emma and Scott. Scott, you should not have low self esteem.

Emma thinks you are good looking and loves your personality. You prayed her into existence.

Your aunt is here and has a message for you. She says she wants you to have more fun. She said she wants to see you married. It is time. She wants you to recognize that your masculinity is priceless.

She wants you to take that step with Emma and not be scared. She said that you should stop and change the way you think of yourself as a man and your self-image. She said you have charisma and you are desirable. She said that she could tell Emma desires you and that you are lucky that you found her. She approves of Emma.

She wants you to know that you as well are good enough for her and Emma is lucky to have you. She said that you deserve love and you deserve contact.

The word "complacency" is coming up. She said stop being complacent. She said fix your shit and stop stalling. She said be more active and stop worrying.

Your aunt loves you. She said Emma loves you. Your aunt sees how Emma makes you feel.

She is saying if you pressure her she will be into you more. The more masculine you are the more she will be into you. Your aunt keeps saying over and over that she approves of Emma. Emma is curious, loving and will bring you peace of mind.

Beautiful Souls

Emma needs to feel better about herself. Scott, you need to speak to yourself in a more blissful way. You are not seeing the value in yourself. Your "one on one" relationship with yourself must improve.

Your aunt says she loves you and is always with you.

"Complacency" is coming up again. She is not happy with your living arrangements. She fears you are going to get sick. She wants you to love yourself and wants you to want more for yourself.

If you choose the right path you will have what you want. Your aunt sees you working hard but wants you to think differently about what you are doing. It is okay to plan around Emma and a future with her. She said, "build a nest and she will come." The nest she sees increases her fear and dampens the truth in her soul from coming out.

Emma wants security and safety.

She sees that you put others before yourself too much. Your aunt is asking you to be curious about this and think about it. Your aunt has only one disapproval of you.

You are serving too much. Your aunt sees your fear that you do not want to have regret. God saves the world, not you. God wants you to be happy and have fun. God wants Emma to be happy. You are both a gift to many people and many people on this planet are gifts yet to be discovered.

This is your ego Scott. You do not have to do as much as you think.

You are a gift to so many Scott and without you they would be more lost and bumping around more but this is okay. Your aunt says she has nothing to do with bringing Emma to you. She said that was God but she likes Emma a lot.

She likes that Emma makes you happy and she likes seeing you happy.

Your aunt sees that you are exhausted and asks that you take care of yourself. She is concerned about your health. Your aunt says she will help you in your future life. Just ask and speak to her. She is hoping that your life is about to get really good and she is hoping that it is with Emma.

She also knows you are sorry and she forgives you. She has nothing but love for you. She is giving you a hug now and is saying that she knows who you are, what you want and who you are becoming.

Your aunt sees your regrets, and wants you to be more blissful.

She knows God and wants you to know that you are on the right spiritual love path. She is also in the light and on the right path. This *reading and asking her for help supports her in taking a step on the right path on her side.*

We can help her in prayer by keeping her in our hearts about her transitioning up. She is definitely ascending but will not leave you. The Circle of Angels are real and are from the creator. She can see that now.

Communication is always key.

Your aunt says love yourself, give lots of hugs, love yourself, your job is good, but you will need to stay grounded and in time you will need to lean on Emma. She will need to lean on you as well. You will both know in that job when it is time that all you have to count on is each other. You need each other. You heal each other. You cause one another to grow even when you do not realize. You will help many people in this world.

Be honest and straight with her. She will accept you. The future is much bigger than the past. Go get her. Do not give up.'

Morena sat there with her hand propping up her head.

'Well,' I asked her.

"Well, what?"

'What do you think about everything?'

"You want me to sum up everything you just read in a matter of a few words?"

'Yeah,' I started. 'I trust your judgment.'

"Thank you," she crossed her legs and propped herself up against the pew in the sanctuary.

A long silence stood before us. Morena just looked at me with a distinct curiosity, then shifted her head to the right.

'Are you going to say anything?' I sat beside her.

"No," she smiled. "I don't think I will."

'Why?'

"Because you need to listen to your inner voice," she stood up and walked over to one of the stained-glass windows. "You need to make your own decisions, Scott."

'Okay, that's all you got out of that?'

"No," she gently rested her fingers on the glass. "But you need to be the one to carve your own path."

I rolled my eyes and walked over to her. The two of us stood perpendicular to one another while I waited for another response.

"It is time you made your own decisions," her voice grew stern and more purposeful. "The angels will support you, but you need to support yourself above all."

I scoffed at Morena. She was hiding something she just did not want to speak about. I never understood why she would tend to try to wholeheartedly reserve her judgment, even when I would ask her to tell me what was on her mind.

'Tell me,' I rested my body against the wall. 'What are you thinking?'

She sighed and flashed a smile towards me, "Just go within. Listen. Try to hear what that inner voice is telling you."

Yet every time I tried to listen to whatever my heart was saying, I was caught up in believing that Emma and I had a chance.

Our story was far from over. I devoutly believed it had to be the beginning of our story, and so it was.

∞ ∞ ∞ ∞ ∞ ∞ ∞ ∞

On the day of Lincoln Memorial High School's holiday party, I was nervous beyond belief. Emma seemed to be a lot happier than usual, which I hoped was due in part from the rekindling of our relationship.

Outlet was going to be performing at the Queens Community Church later in the evening, and Emma promised that her and Joy would make an appearance at the concert, before attending the holiday party. I wondered if life would be different after tonight or this weekend.

There is a famous saying that things change in a "New York minute," and I realized that my life would soon embody that phrase quite well.

Emma was wearing a black dress at work, which she looked utterly exquisite in, and her mere presence took my breath away. I always wanted it to be like that. I always wanted to bask in the glory that was her vibrant love.

As the hours marched on, I was anxious to be in the same room as Emma and get to experience her seeing me pursue my passion: drumming. Music was such a special part of my life for so long, and I was hoping that Emma would sense how important she was to me considering I wanted to share the experience of playing with Outlet with her in the audience.

Refuse to Sink

Whether it's the words Emma wrote in "The Vault" or just sitting across from Emma, everything she did during those pivotal weeks of our relationship was sheer magic. I felt that I was experiencing an entirely different mindset be it spiritual or just in terms of insight.

Every breath I took was in honor of the love I shared with Emma. Each moment that passed made me think of the future we could have together.

With each beat of the drum that was located on the altar of the sanctuary, I could see Emma's smile getting wider and wider. Joy sat with her head resting against Emma, the two of them looked on arm and arm with a beaming sense of pride. Their friendship and compassion towards me, above all, made me feel as if all of my dreams in education were possible.

Both of them were helping me lead the way to a better tomorrow, and at that point I didn't want it any other way.

A day later I was meeting Emma, Joy, and a few people from Lincoln Memorial at a local bar in the area. Although Joy was Emma's best friend, neither of us were comfortable telling Joy about our relationship. Emma stood steadfast when it came to hiding our relationship from everyone. As she said, our reputations and our careers were more important than what the world would see.

At the bar, once Emma had a bit of alcohol in her, the two of us could not keep our hands off of each other. Part of me wanted to say that I really didn't care because I was crazy about her, but I respected who Emma was and what she wanted.

That night, Joy looked on as Emma and I were moving closer and closer at the edge of the bar. Joy recognized how Emma's eyes were glistening each time they shifted towards me, and part of me did not care what she thought.

Part of me did not care what anyone thought of us.

Part of me thought that Emma's seemingly newfound liberation meant that she was coming to terms with the fact that our relationship was real. In my eyes, it didn't really matter what people were going to say.

Feelings are feelings, and our connection was proof that reality can be just as satisfying as fantasy.

In Emma's drunken stupor, she began to caress my back and smile intently as she continued sipping on her drink.

Beautiful Souls

"I don't get it," she whispered in my ear. "Why now?"

'What do you mean why now?' Joy shifted her eyes away from Emma and I.

"Why now?" Emma moved closer to me and started to giggle.

I smiled at Joy and she rolled her eyes.

I mouthed the word 'What?' to Joy, but she turned away.

In those moments with Emma resting against me, I realized that you could plan and plan as much as you want, but you never know when something or someone life-changing will appear.

As I watched her saunter away to the bathroom with Joy attached to her arm, part of me thought that maybe I should just leave. At that very moment, I wondered if I should just walk away and let Emma have a life that she planned out for herself.

Though I knew in my soul that we were meant for each other, something from deep within me said that Emma needed to make her own decisions. I made millions of decisions in my life that just never felt right, yet I followed them anyway because I didn't think happiness had any other definition.

But then there was Emma… and everything seemed to make sense.

I believed that years of fake smiles and just getting by finally had a purpose: to find her.

I thought I knew who I was and what I wanted in life, and once I found her; I figured that I could never let her go. I came to the irreconcilable conclusion that somehow and, in some way, Emma would manage to slip through my fingertips. Still, I vowed to hang onto her as long as I could.

When Joy and Emma came back from the bathroom, Emma fell into my arms accidentally and yelped loud enough for everyone in the bar to hear. As the eyes of our co-workers shot directly in our path, Emma jumped backwards and fell into Joy.

Joy appeared to be startled, but she did not take her eyes off of me.

"What the hell, Scott?" Emma beamed her inebriated eyes in my direction.

'What?'

"Do *not* grab me. That is inappropriate!" Emma seemed to be incredibly bothered by my presence.

'You fell into me and I-' Everyone was watching us intently and some were even giggling. I figured that this would be the very moment when our secret relationship was about to spring forth from the shadows and into the light.

Instead, Emma was sobering up and realized that she, in her eyes, just made it obvious that we were together.

And that was something she did not want.

The two of us argued as we made our way through the crowd and onto the rooftop of the bar. The lights from the street below glimmered with the hope that this brisk December night in Queens would turn to a romantic evening between Emma and I. However, as we continued to bicker, that idea seemed as if it were fleeting.

Joy followed us upstairs and stood in the doorway as the two of us sat at the wooden tables nearby. We barely noticed her for she was doing her best to seem invisible. The fabric awning whipped in the gentle breeze above us.

"You need to understand where I am coming from," Emma shouted at me.

'I do,' I yelled back. 'I understand you more than you know.'

Despite reaching out my hand to comfort her, she was still aggravated.

"No," she screamed. "No, you don't!"

'Hey,' I shouted back.

Joy began to recede into the staircase, though I could see her head peering over the window.

Emma strained to speak her mind: "You don't *get* me."

'I get your soul,' I extended my hand to Emma again, but this time she rushed towards me and kissed me.

The two of us embraced in that picturesque scene on the rooftop for a few moments, which made me feel as if nothing else mattered in this world.

As we looked into each other's eyes and made our way hand in hand down the steps, Joy reached out and tapped me on the shoulder. I released Emma's hand as she made her way back down to the party.

"I never want to be a third wheel to you two ever again," Joy spoke sternly and followed Emma downstairs before I could even respond.

Hours later, Emma and I decided to rent a hotel room and allow the rest of the night to unravel before us as the ribbons of time eloquently made their way down our merging pathways through life.

Beautiful Souls

The intimacy the two of us shared could not even be expressed in words.

Emma and I shared our fears, our hopes, and our ambitions for the future. I caught her scratching at her thighs and we spoke about how nervous she was to finally be in a bed with me.

"Do you want to feel them?" Emma asked awkwardly.

'What?'

"The scratches," she pointed at the gentle scars on her skin.

Instinctively I wrapped my fingers around her insecurities in hopes of making her see just how beautiful she was, both inside and out.

It was an intricate moment in time, almost as if the two of us were in a movie.

Emma was vulnerable and allowed me to fall in love with every touch of her supple skin: her perceived imperfections were exquisite from my point of view.

Letting someone into your world is difficult, whether you are intoxicated or sober, and I knew that first hand. It spoke volumes about our relationship and where we were going.

I loved every inch of her body, and there was nothing she could say or do to tell me otherwise. The intermingling of our hands and the sinuous peace that appeared as she smiled with her head on my chest granted me with the notion that life was and would forever be composed of our love's sweet music.

Yet the first line in a song about our love seemed to scream out, *"I should walk away from you forever…"*

And that would have seemed to be another sign that something was so wrong in thinking we were so right, though I could not fight the feelings that arose when her hair brushed against my bare chest.

∞ ∞ ∞ ∞ ∞ ∞ ∞ ∞

'I don't know what it is, but I feel like I am going to screw up.' I looked in Morena's eyes and she seemed to change her demeanor.

Morena knew that I loved Emma deeply, but she seemed to fall short when it came to the words of wisdom that would usually be so natural for Morena to conjure up.

"If you feel like you are going to screw up," she began. "Then you are willing that into the universe."

'But,' I rested my forehead on the pew in front of me. 'I am terrified of losing her.'

The sanctuary provided us with the comfort of talking about practically anything, though I knew that God was granting us the elegant space to express ourselves.

A resounding silence echoed through the room.

'Morena,' I whipped my head towards her. 'Speak to me. Tell me what to do. I need help.'

"I know," she smiled. "I just want you to finally make a decision that will be yours and yours alone."

No one ever wanted that for me before.

'Thank you,' my impatience simmered in the dust particles that spread throughout the room.

"Ask yourself why you love Emma," Morena started. "Why do you want to choose her?"

'Because,' tears welled in my eyes. I took a deep breath and exhaled in such a resilient manner. 'Because I want her to be my everything. I do not want to imagine my life without her. I do not want to be alone.'

Morena grinned and stood up. She smoothed out her pants and stretched slightly as she stepped towards the altar. As the sole beam of sunlight wrapped itself around her shadow, her glance took on a more devout meaning.

"If you truly, deeply believe she could be your everything," Morena's voice took on a stern tone. "Then you need to do everything in your power to grow your own soul."

'What?'

"You need to make sure that the image that looks back at you in the mirror is someone you are comfortable with. Be comfortable with your skin, and then you'll be comfortable within."

'I hear you.'

The two of us stood there, looking at each other, just smiling.

'I'm working on loving myself, honestly.'

"Keep working at it, Scott," she began walking down the aisle, brushing past me slightly as she left. "Everything is going to be okay."

Something within me felt ready. A sense of purpose was growing from the depths of my soul: Emma and I could be the ultimate power couple. There would never be a love like ours and I had never experienced what the two of us were going through.

I thought possibly I had finally found the one.

Days later at work, I was building up the courage to speak to Emma about potentially taking our relationship to the next level. I knew in my heart that Greg could never be the soulmate she was looking for, and that I loved her more than he ever could.

When I woke up in the morning, it felt as if the air became less dense overnight. I could finally breathe fresh air without worrying about what would happen next.

For all intents and purposes, Emma was my future.

As I walked into work later that afternoon, there was an extra pep in my step. I could not wait to counsel the students and speak to Emma about my future… well, our future.

The minutes passed before me and the next thing I knew, I was nervously staring into the mirror at my reflection. Morena's words floated through my head, but they paled in comparison to the majestic eloquence that was Emma's abrupt entrance into the room.

When I leaned forward to kiss her, she put her hand up and crinkled her face.

"Who is Bryan?" Her tone was partially furious and partially spiteful.

I never told her about Bryan, for I didn't share with her every aspect of my past. Our relationship was moving so fast that I did not think to tell her. It is not that I was ashamed of my son or my experiences, but parts of my private life simply did not come up.

Bryan is the most important person in my life, but maybe I had this subconscious weird feeling that she would not accept that I have a son. In hindsight, I realize it is a very poor excuse because lying is never a good thing in any relationship.

Still, I do not think that I was ever outright lying.

I wanted to find the right words to tell her how complicated my past was, but I struggled inside.

I loved her, though I did not know how to balance the deep pain from my past relationships and the emotions I felt each time I thought of Emma.

Refuse to Sink

The two of us sat on the couch and she expressed how angry she was with me, although she said she loved me so. I apologized immensely for hiding part of my life from her, but she said that we would be okay.

We walked back towards the parking lot and began listening to music while sitting in my Monte Carlo. Emma ran her fingers along the leather passenger seat looking to find something to say.

"Empty Apartment" from Yellowcard came on the radio, which made Emma's eyes well up with tears. It seemed that she was lost in the lyrics to the song:

> *"Call me out*
> *You stayed inside*
> *One you love*
> *Is where you hide*
> *Shot me down*
> *As I flew by*
> *Crash and burn*
> *I think sometimes*
> *You forget where the heart is."*

I looked over at her and brushed my fingers along her cheek. She leaned over and fell into my arms instinctively.

Deep down, she knew I loved her and I knew that she loved me.

"It will always be us," floated from her lips and directly to my heart.

Nothing could stop us.

∞ ∞ ∞ ∞ ∞ ∞ ∞ ∞

Joy texted me as the weekend rolled around.

She said that her and Emma were definitely excited to see Outlet play later that night, though Emma told me privately that she was thinking of staying home that night.

The band was performing at a local bar in Queens and I was thrilled to get behind the drums again. I had begged the band to learn to play "Empty Apartment," which I discovered was Emma's favorite song.

Beautiful Souls

Though as the night closed in upon us, and Emma and Joy looked on with excitement in their eyes, I discovered that I created a door for Emma to escape from.

As the band played "Empty Apartment," Emma's face instantly went sour. Little did I know that her favorite song harnessed such a tragic memory for her.

That was the second strike in less than 24 hours.

I was not doing too well.

Emma stormed off and Joy watched the love drain from my eyes as she walked away.

"It'll be okay," Joy smiled and placed her hand on my shoulder. "It will all be okay."

∞ ∞ ∞ ∞ ∞ ∞ ∞ ∞

The following day I went to Alley Pond Park and wrote Emma a five-page letter. I did a lot of soul searching: Why did I hold back parts of my life from her? Who am I? Why would I hide myself from someone who meant so much to me?

Emma did say she never wanted to lose me, so why was I so afraid?

I watched a squirrel dive in and out of a dead pile of leaves then scurry up a tree. It reminded me of the life Emma and I were creating. We were playing in the leaves in such a joyous manner, and neither one of us wanted to climb up the tree just yet. Though if we dug our nails into the tree and climbed together, would we find what existed beyond the surface?

When I returned to work that Monday, there was a note on my desk:

Scott,

Sorry this world can suck sometimes but it could be worse - Anna Kendrick could be dead and octagons could be declassified as a shape.

Love,
Emma

Octagon was our code word. It came about one night when she was drunk and trying to make a shape out of her hand gestures. It was a silly moment that stuck and became our inside joke, our code word, our everything. There was even an octagon building near our job that we would make jokes about.

She was struggling. I was struggling. I had to let go.

Greg was back in the picture and she was wholeheartedly torn: she had to choose one of us, and I was fearful that it would take her too long for her to realize that she should choose me. I guess that idea is selfish in a sense, because no one should ever feel pressured to choose between two people.

Still, I loved her so much. She knew that. It was a deep-rooted truth that lingered in her soul.

In the days that followed, I was working with the students at Lincoln Memorial on a puzzle piece-shaped project we were hanging on the walls. Every person in the school had to add a positive message on the puzzle piece in order to spread some semblance of joy around the school.

One puzzle piece struck me with such a sense of profound love:

"Dear Scott,
Thank you for giving me the power to challenge my independence.
Love, Emma"

I was not crazy. She loved me.

Emma ended up giving me two beautiful paintings she created, along with a magnificent sketch of an infinity sign and an anchor, which had an inscription that said, "Refuse to Sink" on the right side.

The first painting was an image of her silhouette adorned with the lyrics to one of her favorite songs, "Rinse" by Vanessa Carlton:

"...If she runs away she fears she won't be followed.
What could be worse than leaving something behind?"

The second painting was an image of a Christmas tree in front of a cross, for she knew how spiritual I was and how much I loved Christmas.

I wanted nothing more than to do something special with the sketch she gave me, so I chose to carve her image into my soul forever: it became the forearm tattoo that runs through my veins day in and day out.

The anchor and infinity sign wholeheartedly represent who I am and what I stand for: I refuse to sink.

And as the tattoo needle burned her artwork into my skin, I knew I never would sink. When she saw her artwork adorned on my body, her facial expression was a mixture of shock, awe, and elation. At the time, I just couldn't tell what she felt more.

In the days leading up to the school's weeklong winter break, a sense of trepidation lurked in my mind again.

I left the notebook, "The Vault," in Emma's mailbox at work and she left me with this last entry of the year before we left the building:

Dear Scott,

With 4 minutes left to this night, I do not really know what I want to write about. I feel guilty holding this book for so long because so much has happened and been said that there is a gap in our entries... in our story.

Today was a long day and I wasn't exactly the nicest person to you. You didn't deserve it but subconsciously I think I was mad at you. So so so much has unfolded and with every word, as much as I can expect it, they are still unexpected. Waves keep breaking and I am taking them each time to stay afloat. I had a large agenda today and reflecting back I think that thinking about the day, all I was dealing with, keeping up with "us" was not on the agenda.

It was too much.

I wanted to push it all out of my head today and not deal with it. Do not get me wrong. Some amazing things have happened between us and I really do treasure you, but wow, when I take a breath I am blown away on how I can still be a functioning human. I got thrown into this ring of love, taking punch after punch to my soul, and trying to stay ahead calm and cool, and it just all caught up to me today.

I needed to push you away.

Also, after the tattoo yesterday... I know I did this for you.... And for us, but it hit me hard.... You got this grand permanent ink on your body

Refuse to Sink

and what if days later I am faced with this ring... how do I say no to that? Maybe I am feeling guilt.

Now I am feeling should I have not drawn it?

Should I have not given you this for Christmas?

Yet, I did and I was determined to give it to you. I wanted you to have this. I wanted this on you. I wanted on some level for us to be permanent. All I wanted in that moment was to surprise you and make you smile as you make me smile always. I wanted you to have this before I left for my weekend. I wanted you to have this piece of us to hold and to treasure. What does that say about me? It is all confusing. So confusing.

It scares me and it is sitting in my throat.

Please please do not freak out and lose it. Maybe I just need to write this out so we can talk through it. I do not want to hide these feelings from you and maybe writing it out will make me feel better.

I do not want to say anything else to upset you. I really do care for you. It is my turn to have a bad day.

This may be the last entry from me before the break. RELAX! I am so excited to come back to reading all your entries. I love when you write. It makes my cheeks hurt from smiling so much!

Everything will be fine!

ALWAYS remember that.

Does the earth stop moving? No. So why should we? Take deep breaths and treasure the moments, don't count them. Wasteful habits are horrid. Even though I do not have anything imprinted on me, you have left marks on my soul that will never go away.

This is not a one-way street.

We will talk a bunch I am sure of it, but when I am up in the woods, talk to me here. Each entry is like a surprise and I love surprises. It has definitely been an incredibly crazy adventurous and emotional end to the year but it has all been something I know I am tremendously grateful for.

Just remember, whenever you are having bad thoughts, picture my hurting cheeks smiling, my "ughing" and saying "its finnnnne Scott." Okay? Ok. Great!

You got this.

Please forgive me. It will all be fine.

We will be fine. Write me back. I like when you write.

Beautiful Souls

I love you.

Always,

Emma

Despite acknowledging that Greg could propose to her over the break, I wrote back. I was supportive and loving. I told her I would take things slow, give her space, and just be there for her.

For Christmas I gave her two charms on a bracelet: the anchor and infinity sign looked beautiful in silver.

She placed it on her ankle and wore it with such pride in our love.

She struggled for days and we texted on and off, but we were never apart.

We continued to call each other; the journals and adoring words were exchanged.

We were on borrowed time, but I did not want to give her up just yet.

∞ ∞ ∞ ∞ ∞ ∞ ∞ ∞

I gazed out into the darkness of the sanctuary. My chest felt heavy as my heaving sighs and sweat-drenched forehead registered some semblance of balance while scurrying to my feet. The curtains rustled in the wind that burst into the room. I don't remember leaving the window open, but I must have, because I was the only one there.

Remnants of Emma's hair lay strewn across the floor as I teetered over to slam the window. If I hadn't known any better, I would think that she had just got up to use the bathroom and in her infinite wisdom, opened the window on one of the coldest nights of the winter season. Though I knew deep in my heart that she was not there and I had to have been the one to crack open the window. I was all alone; it couldn't have been anyone else.

A sudden creaking noise drew my attention to the corner of the room, only to be met with the silhouette of my robust figure being cast on the glimmering wall. It took looking in the reflection of the shadow that I realized I gained some weight. It was a harsh reality that only sunk me deeper into a depressed state. The door swung open and I was startled by the figure of a small woman standing in the shadows.

"Scott, what are you doing out of bed," the voice whispered, "You'll wake the baby."

I rushed closer to the figure, 'Baby,' I gasped, 'What baby?'

The window burst open and I heard loud screams. I actually woke up this time, my head resting against the car window. As I watched my breath collect in the form of fog on the window, I realized that Emma would always be with me in my dreams, even if she did physically leave me.

Each day that passed, Morena watched me putter around the sanctuary. I think both of us expected that Emma would call at any moment saying she was engaged.

One night, Morena found me passed out on a pew with my phone still on. Emma and I had passed out on each other while we were on an intense call together.

On Christmas Day, I went to the school and sat in an exterior doorway with just a lawn separating me, and the windows to her classroom. I had nowhere to be and nobody wanted to see me. Bryan was in Florida and I just wanted to be near Emma.

I sat there in the snow for over an hour and cried.

It felt like a bad 80s romance movie, or that scene in *The Notebook* where Allie was proposed to, though she had the image of Noah in her head.

I wondered if I could be her Noah.

Then it hit me: I could not experience a painful love like Faith's ever again.

This was exactly why I didn't want a relationship.

My head smashed down into the snow as I heaved and felt nauseous.

"What are you doing to yourself?" Morena stood before me; her tracks traced her purposeful steps in the snow.

'What are you doing here? How did you find me?' I wiped my tears.

"I know you well enough by now, Scott." She sat beside me, and the two of us shivered in the snow for a while just watching Emma's classroom windows.

It was there, with the pristine snow falling before us, and our bodies shivering, that I realized that Morena was not as she appeared. I spent years upon years asking the universe questions, but she seemed to have the answers. Maybe that fateful day when we met in the coffee shop the universe was telling us that we were destined for more than just the trivial day-to-day nonsense that pandered before us.

"If you want the love you deserve," Morena put her frigid hand on my shoulder. "Then you need to go within."

A solitary tear rolled down my cheek.

'I know, Morena,' I let out a deep sigh. 'I know.'

Minutes later she stood up and extended a hand towards me.

"Let's get you out of this cold," Morena hoisted me up and we walked to the nearest coffee shop to warm up.

Emma ended up calling the day after Christmas while I was on a five-mile walk. She was upset that Greg did not propose to her and her sadness confused me. I was supportive, but I was secretly devastated: there I was, loving her and appreciating her, but she did not honor my role in her life at the time.

She admitted that she felt guilty, but I reassured her that I was there for her. I would comfort her soul and I would help her work through her emotions. I also told her that if he were playing games with her heart, I would step in.

Her voice suddenly took on a stark contrast to what I expected would happen.

Emma told me she was uncomfortable and a fight ensued.

"I have to go. Greg is coming now." Her curt tone left me with a sour taste in my mouth.

The two of us didn't speak again until the New Year started, but it gave me the strength to start writing some of my story down. I firmly believed that every great love started with a great story, but I just didn't realize the gravity that this relationship would have and weigh upon my soul at the time.

As I rummaged through my private journal and the papers in my bag at the time, I stumbled across the card Emma gave me for Christmas:

Refuse to Sink

Scott,

"You have a special place in my heart. As I thank God for all the blessings He gives, I'm thanking Him especially for you because you <u>mean so much to me</u>, and I'm so glad you're part of my life! We have shared together the blessings of God." Philippians 1:7

I hope you like this card and know I went a "little bit" out of my comfort zone for it. It was the first one I spotted, and when I picked it up, it just seemed so "Scott." What I write here is all separate from the vault and I just want you to know that over these next days, I'll miss you. I'll also be wishing for you to have the best Christmas and New Years. You're an amazing guy who deserves it. Looking back on this year and more so the past few months, you taught me a lot about myself and just been the first person to walk into my life that I can share this way with. You get <u>ALL</u> of me. Yes, it is rare. This journey we take moment by moment, <u>uncounted</u>, that is key. Each day is a gift, and blessing, and life is life with its own rules and ways. Right now, it's chosen for US to be here at these crossroads. Let life happen. Everything is fine always and thank you for the most precious gift this year I could receive. Have a wonderful Christmas, and a Happy New Year.

Love "Always,"
Emma

P.S. Breathe!

I threw everything back in my bag and dashed out the door to the church. I had to go to the bridge.

Red and blue flashing lights in my rear-view mirror were a poignant ending to this day. It had been days since I last heard from Emma, and I was beginning to think that bottling up everything from today meant that I would burst momentarily.

In the hustle and bustle of the chaos around me, I felt sick to my stomach. Maybe it was a bad day, but it certainly was not a bad life. Though she will never realize how much those words in her card meant to me after everything, I pray she felt the extra positivity I sent to her that night in my dreams.

∞ ∞ ∞ ∞ ∞ ∞ ∞ ∞

When the two of us were in flow and in our prime, we were working together and splitting up counseling meetings with students. Anytime Joy needed help, the two of us supported her and friends and beacons of infinitesimal hope. For all intents and purposes, Greg did not exist.

Our conversations consisted of philosophical questions like "Where do you go when you die?" and Emma would sit in the church with me for hours talking about her spirituality. The two of us would lay on the mattress I had in the attic of the church, which was situated above the sanctuary. We would talk for hours upon hours and our conversations never seemed like they would have a concrete ending.

Leading up to her birthday in late January, the two of us were in the midst of a rollercoaster of emotions. Emma continued to flip flop between pursuing the life she created for herself with Greg and the relationship she had with me.

She continued leaving cute things on my desk like homemade pies and cards, which usually sounded endearing, like this one:

Dear Scott,

You asked me once about my standards and I said that they have only gotten higher, so let me name some and just say you can take a breath because you over achieved them all:
- *HAS to make me laugh*
- *HAS to know and do what I want/need without asking (because I am a girl, duh!)*
- *CANNOT be afraid of my extreme weirdness moments but can join me and be just as weird.*
- *Understand how hard I work (physical job)*
- *Understand that deep down at my core I am a people pleaser that does anything and anything for someone.*
- *Shows me appreciation and affection.*

Of course, a girl like me has more than six, but those are the tops. I do not want to kill you with expectations. You are doing great!

Love Always,
Emma

I would spend hours looking at the paintings she made me and reading her words. Her presence and how she loved me seemed so real, but I could not fully fathom how she was ensnared between two seemingly different relationships: one with me, and one with Greg.

When her birthday finally rolled around, I watched her favorite movie, *Galaxy Quest*, alone in the church. As a blizzard roared around the edges of the building, she called and told me she was devastated that everyone decided to stay home and forego her birthday party plans.

It was clear that she was in pain, and there were a lot of romantic exchanges between the two of us, but Greg was on the forefront of her mind. I gave her plenty of my own philosophy on true love, her soul, and how she should embrace her inner power. Emma appeared to hear what I was telling her, but she seemed hesitant in terms of embracing my words in her own soul.

That weekend, the two of us met at a hotel and we celebrated her birthday with much less pomp and circumstance, but with the utmost love I had in my heart. Hours passed by and she ended up having to leave earlier than expected, so I left her to gather her thoughts and allow myself the space to think about our relationship.

I stood trapped between reality and our passionate love dwindling in the setting sun. As I leaned on the railing to the church, glaring out at the majestic colors fading into the horizon, the moon was a reminder that all things, including the end of a day, were beautiful.

Leaving Emma in the bed, wrapped in the sheets and too pristine for this world, I came to the stark realization that true love can wear a person out. Flashes of our love danced in front of my eyes as I sincerely missed her hands intertwined between mine.

Just a mere thirty minutes had passed since I last kissed her forehead. Just a miniscule hour ago, we were skin to skin. Our hearts beat rapidly and as one. Our souls collided in the most humanistic and ravishing ways.

We were infinite. We were doused in each other's sweat and adoration. We reached the peak in any physical relationship, and we dropped to the sheets knowing the effect we had on each other: passionate love is passionate love. A deep, sensual love exists in those who have collided skin before… it was an accident that carried so much merit. It was a cataclysmic event where you are holistically vulnerable.

As images of her body rocking close to mine danced away in the night sky, I dragged my exhausted frame into the church. Still, I knew full and well that I had to resist the urge to run back to her. I had to force myself to linger in the melodic chimes of the church building, for if I went back to Emma now, the odds of one of us passing out would be probable.

I eagerly and impatiently waited for the next moment I could cling to her body. I yearned to be in her arms again… holding her gently and caressing her supple skin…

Yet I knew I had to wait for tomorrow…

But tomorrow was just one day away…

She continued to leave little notes on my desk, while I texted her my thoughts. Emma was worried that people may notice me walking in and out of her classroom, so I stopped leaving things for her where someone may stumble across them.

She would tell me in texts that she loved me and that it would "always be us." Emma said we would get through this and that she missed me.

In the dwindling days before February began, the two of us had one of our rendezvous in Kissena Park. We would meet far from the building so that no one would see us together.

I would pull into the parking lot of the park and watch her leave her car. Sitting back in the driver's seat of my Monte Carlo, I could see the outline of her silhouette appear more defined. A gentle gust of wind grasped her hair and whipped it forward each time she leaned back. Her eyes were far shallower now than they had ever been, and her lips were far too dry for a kiss.

As she got into the car, she leaned into my chest and began to cry openly. As the snow flurried down upon the windshield, our intertwined bodies merged in the symphony that surrounded us. The flakes cascading down the car emulated the sweat that beaded down our foreheads.

Refuse to Sink

We were flooded by both the intense passion enveloping our bodies and the snowfall that began to encompass the car. The gentle fog sealed us away in our compassionate love as the lyrics to "Keep on Loving You" by REO Speedwagon wrapped around our skin. Our heated embrace and sweet whispers were exchanged over and over again. Two hearts beat as one, a rhythmic entity that refused to part ways.

And despite threats of Greg's engagement, I sensed that she would end up choosing me.

After we cleaned up from our afternoon delight, she told me about how she prayed for me each and every night. Emma had a ritualistic nature to her, as she called them, "bedtime prayers," that ushered her into a tranquil night of sleep. She told me that I was consistently on her mind, especially before she went to bed.

Our nightly texts continued, but our daytime fights were running rampant through my soul. I started feeling an aching sensation in my core, but I knew I did not know how to process losing and loving Emma all at once.

My greatest fears were being actualized, but I was clinging to some semblance of her love.

Then in the midst of everything, Bryan told me he was going to move to Florida to be closer to his mother. I was crushed, but I knew that he was free to live his life how he pleased. Bryan told me that he was miserable and had to try something new. Emma was supportive throughout my emotional turmoil, and she assured me she would be with me throughout this difficult time.

I found a purple envelope with a peacock on it that said, "A thank you for being you" on it. Emma must have left it on the passenger seat of my car at some point. It read:

Dear Scott,

Simply saying "Thank You" couldn't begin to cover the gratitude I have towards you. Not only have you shown me so much but you've let me be the inside me on the outside. Thank you for that connection. Thank you for always being there. Thank you for coming back after I left. Thank you for making endless time for me. For making me feel unique, one of a kind, and special. You have such an influence on me as well as others and you do not hear appreciation enough. You are an amazing magical soul. Thank you for allowing the world, and especially myself to see that.

*Love Always,
Emma*

This would be one of the last notes she would leave for me. The last one was a vertical infinity sign that was superimposed over an anchor. At the bottom she inscribed, "I love you" in big, bold letters.

She did love me. I was sure of it. Sometimes she was scared to say, "I love you," so she would tell me that she "liked me a little bit." "A little bit" became our inside joke and our way of saying we loved each other without actually saying it.

The two of us joined Joy and a handful of other co-workers at one of the local bars for a few drinks after work. Although my drinking days were in the distant past, I liked socializing with everyone.

No one suspected anything between me and Emma, except for Joy, though Emma and I were comfortable enough knowing that Joy would never say anything to anyone.

The bar was packed with idle chatter and clinking glasses, but Emma was the only person I was focused on. She was swallowing alcohol almost as fast as she was breathing in air; I could tell she was nervous. I didn't understand why at the time.

Soon after she finished guzzling down what appeared to be her fourth drink in less than a few hours, Greg showed up.

I wanted to walk up to him and address him, man to man. The chill crept up my spine and split itself down the center of my core. A solitary thought whipped through my mind: Do you kiss her goodnight just as easily as you shatter every fiber of my existence?

The two of them got into a heated argument and they left together. Emma walked right past me without saying anything. She was being nasty on purpose and I never saw that side of her before.

I was crushed. What did I do?

Upon walking out the back door of the bar, I didn't hear Joy follow me into the bitter cold. I threw myself onto the floor sobbing hysterically, almost throwing up in the process, and tried everything in my power to prevent my wailing from disturbing the people who lived in the nearby houses.

Joy bent down and hoisted me from the floor with such sincerity.

"Do you want to go talk somewhere?" Joy's concern was adorned across her face.

'Yeah,' I swallowed. 'Yeah I would really like that.'

This was the first night that triggered a deep-rooted friendship with Joy. We spoke about our lives and I poured my heart out to her without any guilt.

I began to hang out with Joy to make Emma incredibly jealous. It was absurd that Emma did not treat me with the same respect that Joy bestowed upon me. This eventually led to "The Vault" slamming shut for the rest of eternity.

Joy started to pull away from Emma as she coached me on how to get back with her. As Emma's demeanor and nastiness began to rise to the surface, I could see Joy getting crushed by the dissolving bond that was once sturdy and true. Joy and I would reminisce about the "old" Emma and I started to tuck away my emotions.

Both Joy and I realized that a concrete line drifted between myself and Emma, but I was resisting it wholeheartedly.

Even in the resolute silence that existed between myself and Emma, and after several weeks of silence and pain, I came to a spiritual crossroad. I had never felt more betrayed or misunderstood by anyone.

Losing Emma was dragging me to my knees.

I saw a family in our future, I saw a life together; I saw so much that we could accomplish, but with Greg's looming proposal, everything was starting to fade.

Nobody knows my true soul and my inner search for God and divine love, but in sharing snapshots and thoughts that fluttered through my head I thought I might have had a glistening moment in time. Who would have thought that another human being, who I admired and respected, would demolish those snapshots?

Morena watched me sit in the sanctuary night after night again.

"Don't try to bury your pain," she would reassure me. "Let it all out. Crying is pain leaving the soul."

Beautiful Souls

I had a nightmare in the true definition of exquisite horror. There was a little girl standing in the center of a long corridor. It looked like the wing of a hospital. There she stood, in a small gown, glaring into the darkness. The fluorescent lights flickered and scattered hospital equipment lay strewn around the floor. The linoleum tiles, though white in reality, were bloodstained almost as bright as the streaks on the walls.

"Come play with me, Scott," the little girl whimpered. Upon turning, a concrete wall lay blocking my return path. The only way to go was forward. I reluctantly followed her. Her blonde hairs spread across her head like static. She could not have been older than 8 or 9… maybe 7.

We walked through the hospital knocking into broken wheelchairs and boxes along the way.

'What happened,' I asked inquisitively.

"They attacked," she said, a sullen tone emulating from her. We stopped walking and I looked down at her.

'Who attacked you?' I bent down and met her glassy eyes.

She shrugged and merely said, "the bad people." Her arm rose suddenly and three people stood at the end of the hallway, dressed in heavy black clothes and covered in blood. The scene shifted to a school hallway, dimly lit, with the three walking down it.

"You're next, Scott… run," a voice echoed down the hall.

I planted my feet firmly and boomed: 'No. I don't run."

The three sets of eyes I didn't recognize locked on my gaze.

'You run, run now,' my voice echoed down the hallway. Their stern faces transformed into fearful ones. They darted down the hall and one tripped in her retreat. I scampered over to pick her up from the floor.

'Here,' I said, 'Take my hand.' I tried pulling her up, but she refused my help. Her hazel eyes sunk into her skull with devout fear stemming from her body.

"I did this to me," she yelled. Her head twisted into the pit of her elbow and she retreated further back. "I'm sorry" were the last audible words that she muttered before bursting into mere ash.

"Save them, Scott," boomed from somewhere. "Save them now."

Then I woke up as a bright light ascended over me. Morena looked at me with a tinge of panic in her eye.

"Are you okay?" She was sifting through papers.

I didn't have to lie to her and say that I was fine; Morena knew that I was struggling and she continued to reassure me that everything was going to be okay.

∞ ∞ ∞ ∞ ∞ ∞ ∞ ∞

The frigid wind whisked through my hair with intense violence. The air was still, but turbulent enough to catch whomever was in its path in a whirl, a twirl, and an instinctive squint.

Looking down at my watch, the numbers read 2:22 A.M. A sigh pulled my breath in front of my face, as my shivering kept me awake and from feeling fundamentally alone on that dimly lit street.

The little dance I did to warm me up did not prevail. My shivering was unending. 'Where is he, where is he,' managed to leak from my frostbitten lips.

Time kept progressing under that streetlight in the harsh darkness of that bitter morning.

I stood impatiently waiting for something. Anything. A sign.

I had been summoned here under the pretense that a sign would materialize. Something would happen, and that something would be clear.

Faint music could be heard from a car radio in the distance. Could this be it? The sign?

No, it is just a passing motorist.

Great, 2:48 A.M.

Another few minutes ushered themselves through the floating garbage in the street. The wind showed mercy to not a thing, nor a soul, in the morning air.

Footsteps echoed in the air. A faint memory of someone who should have been standing there with me, yet somehow dissipated into the atmosphere.

The feeling was rather haunting. It was a terse reminder of how we spend so much time trying to please others, yet falter in actually trying to do what is best for ourselves.

I would say it is sickening, but it is yet another part of being a wholesome soul… or at least something to that extent.

Beautiful Souls

Dancing with my shadow in the streetlight, I saw another figure moving slowly in the dark. I relaxed my back against the streetlight's post, hoping this was the foretold sign.

3:03 A.M.

The figure slowly dragged its frame closer and closer, without a hint of personality lurking underneath its hood.

Pensively, I squinted at the sight of what was nearing my aura. I could not read the person's intentions.

The click of their shoes meeting the pavement grew louder.

3:04 A.M.

As the person approached me, their dark hood waved in the wind. The suspense of who this figure was grew. I was struck by silence.

The dark hood stood inches from my face without showing its face. All that was visible was a shadowy chin, cast upon by the overhead light.

3:05 A.M.

A frigid peep lurched from my mouth. 'What do you want? Why am I here?'

A stern voice crept from under the hood. It shook me to my core as I heard it echo through my soul.

"You wanted answers, well here I am," the hood flew back, revealing her pristine face. A face that had melted somewhere into my past many many moments ago. Wrinkles pooled themselves at the edges of her eyes, as they met my gaze with a harsh tone.

"Well," fell from her lips, almost as if she were impatiently waiting for some sort of response.

A surprised look must have been the first thing she expected, because she was unfazed by the cold. She was locked onto my gaze.

"Say something Scott, no one knows I am here, just say it," she clattered her teeth.

'Hello Emma,' 3:06 A.M.

Emma and I rekindled some romantic moments in Kissena Park in the privacy of our cars, but she would ignore me at work. I was no longer permitted near her or her classroom when the two of us were in the building.

As my eyes fluttered open, I could feel last night on my skin. The words clung to my body like the sticky residue from an old movie theatre's

Refuse to Sink

floor. Switching masks had become a painful reminder that not a single person saw 100% of the pain I am in. As each mask was removed and laid on the floor, I couldn't help looking at the scattered existence of what once was and what could never be.

We would have long winded fights on the phone. It grew ugly but she assured me that we were still us, and we were still together.

Being considered a passenger in your own life is fundamentally depressing. With each step, each movement, your strings are being pulled left and right with no control. It burns to the core and cuts way deeper than anyone could fathom.

Knowing all this, I stood in front of the mirror gazing at the image of a fractured man. Looking into his eyes and watching life slowly drain from them was painful. Almost as if he knows what he is doing, yet he can't control himself. He doesn't know what the truth is, so he feeds into his own misery because he became devoid of emotion a long time ago. However, he's trying to find the pieces of his heart in the shadows of what once was and what was never meant to be.

In being everyone's rock, he's chipped away at his values and core beliefs until nothing but silenced echoes remain. He is lost in emotion and caught between doing what is right for him and what his heart is trying to whisper to him in the balance of dawn and dusk.

His joy disappeared the day it was created. His life became a puzzle with the right shapes but the wrong pieces. Now he is more isolated than ever, for he is an island and desolated the water encompassing him.

Who would be brave enough to risk treacherous waters in order to try to reach him?

In the midst of my downward spiral, I figured that the image of being half of a power couple was fleeting, and then I got some reassurance from the universe that there was hope. There was an ounce of yearning and an ounce of ambition left within me.

With a single phone call, I thought my life was about to turn around again… I just didn't know whether to take a step towards the light.

For even in the depths of what seemed to be my soul's darkest chapter, a solitary beam of light beckoned towards me.

"Hello Scott," the sultry voice at the other end of the phone was so familiar. "I miss you."

With trepidation in my voice, I replied instinctively: 'I miss you, too, Faith.'

CHAPTER 4

Keep the Faith

"I'll do what I got to, the truth is you could slit my throat, and with my one last gasping breath, I'd apologize for bleeding on your shirt"

- Taking Back Sunday, American Rock Band, Long Island, New York

Beautiful Souls

Fractured fairy tales laid open in front of me: their textured words emulating from empty pages of a love that never was. All that remained was the sinking feeling that the words dripping off my diaries were that of a mistaken goddess.

Her words, though once airy and gorgeous elements of all that was pure in this world, echoed the halls that stung from her loneliness.

And there I was, a knight without armor or a white horse, standing at the edge of tomorrow… hoping that one day, some way, somehow… she would realize that she could come down from the tower all on her own.

She would need saving… but she only needed saving from her own soul.

And that is the hardest fairy tale to tell after all: what do you do when you are the heroine masked by the darkness that you allowed to consume your soul? What do you build when your castle was merely made out of sand?

You cannot wash away the shame and pain that is your personality, but you have a chance to show a little bit of compassion and consideration for yourself.

The bitter cold pushed against me as the alarm clock blared its usual scream. The weight of the frigid air heavily compressed my chest as I waited for the tears to subside.

Another day.

I slid out from under the shelter of the blankets and gazed up at the moon peering through the window. It looked lonely. I knew that exact same feeling.

Scurrying into the bathroom, I felt my toes wrap around each frosted over floorboard. Upon flipping the lights on, I glared into the mirror and saw someone I did not recognize: it looked like a version of me, but one that very scarcely resembled what I thought I had become.

This second version of me reached through the mirror with the fervor of rage visibly running through their veins.

"It's coming," the mirror image blurted out, almost sing songy. It grasped my neck and ripped me against the glass.

With its frosted fingers around my neck, its horrid breath graced my ear, "It's coming. Be ready."

Glancing down at my body, I saw blood rushing from my shoulder mercilessly. A gunshot wound of some sort materialized on the surface of my skin. The reflection laughed maniacally and transformed into a person whom I had seen many times: a vivid image of my past manifesting inches from my face.

"Face your demons. Now." were the last words thrusted into the cold air before the image disappeared.

My eyes slammed shut and flew open between my rapidly beating heart. The illuminated digits on the clock read 3:14 A.M.

3:14 A.M. 3:15 A.M. 3:16 A.M. Time stands still for no one. Time relinquishes no control. Yet through the pangs of a heavily beating heart, there is solace in knowing strength overpowers malice every. Single. Time.

Last night began playing over in my mind like an old film. The reel was getting snagged in the machine, but the images cast on the wall haunted me so.

I grabbed my ratty old towel and started the cold water in the small church sink. The grime and mold on the walls appeared to scowl at the sad excuse of a man cleaning himself up in the miniscule bathroom.

Desperately and diligently, I was doing everything in my power to care for the building and save money so that one day, Windows of Opportunity would have a home within the walls of the Queens Community Church.

Still, Eve treated me as if I was under her merciless thumb.

We argued almost as much as I was arguing with Emma. Except with Eve, the hounding did not stop. She was wholeheartedly unaware that I was practically living in the church, though she knew I was sleeping in my car a few nights a week.

Emma wanted to have the white-picket fence and cute little house in the suburbs, and I was praying that one day I could provide that for her.

In this tumultuous time in my life, Morena came to the church bright and early to help me through my suffering.

She waltzed into the basement where I was washing my hair and brought me a fresh cup of coffee.

"You ready to get to work?" She passed me the cup and smiled.

As I grasped it from her, I looked up and asked if we could sit in the sanctuary for a bit.

The two of us made our way up the paint-chipped steps and through the glass doors. I could tell there was an energy shift the moment I walked in, for Morena and I stopped in our tracks.

I turned to her for a moment: 'Can we just talk?'

"I thought you would never ask," she replied, motioning to the seventh pew to our right. I usually sat there and had philosophical talks with God. In addition, my favorite stained-glass window was diagonal that pew.

I read her Psalm 42:5:

"Why am I so depressed? Why is this turmoil within me? Put your hope in God, for I still praise Him, my Savior and my God."

The two of us sat in silence for a moment, taking in the meaning of the words that I just said. I cut the silence between us with a realization:

'I wrote a lot during the years and most of my journals capture my daily life, love, or challenging aspects of my life. I don't know what is going on, but I feel like God is responding to what I have asked for.'

"Why do you think that," Morena asked.

'It's a song, it's a conversation, it's a movie, or a random moment,' I started. 'I just feel this overwhelming sense of faith growing within me. I just... I feel everything is happening for a reason.'

"Well, your life has been a test of faith through and through."

'You got that right.'

We let the silence boil over for a few more moments.

'The church seems like a gift from God, right?'

"What do you mean?"

'It's like God brought me a window of opportunity in allowing Windows of Opportunity to thrive here. We can truly make this place something special.'

"We can," Morena looked at me wistfully. "We can."

∞ ∞ ∞ ∞ ∞ ∞ ∞ ∞

February 2016 was a particularly bitter month for many reasons: Emma and I were caught in a tumultuous love story, where I didn't know if I was losing her or not, and I was running myself into the ground to keep the youth of Queens engaged in leadership programs.

Paul and Eve were beyond happy to have youth fill the halls of Queens Community Church, which meant that I was at the church well past

10:00 in the evening on school nights and often cleaned the community room in the basement.

After all, I was sleeping in the musty attic on a mattress I kept on the floor.

During the middle of a terrible snowstorm one weekend, Eve still insisted that a group that rented the church was still going to host an event in the community room. A gang of rowdy people showed up and ended up trying to attack me while I was attempting to break up a fight. A bunch of people spilled out onto the lawn of the church and they were trying to bring in drugs and alcohol.

Someone pulled a knife on me and before I knew it, I was trifling through terrible flashbacks of my time in Texas.

A rock flew through the church window and my hope of having a quiet night in during the storm was shattered.

Over a hundred people had to be thrown out of the church and Eve didn't care. We argued about having boisterous events late at night, but Paul told me the argument was not worth it.

"Let her be," Paul assured me. "Just let her be."

Morena and I continued our daily spiritual talks throughout the month, and though Emma was texting me, Faith was calling me consistently.

At this point I had been hurt, I was weak, I was in need of some serious soul nourishing moments. The sanctuary and the cross at Queens Community Church were peaceful and granted me with no clear direction in terms of what to do or say with regard to Emma and Faith.

"What does your heart say?" Morena asked me.

'It doesn't,' I would reply. 'It just doesn't want to say anything.'

I texted Emma and told her about my talks with God in the sanctuary. I didn't want her knowing I was speaking with Joy or Morena at that point, but I wanted her to know that I was doing some soul searching.

"Lighten up on the God stuff," was the only response Emma left me with.

I didn't know what else to say, but all I knew was that my soul was crying out.

When it came to Emma, it became difficult to determine where the illusion of our relationship seemed to end and when our reality cut in.

Love comes in all shapes and sizes, and I suspect many often misunderstand love. Love can be in the beginning of a smile or a silent exchange between two people that nobody else comprehends. Real love is a friendship that has caught on fire and still has faint embers burning after the test of time.

No matter how deep the test, and how much water has been tossed on the flame, you cannot extinguish it.

It can be a quiet understanding, a mutual confidence, or the sharing and the forgiving of past expressions. Every moment we experience is an opportunity to learn, and even through mistakes or choices, real love cannot, and will not die.

Love is a quiet truth in your soul that burns through good and bad times, no matter how the exterior of your life is perceived by yourself and others. Love never truly admits defeat to our human desires for perfection and makes allowances for human weaknesses.

It is not a fairytale. It is not a story you have to dive in with the hope of a specific ending. It should not be forced into the idealistic vision we were taught growing up. Love can be facing challenges together, overcoming those obstacles, and never letting go knowing it is real in your soul.

It can be a passion of different sorts: creating together, supporting one another, reaching out when needed, and just knowing you have someone to lean on. It doesn't have to be more than that realization but isn't that everything?

Love is an undeniable energy that should not be a label and recognized as such. Allow yourself to be loved by the people who truly love you, the people who want to give you their heart, and who will never sway from that.

Morena told me, "Don't be blinded by society's definition of love or pushing people into a box, because we want someone to love us so badly."

Despite the quiet embers true, real, rare love can look you in the eyes, set your soul ablaze, allowing you to reach down and ignite the night like a phoenix. It is the process of supporting your soul's growth and enjoying the enlightening moments that present themselves on your doorstep.

By those criteria, I was not sure if Emma or Faith fit that bill.

Morena took me to a coffee shop to clear my head, where we ruminated about life's most pervasive questions and ideas.

I placed down my coffee cup and turned to Morena with a plethora of questions: 'Why does clarity find us when we are picking up the missing pieces of the soul we once believed was whole? Trapped between the tragedy that was a love painted gold and placated as a trophy and one that devoutly hangs in the balance of the contrasted state of why did she pursue him and why didn't she love me?'

Morena read my face blatantly. She could see me caught up in the net that was Faith's love hoisting me from the ocean and smashing me onto the shore.

'Do I go after Emma or do I choose Faith?'

Morena's eyes were fixated on something in the distance. She was not spiritually involved in our conversation. I turned to see what or whom she was staring at and my eyes locked with Faith's. When I turned back around to speak to Morena, a sole white napkin sat in her place.

"Scott, I thought I would find you here," Faith stood beside me in the coffee shop. Morena disappeared without a trace and Faith treated her presence as if it were a dream.

My mind went wild thinking about how Morena could disappear so quickly... but Faith's abrupt kiss on my cheek brought my attention directly into wanting to feel her lips pressed against mine with each passing second.

Faith was in, Emma was no more.

Or so I thought.

I felt my mind shutting down with each passing moment, for I never thought Faith would walk back into my life like a hurricane.

∞ ∞ ∞ ∞ ∞ ∞ ∞ ∞

Just when I thought Faith was about to re-enter my life as the other half of my power couple, I was struck by feelings of utter confusion. As I arrived at the church, I found Emma sitting on the steps leading up to the entrance.

"Hey," tears were streaming down her face. "Can we talk?"

I let Emma come into the church and the two of us sat for a bit and spoke.

She cried on my shoulder wondering why Greg wouldn't propose to her yet. It was a universal juxtaposition of sorts: there I was, the man who would do absolutely anything for her, helping her through an emotionally difficult time for her.

Beautiful Souls

When you see or experience so much hurt in the world, you start to question the notion of love. Then when you finally experience it for yourself, you see what all the fuss is about. You can't imagine not having that person in your life, and you feel like the luckiest person in the world. You would do anything to make them feel the same way about you.

There is a difference between feeling like the luckiest person in the world, and actually being the luckiest person in the world.

Emma wore a mask adorned with her crooked smile and my leather heart, which she beat mercilessly until I bled acidic tears. They dropped as I screamed in agonizing pain, for when she asked me how I was feeling in that moment, the only words I could muster up were: 'I'm fine.'

Greg appeared to be stringing her along while I was more than ready to love Emma the way she needed to be loved.

How come the most beautiful souls on this planet are the ones who seem to get hurt the deepest? Why does one human being get away with damaging someone's soul, especially one that is so uniquely precious? Does he get away with doing this to her?

The pain in my heart was so difficult to mask. I had never experienced the magnitude of that feeling before. You had someone, a literal angel on earth, who was so powerful in spirit and had rare strong values, with whom I connected with like no one I had ever connected with. I was so ashamed that in my erratic emotions of loving this blessing you provided me, that I was blind to the pain she was in, and in turn hurt her myself by my constant wanting to "win her."

Life isn't a contest and neither is love, and even if she could not see it, all I wanted was her true happiness, if she could recognize the reality of "truth."

Did I even know what the truth was? I thought I knew, but I was so angry at my actions of being a selfish man. She was just so rare that I took my wall down in overwhelming excitement and put my blinders on to all else.

After Faith, I swore I was done. I missed Emma when she was with Greg more than words could begin to describe.

How do you show someone that you are deeply genuine, who lost trust in you? Did she lose trust in me? Was our energy just off? But she continued to come to me for support.

She didn't get the spiritual connection but she responded to it… and then ran away from it.

There was not a bad bone in my body, and how could she realize that I was not like anyone who had ever hurt her before?

I saw the world differently. I still see love differently.

How do you show someone that their soul and energy is the greatest feeling you have ever felt, and that all you wanted for them was to truly be happy – no matter what that looked like or whom that was with?

How do you say to someone I want you back, when you were never even technically with them in the first place?

Physical and emotional love unknown to the world does not exist in the reality we call the sands of time, or does it? How do you show someone that your words were true when you told them "you saved my life?" How do you show someone you unconditionally love them with no desired outcome and that you respect them and do not have an ulterior motive?

There was this constant gnawing slow pain in my chest that would not go away. I simply couldn't imagine my life or a world without her. I saw her struggle with me, and with life.

When she left, I found myself in the sanctuary saying, 'God, please help her. I ask you that any blessings you have stored for me, please trade them in and hand them to her. I do not need to be with her ultimately.'

I wanted her and I loved her, but truth be told in the silence of this church, I wanted her to stay with Greg if that's where her heart was. If someone truly wants to be with you, their heart will be there and show up. If not, they will stay with where their heart truly feels like home. It is that simple.

If she couldn't see my love and energy, though she acted on the energy subconsciously, then I wanted her to be where she was.

That was her truth in the universe, even if it was not mine.

I figured it would crush me to see her married and build a family, but if she wanted my shoulder and unconditional love, I would give it to her. I figured I would do so gladly and without showing her any pain I may have had in my soul.

She had been tested and she would rise above it all, I had no doubt in my mind. I would help her from whatever position she allowed me to help her, but I prayed she would come to me eventually and let me in.

I wanted to be her real friend. I wanted to show her what she was truly worth. I wanted to grow with her and make sure she knew how much she mattered. Instead of pursuing what "I want," which only perpetuates the cycle of selfishness and a message that I do not have energetically, I could only provide her with what she wanted.

It was truly not about me.

It never was.

Before I went to sleep, I let my mind wander. When I shut my eyes and reopened them, I was standing at the bridge, watching her lean over a bucket filled with flames and ash. She was kindling a small fire.

'Emma,' I called out. 'What are you doing?'

She tilted her head slightly and met my gaze. She didn't look well. We stood glaring at one another.

'Emma,' I shouted desperately. She remained silent. The fire raged on in the bucket. She moved towards me and handed me the pen I keep in my pocket.

"Tell me the truth," she murmured. I stood gazing at her in astonishment for a moment.

'What truth?' I whispered. We stood there for a moment longer and watched each other's every move.

Then someone I didn't know handed me a pen and paper. They told me to write a letter to my past self. So, I did:

"Dearly Beloved,

You weep for a heart that was never meant to break. You shatter bits of your soul so others could be rebuilt. You are the definition of an empath. You embody the spirit of those whose journeys were cut short. You bend and break, but don't you ever waver. Don't give in, not for one moment, to the voices in your head. Burn your demons and inhale the smell of your soul being reduced to ash. Find the goodness. Find the happiness. Feel the wind break through your skeleton, renewing all that once was and all that can be more powerful. Exhale the stress, the agony, the pain, the suffering. You were not born to be a minute. You're an infinite amount of time. You are a living legacy. You need to wake up. Please wake up. I can push at your heartstrings and head for so long. You are sleeping. Please remember to wake up. You have fight within you. Do not succumb and fall into the darkness. A beautiful soul is often beaten, but just bruised. Get up. Wake up. Wake. Up. Now. I am sorry you are here at this point, but I am overjoyed that you can have the satisfaction of growing again. You are a seed; you have been planted. Blossom. Not into a flower, no, something bigger than your imagination. See yourself from my eyes. You say you aren't that person. You say I am better. You are blind. Open your eyes. Wake up. I will always be on either side. Live. I got to see what your life becomes. Cling to hope. You have your faith. Do not falter. You are a beautiful soul, just wake up."

∞ ∞ ∞ ∞ ∞ ∞ ∞ ∞

Upon waking up the next day, I got the answers my soul was trying so hard to tell. A story fluttered within a story. A name trapped within a name:

Faith in love and a future wholeheartedly existed within her, within Faith, within the words we could not say to one another.

I felt as if I was cheating on Emma, but I knew she had made her decision. She didn't want me. She didn't want me…

The phone trilled and I jumped up…

3 Missed Calls: Emma

1 New Voicemail

Dare I listen? Dare I hear her smashing my heart to bits? No, I couldn't. I wouldn't. I couldn't face the hurt or the pain. I was not the one.

Incoming Call: Emma.

Do I answer it? Do I go for it?

No, no, no, no… I couldn't do this. I made my choice. Stay true to your faith.

'Stay true to your faith,' I told myself. Though I knew in my heart that Emma was the one for me.

Images of months past flickered innocently across my line of sight. The feel of her skin against mine lingered between my fingers, as a reminder that what once was is just a pleasant memory ruminating in my mind.

The connection between two souls can be severed. A bond of togetherness can simultaneously collapse with the fluttering of false eyelashes and genuine beauty.

Beautiful Souls

I wondered if she, too, looked up at the sky and reminisced about our hands and minds intertwined on that luxurious park bench we called home. I wonder if my name floated through her brain waves on a daily basis. For in my own mind, I still felt the ebb and flow of her hips crashing through my mind. I sensed my mouth forming her name on my lips, but the crisp air caught the words before they slid out of my cracked lips.

Her energy gave me the intensity and the hydration that no other soul could ever manifest.

And for her presence, I would forever be grateful.

But I know when it is time to let the universe consume a connection, for when one bridge collapses, another will be built in its place. Though she was fundamentally irreplaceable, I knew in my heart, another beautiful soul would fill the void she left within me.

For Faith may be strong; but my personal faith is much stronger.

I think Ella Wheeler Wilcox said it best:

"Lean on thyself until thy strength is tried; Then ask for God's help; it will not be denied. Use thy own sight to see the way to go; When darkness falls, ask God the path to show."

My path was not complete darkness, but I was spiritually searching for strength. I had entered a transitional period I found myself lost in, not expecting to be in, and felt the pain of all my scars.

I was scared and found strength in the idealism I had set myself up to be. Many people count on me and there is a reason for that. I have been given a gift. My difficulty was in sharing that gift when I felt so hurt and hypocritical inside.

I prayed every night in the church for wisdom. I did not want to pray for strength, as I did not want to face any more tests of strength.

My past and my history have made me strong.

I wanted to release my worries and exhaustion to a higher power, so I could have the unconditional love and positive energy to share with humanity. This was where my journey led me and where I was stuck.

The phone rang and I found myself begging for Emma's name to be the one looking back up at me.

Keep the Faith

It ended up being Faith who was calling and who wanted to meet up. At a loss for words and in the midst of utter confusion, I obliged.

Faith and I agreed to meet at a new restaurant in the neighborhood. I didn't consider it a date, but I told Emma where I was going and who I was meeting.

Although she was pissed and incredibly jealous, I had a feeling Emma was not going to do anything about it. Deep down inside she had to know I loved her, and I was trying desperately not to make her choose between Greg or me.

It was my devout and firm belief that Emma needed to choose herself above anyone else. For though I hoped she would choose me over Greg, something told me she was not going to choose herself.

On my way to see Faith I realized that I could feel so lost at times. My only comfort was knowing that I was exploring my faith and growing spiritually. You can be on one path at one point, and be on a totally different one in mere minutes. That is the beauty of life, I guess… times change and people change as well.

We all just need to ensure that we are all changing for the right reasons.

Faith and I met up, but as soon as we sat down, she had to rush home. It was almost as if the universe did not want us to meet. I texted Emma to tell her what was happening, and she almost sounded relieved.

In a way, I knew that our love would triumph over anything her and Greg had, for I believed that Emma knew her own soul at the time.

When I returned to the church, I spoke with the angels and the universe. Morena came by for a while and we spoke about both Faith and Emma.

"Why do you think you are so torn?" Morena ran her fingernails along the pew.

'I don't know,' I rested my head on the wall next to my favorite stained-glass window. 'I mean I have a history with both of them and I love both of them in different ways.'

There comes a point when you suddenly realize you're in a moment that would normally debilitate you, and you find yourself automatically turning the situation over to faith. When you're feeling every moment of letting go and letting God, there is a sense of peace.

Beautiful Souls

I knew my faith was getting stronger. I remained alone with my thoughts and misunderstood by many, but it was okay. I learned that someone you used to easily speak to and express love towards could become the hardest person to speak to, and someone you desperately want to scream the words of love to may not have anything to say.

A momentary smile and a quick and embrace could mean the world to someone. God is at work in both scenarios. I didn't quite understand the methodology and though I tried to figure it out, I trusted God, and the mantra "what shall be shall be."

Sometimes emotionally removing yourself from something you want so badly helps you to see things from a perspective you were not aware lies within you, and herein lies personal growth.

To love someone enough to let them go, to love someone enough to have space and time to learn their own soul and power, to love humanity and dedicate my existence to making a difference on our planet, is powerful. There was a powerful love present. I was excited to watch and feel it unfold. I was aware of it, and I stood for it, eternally grateful.

I started allowing Emma and Faith's respective images to pass through my mind. Morena sat before me watching everything register in my hollow expression.

The fond memories I had with Faith floated to the surface. I felt a warm sensation reminiscing about long, spiritual talks with Faith. Her hair brushing against my skin while we spoke of ideas that seemed so much bigger than us. Her kids came to mind. I could feel the gravel beneath my feet from the long walks we took in the park. I smelt the cultural cuisine we would have.

Despite the beautiful memories that reminded me of why Faith seemed like the one, I could not shake the pure, unconditional love I had for Emma. I would not dare sever the connection I had with her. The sacred "vault" we kept together and our scribblings transcended the definition of what love is. We poured our souls into every conversation we had and each day seemed like a poignant fairy tale. If God had answered my prayers years ago, I would have never had the relationship I created with Emma.

I must trust in the process and keep the faith. I must refuse to sink, as I had always wholeheartedly believed, and as Emma endearingly says.

One day this journey and this stage would make sense, and until then I needed to be the best human being I could be.

Morena seemed to gaze into my soul as she smiled.

"So, you know what you must do," she spoke as if she was asking a question, though with slight hesitation.

'Yes,' I replied.

I stood up from the pew and left the sanctuary. When I turned around, Morena had disappeared. It was a pervasive thought in my mind that she was almost an apparition of sorts. Whenever I needed Morena, she appeared before me and seemed to know what to do or say, though I must admit she was holistically a ghost in the body of a human being… or at least that's what I thought for the time being.

I called Faith who surprisingly picked up the phone within moments.

"Hey," her sultry voice made it sound like she was reaching through the receiver and caressing my cheek. "I miss you, when are we meeting for dinner?"

'Hey,' was all I could get out of my mouth.

"What's wrong?"

'Nothing,' I knew she would sense that something was up, and she did. We spoke for a while longer, and I ended up meeting with Faith that night for a quick bite to eat.

When we sat down, Emma was the only one who I wanted sitting across from me. Although Faith said that she finally made up her mind and realized she wanted to be with me, it was like we could never get the timing right.

I always wanted her when she did not want me and vice versa. We were on a carousel of emotions, constantly getting on and off of the colorful wooden animals we chose to sit upon, but at the end of the day we were just going in circles.

It was time to get off of the carousel and just enjoy the carnival of life.

'No,' I told Faith.

"No?" She dropped her fork in the most dramatic way.

'I am with someone now,' I began. 'She's the one.'

I smiled, waiting for a response from Faith, who looked at me in awe.

"Well, I didn't think about that," she chuckled. Faith stood up and hugged me, "She must be something awful special."

Beautiful Souls

'She is,' I put my hand on her back and gave her a reassuring pat.

"Goodbye for now, Scott," she began walking away. "Until next time."

Faith took our conversation in stride. She appeared to understand my soul, as I understood hers. I think it was the first time in years we spoke the same language without having to interpret each other's words or actions.

I was incredibly thankful for her understanding.

For all intents and purposes, Emma was the one I wanted to spend my life with, and I knew I would stop at nothing to make her mine.

This is how it was going to be.

∞ ∞ ∞ ∞ ∞ ∞ ∞ ∞

Now that I had made my mind up, I chose to keep my decision between Morena, God, and myself. No one else really knew how much I adored Emma at this point, and I wanted to keep my next move a secret.

I loved Emma. Nothing and no one would stand in my way of confessing my unconditional love for her. She knew, deep down inside, that I loved her more than anything else in the world. Oftentimes, I convinced myself that I loved Emma more than I loved my own soul.

My nightly ritual of pacing the sanctuary re-ignited a flame in me. At the time it seemed to feel like there were rocks churning around in my abdomen; this should have been one of the first signs that something else was manifesting inside of me.

I continued to see Emma in the halls at work, but I was careful not to approach her and make it obvious to others that my eyes utterly adored every inch of her body and her soul.

Emma would occasionally flash me a coy smile while we were at Lincoln Memorial, but our relationship was contained to rendezvous in the park and long phone conversations after work.

On the morning my life was about to shift forever, I did not suspect anything was wrong. Emma and I had a lengthy phone conversation about some trivial matters, though by the end of the conversation we were both consumed in a flurry of "I love you's" and "I am grateful for you's."

I never would have hung up the phone if I knew what was coming next.

Morena and I were spending a quiet evening organizing papers for Windows of Opportunity, as we were in the midst of structuring one of our programs for the kids.

Laughter and spiritual conversations flooded the air that night in the church, until a chime from my phone brought our frivolity to an abrupt halt.

I remember looking over at my phone and seeing the message from her. I was excited that although Emma was with her family and busy doing her ritualistic weekend activities, she would still be sweet enough to find the time to text me.

After looking at my phone, I fell to the floor so tragically that Morena leapt across the table thinking that I was having a severe heart attack. To me, it was worse: my entire soul shattered.

As I cried and clutched my abdomen in pain, Morena picked up my phone.

Her face dropped almost as fast as the tears rolled down from my eyes.

"Scott, I-" Morena's words drowned in the sorrows I quickly succumbed to.

I had hoped that what I read was just a misunderstanding, until I took my phone from Morena's hand and re-read the text message from Emma:

"Scott,
There is no right way to tell you or a good way, but today Greg asked me to marry him and I said yes.
It's just another day. Breathe.
Love "Always,"
Emma"

CHAPTER 5

Always Just Another Day

*"You're not listening now. Can't you see something's missing?
You forget where the heart is."*

- Yellowcard, American Rock Band, Jacksonville, Florida

Beautiful Souls

The sensation of reality slammed into my head. Emma had chosen Greg and I was at a loss for words.

Two days after her engagement, Emma left this note on my desk:

Scott,
I feel like I don't know where to begin. All I have playing over and over in my head is how this was already such a hard time for you, especially with Bryan. I figured you got my message and it was one of your worst nightmares coming true. With that said I've wanted to give you space. I know you are hurting and I'm going to hold back from saying much more because the last thing I want to do is add more hurt. I want to be there for you like you've been for me but I also know you might not want me to. So the ball lies in your court. Just remember the conversations we've had before about when this moment came. It's just another day...

Love,
Emma

Is it really just another day?

Maybe it was time to emerge from sadness into a state of higher consciousness where "another day" represents a chance to spiritually awaken from who I once was. There is a realm of possibilities and new perspectives, although I knew I needed to pull the dagger from my back, which was laced with Emma's words and her fleeting love.

We are all angelic beings masked by our human attributes. You can recognize those who are moving towards enlightenment when you yourself open up your very own eyes.

The moment I laid eyes on Emma, I knew I had found one. The moment I saw Emma, our intermingled lives flickered through my mind. In seconds, I was struck by a pull so indescribable that gravity itself was nonexistent compared to our energy.

Souls' crashing into each other is the greatest feeling in the universe. When your soul burns with passion, and your faith is operating on overload, life seems to shift. The positive shift and vibration is almost overwhelming, but the most devout and unwavering feeling of awareness ever experienced.

It's so important as we build our futures, implement our strategies, and search for our dreams, that we go deeper than we could ever fathom.

It was crucial to believe in a path beyond the physical eye and pass the point of should, could, and would.

It was painful, but I had to accept living life in the exorbitant now, patiently waiting for us to succumb to what is and not what should be.

There is a light that shines bright, not only from inside our souls but upon us from above. There is an energy that could fill your half full cup to the brim with unconditional love and overflow it with joyous life experiences. Think it, see it, and live it. For after all, we deserve to live a life of enlightenment.

I had to awaken the voice within, because it is not just another day anymore.

The "one" who I thought would never destroy me ended up being the "one" who would shatter my soul and shred me to pieces. There was never a love like ours before, and clearly this love never would be.

Was it ever love to begin with?

Music seemed to be the only thing that would fill the cracks of what once was. I figured that the lyrics would take the place of the words she left in her last entry in "The Vault," which was melting off of the pages due to my incessant crying.

Oddly enough, the first song to shuffle on was "You're No Match" from Bayside:

> *"You are the monster I was scared you'd be*
> *And now you're blaming it on your surroundings*
> *And your horns came out so gradually*
> *But honey, you're no match for me."*

The song reminded me of my connection with the band. The lead singer of Bayside was a former student of Elyza's, and over the years we ended up becoming good friends. The band was incredibly popular in the underground music scene in New York, and after they made it big the only show the band actually performed in Bayside was due to the Musicapalooza event I coordinated.

The next morning after their performance, I was walking through the parking lot and heard the principal blasting Bayside's album from his car. The two of us made eye contact and he gave me a thumbs up.

He cracked his window and said, "This is good, I am glad we had them here."

They are truly amazing musicians who deserve to be admired with the likes of Bon Jovi, and I am not just saying that because I know the band members personally. Each of them truly connected with their fans at shows. Bayside became one of those bands that you genuinely admired because of their musicality, their lyrics, and just how thrilling they were to listen to or see live.

Bayside's songs have a true, devout message. Their lyrics have something powerful to say.

I was devastated the day their drummer passed away, and I carry and cherish his memory with me day after day.

The band is resilient and unwavering in their commitment to music and their fans. Their message to the world is inspiring. Words that they pieced together illustrate the melody people never realized they needed in their souls.

One day they will gain the notoriety they deserve.

As I listened to more music seeping through the speakers, these tears tasted familiar and these songs sounded the same. I was stuck in a music box, except I was the ironic ballerina spinning on the spindle, waiting for the lid to slam down hard and the music to stop.

∞ ∞ ∞ ∞ ∞ ∞ ∞ ∞

Dawn was creeping through the wind. Fresh beams of light were reaching out and caressing my face ever so gently as to lull me back to sleep.

Too late, I was already awake. I hadn't slept all night. All I could do was think of her. I imagined her rolling over in bed, her amber eyes flashing open slowly to greet the new day. Locks of her luscious brunette hair dance over her pillow and land on her pure face.

"Good morning," she says groggily. Only it isn't to me: it's to Greg.

I wondered if her fiancé cherished her as much as I do? I wondered if he shivered as I once did, as she tenderly presents her kisses. I wondered if she left him adorable notes on crinkled pieces of paper. I wondered if he looks at her in awe as I have done. I could not help but ask: Does he take her for granted as much as I had?

There is that old saying, "All good things come to an end," and I consider the notion all the time. Then again, were we ever a "thing," or just two lost souls floating in the ocean? Or was she just looking for a temporary shelter from her soul's pain.

Turning the page on a chapter that was barely written is echoic of the inner turmoil that flooded my soul for years. A single page blank in the greater landscape of the epic saga that is my life.

Looking skyward, I felt the sunlight embrace my skin with each breath I exhaled. Our story lay cemented into pages at my feet: an entire love story whittled down to ash in moments. The match hung shakily in my hand, about to take its final descent.

Memories flickering past me reminded me how love was a temporary flame. We burn out eventually. We go up in smoke with the dissipation of the flame. We turn and we catch fire.

We were everything and nothing in the passing remnants of a solitary day.

And we were bright.

And we were everything love needed to be at that time.

But we were a lesson: hearts cease, but they beat on eventually.

And with the drop of the match, I could feel her wrapped in the arms of another just miles away.

Everything. Gone.

The ashes danced towards the sky in the most majestic way imaginable.

And our souls lay scattered in the bucket, doused in the tears from years past, yet burning vigorously as a means of sealing our fate forever and a day. Yet again, "just another day" rocked through my mind and pushed any semblance of love far from the depth of my own, decimated soul.

I was a mess without her, but it felt like my soul wanted absolutely nothing to do with her. How do you manage to miss someone terribly while still acknowledging that person shredded your heart?

After everything we went through, part of me could not believe that she still said yes to Greg and must now live with the story she perpetuated each and every day.

I spent over an hour and a half after school counseling a student who recognized that the two of us loved each other. She sat there in my office while I had to calm her down and explain to her that it was okay that we were not getting married.

Still, the student turned around and said, "I don't get it. You are both the definition of true love! I see it when you look at each other."

Deep inside I wanted to tell the girl that although she saw it, you were eclipsed by the shiny diamond ring precariously sitting on your fragile hand.

Emma's happiness and my stinging agony were slammed in my face every single second while I was at work. It got to the point where I didn't even want to work there anymore.

Just a week prior, Emma painted my soul with ornate words of grandeur, claiming that I was her soul mate. Then in one fatal swoop, with four words symbolizing a humanistic commitment, Emma started to nonchalantly talk about how her and Greg would grow old together.

I am happy she found the love she wanted to connect with at the time, but I knew in my soul our relationship was bonded on a deeper level.

Greg's love was a thrill.

Emma began to ignore me in the hallways. Our moments and glances faded into the illusory distance.

Her voice, her life, and her dreams began to beat my soul to the senseless point where it seemed as if there was no return.

I wanted to talk to her. I wanted to tell her how much I loved her, but it did not seem to matter and she did not seem to care. Reality seemed to dictate that the two of us were not true love. The way she kicked me aside made it appear as if we were a total farce.

It appeared that I was all that Emma needed for the time being, so she could fill the void of loneliness until Greg chose to stand up to her expectations. Emma needed a story to tell and she was setting the stage: she got the boy, she got the ring, and she was on the verge of getting the white picket fence she so desperately yearned for.

But where was the love?

There was no room for a man who bared his entire soul in hopes that Emma would see just how much of a treasure she truly was.

The moment the ring slid onto her finger, the circle was complete: the love they had fit into that continuous flow. Meanwhile, I existed outside the ultimatum she put forth months before I even had a chance to deeply adore who she was.

Though weeks prior she proclaimed that I was hers and she was mine, there was an asterisk on Emma's love. The disclaimer read, "I will love you, until Greg gives me a ring."

The truth was that she wanted the commitment from Greg. I was nothing.

I wonder if she even thought of me when he put the ring on her finger. Devastated was an understatement at that point, and I couldn't even show it to anyone. Within weeks, I lost Emma and I lost Bryan… and I lost myself.

I was numb with the exquisite exception of the uncontrollable moments when a few solitary tears would slide down my cheek.

The walls went back up.

Who cares about feelings?

Who cares about love?

I was hurt so many times, and despite my better judgment telling me to resist… I risked everything. I risked my soul and my sanity…

And despite it all, I was left with one conclusion: just settle.

I found myself sitting at the bridge for hours upon hours, brushing my fingers against the peeling pine-green paint on the bench where Emma and I once sat together. I longed for the days when we were truly us. Though our meetings in Kissena Park were sensual in nature, I was craving a day where Emma and I could meet there again and just talk.

Without her in my life, I felt that my reality, all of my hopes, and every single one of my dreams were gone.

It took so much effort to walk into work each day and put a fake smile on.

How could it be just another day, considering she was no longer in it?

How could an engagement be whittled down to three words: just another day?

Emma was craving true love and it appeared that I was not the flavor of the week. It made me feel like our few months of passion and promises were an absolute lie.

How did this happen? How did I get here?

Why would the universe put someone so perfect in front of me, just to have her rip my soul to shreds?

∞ ∞ ∞ ∞ ∞ ∞ ∞ ∞

I found myself roaming through Alley Pond Park once again.

The sunlight cut through the trees and ceased on its journey through the woods to rest on my face. I could not help but let the tears rush down my face with the fervor of a coursing river: I truly missed Emma.

Morena sat pensively in the shallow dirt by my feet, gazing up at the shell of a man heaving and filling his head with grandeur of a once beautiful, passionate love that was shredded to its core.

All because of Emma.

All because she did not love herself as much as I could ever love someone so toxically beautiful.

And there I was crying again to mourn the soul of a woman who never died, but rather killed her chance of a beautiful relationship smothered in true, impartial divine love. She killed us with a slender knife to the heart.

Yet, all this time later, there we were, sitting in the woods discussing her lost soul.

And my fleeting hope sewn together by the sliver of hope screaming, "you have a chance."

What chance? What chance if she is not willing to accept our love? Our bond?

I would die for her, while she would just let me drown in the misery that is her absence.

Through strife and tears, I could see Morena's face slowly forming a more compassionate demeanor. The devout pain was burning a gaping hole in my soul... and all she could do was look on and watch me shrivel and fold into itself.

A devastating scene grew more contrastive to the silent trees bending into our conversation to hold me back from falling into a pit of despair and tragedy mounting on the edge of the rotted log I perched myself upon.

I was drowning in tears. Scoffing off any positive energy that inched closer to my frame: Morena's frozen hand reaching out to pull me out of the shattered existence before her.

I could not reach out for her. Emma's absence clasped around me and ripped me further into an ocean of this depressive state.

Morena stood before me, and I could see her smile tear through my shallow tears.

"Scott, it will be okay, don't let go," Morena wrapped her tired body around mine. She clung to my tears, absorbing them as her own as to shield me from the pain and agony that crashed down onto the dirt before us. Heavy drops of emotion spewed from every ounce of my soul and split the air in a matter of seconds. I could not hold in the pain any longer. The pressure mounted.

I needed Emma more than I needed anything in the world... but she was too blind to see that.

There was a quote I read somewhere, I am certain it was from Yann Martel's *Life of Pi*: *"You cannot know the strength of your faith until it has been tested."*

If I only knew the truth in those words when I met Emma, I am unsure what I would have done. I tended to let my mind drift to a realm where Emma chose me over Greg. I wondered what it would have looked like if I was hers.

Questions fluttered through my mind: Would we have had the white picket fence? Would the two of us be everything she wanted in a relationship? Or was she assuming that I could never give her what she wanted?

The truth is you never really know what the next moment holds.

You can have your whole future planned out, and it can finally make sense, and then all of a sudden it evaporates in between the seemingly innocent tears you shed. You could have a love that is an absolute blessing, only to discover their love is being bestowed upon another person.

You could be an inspiration to so many lives yet hate the person you have become.

Morena interrupted my spiritual derailment of sorts to release me from her grasp. She walked towards one of the trees and brushed her fingers along the rugged bark.

"Tell me," she began. "You can hear the whispers of the universe and know that the truth in your heart is real, and yet you are still scared."

I looked over at her and allowed a teardrop to cut between my bashful smirk.

'The truth is I would give it all up if the trade off would mean she would find her true inner power that she hides from the universe.'

"It is more than that," Morena's eyes shifted towards me. "You know that."

'Do I?'

"Listen to the voice from deep within your soul, Scott. What does it say?"

I sat silently for a few moments.

'You can be in the same room with the person you are spiritually devoted to, yet as she talks about another man she loves, hear everything inside you scream. She is just impressing society's demands. She has to be.'

Morena rolled her eyes and plopped beside me.

"It is more than that."

'I fall asleep in the sanctuary sometimes with her as the last thing on my mind.'

"Maybe the stars just don't align for your souls."

'But she was the one who initiated the relationship!'

"And?" Morena gripped the edges of the rocks we were sitting on.

'And shouldn't that mean something?'

"It does," she paused. "Maybe what you are searching for is not what you are looking for."

'I am looking for her,' I felt my ears burning up. 'I know she is the one for me. With one smile, one hug, one look with those eyes of hers… all my pain goes away.'

"Is that your pain dissipating, or your soul?"

'Morena, what does that even mean?'

"Think about it," she stood up and brushed the dirt from her hands.

'Maybe my *greatness* and *worthiness* is all in my mind.'

Morena sighed, "Why do you instantly jump to the conclusion that you are not worth it?"

I looked at her blankly for a moment.

"The truth is judgment and society will tear you to shreds if you let it. If you do not trust in true love, you can't overcome the maliciousness that others may cast upon you."

We glared at each other with empathetic eyes.

'I am mad at her.'

"Good," Morena said. "Why?"

'Because I am so scared of losing her.'

"What does 'losing' mean?"

Morena was right; I didn't know what it *really* meant. I could not fathom what loss even looked like in that moment, for Emma was truly just a call or text away.

'No one would defend their love for me, they would rather walk away.'

"Did she truly walk away?"

'Um, yes?'

"Maybe you are just looking at things the wrong way."

'Well if you are going to be that insightful,' I quipped. 'Then where should I look?'

Morena put her hand on my chest and gazed up at me. When our glances met, it was like I could see the entire universe sprinkled throughout her eyes.

"Within yourself," she replied.

Every great hero has a phenomenal love story to catalogue the reward for their perils. Emma was the love I needed to change the world.

I felt it wholeheartedly. Though it dawned on me: what if I wanted love so bad, but I was looking in all the wrong places? How would I know?

'Morena,' the two of us turned and started walking away in unison. 'I searched my entire lifetime for love, and she has to be the one. I am tired of searching. I miss her. I dream about her. I love her.'

She did not respond.

'The next time she falls into my arms, I will treasure her more. I will show her that I love her because we just make sense.'

The two of us got to the edge of Alley Pond Park and I found myself alone again.

It was becoming a natural occurrence at this point.

∞ ∞ ∞ ∞ ∞ ∞ ∞ ∞

There is nothing like a rainy morning in the spring. As I was laying on the mattress in the attic of the church, listening to the rain pelt the roof, I felt the ghost of her cuddling into my arms. I wondered if she missed our cuddling sessions where we curled into each other and felt the warmth of love.

I couldn't get out of bed. I was debilitated by my loneliness and what I took for granted for so long.

Beautiful Souls

My pain was my punishment and it cut through me with such tenacity.

I was stuck inside my own love story, yet the rest of the tale was stuck between the pages of someone else's journey.

I went into work with my head hung low, only to find her waiting in my doorway as my students were coming in.

"Hey," Emma spoke coyly, though I could see the light reflect from her engagement ring.

'Hi.' I wasn't sure if I could hold my tears back in front of the kids. I tried to forget her and move on, but then I felt her love spilling over from my soul. Then almost poetically, I looked up and there she was.

Emma sat down and started to counsel students with me. I almost wanted to run up to her and kiss her on the spot, just to see if she was truly real.

When the students left hours later, she reached up and touched my face as a breathy, "Hey," escaped her lips.

Touching her was getting easier. Kissing her hand evoked a genuine smile.

Embracing her made every ounce of pain instantly disappear.

I was under a spell, knowing in the recesses of my mind that ruin was about to be the road to transformation.

My soul shivered out of fear: I was petrified that she would have wanted to stay with him and I would be hurt forever.

I found my heart of gold.

She makes me want to be a better man. It's loving her that drove me to push my body, mind, and soul to a greater awareness.

Now I stayed in the moment.

I refused to pressure her. She chose him and he has the financial resources they need. I couldn't compete with that. Still, though I loved her from afar, she became a permanent part of my soul.

How do you let go when you don't want to?

I was so confused. The situation seemed like we would never be together again, but then she reaches out to me in her own quiet way and it feels like we are the true love I believed in.

Prayers hung against the back of my lips. I hoped she could admit she was fighting her feelings, so I would have at least known that our love was real and that I was not insane.

I wondered why I kept falling harder for her.

With her in my arms, pressed against my chest, I wondered: Why am I afraid to lose you when you are not even mine?

I saw a story in her eyes, but I must have been reading the wrong book.

"I missed you," she murmured those sweet words in my ear without remorse.

Instinctively, I leaned towards her and pressed my lips against hers. She reciprocated the kiss, which made me feel that something was happening between us again.

The two of us sat and she cried on my shoulder. I tried to sit in silence just for the sake of being. My mind was on the verge of bursting, but I had to just be. I had to just exist.

I was so lost without her. Just having her with me for a few moments meant the world to me.

As tears streamed down her face and I embraced her, I tried to rise above the pain of nursing a shattered heart.

I would have shattered my own heart into teensy bits, if only it meant giving Emma the pieces that would make her whole again.

Her phone rang and she scrambled to pick it up, almost as if I was not mere inches in front of her. Emma and Greg were bickering back and forth about something I struggled to hear.

Within moments, Emma apologized to me and rushed out of the room almost as quickly as she seemed to enter my life. While standing alone in my office once again, I realized that I had to stop teetering between wanting her love and genuinely loving myself. Although it is honestly easier to speak something into existence than to physically will yourself to do something.

The worst crime I have committed against myself was to expect someone to love me the way I loved them. I had hoped she would feel that same jolt of energy I felt when I saw her smile.

I prayed she would hang on each word I would say. I aspired to be her everything, and not just her something.

I think I had said this time and time again, but I truly meant the words: I would rip my heart from my chest, slam it against the ground, and pick up the shattered pieces and give them over to her. Maybe that was my problem: I would sooner break myself further and further into a pit of despair so that she could become whole again.

Beautiful Souls

Maybe that has been my problem all along. Shattering my very core and my dreams seemed like the right thing to do, since she seemed to replace any aspiration I could ever imagine.

So that's my problem… I would rather break down than see her suffer, but she is not worthy of my love. She should stand in the shadows while I claw my way back into the sun. Let her feel my pain rush over her like the wave of agony she thrust upon me. Let her feel her blood boil when she reads this. Let her see how painful it is to look at yourself in the mirror and beg yourself to be okay again.

Maybe it was time I stood firmly rooted in the ground…

Maybe it was time I grew…

Maybe it was time I stopped discounting myself…

Maybe it was time I rose from the ashes and truly "keep the faith…"

Although I was speaking such a devout series of truths to myself in the quiet solace of the office, something was physically preventing me from living out these truths.

I promptly ran home to the silence of the sanctuary so that I could speak to God and the universe. The whispers I released into the universe were of a purposeful nature: I believed that if I truly proved I believed in my faith, I would be able to attract Emma back into my life.

As the night sky enclosed upon the stained-glass windows, I felt a sense that something was shifting. My mind was filled with intentions for my future, though I felt that it went beyond the typical "power couple" idea I always considered.

I felt my spirit was being renewed over time and I was thankful for that miracle.

However, with such a great blessing, namely a growing sense of being and self, I felt more burdened as I absorbed the pain of those around me. Countless youth were being belittled or disregarded for their respective passions and interests, people in my life were suffering from battles they could not even articulate, and in general, I felt that Emma was the epitome of what happens when you love someone and can't outwardly pursue that love.

Asking God and the universe to heal the souls of those in pain seemed to be the only thing I could do in those moments. I needed help with people on my team. The intricate and hidden pain within their souls is hindering them from moving to a state of higher consciousness.

I recognized that I was also stuck, but I knew I could rise above. I just needed to see what I was capable of. I needed to remind myself of how strong I was and what path I was on.

In a sense, I did not know what I wanted other than divine love.

I wanted to be outstanding. I wanted to develop and design programs for youth. All of my life lessons, celebrations, and challenges were preparing me for the moments ahead.

The next inspirational chapter of my life was on the verge of appearing; I just hoped that the one narrating those chapters would be Emma. Her voice and her presence was all I truly wanted in my life. Although Bryan was my source of true happiness, his departure to Florida provided me with less of a daily reminder that love was close.

Emma's sudden exit and engagement was a blow to my ego, though I had to know in some respect that love had to be a feeling beyond just the human ego. Everyone has their own gifts and talents, and mine seemed to be providing love and inspiring others to see how they could pursue their passions.

There is so much potential and insight brewing in the minds of people in this universe, and I hoped that Emma would see that as well. I prayed Emma would discover that for herself and come back to me at that moment.

Just as I sent God a prayer and yearned for Emma to feel her innate power, I heard my phone's vibrations echo through the sanctuary.

A solitary text message was glaring up at me. Emma sent one statement: "I don't want to lose your friendship, but Greg is very special to me."

I felt my spine go up in flames. I sensed the hairs on the back of my neck stand at attention. All of my prayers and ambitions appeared to melt away.

Emma used the term, "friendship," as if that was all we were. Oftentimes she made it seem like so much more than that, both emotionally and physically. I had years upon years of a connection with Faith, yet I was willing to throw it all away just for Emma. I could tell she was worried about Greg getting jealous of what Emma and I had.

In my mind, it did not change the truth I knew about us, or what we felt. However, in her fear-laced words I sensed that everything between us seemed to be a lie. Yet before she had that ring on her finger, her messages never harbored that tone.

Beautiful Souls

Time and time again, she said it would always be us. Though once one of "us" had a ring on their finger, I guess our memories were erased.

Once upon a time, as most fairytales begin, I was Emma's "rock" and "soul mate," though those words crumbled as soon as Greg sealed their love with a ring. How poignant: she ended up with the charming prince in a story she wrote long before my character crashed through her happily ever after.

I wondered what happened in her mind when she would roll her eyes at him and saw what she created.

Part of me was glad it was Greg who she chose instead of me. She caused me so much pain in teetering between her self-developed games of, "Whom do I want more?"

It dawned on me that I became a secret because I did not fit in the quintessential picture she wished to place in her frame. My mind plummeted into a realm of "what ifs" and broken promises. What if the words I spoke to her were not real? What if the love I showed to her was all a dream?

I loved Emma wholeheartedly, yet she denied our existence with her perturbed notion that I was "just a friend." Months of loving her came to a screeching halt, for the second she sent that text shattered what was left of me.

As tears dripped down my cheeks, I was practically paralyzed by the many thoughts left unsaid. I wondered if she was just living a lie; honesty was not her strongpoint, as she had an entire life planned before we met. Part of me hoped Emma just forgot to tell me about the life she had planned, but how do you hide so much of your soul from someone who you supposedly love?

The painting, the silhouette of her shadow, hours upon hours of our texts, the vault, was it real? How do we even perceive reality in its most reverent form? I considered it to be a deep connection.

However, what is a deep connection?

Is it defined by the euphoria a person feels the moment they rest their eyes upon another soul?

For if that were so, then the definition of euphoria would be up to the person caught up in that sensation. Greg might feel euphoria when he looks at her, but does she mirror that feeling?

Does she paint him her soul as she did for me?
Even if she did, would he receive it the same way my soul did?

The unanswered questions in the shadows clung to the desperate parts of my soul. My tortured soul was plagued with loneliness, and I assumed that was how it was going to be for years upon years to come.

I felt cast aside.

I felt used.

My heart was just a tattered rag doll at her disposal.

I wondered if she would flinch when she looked into my eyes each day at work, for she would be the one who made me take down my walls, only to destroy any and everything I had left within me.

As I made my way out of the sanctuary and onto the mattress where we once held each other, I saw an old copy of Nicholas Sparks' *The Notebook* sitting on the floor. Its pages were torn, just like my soul, and it was a pitiful reminder that like Noah and Allie, Emma and I would just be "friends."

∞ ∞ ∞ ∞ ∞ ∞ ∞ ∞

The storms and rough tides that plague our waters are echoic of our innate existence. We are an ocean of opportunities encased in a heart, mind, body, soul, and spirit, though sometimes the facets that make us whole are not as we make them out to be.

Other souls touch the fundamental parts of our being. Other people can raise our spirits. We can bestow empowerment on ourselves and on those who are around us.

We are the leaders of our lives, and it was my belief we started to act with that strength brewing deep within us… yet in those moments of mourning what I thought I had with Emma, heartbreak and notions I could have had a divine love with her masked my true energy in this universe.

Despite all of the apparent blessings around me, I often felt lost more than ever. I was intellectual and passionate enough to comprehend that all of this would make sense one day, though I did not know how long I would have to battle my way through the trenches.

I was praying for a sign in the attic of that church. I was praying for someone to come rescue me.

Something had to be out there, and I was sure of it.

A murmured thud snapped me out of my trance-like state.

Footsteps began to make their way up the steps and just behind the door. I did not know what was about to happen, but I figured that since I was asking the universe for a sign, whatever was about to make its way into the room would create a massive shift in my soul.

The door creaked open and I was met with a familiar face and a smile. It figures, when I usually ask the universe for a sign, it does deliver. No matter what was about to happen, I sensed that it would be just what I needed.

Morena's face appeared in the door and my heart sank a little. I was hoping that Emma would be the one standing in the doorway, but I guess it was not meant to be at that moment.

"You wanted a sign," Morena moved slowly across the room. "Here I am."

'*You* aren't what I expected,' I rolled over on the mattress and pulled the blanket over my head.

"I may not be what you expected, but I am what you have." She plopped down on the mattress and looked at the mirror across the room. It was difficult to make out her reflection, which is why sometimes I figured she wasn't real. Morena also always seemed to show up just when I was asking the universe for a sign.

Yet in some twisted way, she seemed to be the sign. It was strange.

"Scott," she spoke softly. "You can't do this to yourself."

'Do what?'

"Beat yourself up over Emma."

'I am not–'

"You are," she cut me off. "You are, don't lie."

I sat up and whipped my head around, 'Okay, so what if I am?'

"You are so focused on divine love and Emma, but what do you *really* want Scott?" She stood up and walked to the edge of the room. "What do *you* want?"

'I want love,' I shouted. At this point I was exhausted beyond belief. Tears started streaming down my face again, 'I just want love.'

"Think beyond that," Morena turned back around. "You have a company and you have a vision… yet you are stuck on her. Why?"

'It is more than that, Morena.'

"Then tell me, tell me what it is."

'I want to give people jobs and reach youth around the world. However, there's one problem–'

Morena cut me off again, "Think beyond divine love for Emma for a moment."

'Something is not right with the pieces of this puzzle. They are being forced together and not clicking naturally. Someone is always upset, angry, or sick, and it's not just a momentary thing.'

"What do you mean?"

'There's always something going on with Eve and the church, my program directors are going through so much, and this lonely, broken heart is a mess.'

Morena's face was partially obscured by the faint darkness in the room. It reminded me of the first time we met when she was covered in bruises. So much had changed since then, I sensed the fire burning within her soul, yet I barely knew her real story.

'How do you mend a broken heart? You must know.'

A lingering silence hung in the air.

"Love is lost when one does not understand the balance that must exist. It is like yin and yang. Sometimes there is light, sometimes there is darkness, but the most empowering creations happen when we are aware of the strength and beauty within us."

I laughed slightly, 'That is very profound.'

"I have my moments," she smirked.

'I have had the most incredible love and moments that have been etched in my soul for eternity, yet why did those moments get destroyed?'

"It's not the memories and moments that get destroyed; it is our expectation that things will be the same forever. People grow, people change, we change," She moved closer. "Our souls grow, and that is what makes them beautiful."

'That makes sense.'

"At the end of the day, the most beautiful souls are the ones who grow and acknowledge the true gift they are to the universe."

'Doesn't that contradict who we innately are?'

"How so?"

'If we see ourselves as a gift, isn't that conceited?'

"You need to own your soul. You need to empower yourself and others... it is who you innately are."

I saw Emma's pain, the walls she put up, her strength, her courage, her heart, her spirituality, and her beauty. The divine love concept embodies her almost perfectly. The possibilities with her seemed endless, yet I was clinging to the love I thought we shared.

Everything within my beautiful soul said that she could be the other half of my power couple. Everything. I could not fathom how Greg could see her. It boggled my mind that Emma could show up for him the way she showed up for me.

I watched Morena drift about the room and fade into the shadows.

As I closed my eyes from sheer exhaustion, I could sense her spirit crawling up my spine. I knew that somewhere else in the universe she had to come across a memory of us. She would have to look at herself in the mirror and try to deny what we had because she could not fathom the guilt: she had me and she had Greg, and she had to choose.

Nothing that she did or said could prove that she could deny the guilt coursing through her veins. Emma did not see the light shining within her, and I sensed that I loved her more that she could even handle.

I was not overromanticizing us.

When two souls collide, as ours once did, the flame never truly goes out. Even in the wake of destruction and in the ashes succumbing my tattered heart, there was a glimmer of hope.

With my last cognizant thoughts, I realized that though I was hurt, it meant that I could still feel.

Our story was not over yet.

Once souls like ours are anchored together, the ship we commandeered together could never sink, even if it was stationed at someone else's port.

∞ ∞ ∞ ∞ ∞ ∞ ∞ ∞

It was an emotionally challenging month, but I figured I was doing okay. I did not know if it was because of my continual spiritual search, however I felt like I was getting stronger.

I was completely helpless, yet full of confidence; I was a walking juxtaposition. I was drowning in the depths of insecurity, though I felt I could do something… anything. The idea of letting go may not be as simple as flicking a switch on or off, rather it was a journey between growing my own faith and shifting elements of internal personal growth. I never could have imagined the tearing apart of my heart and soul as I had experienced during the past few months, but I felt in my heart that we were real.

There was an overwhelming sense of self-doubt and giving up on love, but I had been blessed with love throughout my life. I felt I still had a lot to learn, but I also had a sense that Emma would return.

My pain and sadness were carved into my soul though in some customs and cultures, cracked porcelain was filled with gold to keep broken treasures together.

In a sense, I hoped that I was a broken treasure. I prayed someone would see me as a precious gift.

Trust was becoming a fragile currency, and my love was running out. I prayed for a partner to help me on this journey through life, and little did I know I was perceiving partnerships all wrong at the time.

In the initial weeks of the tears I shed in honor of Emma's love, she would occasionally text me as an indirect reminder that she loved me, but she could not fathom "us." We went from texting every single day, to once a week, to once in a while.

Then the texts seemed to stop. I watched her parade around work, flashing her engagement ring to anyone who would catch a glimpse of it.

In praying for love to return however, I was greeted with a pleasant surprise: Bryan decided to come home from Florida and chose to stay in New York for good this time.

When I went to go pick him up at the airport, I sat in my Monte Carlo and watched raindrops slightly drip down the window. I missed Emma, I truly did. The longing I had for her became a constant pain in my chest.

I shut my eyes for a moment, mourning her disappearance, when my heart suddenly filled with glee.

"Pop?" Bryan's voice provided me with the most love I felt in a long time.

'Son, you've come home.'

He jumped in the car and we embraced quickly. The tears that fell from our eyes were a reminder that we were the definition of unconditional and true love, and we were all we needed.

Bryan began to tell me about how challenging of a time he had in Florida, and asked if we could listen to some music.

The two of us were driving down the highway blasting Bayside's "Head on a Plate:"

> *"With tied wrists we're under their control,*
> *With fists clenched, we're taking on the world.*
> *I write down words with cathartic intentions.*
> *But they spawn revolutions of minds."*

Everything felt natural, everything felt phenomenal, and for a few moments, everything was perfect because my son was home.

∞ ∞ ∞ ∞ ∞ ∞ ∞ ∞

Forgiveness and acceptance seemed to be a theme that spring. Though I was just shy of begging Emma to come back into my life, Faith was contacting me non-stop to talk as friends.

I trusted in God and the universe, so I chose to see what Faith wanted.

The two of us met at a cute café on a busy New York City corner. It was once a popular Italian restaurant, which was turned into an Irish pub that served breakfast early in the morning.

Our small table rested against the tall glass windows. The sunlight beamed towards us and I could not help but admire Faith's exquisite beauty. It was difficult to be around her energy, but I knew that she just wanted a friendship.

"I can't say that I love you anymore," Faith started the conversation. "It's a sign of weakness in me. I have to grow and connect to the universe."

I looked at her over my cup of coffee.

"We are like transmitters trying to find the right tune, so that we can finally realize our power and purpose."

She sounded a lot more aligned with my thoughts and beliefs. What really engaged me was listening to her share what was going on within her soul. It was honorable to see her spiritual expansion happening before my eyes. It made me feel as if I was her sounding board and she was my partner, but in fact, she wasn't.

Though I felt like I was tempted to fall back in love with her, something told me to back off.

Something told me that she was a part of the larger picture, though I was still trying to figure out what that picture was.

The two of us joked about how long we had known each other and how we were both a blessing and a curse. I did not see her as the spiritual love I thought we once were, but that was totally okay. We went through so much, but despite going to hell and back, we were right in front of each other once again.

It is amazing how everything seems to come full circle.

After the two of us spoke about everything, including my fears surrounding Emma, she seemed to echo what Morena told me. Faith's spirituality was growing, and I was proud of who she was becoming. We explored our respective fears and ambitions, and I told her I wanted to do so much more in this universe.

"Then do it," her accent brought a certain thrill to my soul. It was almost as if she knew just what to say to push at my ambitions.

As we left and I was rushing across town to meet Morena, I turned to Faith and put my hand on her shoulder.

'Sometimes it is okay to face your fears, so from me to you: I love you, my dear friend.'

Faith looked at me and smiled: "I love you too… so much. Thank you for listening."

I darted across town and saw Morena sitting on a bench.

'Mo,' I shouted to her.

"Hey," she shut a notebook she was scribbling in.

'What's that?'

"Oh," she pushed her hair behind her ear. "It's my journal. I write ideas in it."

'I never noticed it before.'

"Oh, I'm always writing in it. If I don't have a thought rumbling around in my head, then I am at a loss."

'Can I see?' She passed me her notebook and I opened it somewhat cautiously. Her hopes and dreams were caught between these pages. I flipped through her scribblings until a drawing caught my eye. 'What's that?'

She leaned over and looked at where I was pointing.

"Oh," she grinned and pulled her head further into her chest. "It's the White House."

'The White House?'

"Yeah, you know like in Washington, D.C.?" She looked over at me, almost waiting for a response.

'That's cool.' I was curious. 'Why are you drawing the White House?'

"Um…" she didn't seem to know what to say. "I always wanted to go to Washington, D.C. and see the White House and all the buildings there. I just never got a chance to go."

Something ignited within me at that point. I think this was the first moment that D.C. truly came to mind.

'We should have a leadership program there,' our eyes locked for a moment.

Morena was quiet, but something was churning in her head… I could see it.

"We should," she smiled from ear to ear and grabbed her notebook back. "I think we should build out those curriculums you have. You truly have something exciting."

'That sounds good, but what would we do with them?'

"Oh," she seemed to be holding something back, but I didn't question it.

The two of us stood up from the bench and we started to walk down the sidewalk.

"I am sure you'll find *something*, Scott."

It was almost like she had all of the answers, but did not want to share. It was like she was holding the best kept secret within her mind, and at the time I think she wanted me to see just how empowered I could become.

I spent years inspiring and empowering so many people, little did I know I could do so much more than working in one school. At the time I was thinking of the bigger picture, but I was ensnared in a web of wanting to find the other half of my power couple. I did not see what I had within my own soul.

Time would tell the rest of my story.

Always Just Another Day

∞ ∞ ∞ ∞ ∞ ∞ ∞ ∞

As summer closed in on the leadership programs within the high school, Emma's presence was about to fade into the summer. I was partially terrified; because I did not know what she would do in the months we were apart.

Would she think of me?

Would she call me or text me?

So many thoughts clogged my head and distracted me from what was truly important, though Emma was for all intents and purposes who I wanted to be "my everything."

When the bell rang and all of the students filtered into my room, she was standing behind a few of them. I was unsure of what to say to her, nor did I know what I wanted to say.

"Have a good summer, Ms. Paige," one of the students said to her.

'Yeah,' a somber tone overtook my voice. 'Have a great summer.'

She looked at me and smiled slightly, but she did not say anything. I lost her for good, I was sure of it.

Days later would be her engagement party, and I did not know how she would stand there in a short white dress and pretend she was so just and pure.

Then again all of this sounds judgmental, but it was the story that I told my soul. Part of me thinks that I had to tell this story at the time in order to justify why she ran away from me. She flew right into his arms.

I was not invited to the party, so Morena asked if we could spend the day working on the curriculums. Naturally, I obliged.

That late afternoon, Morena and I were working in the office at Queens Community Church and I was deeply sad. Then my phone chimed and I looked over to see a text message from Emma on the screen.

"Can we talk?"

Emma wanted to speak to me.

I figured that something was wrong; I felt it in my core.

I excused myself and ran outside to speak to her. Emma told me that her and Greg got into a huge fight, and she asked for my advice.

Emma wanted *my* advice about *her* relationship with *Greg.*

Beautiful Souls

I wanted to vomit. I wanted to run away and never look back. I felt sick.

We spoke for a while until I asked the question that I longed to hear the answer to.

'Do you miss me?' I held back the tears.

"A little bit," she said softly. "I have to go. Thanks, bye."

The line went dead and I retreated back into the church.

As the door slammed shut, I could feel my heart drop into the pit of my stomach. The love I felt for her was in its purest form. She was anything and everything I could have hoped for. She was the embodiment of divine love and the retribution for years of my soul's torment.

Then, in moments, she slid through my fingers. No warning. No sirens or flares.

Gone.

I had never figured it would become this sort of fractured fairytale. I painted this image in my head of what our life would grow into: her dream of having the house with the white picket fence in a quiet suburban town, her dog zooming around the backyard, the kids playing in the kitchen while their mother baked cupcakes... the perfect family.

Yeah, maybe the perfect family... but not our family. Not mine and Emma's family.

Greg's family. Greg's house. Greg's yard. Greg's fence. His grass, his trees, his kids... my wife. My love. My divine love and my soulmate.

Emma.

Now she is just a distant memory.

A faded carving in a tree: S + E forever.

I guess forever ended weeks ago.

And all she left me with was "Breathe, it is just another day."

Emma, when you look at me, I often wonder what you see. Do you see a hopeless shell of someone who once was? Do you see a pliable existence bent by a single gust of wind? Do you turn your back and brush off all of the love that could have existed between us.

Oh... wait... *could have.*

I stood there in the darkness, peering out the window where I once glared out of when I was moments away from one of our passionate nights and wrote what came to mind:

If I called out your name in the darkness, would you come running towards me? Would you know just where to find me just by hearing your name? Would my soul beckon you back to the place where you belong, with me, or would these mindless noises tell me I am wrong?

I stared at it for moments before I crumpled up the paper and threw it furiously against the wall.

She wasn't coming home to where she belonged. She was not going to fall into my arms ever again.

Days must have passed by during my depressed state. My hand became caught in the rough stubble that had formed across my face as I waited for her call. Something inside me knew she would never call me engorged with lust ever again, but oh did I pray for the phone to ring.

My Circle of Angels must have heard me, for within an instant my phone began to buzz. The blue and white glow from the phone shouted the name I did not want to see: Morena. Of course, she has a habit of falling into my life at just the wrong moment, but then again, the Circle of Angels keeps tossing her into me nonsensically, almost as if bowling pins were persistently chasing after a bowling ball.

The dreams of Emma and I continued throughout the rest of July and August. I did not know if my soul was detoxing or what, but my subconscious seemed to crave Emma. The two constants, other than Emma, in each of my dreams were Morena's notebook and Morena's voice. Before I woke up each morning, Morena would say, "It's time to wake up."

And there I was, sitting up on the mattress by myself, covered in sweat: slightly confused and wholeheartedly missing Emma.

∞ ∞ ∞ ∞ ∞ ∞ ∞ ∞

When I went back to school in September, Emma and I were walking in the hallway in different directions. We were alone, but we were together.

It was a strange, yet comforting feeling to see her again.

The two of us stopped in the hallway and she looked up at me. I could tell she was reading my energy and she smiled.

Emma giggled a bit: "Still?"

'Still?' I replied. 'I haven't stopped.'

She blushed and rubbed her shoulder.

'Still?'

She began to walk down the hallway. I heard her whisper a faint "Always" as she went into her classroom and slammed the door.

The day flew by and the night was filled with dreams of Emma kissing my lips again. I woke up to find that once again I was alone in the church attic, with a throbbing pain pushing against my lower back.

I drove to the parking lot of Lincoln Memorial High School and watched the rain begin to twist through the sky.

I could hear a solitary heartbeat overhead. It was as if I was walking in another's shoes, wandering this planet as an addendum to someone else's story. My misshapen hair flopped to the side and I dragged myself out of the car and into the pouring rain.

No one can tell you are crying when raindrops grace your cheeks with the same intentions: to cleanse.

My eyes were glazed over and it felt as if I was trouncing around in a daze. I could not feel, rather I could not feel because I had been so numb to her touch for the longest time. The very thought of her pressing against me again made me yearn for yesterday, or maybe the day before, or possibly years before that. Time has melted away since we last had a heart-to-heart conversation, and I so desperately wanted to burst into her room and apologize profusely.

I wanted to get on my hands and knees and bow down to her essence and her soul.

Yet upon walking into the school, rounding the corner, and catching a glimpse of her beautiful brown eyes, I realized that I had to swallow my pain and be patient. Maybe she would not communicate with my soul today, tomorrow, or the next day… but someday.

Just someday.

I caught my breath becoming more and more labored: I was having a full-blown anxiety attack. It was my fourth one that week, and they seemed to come throughout the day at this point.

At night I would wake up discombobulated and I did not know where I was at certain points. Emma's presence, or lack thereof, was beginning to plague my thoughts.

Emma would always visit my dreams.

Night after night I would find myself standing in the doorway to our first hotel room. I could see her silhouette resting patiently in the bed. Her body was tangled in the pure white sheets that reflected every innocent thing about her soul. She was in an incoherent state of peace and tranquility: one she would never experience while being wide-awake.

Then Morena's notebook would appear and I would hear her telling me to wake up.

'You haunt my dreams,' I would tease Morena.

"You're haunting," she would quip sarcastically.

We find symbols when we manifest them. We seek out validation from the mundane and create our own reality. Respectively, if we truly look within, we are all creatures of habit and habitat. If you want a reality, find it. Create it.

Emma always said she fears being a parent. She fears loss and solitude beyond her control.

Everything inside of me pleaded with my soul: Do not allow the wound to fester.

"Look deep within the recesses of your mind," Morena told me. "The key is there. In reality you have much more value than you believe."

'I don't know what I'm supposed to do haunted by the ghost of Emma,' I told her.

It was the essence and the presence: her adorous infatuation with pulling the leash just far enough for the dog to snap back methodically.

A cruel intention was anchoring and weighing on my soul.

A saying and sensation were brewing within me: "Toss the ropes but drop the anchor: if the weight is held, the roots are set. If not, sail on. Another lighthouse beckons with its glow."

If only I knew where the light was, I wonder if my soul would have been this tortured for years upon years.

In late October, almost a full year since Emma and I started on our spiritually shifting, yet tumultuous relationship, a glimmer of hope presented itself before me. As I was packing up to leave one night, one

Beautiful Souls

of my students rushed downstairs to my office to proclaim that Emma was still in her classroom.

Something about it did not seem right.

Part of my soul was frozen in its tracks, wondering why, after so many months of beating myself up over the lack of her presence, someone would rush into my room and proclaim she was still in her room.

Something within me said to trust in the universe and take the leap of faith.

I walked up to her room, where she was sitting with a restless look on her face, and offered her a hand.

'Are you okay?'

We gazed at each other in a moment that could rival even the most romantic scene in a movie. I felt it: our love was real.

"You know," Emma said matter of factly. "You know my rule about us at work."

Her comment caught me off guard. I did not understand what she was getting at exactly.

'You look like you need a shoulder to cry on.'

"I need a *lot* more than a shoulder," I heard her voice breaking.

'Do you want to go get some coffee or something?'

"That would be great."

The two of us walked out the door, went our separate ways, and met up at a place fifteen minutes away from the school.

"Greg and I keep fighting," were the first words she spoke when she sat down.

'You can talk about it if you want.'

She laughed, "That's why I am here."

I sipped my coffee. 'Is that the only reason why?'

Emma glared at me with her chocolate brown eyes. "You know it will *always* be us." She reached out and grabbed my hand. As I maneuvered my fingers between hers, something felt different.

"You okay?" She looked concerned.

I sensed that the pain and agony stirring within me were ensnared in the conflicting feelings I had for her: I loved her, but she hurt me so much.

How do you look into the eyes of someone you were once so vulnerable with, someone who you were once so in love with, and allow yourself to say those three words?

'I am fine.'

We continued to talk about her and Greg, ignoring the fact that our relationship was once so much more than spiritual pillowtalk. We were the embodiment of love.

At least I thought we were at the time.

As I walked her to her car and wished her a goodnight, she looked at my lips and spoke softly, "Scott?"

'Yeah,' I put my hands in my pockets.

"Thanks."

She got into her car and slammed the door.

I began walking down the block, crumpling leaves on my way to my car, when a homeless man approached me. I don't know if he was really homeless, but he was definitely poor and in shambles.

Though I thought he was going to ask me for some spare change, he merely said, "Buddy, try smiling… you may actually start to have fun."

It made me laugh and, in that moment, I realized how sad I was. The energy I was putting out must have been incredibly desolate.

Faking it gets hard sometimes.

Why I allowed her to anchor my soul this way is unknown to me, but I must raise the weight and sail on.

This was just a case of two ships passing and briefly touching… yet it's an ocean I want to swim in. Is there anything wrong with that?

I miss watching our natural flow.

It led to paradise, yet now I am drowning.

I refuse to sink with or without the anchor.

I have a huge future and I had to begin acting like it.

The voice within me said that I should just sacrifice true love once and for all. Did I really need love if I knew I was destined for much more than the physical?

My innate existence had to be of a metaphysical nature. Why would I continue to survive through all of these trials and tribulations?

However, my soul kept saying do not let go.

When I got into my car and thrusted the key into the ignition, the radio hummed with the melodic tune of "Patience" by Guns N' Roses:

Beautiful Souls

"Said 'woman take it slow, and it'll work itself out fine'
All we need is just a little patience"

Stacey was with me. I sensed it.

Maybe at the time I did just need a little bit more patience, though I was too blind to that notion.

Emma's love, or lack thereof, was extremely loud and incredibly close. Still, I was wading in the waters of chance: Maybe, just maybe, she did love me.

When I got back to the church, I felt exhausted. For some strange reason, Eve and Paul were standing out front arguing loudly about something.

As I got out of the car and slammed the door, Eve whipped her head around towards me.

"*What* are you doing here?" she hollered.

'Oh hi,' I said quietly. 'I-'

Paul cut me off: "Eve, Windows' office is here. Let the man be."

"Fine," she snapped sarcastically. "Fine by me. People come and go as they please."

She retreated into their car without saying anything else, and Paul apologized to me for the scene.

'Is everything okay?' I asked innocently, knowing that something strange happened.

"No, but it will be my son." Paul put a reassuring hand on my shoulder and smiled.

'Okay, well if you need anything, just call.'

"One day," he wrapped his hand around my shoulder. "One day this building will be yours and it will truly bless this community. I know it."

Eve rolled the window down and shouted for Paul to get into the car. He wished me a blessed night and scurried away.

I did not know what to think about the conversation, but maybe that was what I needed to be patient for: Windows of Opportunity might have a true home, and not just an office, at Queens Community Church.

I felt so blessed for everything, for who I was in those moments, for what I knew, for what I felt, and for what I connected to.

The universe has always been incredibly kind to me, and I just didn't really understand why at that point.

Why me?

Why did I have to see the things I had seen and loved as deeply as I did? I did not understand my role.

I knew at the heart of things that people had to be happy and that we are all here to find our innate happiness.

For the most part, I was happy.

When I looked at my life, who I had loved, and who loved me, I knew everyone was teaching me some sort of lesson about myself. I just did not understand what lesson Emma was teaching me as of yet.

My heart was crippled in the unresolved situations I was a part of. Emma and Faith's respective love unearthed my soul, yet I could have a peaceful conversation with Faith. Emma's conversations left me feeling dreary and longing for what we had.

The moments were deafening to my soul and I could barely hear the voice I had within me.

At this point it was midnight and I could not sleep. I jumped into my car and found it almost pathetic that I was sitting there, at 12:30 in the morning, looking at Emma's darkened classroom windows and waiting for the gym to open so I could shower. My mind was wandering. My sacrifices were mounting. My lower back began to ache at the very thought of how much real change I knew I needed to make in my life.

I wondered if anything mattered at all if Emma was not going to share my life.

My voice took on a solemn tone as I whispered Bon Jovi's lyrics into the brisk night sky:

> *"What do you got, if you ain't got love*
> *Whatever you got, it just ain't enough*
> *You're walkin' the road, but you're goin' nowhere*
> *You're tryin' to find your way home, but there's no one there*
> *Who do you hold, in the dark of night*
> *You wanna give up, but it's worth the fight*
> *You have all the things, that you've been dreamin' of."*

I drifted off to sleep feeling grateful for what I had, a roof over my head, even if it was just a car.

∞ ∞ ∞ ∞ ∞ ∞ ∞ ∞

Glass ricocheted as screaming rang out through the room. In those brief moments between the heaving breaths and wallowing, it was almost peaceful. I could not find the appropriate words to materialize any sort of thoughts, so my mind just went blank.

All the memories from the past few months flickered by as if a film was being made about what she meant to me.

But she was gone.

She was a shattered existence of the woman I once knew.

And I was okay with it.

And I was no longer the morose figure dancing just past her line of sight, beckoning her to step closer.

To come closer.

Loneliness was no longer the moniker that would cling mercilessly to the depths of my soul. She was released from the fundamental roots that once ruptured this tree.

I am past tense and he is future perfect. I was the one, but I hope he will be worth it.

She no longer controls every aspect of my gaze. She does not have the privilege to see me soar and fly. She does not have the honor of standing beside me when I genuinely shift this world into a more positive space.

I miss her. I do. Do not, for one split second, believe that this is my whimpering plea to earn her back.

This is my Declaration of Independence. This is my Magna Carta.

I was standing with my eyes closed near a still body of water.

When I opened my eyes, the Washington Monument was directly in front of me.

'Take care of yourself, Emma. I am proud of you.' I whispered as I turned and glared at the Lincoln Memorial. 'I hope you find the solace from our severed love that you so deserve. Rest in peace, or rather, rest in the pieces of our memories that you choose to savor. Rest in the pieces of us.'

Because something is shattered, that does not mean it is broken.
"And now neither are you," A voice echoed throughout the monument.
'What?' I shouted. 'Who is there?'
Morena emerged from the shadows and held out her notebook.
"The question is, are you ready?"
I jolted awake to find the sunlight peeking through the urban cityscape.
I did not know what any of that meant, but I sensed that Morena had to have some sort of answer for me.
Her notebook had to be what was holding all of the answers.

∞ ∞ ∞ ∞ ∞ ∞ ∞ ∞

After I got in and out of the shower quickly, I rushed to the school to start going through some papers I had in the office.
Joy appeared in the doorway and said good morning.
A few students filtered in and out of the room.
I did not really know what I was looking for, but I needed to find an excuse to get closer to Emma again.
"What are you doing?" Joy was standing over me looking at all of the papers scattered on my floor.
'I am looking for something.'
"Okay," she said. She shrugged and grabbed her lunch from the fridge.
'I look a little crazy, don't I?'
"A little bit," she quipped back.
A little bit. She said one of Emma's catchphrases.
I figured I would just walk past Emma's classroom and see what she was up to. Odds are she was teaching, I mean it was the middle of the school day.
When I walked up the stairs, a sense of existential dread washed over me. I noticed that her classroom was empty and she was nowhere to be found. There must have been an assembly or something.
I walked into the room and saw the picture of her and Greg on her desk. The two of them looked nauseatingly in love with one another, though Emma's eyes looked dead compared to the way she once looked at me.
It was pitiful.

Beautiful Souls

My mind drifted to a series of questions, as per usual. All of them were focused on Emma:

If you came into this room right now and whispered the words I longed to hear, would you mean them? Would your soul collide with mine in the most breathtakingly cataclysmic way? Would you linger on my kisses a bit too perfectly?

Would you capture the essence of a love paused in time, only to return to the scene of the crime and steal my heart again?

Would your eyes drag themselves along the outline of my sunken shoulders? Would you caress my skin with the intention of leaving your fingerprints along them in the most delicate of ways?

Would you realize the hurt you caused me in the most shattering of ways? Would you walk on eggshells around my soul for the rest of my life, knowing you damaged the pieces that were already broken?

Would you lay awake watching me rest in your comforting arms? Would you brush the tears you placed on my cheeks? Would you fall into my arms like it was four years ago? Would you cling to my soul because you realized you left me when you needed me the most?

Do you also think about these questions, day in and day out, with the same dragging feeling in your chest? Or do you beat on, ignorant to how much you have hurt me and continue to drive the knife further in my back each moment we are apart?

As I looked at the picture of Emma and Greg again, wisdom filtered into my soul. If I could have spoken to her in those moments, I would have said so much with so little.

'May you never feel the pain you have caused me. May you always be loved twice as much as you ever loved me. May you recognize my face in the crowd when our paths cross again. May you feel my touch against your neck when your back is turned to him, for he may touch you now... but our love will touch you for the rest of your life. And don't you ever dare forget it.'

I left her room and caught a glance of her walking up the hallway.

Our eyes locked in an attempt to remind each other of the days when we were us... and in those solitary, rare moments that arise... I can tell, just with the gaze she bestowed upon me... that she remembered, too.

When I got back into my office, Joy was gone.

I started to pick up my papers from the floor and came across the original infinity sign and anchor tattoo drawing Emma created for me. Instantly, I felt sick.

My fingers traced the infinity sign tattoo on my forearm. The number 88 and the infinity sign have always held such a profound meaning to me.

For as long as I could remember, I was always attracted to the number 8. Eighty-eight was the number on my lacrosse jersey. At some point, I made the mental connection that the number was the same shape as the infinity sign.

To me, infinity meant that life was ongoing, strong, and unbreakable. It was the metaphor for how things should be. It provides power and energy to my soul.

Emma understood what 88 meant to me, both physically and spiritually. Once upon a time she had the desire to get to know me. She connected to my soul and I shared this part of my spirit with her. She explained to me that her favorite symbol was the anchor. To her, it was a constant reminder that she had to "refuse to sink" in life.

Her words echoed through my head as the ghost of who she was to me floated through the room: "I refuse to give up on us, on life, on love, on humanity."

No matter what was going to happen to us in life, she was etched into my soul. Her soul was drawn in ink on my skin, as her love was permanently inscribed in my spirit.

Our fleeting moments were drifting into the distance, so I quickly collected my tears and chose to continue with my day.

As the night fell upon me, I looked at my phone for some semblance of hope. Still, Emma did not text or call. I was holistically alone with my thoughts once again.

Upon returning to the church, I heard rustling in the Windows of Opportunity office. I assumed Morena let herself in to work on something, and I intended to ask her about her journal that kept appearing in my dreams.

Instead of being greeted by Morena, Eve was the one rummaging through the office.

'Hi Eve, how are-' Her eyes narrowed and cut directly through me.

"What are *you* doing here so late?" Eve was not happy.

'I was going to work on some stuff.'

I could not tell Eve that I was home for the night, and that I was about to pass out on my mattress in the attic.

"You are *lying*," she shouted. "You *live* in this church!"

I did not know what to say. Yes, technically I was sleeping at the church and all of my clothes were here, but there was no shower or real place for me to stay here.

'I-' the words I wanted to say were trapped at the tip of my tongue.

"Get out," she screamed. "You can keep your office here, but all of your stuff needs to go. *Now.*"

I wondered if Paul knew. If he realized I was homeless, would he make me leave?

Within 24 hours, I packed everything up. Eve told me that we were going to get reported, though we never were. It had to look like I never stayed there.

Those moments where I had to launch all of my belongings in bags and boxes were insane and sickening. Morena assured me that everything would be okay, and that this was all happening for a reason. At the time, I did not think to ask her about the journal she had just yet.

"It is all a part of your spiritual journey," she said.

Faith offered me a place to stay, but I humbly denied her. I could not impose upon her or her sons, for I thought our friendship was fragile and something I did not want to test.

For me, sleeping in my car meant that it was just another day. My life was filled with just another sacrifice.

I fell asleep, night after night, in the front seat of my car. The faint murmur of my engine reminded me that my heart was still beating and life was still worth living.

One early morning the phrase "It was not just a dream" faded out into a distant echo as I awoke to find a man knocking on my car window. A police officer, neatly dressed and too eager with his flashlight, clanging on my window, stood before me.

I rolled down the window and shielded my eyes from his bitter existence. He looked tired, defeated even, in the rising sun. The shadows dragged along his face with unwavering certainty.

"Sir, are you okay?" He boomed. His eyes pierced into my soul.

'What-' I groggily lowered the heat in the car. The fan burst its hot air before succumbing to the contrastive cold air outside.

"Sir, you were passed out, do you need medical attention?" He beamed the light into my car as his radio murmured at his waist.

I hastily responded with a jumble of words. I drummed up some concoction of 'just tired' and 'I work in the church.' He retreated to his car and left me alone in the dusk that settles right before the sun creeps up the horizon.

I savored the dream I just experienced as I drove off to a coffee shop. I was in a freshly polished pair of shoes. My suit was crisp and dark blue. I was standing on the steps of a grand building... it looked like Washington, D.C., but, no... why would I be there?

Maybe these visions of grandeur are just a manifestation of Morena's wishful thinking... After all, she did say she wanted to go there.

Yet as I glared up at the sun rising over Northern Boulevard, I could see a majestic flag billowing in the morning air. It flattered the hollow parts of my soul. It squeezed my heart and yelled, "Beat on."

As the light turned green and a man violently honked his horn to interrupt my destiny, I inched forward and towards the shop. As I parked my car, the realization hit me...

I just said destiny.

This was not a dream. This was real life intermingling with the hand of reality, hoisting me high above the turmoil flooding my soul.

D.C. was coming... it was speeding like a train bolstered tightly to the tracks: remaining constant and unabashed by the speed and tenacity it so desperately clung to.

This dream would not be derailed... no, no... no. This was reality. This is the reality I would manifest and create.

I just did not know what Washington, D.C. would mean to me at that point.

My life revolved around running leadership programs in a high school and living in a car. It was then I realized that you can be homeless, but you can still have a home in the hearts of those you help heal.

I am awake.

I am in pain.

I should be sleeping, I figured.

What message does the universe want me to give the world?

There were hints, the moonlight peeking in through the darkness, the sounds still heard in the silence, the rustling of tree branches I see through my sunroof, the lyrics in a song, the look in someone else's eyes, a text message, and the vibration felt in closing my eyes and clearing my thoughts.

Morena had to be the key.

Our stories intertwined and it was all for a higher purpose.

I was ready to step into the bigger role... the larger frame.

I knew Morena was part of that puzzle. A huge part. Her strange gift combined with my story and our mutual support could spread messages from the universe in a way that has never been done before.

While Morena and I were at the church one afternoon just before the new year fell upon us, I looked over at her and asked for her journal.

'It is time I know what the scribblings in your book mean.'

She rose from the chair and handed me her book. Her fingers were still wrapped around it.

"Remember," she spoke solemnly. "We complement one another and it isn't a contest. You getting down on yourself cuts off your flow of positive energy. Avoid all of that negative nonsense."

'I'll try.'

"Trying is all SHE could ask for," she released the book.

'SHE?'

Morena seemed to ignore my question: "You are loved and your journey began way before you were manifested into this timeline. You have made what you call mistakes, you have learned, and you have evolved. Each lesson makes you wiser."

'What do I need to do?' I asked, wondering what was happening.

"This world needs higher conscious-thinking leaders. Some will refer to these souls as thought leaders. The next generation will be progressive, but needs spiritual guidance. You are damaging your body and it is the vessel to bring you higher. Do you want to go higher?"

I hesitated and thought of Emma.

'What lesson was she bringing me?' Morena instantly knew what I was talking about.

"You aren't ready." She pulled the book from my grasp and tucked it back into her bag.

We did not speak of that journal for quite some time after that incident.

'Why,' I yelled at her. 'Why am I not ready?'

"You aren't," she did not look up from the paper she was reading. "Stop punishing yourself, for you are love. When you are ready, you will know."

We sat in silence for a while and I figured I would just drop it.

Her words echoed in my head, "When you are ready, you will know."

∞ ∞ ∞ ∞ ∞ ∞ ∞ ∞

An unspecified longing for Emma's presence haunted me daily at work. To make matters worse I began to work at Lincoln Memorial High School full-time, which meant that I had to see Emma trounce around for an entire school day.

While on my way to a meeting one morning, I rushed out of my office and there she was. Emma stood before me in fuchsia pants and beige platform shoes. That odd walk that she has made me melt. She looked beautiful and her energy consumed the hallway.

No one else was there. Nothing was between us.

She had her back towards me and was walking away from me. The only sound gracing the hallways was the pitter-patter of her shoes.

I wanted to call out her name.

I wanted her to see the pain in my eyes.

Yet the only thing that escaped my lips was a breathy sigh, it was the residue of months of love and affection whittled down to the fact that she still took my breath away. She had no idea I was there. She could no longer feel my presence like once upon a time.

Emma slid into a classroom and vanished from the physical space between us.

Sadness consumed me, and I realized that was the first time I actually saw her all week. Why did her existence have to be one of the last images I had to see before the end of the year? 2016 had been a violently sickening experience in my soul.

It was almost a poignant metaphor that she slipped into the abyss.

I had to pause for a moment and ask myself: What is wrong with me?

My emotions flooded my throat and I was trying desperately not to lose it.

Beautiful Souls

Damn you, Emma.

The night we were in the hotel room pulsated in my mind. Her apparition was a painstaking one.

It was almost as if she was directly in front of me on the hotel bed, *our hotel bed*, in my mind. The rustling curtains and the dimly shivering red letters from the hotel's sign shimmered at the back of my eyelids.

Sitting across from Emma in the vision I had in my head brought me such sorrow. I realized that selflessness had a name, a concrete voice, and a shattered heart.

I had an epiphany: I was so much stronger for going through hell and back, and back and forth, countless times. The pendulum has to swing at some point: gravity has a funny way of drawing us back to where we are meant to be just before we tip over the edge and crash.

"Say something," Emma's ghost spoke to me.

My eyes filled with tears as I reached out to stroke her face.

'You were an accident, you were a coincidence, and you were the best I never had,' my words were shattering as they escaped my mouth.

'You were the best I always wanted and always deserved, but I knew that a soul as gentle as mine could never feel true and honest comfort. There's that old adage: forged in flames, a soul set on fire, or something like that, I don't know.'

The room grew warm and as I pivoted to see what was illuminating her face, a fire ensnared the room.

Beauty can come out of ashes. I am the living, breathing, agonizing truth clawing my way up from rock bottom. I may burn myself into despair trying to light another's fire, but that will not stop me from glowing bright before burning myself out.

Her voice grew louder as the flames climbed up the walls: "I will be your flame, I will be your burning passion, I will be whatever light you need... well, could be or could have been."

Emma disappeared and my daydream brought me back to the dingy, crackling paint. The school was brighter than I had realized.

A star shines brightest before it burns out... right? Emma was an accident, a coincidence, and was the best I never had... but I will always be thankful for her. Despite the pain and whether she would ever really catch my silent glow emulating from the shadows or not, I figured I would always be that faint flicker she saw in her peripheral vision. However, it became a sick reality that I would never be in front of her again.

And that is the hardest truth of them all, and the hardest one I had to swallow in those desolate, passing seconds.

When I returned to the church that night, just to churn some work out before the darkness fell upon me, I pulled up the application on my phone that we used to use to text each other. She was always petrified of texting back and forth with me, for she did not want anyone to grab her phone and see it, so we used a special texting app to keep our conversations a thrilling secret.

This should have been the first sign that something was wrong.

Who was she hiding from?

Oh, yeah, I guess Greg.

After a while she stopped responding on the app, which must have been her definition of "pulling the plug."

I kept writing to her, but I assume that she never saw the messages, for she never responded there after some point. I don't really remember when that was.

Morena appeared in the shadows. I caught a glimpse of the side of her face in the reflected light from my phone: "What are you doing?"

'Nothing,' I tucked my phone back in my pocket. 'Nothing, nothing.'

"You are still hooked on her," she locked eyes with me.

'No.'

"You are lying to yourself. You are not lying to me. I know your truth."

I felt a sharp pain in my lower back again… Emma still had control over me, even though I knew I had to let her go in order for my soul to grow.

If only…

If only I could let go then.

∞ ∞ ∞ ∞ ∞ ∞ ∞ ∞

January 2017.
February 2017.
March 2017.
April 2017.

May 2017.
June 2017.
The days were filled with leading students and organizing conferences, empowering and counseling students, running events that displayed great attendance, and staying ahead of the curve, yet regardless of what I did, Emma's curves were all that I wanted to see.

Even the lyrics to Bon Jovi's "Novocaine" could not dull the pain in my chest:

> "I guess there'll be no happy endings
> When 'once upon' is doing time
> There's a different kind of meaning now
> To livin' on a prayer
> Some don't seem to notice
> And the rest don't seem to care."

It was oddly damp and frigid for a summer day in June, but I did not seem to truly care. Once it started to downpour, all sense left my mind.

I sat there frozen.

It was happening again.

The windows fogged up but through the pelting rain, my eyes were affixed on the memory playing over and over again. Ghosts echoed through the stereo: "Goodbye to Romance."

A love lost revitalized in the lyrics of a song from long ago.

The ghost of Emma appeared in the parking lot.

"He hinted he is going to propose to me," reverberated in my soul. "He misses me and I think I miss him too. I'm sorry."

"I don't know if I am going to say yes."

I should have walked away then.

I should have run.

Instead, I braced for impact.

Getting out of the car did nothing to soothe my soul.

Wiping the rain from my eyes that I could feel were mixed with my salty tears, I recalled planting my soul firmly within her hands.

'This is going to be a long ride, but I will wait.'

Always Just Another Day

I shook my head to try and erase the memory. The rain was pounding hard just as it was that same dreadful November day.

Guns n' Roses poetically seeped into my soul. Thoughts of missing Stacey added to the moment.

> *"Nothin' lasts forever*
> *And we both know hearts can change*
> *And it's hard to hold a candle*
> *In the cold November rain"*

It is the same lot. It is in the same spot. It is the same type of rain.

And my heart is still shredded, just the same.

I finally peeled myself from that spot and forced myself to walk into the building.

The same tears flowed from my eyes; will she ever know how much I still love her?

Did it even matter anymore?

I needed to wipe my eyes and dry off before I began my day. I walked into the building, the play by play of days past running through my mind.

I did not think she would ever know how much this still pained me daily and how much I would have done anything for her to know what was going on in my soul.

"Hey... hi..." I didn't realize I was looking down at my feet in shame and was lost in the memory of Emma when I heard that familiar voice.

I looked up.

Emma's huge beautiful eyes locked on to mine.

It took a matter of three seconds for her to download all I was feeling at that moment and know exactly where I was at.

She smiled and said, "It will be okay."

I didn't have to say a word.

She knew.

I went into the app where we used to text one another and sent her a message:

Beautiful Souls

Dear Emma,

I haven't written on here in a long time, though there were so many times I wanted to. Today was the last day of the year and there were so many things I wanted to say to you. I am just hoping you are well... that you have a great summer... and that one day our friendship will find its way back to one another. Please take care of you. Keep the faith...

Always,
Scott

The summer would greet me with a downward spiral lodged between prayers and a broken heart. Two people who were affiliated with Windows of Opportunity committed suicide.

A friend of mine died of cancer.

I was begging God that Emma's friendship would reappear in my life, yet I was met with utter silence in the dark shadows of the sanctuary.

Morena continued to work with me each day on building Windows of Opportunity, sitting in silence and denying me the chance to see the journal she so highly coveted.

A wave of existential dread washed over me, knowing I would have to face her sneering once again. Emma's wedding was within the coming months, and I had run out of options. Visions and sounds swirled between my ears, simulating the harsh reality that this was no nightmare: this was my life. This is what it had to be.

I had no tears left to cry for her, yet I was nursing the harsh hole brewing within my core. Only the tears that reminded me of her shattered soul dripped from the edges of my eyes.

Out of habit, I continued to write to her on Viber, our secret texting app:

Em,

28 days. You must be in that last-minute tunnel vision exciting anxiety. I truly hope you are well and soaking in the moments. So much I wish I could talk to you about. Sending you positive love and prayers.

Always,
S

I reminded myself that she made her choices, and I had to make mine, and her choices were a stark contrast to all of our combined hopes and dreams. I once thought that it would always be Scott and Emma, but now I found myself in a place where her touch is a fond memory.

There were moments in the sanctuary where I prayed for her to return, then promptly texted her in hopes that she would remember me.

Dear Emma,

19 days. You must be sooo thrilled! Hope all is coming together for your wedding. Just left a concert and so many lyrics... well, so many songs I think you would have enjoyed. Wishing you the best!

Love Always,
S

Still, there was silence.

Days passed by rapidly, yet I continued to hold out for her to be my hero. I wished devoutly that she would come back to my arms.

Desperation hung in my texts to her:

Emma,

5 days to go. You must be excited. Hope you're doing well!!

Love Always,
S

Emma still did not check our secret texts. The scripture of our love lay dormant in her phone, though she had no clue I was still waiting for her.

She chose her path and I chose mine. At that moment I figured it is a shame that our roads may never cross, but maybe it is just meant to be that way.

Beautiful Souls

Day after day at work, once school started back up again for the year, I was petrified of what was to come. She would run off and marry Greg, and I would still be sitting in the sanctuary, night after night, with pieces of my shattered heart grasped loosely between my fingertips.

As a last-ditch effort, I figured I would lay everything out on the table.

I sent her one last text as I sat in the sanctuary, tears flowing from my eyes, thinking she would read it and find me:

Dear Emma,

Night before... sitting in the church and praying something guides you here. I keep sending you messages here hoping the universe will intervene and cause you to download the app again because I really miss the friendship and connection part of our relationship. Would love one more conversation and to send you positive vibes of support and to know if you're ok and what you are thinking. I know it will be magical for you. Congratulations! Xoxo

Always,
Scott

After I hit send, I hung my head in utter disgrace.

She was not coming.

She did not care anymore.

I wondered if she ever cared.

I dragged my body out of the church and into the driver's seat of my car. My bed for the night used to be where Emma and I made one of our first daring memories.

As my eyes slammed shut, I imagined she was in the driver's seat next to me, though as I reached my hand out to grab for her, Emma was probably in bed with her soon-to-be husband.

∞ ∞ ∞ ∞ ∞ ∞ ∞ ∞

Dread hung over me as if it were I who was on a hanger, and not the jacket in front of me. I slid the coat off of the hanger and draped it over my back: this would be the only warm hug I would receive that day.

Not a single person I would see would know that.

Nor would anyone who interacted with me understand how you could be surrounded by people, yet fundamentally alone.

Loneliness is that sharp knife that people warn you about: do not use it unless you really have to.

But what if you grab it by mistake?

I felt that with each step forward, I got two steps further from reality. I had been six steps closer to the edge with each passing moment. With each passing second.

Yet something always drew me back.

A light. A beam pushing me into a realm I just did not understand.

I felt like I died every solitary night since she left me. Every movement from the second hand ticked closer to the end of Emma's fateful, adoring glance…

Or to the start of something bigger.

I kept a countdown in the back of my mind leading up to her wedding. Her white, perfectly laced gown would never run through my fingertips that fateful fall day.

On the exact day of her wedding, I woke with a sense of longing on my chest. Something or someone was pulling me towards them in a manner I could not articulately describe in concrete words.

The passenger seat was empty next to me. The blankets coddled me in their everlasting warmth: comfort wrapped me in its confines. Yet I wanted more. We develop comfort when we think we are in a stable space. We push ourselves into this comatose state of, "No, everything is fine."

But it isn't. Nothing is fine when you are missing a crucial piece of your spirit.

Fine is an illusion, existing merely to convince us that we are not settling. But then aren't we? Are we not clinging to the past as a means of comfort? As a means of lying to ourselves that we can't reach our full potential because we do not or cannot face the treacherous path to earning everything greater than our hearts could imagine?

It is all there. It is all out there.

It just takes a moment: a wince, a flinch, a smile, the upward roll of another's eyes… to simply see everything we never knew we could fathom or define…

We push on. We persevere. We launch our rockets into the sky and enter an entirely new atmosphere.

We become the stars, and if we are lost, we are shooting stars that illuminate the right of the night's beauty.

We harbor the generosity to love ourselves; we just need to release the pain within in order to do so.

It is time to let go.

I found myself driving towards the church and praying that something would guide her there. I would have loved one more conversation with her before everything came to a screeching halt.

I looked down at my watch and prayed one last time.

I hoped for one last *"Thinking of you"* text or something that would show she was still there.

Nothing.

Naturally, I decided to go to where I felt most at home: the bridge.

It had been quite some time since I last approached the bench, our bench, by the bridge. The wooden planks looked almost bleaker and drearier now, maybe because it was almost winter, but in reality, it could be the semblance of memories and her perfume that hung in the air. Regardless, everything here was gray and tiresome.

Upon approaching the fence, I felt the wind whisk around my body. The voices of nearby children contrasted the bleak image being painted in the bitter aroma that clung to the scene. I turned to see where their laughter was emulating from, but all I could find were playground swings drifting in the air.

Beyond the fence, the water calmly ebbed and flowed with the fervor of a gentle breeze. It seemed that no matter where you looked: the water, the bench, the playground, everything was still.

But not the bridge.

The bridge contrasted the entire scene. With its expansive length that appropriately framed the drab winter scene, it beckoned me to sit for a moment. To take in the entire scene. To bask in the emotional glory that awaits me.

The twinkling lights from atop the bridge were breathtaking. So I inhaled deeply, sat upon the old bench, and invited my eyes to drift shut.

Within moments, the cold winter air dissipated and memories of what felt like yesterday shifted into the scene.

A haze of lights flickered across my sealed eyelids, and a familiar voice sat upon my ear: "Scott, isn't it beautiful."

It was Emma.

My eyes jetted open at once, and she was sitting in my presence once again. I could hear my heart beating from within my ribcage.

"Isn't it a little bit chilly," she questioned, wrapping her arm around mine almost naturally. Her head rested on my shoulder as her weight shifted against me.

In disbelief of being next to her, I asked her why she was there. She looked at me quizzically for a moment.

"I'm here to say goodbye," she murmured. Instinctively, I responded: 'I know.'

"You know," she quipped back.

'Yeah,' a sigh released from my body.

"Okay then," she said almost happily. I could sense a tinge of hesitation on her lips. She stood robotically and walked toward the fence. Her hair whipped in the sudden wind that filled the air.

"Ok Scott, remember what I said," she seemed almost stoic in nature.

'What's that?' The wind picked up and my eyelids began drooping. They slammed shut almost signifying her chapter was just about over.

Her voice trailed off and I felt a hand fold within mine. A new voice, pristine in nature, relaxed itself within my ear.

"Scott, you know you must keep moving forward," the hand clutched mine tighter. Upon opening my eyes, Faith sat pensively against my arm. Almost hurriedly she said, "You have to do what your soul calls upon you to do."

My eyes ripped shut again. The water became more turbulent and rancid. Another voice faded in as the wind picked up.

"Scott, focus on me, it will all be okay," Joy's voice faded in as Faith's dropped into the background. My eyes were greeted with a colorful fall scene: leaves cascading in the wind. Vibrant yellows, succulent oranges, deep reds: the scene was picturesque. The bridge was illuminated in the late autumn sky.

A genuine grin spread across her face. Through a smile and wispy hairs flowing across her face, she gave me a sweet kiss on the cheek. "Seasons change," she began, "and so will you. Never forget your roots."

Beautiful Souls

My eyes shut violently as the cold air pushed against me. Another voice faded into the setting. Warmth encompassed my frame. Upon opening my eyes, I saw a figure standing in front of me: her back towards me with her brown locks floating in the dry air.

"Hey smartass, why don't you just shut your eyes and meditate? That is why you're here."

Morena.

'Do you always have to be this-' the words were cut short as they flowed from my mouth.

"Blunt? Sadly, yeah, I do," she grinned and turned towards me. She sauntered next to me and plopped down. "What's up?" She placed her elbow on my shoulder and rested her head in her hand.

A smirk crawled across my face.

'Nothing,' I nonchalantly responded.

She began sniffing the air passive aggressively. "I smell," she began, whiffing again, "Bullshit," she pronounced confidently.

My eyes shut as I laughed, but when I opened them, she was gone. A sole hand lay on my shoulder as a ray of light shone down on me.

Aunt Barbara.

"Hey cookie," she spoke sweetly. I could not contain my happiness. I stood up and lunged at her, embracing her joyfully.

'Thank you, thank you, thank you,' tears sprung from my eyes and froze as soon as they manifested at the edges of my tear ducts.

She stood there, gleefully holding my shoulders, on the verge of tears herself.

"My baby, you always will be," clung to her lips as a light encircled us both. "It is time you realize how important you are to this world. Be the light, Scott, shine," were the last words she said before she evaporated before my very eyes.

'Aunt Barbara, this is in your honor,' flew from my lips as the cold air re-attached itself to my face. I could hear the water flooding against the retaining wall.

The light glowed deeper as I re-opened my eyes to greet the bitter air.

She was gone. They all were, or at least from this stark winter scene. All that remained was a distant memory of words digging deep into my ears.

Look into my soul. Okay. I can do this.

The stale air, though once hurtful to the touch, reminded me I was alive. The American flag across the water waved valiantly to the pace of the wind and my heartbeat.

I was alive.

The bridge burned brighter. The water was clearer. The ebb and flow moved rhythmically.

I was reborn.

I have another chance.

For the world, for the kids, for Aunt Barbara, for the angels, for Morena, for all those past and present.

For the future.

My breath materialized as I exhaled, leaving its mark on the painting that illustrated my past, present, and my future.

A sole man stood gazing out at the bridge: me. My passion, ambition, and resiliency miles from the American flag, but realizing it was my symbol of hope. This country's symbol of unity.

All I have to do is bridge the gap between love and misunderstanding. Between tenacity and diligent strength.

Between divine love and faith.

This may seem to be no easy task, but I will make it happen. I have to. For me, for every window of opportunity I can construct.

To empower and encourage tomorrow's leaders.

Anything can be right in front of your eyes: even a bridge between two beautiful souls finding themselves for the first time.

For my rebirth, for the world's rebirth.

This is the start of a whole new story.

Now… to lift the pen higher than it has ever gone before.

To bridge the gap between eternal light and misunderstood darkness.

'Just keep the faith,' faded from my mouth into the brisk winter air.

The bridge peered over my shoulder as I left the park, wondering what emotional and spiritual journey transpired in front of it just moments ago.

She haunts me.

Emma wholeheartedly haunts me.

She gave me the chance to see the beauty within my own soul after years and years of being at a loss for divine love. Emma handed me the mirror to see the best version of myself.

Beautiful Souls

Then she left.

She left in the prime of our devout bond. Emma left a gaping hole in the man I was becoming. The team we were becoming. She knew how much I loved her. I would die for her to look my way. Still, she hid her true feelings and everything she could be.

She broke the foundational elements of a man who was already praying for somebody to love. And she just walked into my life like a hurricane.

Then she blew through my soul and took everything with her.

And she won't let it go.

And she can't let it fester inside of her… our love, that is. She walks this Earth day by day silently moaning to herself about her life, ambitions, and Greg, yet Emma is blind to the fact that while she whittles away her energy on a man who loves her to the best of his abilities, I still loved her. I am rambling. I know I am.

But there was something that drew me to her soul. Something that drew me into the inseparable beauty that she has within her.

We always want what we can't have and we always hope for what's next, but what about what's in the past? What about what we inherently believe will feed our souls? What about divine love? What about our resolute promises that we exchanged in the joining of our lips?

What about me?

As I continued to look down at my watch, I assumed that the vows had already been exchanged and that Emma and Greg were embarking on their coveted relationship as Mr. and Mrs. Whatever-his-last-name-is.

∞ ∞ ∞ ∞ ∞ ∞ ∞ ∞

I did not see Emma for about a week, and during that time I found myself needing to take shelter from the cold weather that was burdening New York.

I missed Emma, I really did, so I went to where we once slept cuddled up against each other: our hotel.

The warm radiator buzzed as I wrapped myself in the crisp sheets. I was homeless, but between these sheets I felt closer to home: I felt closer to her.

Static from the television illuminated the room as a reminder that I was fundamentally alone. My body lurched towards the floor, as I allowed my feet to drop onto the solid wood.

My toes gripped the cold floor, clinging to a little bit of hope that lingered in the air. Looking around, I felt the world get heavier almost instantaneously: she was gone. It was true. It was over.

Out of habit, I messaged her on our secret app again:

Dear Emma,

I wish we were still talking because you would never guess in a million years where I am tonight. The universe is crazy how it works.

Always,
Scott

While lying in our bed, I came to realize that begging for affection has to be one of the saddest things in this entire universe. To have to ask someone for a hug is utterly repulsive.

Have human beings forgotten how to be there for one another?

Have we fallen so far from grace that we forget how to treat one another?

It rattles me to my core.

How do you, as a breathing human being, resist the ability to make someone genuinely happy by just smiling at them? It makes me want to run up to someone, grip their shoulders, and scream, "Look at me, damnit, I am suffering."

She wouldn't bother acknowledging my presence still. To her, I am transparent. To her, I am a ghost of a life past.

That's okay, though. Let her lose out on having someone amazing in her life. Her loss, honestly. Though if one day she did come back into my life in some way, shape, or form, I know I would show her devout kindness. That is just who I am in the universe: the one who heals and the one who accepts flaws.

I was blasting "Unwell" from Matchbox Twenty from my phone. The music radiated through my fingers. I was still trying to process everything.

Beautiful Souls

I'm not crazy; I'm just a little unwell
I know right now you can't tell
But stay awhile and maybe then you'll see
A different side of me

Losing a dear friend without saying goodbye is painful… and she is still there, just miserable and broken because someone else decided her fate.

I was told I had a hero complex, and in a sense I did. I still do. I never had anyone rescue me, and so I went around making up for that.

I made up for the people that couldn't save me.

I saved others. I struggled to save myself.

Those around me barely realized what was going on.

Did they see the papier-mâché skeleton I had?

I was a mere shell of who I used to be, but I am damn sure this shell is a thousand times stronger than I expected.

I was trying not to drown. I was swimming as hard as I could.

I was diving face first into an inaudible scream.

I ended up in the right place at the wrong time.

Maybe it wasn't the wrong time… maybe I was just walking into a shitstorm with the ultimate bucket.

I begged, 'Please universe, please stand by me. Please show me the way. Even if you aren't a guiding light, be a hand to hold when the sharpest words try to cut me down. How can I fit in on Earth when I was born to be a consolation?'

Yet the desolation continued to leave my soul dripping with pieces of the man I once was, and the man I was yet to become.

∞ ∞ ∞ ∞ ∞ ∞ ∞ ∞

On the verge of the New Year, I seemed to be losing even more of a grip on the vision I had for my life and for Windows of Opportunity. Day after day I was tucked away in my office at work, watching the door intently to see if Emma would walk in and remind me that it would "always be us."

Morena continued to remind me that I had to focus on my future, but for all intents and purposes, Emma seemed like she would be my future.

Working on the curriculums and leadership programs was fulfilling, but I still felt like I was leaning towards being "half-empty" instead of feeling "half-full."

At night and on the weekends, I felt myself doing anything I could to occupy myself from thinking of the memories I made with Emma.

Sure, I went on some dates here and there, but no one else made me as happy as I was when I was with Emma.

One evening as a light snowfall cascaded along the roof of the church, I stood looking out at my jet-black Dodge Charger. I felt terrible replacing the Monte Carlo, but after the air conditioning and heating systems gave out, it was necessary. After all if I was going to be sleeping in my car, I figured I might as well be comfortable.

As I was glaring off into the distance, Paul drove up to the church and got out of the car.

He seemed excited to see me, "Hey, Scott!"

'Hey brother, what's going on?'

"Nothing much," he began rubbing his hands together. "It feels like it is just getting colder and colder."

'Yeah,' I stuffed my hands in my pockets. 'It is freezing.'

"Let's go inside," Paul held the door open for me and we walked in.

As the two of us stomped the light dusting of snow off of our shoes in the doorway, we chatted about the high school and the programs I was creating.

"You know," he said as we walked into the sanctuary. "You have a big heart and a lot of great ideas."

'Thanks, I try.'

"It's astonishing how you just keep building new things, how do you do it?"

'It's my team,' my voice became solemn. 'My team sparks passion in these programs.'

"Passion," he laughed. "It's passion, it's promise, it's so much more than that. It's doing things for the right reasons."

'I've always been about all of that.'

"I know, son." Paul wrapped his arm around my shoulders. "And I am grateful you came to Queens Community Church."

'I am grateful, too, Paul.'

Beautiful Souls

We locked eyes and I felt that something more powerful than us was building.

The two of us continued to talk about programs and initiatives we hoped the church could host. Over the years, Windows of Opportunity's various leadership programs found a home in the church, and sharing the space was the utmost example of how giving and loving people can be.

Queens Community Church embodied the essence of connectedness. Paul was sure to include Windows' programs in any conversation he had related to the church, and that helped to grow our impact on many different levels.

After a long conversation, the two of us walked out the door and back into the cold air.

As he slammed the door and locked it for the night, he laughed softly.

'Thank you, Paul.'

"No, thank you, Scott."

'For what?'

"You have given this community a beacon of hope. I am a better person for knowing you."

'Same here, Paul.'

We stared at each other with the innate sense that both of us played a larger role in each other's lives than we thought.

"By the way," he said inquisitively. "What was it you were thanking me for?"

'I am just thankful for you.'

Paul grinned again. The snow was falling more fervently upon us.

"One day this church will be Windows' permanent home, not just a small office and an attic. I promise you this."

We spoke for a bit longer until the two of us decided it was getting too late and too cold to stand outside.

"I'm going to get home, are you going to be okay?"

'Yeah, I think so.'

"Keep the faith, Scott."

Paul got into his car and before he drove off, I whispered 'Yeah, keep the faith.'

Naturally, I would always keep the faith. The phrase has always been a part of my soul, and is something I strongly live by.

No matter what, I could never go against the voice in my soul. Though sometimes I have had trouble listening to what the voice was trying to tell me, I learned that it often takes time to comprehend what your soul's purpose is.

Even when you think you know who you are and what you are destined for, the universe has a way of showing you another path is out there.

As I left the church and drove off in the car, I felt a humbled sense of relief: Windows of Opportunity would finally have a real home. With an entire building, we could host about any program imaginable.

Finally, everything seemed to be coming together despite Emma's absence.

Then days later as I was sitting in the sanctuary praying for clarity, I got the phone call that would change my path yet again.

In the middle of the night, Paul passed away.

∞ ∞ ∞ ∞ ∞ ∞ ∞ ∞

To say I was devastated to hear about Paul's passing is an utter understatement. After years of seeing his positive presence at the church, now I was left with the stark reality that he would never walk through the sanctuary doors again.

It was a bitter truth that I did not want to swallow.

In the weeks after his passing, I found myself praying even harder than before. Losing Emma was a nightmare, but losing such a kind soul was something I could not fathom.

Life was tilted on its axis and I desperately needed gravity to kick in.

When I returned to work the following week, Emma was standing nearby and I instinctively walked over to her. Though she was with a number of different teachers at the time, I hoped that my presence would not seem suspicious. Above all, I missed the spiritual friendship the two of us had, and I had hoped she would sense my sadness and attempt to connect to me.

Instead, she dismissed me and was angry that I would dare walk up to her while other people were around. I sent her a text message on our secret app in hopes she would understand I was not out to get her, although I did miss our connection:

Beautiful Souls

Dear Emma,

I feel horrible and embarrassed that I put myself out on the line to try and reignite this friendship. Your actions and your curt words, and then lack of response to my last text on friendship, really hurt more deeply than any words can describe. There's so much I wanted to share with you about my life. So much I know I missed in yours. I truly cared about this friendship and needed it. 4 suicides and 1 friend passed in the last 6 months leaving me distraught and changed.... but mourning the loss of you has been the worst of all.

I know you will never see this but this is my last message. My last attempt to reach you as your soul is long gone. I will no longer be a bother. I'm happy for you and your support system. I wish you the best always. Thank you for the brief moments of whatever it was we had - even if it wasn't real. Take care and God Bless.

Scott

Sometimes words and actions burden us more than we realize. Sometimes it's not "just another day." Years of "friendship" should be silently celebrated with "rainbows, butterflies, and compromise."

In the months that followed, I continued to spiral and transform into a man I did not recognize.

I could not shake the fact that Emma was resistant towards my presence. Day in and day out I wanted to spill my heart to her, but I was shattered.

Everything within me screamed that Emma was a part of my long-term vision.

The Titanic was wholeheartedly human error in guidance, not in structure. You can have the foundation but if the leadership and vision is off, the ship will still sink. No matter how much you refuse to.

I was shrouded in resiliency. In the fundamental respect that laid within having to face each day with a shattered soul and a heart held together by mere shreds. Torn apart did not appropriately describe how I felt in that moment.

There was a gaping hole in the center of my body where bits and pieces of me used to live. I was wholly unwhole and had been desolated to the point of no return. The look in her eyes was blank and shallow, almost as if she was a ghost of what she once was. Having to see her each day, knowing that she had forgotten us in the naturalistic sense, made me want to crawl into a hole and rot there for the rest of eternity.

But why should I? It was true. She destroyed every last fiber of my being with the exception of one: my willingness to stay strong in the face of adversity. Strength is all I had left. The eagerness to fight for a better tomorrow courses through my veins. I am bathed in the blood of try and try again. It took all the strength within me to fall for her, and it took all of the remaining power within me to get back up.

I will survive; I knew I had to. Not everyone in this universe is entitled to the experience that is me. Some are not even granted the authority to be in my presence. No, I am not going on an ego-filled adventure, because there was nothing left.

There was no foundation to stand on, and there is also no solitary soul that would or should ever experience the heart-wrenching grip of despair that she clasped me in. Emma destroyed me. Emma took me and stabbed a knife in my chest without getting close enough to touch me... but she did touch my soul. Once upon a time...

Morena kept texting and calling me, and I asked myself what for.

I don't get her. I can't fathom why she exists in my life or how she even got there. The further I push her away, the quicker she rips herself back in. She went through her own sick and twisted hell, but for some odd reason, she enjoys my company. Morena said she waits to hear from me, almost as if I am the pieces of her that are missing. It was almost as if Morena and I needed each other to be whole in the sense of having some peace.

She is repulsive in the sense that she is resilient and will stand her ground even when she is burned and reduced to mere shreds. Her fight is more devout than her fear, and I wonder just how much do you have to break a person down to push her to that. Morena tells me she is cold and calculated, but it is just a thinly veiled crimson blanket that whispers, "I have an elastic heart, and I am not afraid to let it care again and again." Does she see who I am? Can she fathom my pain? I know she is wrapped up with her own agony and crumbled bits. Still, looking at her tenacity and her wounds do nothing to heal mine.

Beautiful Souls

Morena was calling again. She was bound to leave some motivational message on my phone.

I told her to run, yet she continuously wrapped her hands around my shaken frame and said, "Try me." I tell Emma to come, and she runs faster than ever. Souls are a tricky thing.

I was beginning to think that Morena is not real. She is the working definition of an Earth Angel. She crushes every standard and stereotype she wants, and does whatever she pleases.

She is dangerous, as am I, and I knew that this lethal, peaceful combination will lead us to a higher power one day.

One day or day one. I guess I decide…. With a heavy heart, that is. A bitter chill crept up my spine and through my shallow exterior. I rolled to my right and saw my bag resting next to me on the seat. Another night in my car felt like the beginning to a crude joke.

Only it was just the reality that was my life. Loneliness became a common thread between myself and the plastic bag tumbling down the street in the wind. A brisk gust of air filled my car as I stepped out into the morning sun. This time, I slept only 4 hours during the night. That became my new record, honestly. I didn't think it was possible to find utter peace in sleeping in a car, yet the still air freezes time and space overnight.

They say pain is inevitable, but suffering is optional… so why suffer through when I could have just faced reality: the positivity I exude and the joy I bring to others keeps me warm. It is a devout and refreshing reality, even though my kindred spirit would have loved to have a warm bed, a warm soul is far more worth it.

From where I was parked, my car was overlooking the v-formation of the birds above signal that this frosty air would not cease anytime soon. For me, that was just an honest reality. It doesn't matter who in this world you are, what matters is how you treat each other when you have nothing to gain. The birds fly together to find warmth, but do they know each other's hopes and ambitions? Would that alter their consciousness? I mean… do birds have a consciousness? They must if they fly like that. They must. I certainly do, yet most days I fly alone.

I flew towards the cold, the seasonal changes, the pain. It is a bitter reality that we all must face. Sacrifices have to be made for the greater good... no matter what the cost is. It is more expensive to be as cold as the morning air than to give yourself to the world. You may lose sleep, shelter, salvation, and bits of your soul in the process, but it is far more worth it to see the birds flutter their wings in perfect balance and harmony as a team... even if it means the cost is living in your car and watching this regulatory celebration of togetherness from the comfort of resting your tired body against the hood of your home sweet home... or rather, car sweet car.

The beckoning sun evacuated any sense of pain I felt clinging to my soul. In loss, there is a realization that there is still life. Pain reminds us that we still feel. We still have time to change what tries to settle within us.

Time is, in essence, a reflection of what we choose to manifest and how we choose to impact this world. We spend an inordinate amount of time consuming negative energy around us, yet are blind to the effect it causes on our body. We wrap our souls in papier-mâché shields, claiming that we can hide our scars and sicknesses from the world. Yet the swords, others' words or actions, may not always cause immunity our hearts need to survive. Hatred, in and of itself, is an illness. Vile hostility is a disease we have yet to find a cure for. However, higher consciousness and growth can remedy the hurt consuming our souls.

The moment we realize that the words and pain of others is a prejudicial reflection of their experiences, and choose to abide by that philosophy, is the moment we open our minds to new perspectives. It is not always in our best interest to consistently expose ourselves to certain situations. However, when they arise, oftentimes we must manifest a cloak of protection built on the foundation of the goodness in our souls. We can all embody higher consciousness if we choose to do so. Adversely, we can develop a strong sense of desolation if we so decide that hatred is a better fit for us.

Still, why would you spend your time harboring such sincere feelings of negativity? Don't you owe it to yourself to feel unburdened? Would you rather be weightless or consumed?

It is our inherent responsibility to ourselves, and our society to be positive: to light the darkness with the etchings of our kindness and genuine love for one another.

Be authentically aware of what you put forth into this world. Be cognizant of how to make the world a much better place with

Beautiful Souls

you in it. Solitude is reserved for those developing their souls and concocting an understanding of how to become more spiritually informed individuals.

It is time to harness the knowledge we feel so deeply, yet need to translate into a language we can comprehend. We are the world and we are the universe; it is time we begin to act that way.

Though I knew all of these truths were manifesting, I was not ready to face what my future held. Sometimes we need to progress further than we ever imagined in order to build up the courage we inherently need to go forward.

∞ ∞ ∞ ∞ ∞ ∞ ∞ ∞

Nightly, I would succumb to my fantasies. It was like Emma was haunting me, yet I did not mind. It seemed as if anytime I found the strength to walk away, her presence continued seeping into my soul.

Each time I forced myself to walk down another corridor or stairwell in order to avoid her path, I still caught a glimpse of her classroom or her glance seemingly lingering a bit too long.

We were like two tormented ships passing in the night. The moments were beginning to feel inevitable.

I still tried to remain focused. I was persistent in staying in my element. My team continued to work with me and help build the vision I had for Windows of Opportunity, though the missing piece of my puzzle was centralized in my soul.

Negativity about the casual work-related drama seeped negative vibes through the souls of those in the school, but outside of school my team was cutting through the pessimism with a glorious knack for reform and spiritual grounding.

As my eyes would flutter closed each night, Emma would press her body against mine and sensually whisper in my ear: "I see you and I know you are doing this all for me."

My heart raced as she placed her hands on my lower back.

I felt her breath on my neck as she moved closer to me. We were drawn into the exquisite moment together.

Our lips locked with the fervor of a passionate reconciliation. It was akin to the fire a drug addict feels when he cannot get clean, and finally has that first hit in ages.

Her love filled up my veins.

My heartbeat constricted and pounded against my rib cage.

Why did she keep coming back like this?

Why did she consistently show up how she did?

I wondered if it was God's way of testing me. I wondered if it was a sanctioned rite to truly embody the mantra, "Keep the faith."

Confusion filled my throat. I was lost, discombobulated, and my eyes needed to readjust because I could not believe what was happening before my very eyes.

What was I missing?

What did I not understand?

As my eyes fluttered open in the stale morning air, I came to the exquisite horror that it was just a dream. Her gentle touch, her glances, her hand reaching out for mine: it was all just a dream. The stark reality was that she would never see me or feel me the way I visualize her.

She lived in the catacombs of her own reality, lurking in the basement of positive thought, preying on the energies surrounding her. She had a habit of wrapping her fingers so tightly around the mindset of others in this realistic realm, but is this all truly real? Is she living in the moments that pass before her, or is she trapped in the false clutches of her own past? Does she see her future? Does she want to see her future?

It may be that she possesses the lips of a mistaken goddess: her whisperings hold no merit to the prison bars she clings upon. She is trapped in her own mind, busy convincing the world that her life, the one she forces, is what it appears to be.

It is a harsh reality: we try manifesting false prophets through the flesh entities we project into our lives. However, in playing God and trying to influence the balance between what is meant to be and what we so wistfully hope life will be, we are oblivious to the mounting energy we put forth in the world.

You could spend days, months, or years building bridges between what you anticipate and what you push another soul into, but if you build that bridge on the foundation that "this is the life I want" and "I did this for us," your false words will only bolster and crumble when the water floods. The true test of a bridge comes when we try so diligently to balance weight on its beams. When we make an effort to cross the boundaries put in place, how will your words hold up against your actions? Will you stand or will you fall?

Will you bear the weight of your actions? Will you hold firm to your truth or your fantasy?

The illusion of time marches forward as you emulate the sensations of weary eyes casting downward over your true soul. She ran from me because she knew she could not hide her true self from my prescriptive soul. I am the truth serum, the drug you asphyxiate yourself with to feel life. You want to feel alive, but you occupy your time with the world you create and force upon other souls to try to make them feel.

Try.

Yet I could not help but ponder what I would say to Emma: when you show your true colors and bleed into the sky and its rising sun… will your bridge still be there?

Will he still be there…

Or will I?

I continued to whisper to the image I had of Emma deep within my mind: 'I'll see you in my dreams, while you will see me in your reality. I am the ghost of the life you could have lived. While you are too scared to own your soul… know your words, your actions, and your demons are brewing and conjuring in the light of day. For when you close your eyes to escape from the world you perpetrated, there will come a day that you will open your eyes and maybe… just maybe… the reflection before you could just be your own.'

By morning, she would always disappear from my life. However as the universe would have it, I would see her at work and watch her flash a smile in my direction.

I consistently wondered what was going on behind those chocolate brown eyes of hers.

Still, I was left without a clear response from her: it seemed she was teetering between trying to rekindle a friendship or sorts while resisting whatever story she was telling in her own head.

The cycle would repeat each and every night.

I was convinced my earthly soul was speaking a language that was difficult to interpret: I wondered if I was romanticizing Emma and our potential friendship.

The universe seemed to be utterly silent though I begged for it to answer the same question time and time again: Why did Emma have to leave when she did?

Day in and day out, I would cry myself to sleep after eating my feelings. The car would reek of junk food and I knew I was destroying my body, but part of me did not really care in those desolate moments.

As the weather grew warmer, I would find myself making solo trips to the bridge in order to clear my head. Each time I would bring junk food with me to quell the bitter taste of Emma's lack of compassion.

With an incredibly harsh day in my rear-view mirror, I rushed to grab the greasiest bucket of chicken possible before running to the bridge. As I made my way to the fast food place, I saw Emma's truck parked out in front and panicked.

I rushed to the bridge with tears obscuring my vision, and praying she did not see me.

When I arrived I didn't even lock my car, I just ran down the path and to the pine green benches by the fence.

I froze in fear upon seeing a woman sitting at the bench with a bucket of chicken. Her brown hair was flowing in the wind, and for a moment I was convinced Emma came to answer my prayers.

As the woman turned and placed her arm on the bench, she shook the chicken and smiled: it was Morena, of course.

She grinned and happily shouted, "What took you so long?"

Morena serenaded me with the heaviest melody ever: "If I truly want to admit that I've committed wrongs against myself, then fine, I'd admit that having to deeply love someone who carries so much pain and sorrow in the crevices of their soul, and not being able to help them save themselves, is the worst and most sincere crime ever."

'Mo, I-' as I tried to find the words, I felt them trailing off into the serenity of the sky.

She stood with her hair flowing in the wind. Locks of her hair mimicked the waves of the river as they crashed upon the shore. The bridge was being caressed by the crisp beams of sunlight that gently floated down to Earth.

My heart sank into the recess of my gut in that moment.

As she turned away while brushing against my shoulder, she gazed at me in that stark moonlight, and I could feel the years of pain and agony

Beautiful Souls

emulating from her body. Her brokenness was something so dangerously beautiful and painstakingly cautious.

Broken was her state of mind, her heart's circumstance, and her body's only comfort. All she ever knew was pain, but she glued herself together enough to show me her soft side that had been buried for far too long.

Like a priceless porcelain china doll teetering precariously on a shelf, she was daring herself to collapse regularly. Today was the day she tipped and cracked, but she caught herself just before the fall as she always does.

Nearing closer to my shoulder, she murmured, "Quit your agony and just be your own hero for a change. You don't need to save the world, you just need to save yourself."

Tears welled up in my eyes and I clasped them shut to prevent her from seeing how much those words affected me within seconds. When I had opened my eyes to show her how vulnerable I really was, she seemed to vanish into the setting sun.

Still, I felt her words coursing through my veins and assuring me that tears are part of weakness leaving the body.

I have spent my entire life saving everyone around me and picking up the pieces of their shattered hearts, but what about my own?

'Why can't I-' tears were preventing me from spilling the words out of my mouth.

Softly and with much trepidation, Morena whispered, "Why can't you what?"

The words rumbled as they left my mouth: 'Why can't I hate her?'

A long pause stood between the two of us on that bench as Morena forced herself to say the words she was slightly unsure of: "Because you can't hate what you created."

I stood up and started to run away from where we were sitting.

"What are you running from?"

'You, it's you. I am running from you.'

"Why, why run?"

'Because you aren't real. You can't be real.'

"Why not?"

I stopped in my tracks and looked right at her: 'Because you just seem to know. How do you know?'

"How do I know what?"

The wind whipped between us to fill out solemn silence.

"Why can't you just trust in the universe?"

'I don't know,' I began to cry. 'God, what are you trying to tell me?'

"Our hearts beat on," Morena started. "We all find a way."

Nothing prevented me from crying on Morena's shoulder.

'Please,' I wrapped my hands around her shoulders. 'Help me.'

She put her hands over mine and said, "Then let me."

I had to keep the faith. I had to see there was a vision much brighter than the one I was living through at that moment.

There had to be more.

∞ ∞ ∞ ∞ ∞ ∞ ∞ ∞

The cruel summer continued with my soul being wrought by Emma's absence. I looked at her social media pages over and over again, hoping I would see a sentimental secret message meant for me.

Still, nothing appeared.

The kids at school seemed to be more in tune with my energy come September. The new school year was keeping me inspired and engaged with what future I could have.

The higher calling I was looking for had to be there somewhere in the world, I figured, but my head was still clouded with anticipatory hope for Emma's love or friendship.

As I wandered to the corner deli one day, my head was in a thousand different places. I was examining my surroundings in hopes that Emma would appear out of nowhere, but instead I saw two large boys harassing one of my leadership students. I approached them with caution, but I kept my head held high.

Something seemed off.

'Hey Larissa,' I started. 'Everything okay?'

One of the guys pushed her to the ground and glared at me.

"Can I *fucking* help you bud? I'm with my girlfriend here." His eyes pierced through me.

My inner hero reached out to Larissa.

'Get up,' I gripped her hand. 'We are going back to school.'

With fear flooding over her, she jumped up and ran towards my arms. The two guys surrounded me and looked as if they were going to beat me up. I threw Larissa behind me and the two guys began to verbally belittle me.

I had all of the strength within me to stand up to them when a student needed me. I had the courage to save her when I could barely save myself.

After I grabbed Larissa's hand and the two of us walked back to the building, she began to sob violently as she admitted what I feared: they were about to assault her. There was so much tension in her soul that I could feel it dripping off of her. Larissa's energy was all over the place, though she was grounded in innate fear.

Even though I did not know whether those guys were armed with weapons or not, I knew I had to help her. I knew I needed to step in and do what was right.

Then it hit me: I had to truly stand up and do right by my soul.

After work, I rushed to the church and told Morena that we truly had to kick it into high gear. She looked me in the eyes and smiled.

Morena began rummaging through her bag and asked if I was truly ready to step into my power. I did not know exactly what to say, so I looked at her and grinned.

She pulled her notebook out of her bag and passed it to me.

"Take a look at your future," she smiled at me and I smiled back.

I was still a work in progress, but I needed to truly step into whatever was next. Everyone is always a work in progress, and forward is forward. It was about time I acknowledged that I had to move forward with or without Emma by my side at that moment.

As I opened her journal, the number "1600" was written on almost every single page.

'What is sixteen-zero-zero?'

"It's sixteen-hundred," She scooted next to me.

'Sixteen-hundred, what?'

She stood up and walked away while calling back to me, "You'll see in due time."

Her journal was adorned with curriculum ideas and scribblings I did not understand. Images of buildings were sketched at the center of most pages, and a common theme was the word, "systems."

I sat there and read through her words for hours. They did not make total coherent sense, but I was getting the gist: all of her ideas centered around Washington, D.C., and it seemed like something there called to her.

As I read through everything, D.C. seemed to call to me as well.

Morena watched as my eyes registered the epiphany in my soul: it was time I aimed for true higher consciousness and a realm of higher thinking.

The two of us got to work and began moving various documents around Windows' office.

Instinctively, I wrote to Emma:

Dear Emma,

I'm still having a hard time. It's so crazy. I shouldn't be so lost and hurting after 3 years but I can't help it. I wish you were around to talk it through like we used to. I can't shake you, and I guess I don't want to. I miss your friendship more than anything. We were unstoppable. October 18th is our anniversary. I've been good and strong - so many great things going on that I wish I could share with you and trust you with again. I want that back more than anything. I know you have your new life and I hope you are well. Wishing you love and success from afar.

Always,
Scott

As that fateful "anniversary" of ours rolled around, I took a leap of faith and went into Emma's classroom early in the morning. Before I even knocked on the door, I stood there admiring her soul's beauty.

She was sitting there, cloaked in innocence, dragging her pen along the metal rings of a notebook. At the time, I wished I could take a picture of her and frame it forever. I wished I could preserve her pristine and sweet existence, so that years later I could return to that moment when I needed a moment of peace such as this.

The moment she looked up I felt my nostrils flare and my breathing grow more labored. A subtle sense of panic set in.

"Hey," Emma said nonchalantly.

'Hi Emma.'

"What are you doing here so early?"

She seemed to forget the days when I would come to the school early, just to leave a sweet note on her desk or drop off our journal, The Vault, in her mailbox.

Part of me wanted to run from the room and bury myself in my office.

Part of me was on the verge of tears as a rush of our memories flooded to the edges of my eyes.

'Happy Anniversary,' I blurted it out and instantly felt my heart drop.

I could tell Emma was shaken by what I said; yet she managed to crack a smile.

"Happy Fourth Anniversary, Scott," she cast her eyes downward to her ring.

'Emma, it's only been three years… well, it would have been.'

"No," she quipped. "It's been four."

'Three.'

"No, four." She looked back down at the notebook and continued to run the pen along the side of it.

Considering how much our relationship, or lack thereof, tore me apart, it was shocking that she even remembered our "anniversary." On top of that, I did not know what to make of the fact that she didn't even remember we would have only been together for three years, not four.

I had a cordial conversation with her about a few students before rushing from the room. It amazed me that she was so far from the woman who I first fell in love with, yet she was merely inches away from me each day at work.

I missed her, yet I wondered at the time if I even crossed her mind.

The day flew by and by nightfall, I was immersed in a dream that was far from familiar.

Emma and I were cuddling, hugging, and being romantic, but then she pulled away from me and stood up.

"I'm not in love with you anymore," she told me.

'Why didn't you just outright say so?' I stood to meet her gaze.

She did not reply and I began to walk away.

I could hear her voice calling out for me, but I just appeared to ignore her.

Always Just Another Day

Before I woke up, I remember looking her in the eyes and saying, 'I know this is just a dream. I will always, *always* love you... but I will be okay without you.'

I woke up without tears in my eyes for a change as I felt the winds of change brushing over me.

Her presence was edging further and further from my purview, and I was not too sure what sort of sign the universe was trying to tell me. My soul needed a clearer translation of the message being told, yet I needed a much clearer understanding of the language being presented.

At the time I was blind and deaf to what was before me, for the best was yet to come.

∞ ∞ ∞ ∞ ∞ ∞ ∞ ∞

Days away from her first wedding anniversary, the holiday party for Lincoln Memorial High School was being held at a local bar. Naturally I felt I had to go, for I felt I was practically obligated to go celebrate the holidays with the people I saw each day.

Upon parking my car and trudging through the bitter cold, I found myself alone at the bar sipping a ginger ale.

In the thickness of a dark, lonely night, a small distant light illuminated the corners of the windowpane ever so slightly. Staring through the fog that hovered both inside my mind, and outside the tempered glass, I thought to myself: 'I'm glad she found her wings finally, but I didn't think she would actually fly away.'

The ice cube pushed against my upper lip, creating such a harsh reality: the last person to kiss my lips was Emma.

It had been a year since she chose Greg, and though her lips were graced with his lips each night, I still longed for her kisses on my skin.

I thought that nothing else could hurt me in those fatal moments.

I would have bet my life on her. I would have bet my life that she was more than the impressions society placed upon her. The problem was that she would let me die...

And I would have died for her even after everything she put me through.

People from work started to filter into the bar in groups, with Emma finally arriving with some of her buddies. The other teachers looked on as I nursed my drink, with a handful of them eventually making their way over to me.

She always told me that I looked good in red, so I wore a crimson, button-down shirt in hopes that Emma would notice me.

Her eyes bolted towards me and the small crowd of teachers around me, but Emma was resilient. She tried her best to stay away from me, but a combination of alcohol infiltrating her system and country music blaring throughout the bar drew her closer.

The moment Luke Combs' "Hurricane" graced the speakers; I sensed her impending appearance on my shoulder for the night.

She glared at me, almost as if the lyrics called her closer to what we once were:

> "Hadn't had a go.od time
> Since you know when
> Got talked into goin' out
> With hopes you were stayin' in
> I was feeling like myself for the first time
> In a long time
> 'Till I bumped into some of your friends
> Over there talkin' to mine
> Then you rolled in with your hair in the wind
> Baby without warning
> I was doin' alright but just your sight
> Had my heart stormin'
> The moon went hiding
> Stars quit shining
> Rain was driving
> Thunder 'n lightning
> You wrecked my whole world when you came
> And hit me like a hurricane."

She was pounding back drinks and staring right at me.

Her fingers frosted with chipped nail polish slid across the counter. The damp wood dragged itself along her gentle touch. Her hand jumped from the bar to my hand as she launched herself forward at me in some drunken, involuntary state. It was almost as she longed to grasp my body. Three years of adoration and lonely nights longing to touch each other flew through her fingertips and through the very arm where her heart was etched in forever and ever. Her eyes anchored to my soul and plunged me into her enticing aura.

She was intoxicated beyond all belief, but even in that state, her soul knew that her body had to pursue every fiber in my body that longed for her dignified touch.

A cupcake rested poignantly in her hand.

"Scott," Emma began slurring her words as she bellowed loudly, "Eat my cupcake, I know you *love* my baking." There was an extra emphasis on the "love" that taunted my lips to press firmly against hers. Emma forced the cupcake into my palm as her lingering gaze was pushing into the depths of my soul.

Three years. I wanted her so badly I was ready to drop her cupcake onto the bar, grasp her in my arms, hold her head inches from mine and… and…

I realized at that moment I had to snap out of it! Three years is three years… and she was drunk… and she was beyond the point of remembering these moments…

…But she was talking to me.

She stumbled backwards into the party to converse with her other co-workers. They were stunned to lay their judgmental eyes upon me. My leather jacket nearly dripped from my body with the sheer amount of hot sweat Emma had forced me to develop.

'Ugh,' I thought, 'She isn't coming back over now.'

While fixing my hair in the reflection beyond the bar, I caught her glance fixated on the back of my head.

'Shit.' I whipped my head around.

She had a velvet cherry in her mouth, just hanging from her fingertips and calling her mouth home, even for a moment.

Her eyes screamed, "Come here, now." Though I had a feeling I was misreading her glances.

About 20 minutes passed and my eyes darted to hers for what felt like the thousandth time in seconds. A slender pointer finger beckoned me closer as she pulled apart from her friends. The heat grew between us as a fire burned within me.

Years turned to seconds as she stumbled into my arms and our eyes locked in a passionate, ornate web. I wanted to be tangled in between her legs so badly, my feet hurt from the pressure I felt in resisting the urge to ram her body against mine and start shredding her clothes off with my bare teeth.

Where was my mind going?

She stood before me as years of thoughtful conversation and her once innocent kisses flowed in my brain. Every time I blinked, I expected her to fade somewhere into the recesses of my mind.

Yet this was not a dream.

This was not an apparition materializing in front of me to act as a silent reminder of a past soulful relationship.

No, she was here. She was real.

Our respective journeys from the past few years led us on separate paths...

And yet on this very night, our paths intersected.

I melted into the very words she spoke. I dove head first into the ocean of memories before us... and we began reminiscing.

This could not, in a billion lifetimes, have been more perfect or real, I figured.

Her brown eyes darted around the room, though they always found their way to refocus on my inner light. My soul felt like it was about to burst from my body in a fit of pure, unfiltered higher consciousness: I wished this moment on myself. I persuaded the universe to grant me this moment. I begged on my hands and knees with tears splattering in the midst of the shedding of my soul.

All of the universe's innate magic whittled down to this very second. And this one.

And the ones that followed.

I was asphyxiated by the scent of her beauty. She was intoxicated beyond all realistic definitions because she was fixated on finding answers to her questions at the bottom of glasses upon glasses of beer and hard liquor.

"Scott," she bellowed, "I can't believe you made it!" Her body was moving cyclically, almost in the form of an infinity sign, but that would have been too perfect and too coincidental to be true.

If only she would have fallen forward a bit more in her intoxicated state, she would have melted into my arms and we would have been spiritually intertwined forever... but she was miles away although she was inches in front of me: I was afraid I would be undying and unwavering in the pursuit of touching those fateful, effervescent lips for at least one last time.

Emma continued talking to me as I began to absorb the positive energy the universe bestowed upon me: here I was, in a bar of all places, with the opportunity to turn the page in what could be the greatest chapter in my life to date.

She kept rambling, but all I could hear her say was "Scott, you have hope."

Emma smiled as the speakers in the background of the crowded bar played Queen's "Another One Bites the Dust:"

> *"Are you ready,*
> *Hey, are you ready for this?*
> *Are you hanging on the edge of your seat?*
> *Out of the doorway the bullets rip to the sound of the beat...*
> *Another one bites the dust."*

I felt the driving rhythm give me courage.

She was three sheets to the wind and I felt guilty saying I would want her this drunk nightly if it meant that she would connect and open to me like this all the time.

The two of us stood there in spiritual solitude, almost as if our souls were talking in a manner that synthesized all of our emotions.

"What's *really* going on in that head of yours, Scott Matheson?" She was sliding all over the place and I kept reaching out to hold her up.

'Nothing.' I wanted so badly to profess my love to her, but I figured she was so far gone and we were in public with all of our co-workers. I couldn't betray her image, although her drunken stupor was not helping her.

"Tell me, *everything!*"

'Maybe you should sit down.'

"No," she screamed. "Talk to me."

I took a small leap of faith: 'I can't speak to you anymore, no matter how many times I have wanted to.'

"Yes, you can!" She grabbed my hand.

Everyone turned to look at us. Emma's intoxicated banter was causing a scene.

'I can't,' I whispered. 'You left me. You pushed me away. I have wanted to call you so many times. I couldn't.'

"No," she whispered back.

Then I said it: 'You getting married sucked, and I felt like I lost my best friend.'

"You didn't lose your best friend, I'm right here."

'I have missed you. Do you miss me at all? Our late-night talks and texts?'

"Yes," she began to walk away and I followed her. "Of course, I do."

The two of us stumbled out the side door of the bar and onto the sidewalk.

I caught her before she fell into the gutter and pulled her close. She looked up at me and I kissed her cheek. As the two of us held one another in the frosted air, my mouth edged towards her ear as I whispered, 'I love you.'

"I *know*," she replied quickly. Emma rubbed her hand in a circular motion before releasing from my grasp.

She said I love you a million times without spilling a syllable of it.

I told her what her soul meant to me and how much light she had inside her. The tears that welled up in her eyes told me she hadn't connected to that level of love in awhile. I told her if her nephew and her future kids mean so much to her that the best thing she could do for them is to step into her power and be the role model she was meant to be.

'You have to be the best version of yourself,' I told her.

"You only know my fears," she retorted.

'Yeah, but-' she cut me off.

"You know me, but you don't *know* me," Emma shouted. I followed her back into the bar.

Everyone's eyes turned towards us, and she seemed to panic. The two of us moved back towards the barstools and she knocked into one of them before shooting glances at everyone in the room.

Emma grew hostile upon realizing everyone was looking at her: "You don't get it, do you?"

'Get what?'

"It. *All* of *it*."

'What do you mean?'

Our co-workers looked away, almost as if they were trying to avoid the awkward scene.

"Greg won," she shouted

'Won what?'

"He won. He won me. That's it; you've lost. Get out of here."

Her mood swing shot right through my core: we went from being cordial to a sudden and total dismissal of who I once was to her.

I felt an utter sense of betrayal.

She didn't want me.

Apparently everything was a competition, and my love just was not enough.

At that moment, I was not enough.

The fractured glass representative of my heart was strewn about the floor as I replayed my night in painstakingly slow movements. My heartbeat was the only thing I could hear in the piercing silence. Years upon years of memories flushed down the drain with the dreadful epiphany that anger and violence sometimes run fervently and rampant.

Grief and mourning are not silent reservations for the dearly departed.

No.

Rather they are exquisitely inclusive of those whose love ran out miles before the daggers of emotion pierce through your heart. A tattered soul lies where a field of dreams once existed as lush and bountiful. A broken heart was smashed to bits, mixed with equal parts hurt and unyielding torment. A mind flooded with reeling thoughts and chaotic, melodic confusion. Through it all, a smile and three words held up the illusion that everything was okay.

Emma stormed off and I saw Greg enter the bar. She wrapped her arm between his and cuddled into him.

Joy looked over at me and asked if I was okay.

Three words, 'I am fine' drowned out the sorrows temporarily while my soul resisted succumbing to agony and sheer desolation. And though the world looks on and sees a smile, the truth occasionally seeps out when the levee breaks.

As the water went rushing down the edges of fading smile-induced wrinkles, all I could do was cling to each facet of hope that remained. There was a lot of hope, too. A lot of pain was persuaded to evacuate the recesses of my mind... for there is always faith, a light and a glimmer of decency in realizing that despite being fractured, the light shines brightest when the broken pieces exist.

Broken is beautiful. Lost is found. Love exists in every language, even if that language is anger.

Fractured just means something has fallen... and fractured means that everything can be mended, though the pieces may take longer to place...

Though the one being mended, the beauty emerging from the ashes will be my own soul for a change.

I loved myself enough to realize, I have earned the right to respect myself enough to stand.

And to walk...

Then to run.

As the hammer dropped through the metaphorical glass, screaming filled the room. Every echo and reverberation dove deeper into my consciousness.

Yet life kept on occurring.

Everyone was in tune to their own adventures and excitement, though the droplets of water cascaded down my lungs and into my heart: dampening the love story that was just a figment of my romanticized imagination... or so Emma thought.

We were a fragile entity. We were delicate roses wilting in the frigid, brisk air. We were damaged upon arrival and shattered with two words:

"Greg won."

The incarceration of our love was a hard pill to swallow. She thought we were nothing. She believed in her lies so much that her pupils did not even respond to the quivering of my upper lip.

Gone.

Done.

"Greg won."

What did he win though?

Was Emma suddenly a trophy?

Was she enveloped in a golden arras, clutched in the sentiments of those who adored, but did not touch? Was her ego and confidence so inflated that she ballooned at the very sight of me.

Yet we burst, and not just her bubble of confidence.

Our intertwined hearts drooped to the floor and melted away into the gutters outside of the bar. The river of tears from years and years of heartache evaporated. I had no tears left to cry for her.

I was only imagining that she was all that I fantasized her to be.

I thought she was real.

I thought she would elevate my soul... yet she was just another face in the crowd who devastated her own soul... and in the process, she spray-painted herself gold, masking the crimson traces from the blood of the hearts she mangled.

Oh, dear Emma, if you only recognized that the only heart you would be breaking from here on out would be your own.

One day you would wake up next to Greg and see that his eyes glare into your existence and see a desolated mold of the mess you manifested. One day you will realize that just another day is fragmented in the hearts of those you embraced and ran from... only the most heart-shattering epiphany is that you will always be running from yourself and the messes that you have made.

Always.

You can love someone with all of your heart and soul, but it will never resolve their pain. You can genuinely care for someone in ways they could never fathom, and they will always expect more.

To some, you will never be enough, and that is heartbreaking if you allow that to be your truth. In actuality, if you think about all the pain, hurt, turmoil, and agony you have gone through to appease someone; that is just your perspective.

The thoughts you process and put into fruition will be your reality. What do you want out of your own life?

You may not be their missing puzzle piece.

You may just have been their tale for the time being.

You may have been a set of comfortable arms to embrace them at their worst... and that is all okay.

Beautiful Souls

The best part about life is that there is always something else coming. There is always growth from your experiences, and there is always someone out there looking just for you (though they may not know it yet).

You could be someone's everything. You could be just what someone needs for the time being. It is okay to be a part of someone's growth and journey, but do not forget your own path.

If there was anything I learned from loving Emma, it was "Do not forget to kindle your own light. Do not forget to grow your own soul. You are paramount and primary. You are your own saving grace. Never forget how special you are to yourself, and just how brave you are for saving yourself from a situation that could be harmful to your soul and growth. Love yourself louder than those who try plummeting your existence into absolute desolation. Even if people think they know what is best for you, all in all you are the creator of your own reality."

Someone may love you, but they may just be able to love you as much as they could love. They may not love you how you deserve to be loved. You can't fault someone for loving you less than they can actualize.

You deserve to be treasured, for your soul is a brilliant gem.

You deserve to shine and be seen in your own light.

You deserve everything and anything this universe can offer you, just know you may have to work very hard for it.

This world does not promise anything other than life and death: you choose what you wish to pursue.

You can see your life as a persistent march towards death, or you can choose to live. Death is the tension that motivates you to live to your fullest. You can choose to pursue your passion. You can choose to create your own reality. You can be your savior and the real deal.

Decide what path you want to pursue... then go forth.

If there was anything I could have said to Emma in those moments, I would have said: 'You may have shattered my heart, but that will just be for one day. After everything, you have earned that: one day of my solitude to mourn the beliefs you had bestowed on my soul. You may have desolated bits of my soul and smashed what was left of my compassion, but that will not stop me from being a good person. You will not break me forever and ever. Listen to the lyrics of the songs we have left behind… tell me, do they still speak to your soul?'

And just like that... I didn't feel like crying for her.

I guess I knew the inherent truth all along... I was never enough for her, and I guess I never wanted to be... in the denouement, darling, you were no match for me.

I jumped in my car and sped off into the darkness.

∞ ∞ ∞ ∞ ∞ ∞ ∞ ∞

I barely slept that night. I kept tossing and turning, letting her image seep into my mind and rip me back and forth like a puppeteer. Why did I do this to myself? How could I let one person have so much control over my soul?

Now that I was in too deep, I was afraid that I started sinking too far to the bottom. I figured that I couldn't get out and that I couldn't escape.

I was suspended in a perpetual state of bowing down to her presence, for I thought I was too inadequate to ever be the same.

This was good though, I guessed. I mean, does anyone ever stay the same?

We wake up each day different from the last, and then sunrise, sunset; we rest our heads on a pillow composed of a day's hard-learned truths.

It is how it has to be.

It is how it will always be.

I will always wonder what it would have been like to open my eyes in the morning and rest my gaze on her peaceful existence.

At the time I remember shouting to the universe upon mourning Emma's official exit from my life: 'Do you know how much I loved her? How much I still do?'

If she turned and looked at me and said, "Let's run for it," I would have transformed into a hot air balloon and floated us straight out of the mess we were in.

But at the time she was too fearful of her image, society's perception of her, and how the world wrapped her in a little box, red bow and all.

She is probably reading this right now in a dizzy morning haze, or a dimly lit coffee shop and is thinking, "Wow, you know me so well."

But I don't... Did I ever?

We were just fractured memories of a love that once was. Though day in, day out, I cherished who we once were and who we could have been at the time. We lived in those final seconds before the clock struck midnight; only I never had the right to place my hand on the glass slipper at the time... or did I?

Tell me.

Tell me I was wrong all along.

Whisper in my ear that I am the only one: "You and me, forever and *always*. It will a*lways* be us."

It wasn't just another day, and it took me seemingly countless lifetimes to get over the passion I thought I saw in her eyes back then.

But my darling I lived a thousand lifetimes before, and I wholeheartedly knew one truth: despite her indifference, our passion, and what could have been us, you, Emma, were no match for me.

Yeah, it is even sad to release those words onto the page now, but she helped me learn, the hard way, that she was indeed no match for me at that time.

I had a lot of spiritual rehabilitation to do before moving forward.

Though forward is forward.

Let that roll around in your head for all of eternity... for I thought she would be slipping through my mind and rolling into another's arms...

For the rest of my life.

But all in all, before I slammed the casket shut on the embodiment of who we were at the time, I could not help but come to an epiphany for Emma:

'You say you refuse to sink, well let that sink in.'

CHAPTER 6

This House is Not For Sale

"Look what they've done to this house of love. It's too late to turn river to blood. The saviors come and gone, we're all out of time. The devil's in the temple and he ain't no friend of mine."

- **Bon Jovi, American Rock Band, Sayreville, New Jersey**

"I wish I could tell you that once you realize what's been irking your soul for so long, you are able to just recover from it," Morena spoke solemnly as she stirred her hot chocolate. "But the truth is, it takes patience to inject tranquility into our souls."

'I hear you, I do,' I continued glaring out the window of the coffee shop. My eyes drifted from each person who passed.

"Maybe what you are searching for out there isn't precisely what you are looking for."

'You always say that, but I never understand what you mean.'

She took a faint sip from her cup. "Maybe it is because you are still looking."

'Okay, whatever.'

Morena smirked and let out a sigh. I placed my palm on the window and began tracing an infinity sign with my fingertip.

"You know," she said. "You don't have to look so sad. This is a happy occasion."

'Why does everyone keep saying I look sad? I've had the mask on. Is it falling off?'

"You forget I know your soul."

'Oh, so what, do you and everyone else know my soul better than *I* do?'

"That's not what I said."

'It is what it is, I guess.'

In hindsight, I did not realize how my innate pain seeped out of my soul in the form of crisp words and an irreverent tone.

"It is what it is, but it is so much more."

'Stop it, Morena,' I snapped at her. 'I just want to run away.'

"Then fine," she stood up. "Run away, but what is that going to do for you?"

'I feel sick,' I grasped at my lower back, attempting to ease the sharp pains I was feeling.

Morena softened her tone. "You need to go within, Scott. You can't keep beating yourself up like this, or something bad is going to happen."

'Something bad did happen,' I stood up. 'I'm alone.'

She cast her eyes downward at my tattered black shoes. "Do you really think that?"

'Is it possible to say no and yes at the same time?'

"Yes," she chuckled a little.

'Then no,' I paused. 'Yes.'

The two of us spoke for a while about my sudden wave of solitude as I continued to nurse the stabbing pain in my lower back.

"If this conversation is making you feel pain," Morena motioned towards my back. "We can stop talking about all of this."

'No,' I continued rubbing my back anyway; blind to the emotional turmoil I was feeding my body. 'I'm okay, seriously.'

The two of us decided to get up and go back to the church. We always had our most spiritual conversations there.

She was quietly gazing out the window at the barren trees, their branches drooping downward in the sullen winter air, as we drove past the back of Alley Pond Park.

The car stopped at a red light and the two of us sighed almost in unison.

I began tapping on the steering wheel to the idle nonsense on the radio. Both of us had so many thoughts in our respective heads, but neither of us could speak upon seeing the wave of desolation that hit Alley Pond Park. The lush greenery was obscured by the change of seasons.

As a matter of fact, I was also obscured by winter's harsh frost, though this was a rather mild month for one of New York's infamously cold seasons. Some years we were blasted with multiple feet of snow, yet in recent years everything seemed to hit us in February, March, and sometimes even April.

Our seasons reflected my inner voice: they were equally delayed for some sort of shift prevented the next wave of weather from manifesting in the sky.

The only difference between the seasons and I was that my voice seemed to have stalled from moving onto the next chapter. My soul was irked by a devout sadness and the injustice I was navigating due to a lack of divine love.

I was not okay, but I was so far from admitting it that I often found myself denying my soul's true intentions.

I needed love. I craved love. Yet, in some odd twist of fate, love did not crave me.

As the two of us pulled up to the church, Eve was standing outside of the building with her cellphone in her hand. The moment Morena saw her; she slunk down in the car to avoid eye contact.

'What are you doing?'

"I don't want anyone to see me."

'Why?'

"Just," she paused. "I'll stay here a while."

At risk of questioning Morena's usually odd behavior, I shut off the engine and got out of the car. The condensation from her breath instantly fogged the bottom corner of the passenger side window.

Eve did not appear to see Morena there, for when I got out of the car, she was rather fixated on me.

Eve snapped at me, "What are you doing here?"

'Hey,' I walked over cautiously. 'I'm just getting some work done for Windows.'

"Oh," she said indifferently. "I thought you were sleeping here again."

'I don't stay here anymore, Eve,' I replied. 'I'm homeless, or did you forget?'

She smirked, "I didn't forget. I was just checking."

Eve wrapped her gloved hands around the door handle and ripped the large wooden door open. The creak from the hinges seemed to have been just as scared of her as the rest of the building was.

Since Paul passed away, the building sat barren almost every day and night. If I did not go visit the church, the only people to occupy the church were a community group that met Tuesday and Thursday nights for a few hours. Eve did not approve of a handful of our youth leadership programs hosting events there, so Windows was at somewhat of a standstill.

As the door slammed behind us, the cold air drifted in to denote the sullen sensation floating about the church.

Paul's presence was certainly missed.

'I'm going to just head downstairs and work on some things,' I cut through the silence between us.

Eve was busy looking at the chipping paint, the cracked walls, and the dust resting upon the office that the ministers used each Sunday morning.

"Alrighty," she snapped.

She made her way up the stairs to her office while I continued my descent into the basement.

Morena was sitting quietly in the room shuffling through papers.

'What?' I was startled by her presence. 'How did you—'

She shushed me and pointed upstairs.

I realized that she was trying to hide from Eve, though I did not understand precisely what she was doing.

'What are you doing' I whispered to her.

"Sometimes it is better to work in silence," she shot back.

'But why?'

"Stand in the shadows, adorned in your scars, until you can stand in the light and be who you are."

'That makes no sense.'

She looked up at me, "Do I ever seem to make sense, Scott?"

The two of us chuckled and I pulled up a chair. Both of us were going over the curriculums until about an hour later I stood up.

"Where are you going?"

'I need some time in the sanctuary… alone, if you don't mind.'

Morena smiled at me and motioned towards the door. I left and drifted past Eve, who seemed to be tucked away in the minister's study.

Sitting in the sanctuary alone, I felt the calm silence rain over me.

God appeared to whisper in my ear in a manner that was much clearer than ever before.

"Those in your life are beautiful in their own way, they are not there to choose one over the other, but rather they guide you in your journey. One is not better than the other, for everyone has different, significant qualities that will elevate your soul into a higher realm. Souls compliment one another, not by the rules of humanity, per se, but by the rules of the universe. We are still learning these rules. They surround the notions of love, but not as love is always defined."

'Love is the fuel of the soul,' I responded into the shadows.

"Ask yourself why you are on this spiritual journey, and you will find your way. You will finally see why you have cried so many tears. You will—"

Beautiful Souls

The door to the sanctuary swung open and Eve was standing there. Her firm voice shook me: "What are you doing?"

'I... I am praying.'

"To whom? To God?"

'To whomever will listen.'

I could see the marks on her face where it seemed many tears had cascaded over the past months. Eve sat down in the last pew and bowed her head. She began to silently pray, and I saw the name, "Paul" escape her lips.

She devoutly missed him and nothing was the same without him.

Eve wasn't even the same without him.

I looked up at the cross and blew it a kiss, 'Until next time.'

As I passed by Eve, I placed a hand on her shoulder and said a silent prayer. No one ever deserves to lose the ones they love. I am far too familiar with that notion.

For although I have not experienced a loss of love in the terms she has, many of those who I adored seemed to stop loving me... and that appeared to be both the harshest of realities and the makings of a grand journey to find what truly speaks to my soul.

The things we see as wars, anger, fighting, having a cold personality, or a lack of commitment are just sentiments of a broken heart.

Souls are often filled with pain and sadness, though it is the process of searching for what innately speaks to us that aids us in the ability to become more than what we seek or seem.

I was desperately trying to fight who I was, but it was the person I was fighting, myself, that I needed to listen to.

Oftentimes I was deaf to what I needed to hear and it constantly hurt me.

My health was deteriorating, but I didn't recognize it. I didn't listen. I was blind to my pain and I was blind to my soul's devout ambitions.

Awareness comes from opening your soul and being knowledgeable of trying to search for yourself. That alone puts you on a closer path to whatever awaits you.

I needed to live in the awe and wonder of what this world was meant to be, not what I perceived it to be.

When I returned to the office Morena was still sitting there, but under the light she took on an entirely new persona. She appeared to be doused in angelic beauty; this is not a comment on her physical attributes, but rather who she was intrinsically.

"What are you looking at," she asked.

I gazed at her for a while and realized that nothing seemed to burden her, but she was consistently connecting to whatever idea or concept spoke to her.

I needed to do that.

I needed to channel my energy before it was too late.

It was a good thing I realized this concept then, for who knows what would have happened if I continued to desolate my soul on the winding, dark path I was on.

As Morena continued writing and flipping through pages upon pages of work, I watched her snatch her journal from her bag.

I don't remember falling asleep, but I do remember waking up and seeing Morena passed out across two chairs with her jacket draped over her.

I had this weird dream that I was driving back from Texas to New York in a 24-foot truck with a car attached to the back. Bryan was about three years old at the time, and I was relieved to finally leave that world behind me.

Once I stood up, the intense pain in my lower back rose to the surface again. It was getting worse and I was ignorant to what it could mean.

I walked into the bathroom and took a look at myself in the mirror.

It was a long, hard look.

How did I let myself get like that?

A wave of sadness and depression washed over me as I scoffed at this shallow existence of mine.

When I walked back into the office, Morena had disappeared. All I saw was her notebook basking in the fluorescent light. I picked it up cautiously and decided I had to have a change in scenery.

I drove upstate in my state of utter sadness. The sunrise eventually climbed over the road, as I felt somber.

My soul was occupied and I felt weird. I was not myself. My sense of dignity also abandoned me.

Morena tried calling me.

My boss Shirley did too.

I chose not to answer them because I wanted to go somewhere and think. I wasn't feeling well and I was not too certain I knew where I was going.

The daze I was in forced me to perpetuate the abandonment I felt deep within.

'Maybe I just won't go back,' I told myself.

That day was not a good day and I prayed for healing. I began breathing deeply and found myself meditating. My mind was filled with gratitude for what I have experienced so far, and I was starting to relish in the notion that my emotional pain had to be causing some of the physical pain.

I was certain my emotions were taking a toll on my body; I had to just listen more intently.

It occurred to me that if my emotional pain caused some of the physical pain, then my ailments could be reversed. Digging deeper within my soul would provide me with the reality I was living in now: I was applying too much stress to my body and rejecting any sense that I was truly more powerful than I currently perceived.

Day after day I was driving around upstate New York basking in the illustrious scenery and growth. I travelled through small towns that were quite the juxtaposition of anything Queens could ever conjure up. My soul was detoxing between the quaint general stores and one-engine firehouses I had the privilege of laying my eyes upon.

As usual a plethora of unanswered questions danced around in my head, but I vowed they would not burden my growth.

No.

Rather, these questions would manifest a new version of me. I would return home focused, strong, and positive. An aura of peace would follow me, and though I would be more empowered, I would no longer be flustered by pain or pestilence.

At that point I was unsure of how long I was avoiding people and my responsibilities back home. It had to be about a week, though I was not entirely sure.

I let the mile marker signs guide me home until I finally saw 150 miles to New York City... then 95 miles... then 60 miles.

My whole life I have always been obsessed with countdowns: Countdowns to music releases, to events, to the end of the school year, and so much more. Moments come and go so fast, yet this was a year I had been inundated with stress. The moments did not appear as savory as they once had been.

This House is Not For Sale

I sensed that my childhood had something to do with how obsessive I was over moments and time. Valuable milestones were obscured by countless tragedies and sullen glances.

Soon I would be back at the church and immersed in yet another countdown. After all, the bliss and serenity of nature would become ensnared in the bleak monotony of the day-to-day, which would be contrasted by the love and energy I would put into the world.

I yearned for love, yet I was missing the fundamental elements of what love meant in the grand scheme of life.

As I passed by beautiful lakes and became consumed by the vivid sunset cascading across the sky, the universe's intricate perfection masked my devout sadness.

Everything I was sensing had whittled down to humanistic emotions, though I was picking up on the elements encompassing my soul.

Parts of me were petrified of what countdowns implied: the end of something. Since my Aunt Barbara died at such a young age, and I was edging closer to that number, I was more consumed with fear than what it inherently meant.

I was treating countdowns like some derogatory nuisance, yet they could also be seen as a slow and easy progression: counting could signify possibility and inevitable change.

At about 20 miles to New York City, my body writhed in immense pain. I began sweating and found the safest place to pull over.

My body felt like it was on fire, and not in a good way.

I darted into a dingy bathroom and clasped my back in a state of immense agony.

A clot of blood exited my body, and suddenly I felt better. It was an odd experience, but I assumed that it was a kidney stone.

I was not eating properly or drinking enough water, so I figured I had to start caring for myself a lot better.

On my way out, I grabbed a bottle of water from the vending machine and continued on my way.

∞ ∞ ∞ ∞ ∞ ∞ ∞ ∞

Beautiful Souls

As I drove up to the church, the moonlight encompassed the entire building. In my absence, it did not seem that anyone had even visited the church. Although I was not gone for long, maybe a week and a half at most, the building appeared to remain barren.

To me, it was utterly devastating.

A building of that size could truly be something special for the community. It could be a safe haven for so many people in need. Paul had faith that my programs could bring Queens Community Church to new heights.

However, it was a Friday night and the only living entities filling the church were my tears inundated with past memories.

I went inside to pray for a bit and ended up falling asleep on a pew until 2:30 in the morning.

I think those nights were the hardest to handle mentally. Emotionally and spiritually speaking, I was filled with such harsh loneliness.

Feeling like a hopeless fool began to be the new normal.

No one was looking for me or waiting for me.

I was just left with my own solitude to somewhat keep me company.

As I retreated to my car and drove to a quiet side street to sleep for the night, I was thankful I had a roof over my head. Although I was staying in my car and showering in whatever fast food restaurant's bathroom sink in the morning, I knew that everything was just temporary.

I held out hope that it just had to be.

By Sunday morning, I received a series of bitter text messages from Eve. She said that the church was a mess and that she could not handle any of "this nonsense" in her life anymore.

She began to insult how I ran my music program, and though my program was not in the church at all over the weekend, she blamed her current distaste on Windows of Opportunity.

Arguments ensued between the two of us for years, but it was never this bad. After every fight we had, I did everything in my power to apologize to Eve and Paul. He would always say that it was nothing or just a misunderstanding, yet Eve always saw it as much more than a tart exchange between her and I.

During this latest argument, Paul was not around to allay her discontent.

As her words grew in severity, you could only take "I don't want this in my life anymore" one way: it means that you are unwanted.

Windows of Opportunity was unwanted within the confines of the building.

Eve called me and began to berate me.

She said that I disrespected her and I disrespected Paul's work. I never had an ill intention towards either of them, the members of the church, or Queens Community Church itself.

Enough was enough with the accusations and assumptions.

If someone cannot see the pure intention and passion a person has to build a better life and atmosphere for something, then it is time to leave.

With Emma gone and my hope fleeting, I had to make the challenging decision to uproot Windows of Opportunity from its home.

Eve did not believe me when I said we were going to move Windows of Opportunity out of Queens Community Church. She yelled that I was being selfish and manipulative.

My only selfish intentions were to give the kids I work with a home to continue their memories and their hard work. They had God and faith in the way we administered the program and Eve was taking that away from them. She treated me worse than garbage and left me with no choice but to leave the church.

She said she hated that the kids performed in the music program I held at the church.

Eve screamed over the phone: "The building is not a place for rock and roll, Scott!"

The kids were finding spirituality in a creative manner, but because it was not being enacted by the old school religious ways, she wanted us out.

Although Eve told me that she supported the kids, it was a farce: she would only support them if they would abide by strict views that she appeared to have.

For weeks upon weeks, I argued with her about Windows of Opportunity's place within the church.

'Paul always appreciated us,' I told her.

"Well," she began. "Dragging my husband who is no longer here with us into the conversation shows you are truly disgusting."

Beautiful Souls

The fight continued until Morena walked up to me and mouthed, "Think of your soul, it is not worth it."

My creased face and crinkled nose eased up. I took a few deep breaths as Eve continued to badger me. I decided that I would arrive at the church at the end of Sunday's service to talk with Eve in person.

As I sat with my back against the wooden pew, I closed my eyes and decided to bask in the positive energy from the sanctuary.

There were very few people there, but the families and people who knew one another were sitting clustered together.

I was, once again, one of the odd ones out.

Sitting in my absolute solitude, I could not help but overhear the conversations mingling behind my back.

Some of the members I did not know were talking about Windows of Opportunity and the decimation it was bestowing upon the church.

It was a sinking feeling, realizing you were the topic of conversation and lingering in the mouths of those who had never even seen your face. If they did, they would have known to silence their prejudice.

My presence was an exquisite juxtaposition: here I was, the target of their profanity, sitting a mere few feet from them. Unnoticed and invisible.

Honestly, should I be surprised?

To stand and defend my honor would have meant to force negative energy into the world, yet to sit in silence would mark my complacency.

My voice is not a pawn in another's game. My essence and experience are not invalid because someone else deemed them so.

I stood, my shoulders rising as if they were breaking free from the puppet strings. The marionette has moved on.

I twisted my body in a sort of mechanical way, inching closer and closer to their proverbial conversation. Though the group chittered and chattered away, mocking the experience of someone who was within their purview, I made it my mission to uphold a persistent sense of positivity and sincere humility.

Still, no human or creation on this earth has the right to place someone in a picture frame... especially one whose actions and energy do not fit.

I tapped the woman on the shoulder, gently making my presence known.

'Excuse me,' I spoke in a hushed tone, 'Are you talking about a friend?'

The women stopped, glaring at me as if I had six heads. "No, it is just hearsay, and what is it your business?" The women retorted chuckles and sighs, as if I interrupted their little tea party of malice and diseased hatred.

'Well, if it is hearsay, here I am,' I spread my arms as if to present my aura to dispel their negative comments.

They sat quietly and utterly confused. The invisibility cloak shed itself from my skin.

In those moments between inhaling and exhaling, it dawned on them. The sun rose: I was their topic of conversation.

Their jaws cracked open slightly, their words dripped back into their throats.

'Do not throw stones at glass houses that you have never even laid your eyes upon.'

I pivoted and dropped back into the chair. Their conversations resumed, but they kept cautiously looking at me: praying their judgment would not shatter my own.

The game is no longer a game. It is a life. It is the fulfillment of a legacy...

It is the beginning of a new chapter and a new era.

I did not know where those words came from, but my sudden burst of confidence and strength felt refreshing.

Moments later, Eve came up to me and began to argue with me in hushed tones. People looked on with a mixture of curiosity and guilt on their faces, for they wanted to know what was going on, but no one was willing to stand up and stop what was going on.

After everyone left and people filtered out through the front doors, Eve and a handful of members who I knew receded into the basement of the church. I sat there in the empty sanctuary for a moment, the sun shining up the aisle and resting a solitary beam on the altar, and began to cry hysterically.

'Why, why, why?'

Tears obscured my vision as I looked on at all of the beautiful stained-glass windows. I wondered if it would be the last time I saw those glorious windows.

I tried to listen to God and the angels, hoping that I would find some sort of salvation.

Silence was the only thing that graced my presence.

I felt most connected to my soul and spirituality within the walls of that church, which was such a contrast to what I felt as a child sitting in a temple, yet when I needed guidance most I was left in solitude.

The church became my makeshift home.

I could not tell anyone how much it meant to me, for how could I justify to the world that I was homeless and living out of the building?

All of my money went into keeping Windows of Opportunity alive and well, and if I stopped funding the programs, then who would help the youth of Queens find their inner power?

That night I was not able to sleep. I gazed up at the roof of my car and toyed with the daunting decision I had to make: stay at or leave Queens Community Church.

Overwhelmed by the choices before me, I felt that saving my sanity forced me into a claustrophobic state.

I wanted to cry.

Scream.

Run away.

Go to where I once felt safe, but was now being torn away from.

Thousands upon thousands of my prayers graced those walls, but now the church was becoming just four walls and a roof.

I vowed I would actively work on my soul after Emma's complete dismissal of who I could have been for her, yet I found myself hitting another concrete wall.

Though this one was metaphorical, I felt all of my sacrifices were for naught: the building, Windows of Opportunity's home, was abandoning the partnership we could have created.

It was the neverending story of my life up until that point: everyone and everything ended up leaving to some extent.

Everyone and everything seemed to not want me.

For those who did want me, it was not unconditional, but rather with extreme conditions that humanly could not be met.

I seemed to disappoint many, despite my pure good intentions.

I took verbal beating after verbal beating over the years in order to make sure that there would be a safe space for Windows of Opportunity and youth to grow, yet I was left in the ashes once again. I needed to figure out a whole new plan, but letting go of the church was too strong of a burden to bear.

Naturally, I have always absorbed negative energy, though this situation with the church left me with a gaping hole in my chest.

It was hard to breathe.

It was difficult to sleep.

My soul was decimated prior to this, and Eve's commentary made me feel worse.

The lower back pain I had been dealing with shook at my core again. Regardless, I figured I needed to disregard the pain and fight through. I was certain that what I was on the brink of creating would change the education system for years to come.

I knew in my heart it would shift society over the next twenty or thirty years, and I acknowledged I might not even be around to see everything reach its full potential.

I made a few promises to myself then and there: I cannot accept anyone in my life who will not support that and give me a safe space to be me. I cannot have anyone in my life that does not trust me and love me unconditionally, so that this vision of mine could be obtained.

I needed all of me and I was only a shell.

My cracked outer surface seemed unfixable, and I was petrified that I was going to fall apart at any moment.

I had to heal myself and that meant making some difficult decisions, including the one that kept me up that night.

There was nothing left to say.

My decision was final.

I sighed as tears rolled down the edges of my face. I drifted to sleep with the image of the interior to my car's roof burning into my drooping eyes.

∞ ∞ ∞ ∞ ∞ ∞ ∞ ∞

As I stepped out of my car and into daylight, people were scurrying about and beginning their day. There was no doubt the people who passed me were running through their to do lists in their respective heads.

Everyone was out living their lives.

Beautiful Souls

The morning was such a heavy contrast to the darkness that preceded my days.

I wake up in the comfort of four wheels and a huge secret.

Still, my address did not dictate the world I was creating and inspiring daily.

The mask I wore as a social worker inspired many, but came with great sacrifices.

Regularly, I pushed through delirium in order to embody the transformative soul I had to become. My dreams are an amalgamation of the paths I crossed every day.

By day I kept myself occupied by helping youth in a high school. Then I would meet with different people to create programs for youth.

At night, I parked my car where I could and drifted to sleep.

When I had to use the restroom, which was becoming more frequent, I begged a minimum wage worker at a coffee shop to let me in the bathroom.

I drove around a while longer and brought my car to an abrupt stop when I saw Emma's classroom window.

It was just another night after another.

By day, I would watch people run past me and consider that some of them may be living in their car as well.

The world might never realize it.

What were their stories?

What was my story?

The daylight obscured my dark reality. My daily strengths absorbed my nightly weaknesses.

The journey to find true love masked the broken pieces of my soul: the memories I created with past loves were now gone, but not forgotten.

It broke my heart when I realized a decade of dedication and a sincere appreciation towards Queens Community Church whittled down to a series of volatile text messages from Eve.

It takes a lot to crush someone to their core, but it is possible. I never thought that it would happen at the hands of an individual who claims to be religious, spiritual, and subservient to God and HER ways, but sometimes people genuinely surprise you.

You could have the best intentions for someone or something, yet people would rather misjudge or misunderstand you instead of communicating in a healthy manner.

The act of leaving the church was an act of forgiveness in its utmost form: though I was harboring a broken heart, I felt no malice towards Eve and the members.

We are all on our respective spiritual journeys, and Eve's just so happen to push her to influence my experience. Instead of building a future and a community together, as we had planned, Windows of Opportunity and the Queens Community Church were being forced to part ways at a crucial point in the development of all of our programs. We were deeply doing God's work on a daily basis, and how it can be seen any other way, whether in a fit of rage, mourning, or depression, and stated in any malicious or degrading way, was simply a travesty and the act of a seemingly non-spiritual person who is blinded by misery and in pain.

It was breaking my heart, as I knew some of my programs would now face irreapairable damage, and I also realized that if I continued on swimming in this sea of negative emotions, my soul would also face irrepairable damage.

Throughout our respective periods of spiritual growth, pain may seem like a hindrance to a soul, but it could be a catalyst to help souls grow.

There is a difference between being entitled to your feelings, which we all are, and manipulating the facts to be "right and win an argument." I know God and my angels flow through my veins and guide my spirit. There is nothing I do or decide without speaking to God first; She is with me as these words flow onto the pages you are reading. She agreed that evil was plaguing my soul. I had to sever ties with those who spread negativity or spoke ill of me and my work, in order to protect the youth my team and I consistently empower on a daily basis.

It is disgusting and disrespectful to be subject to anything less than loving and caring feelings, especially when working with a constituent of a church. How can someone preach togetherness and God's words while directing social media posts towards me and my team that say, "You don't get a pat on the back for the SHIT you are supposed to do."

I wondered: Is this the language a Reverend should be using?

In addition, Eve had remarked that "the collar is off" when using vulgar language such as that, and she said that line many times.

This was just one statement, in a collection of many that led up to my heartbreak. If we were able to maintain our partnership, we would have been able to save thousands of lives together. However, I just hoped that those souls would still find a way to stay strong.

Paul always genuinely cared about me, Windows of Opportunity, and our roles at the church. For that I will always be truly grateful. I was in agony over having to leave the church, for I felt like I was losing a part of him in walking away from what he had hoped we would create together.

There was no point in fighting anymore, nor feeding into unhealthy behaviors. I want all of us to find the peace we need to make a difference in this world.

I sat in the sanctuary and I cried there for many nights since I realized I had to leave. I spent my last evenings speaking to God and praying for all of humanity.

I had evolved my relationship with God deeply in that sanctuary. I loved the church building. I love God. I love my faith. I love the work I do. I love myself and God enough to know I could not subject myself to consistent and hurtful badgering.

It was time to go and it was time to grow.

Sleeping seemed near impossible due to my emotions surrounding the church and the persistent pain I was experiencing. Still, I dreamt about the church in its entirety.

I dreamt I went back to the church after what seemed like a few weeks. The entire building was in shambles: it was a pile of stone and dust, which slightly resembled where the rooms once were.

I was alone until I heard voices: two men were trying to pick up the piano as the keys trickled down the rubble. Part of an old drum kit was crushed nearby.

I chose to hide in another part of the destruction, away from the men and the piano. My shelter and salvation were gone, yet I could not do anything about it.

When I woke up, I realized that a music box played "Somewhere Over the Rainbow" over and over in my head. This morning I saw a rainbow halo around the moon. Someone or something is trying to send a message. Call me crazy, but prayer and religion-based songs played all morning on the way to the building. Something wicked this way comes.

We pray on our knees, but resist the willingness to follow through with our atonements when on two feet. We live in verse, only to diminish another's poetry if it does not match our lyrical ear. If "to err is to be human," why do we fixate on flaws and knock each other to the ground, but frown at the sight of someone trying to better themselves?

We were not born this way. We were molded to see this. We need to open our hearts and minds. We need to banish the rain of hatred that tries seeping through the branches and into the roots of our society. It is only natural that we purge ourselves from the disillusionment that we must hate, we must see color in terms of distention and separation, we must see competition, and we must burn our candle at both ends just to make those ends meet. If you are constantly racing to the next goal, the next dream, knocking down the next person to gain notoriety, then consider how much damage this is causing your soul.

Do not place merit on higher consciousness and whatever you deem holy just when you are on your knees. Live the words you seek and preach. Be the shift in light, in prayer, in words, and in actions.

For the universe knows and forgives those who opt to tear down others… but it restores the balance in granting the gifts we so choose to receive. Negativity gets met with the manifestation of those feelings. Positivity is met with its fair share of challenges, but the universe's hand tends kindly towards those who reject hate and ill will.

Born are we of the same consciousness, yet broken down into fundamental components of a global whole. It is our choice then: do we build sandcastles with our words? (Beautiful and eloquent, yet able to be discombobulated with the presence of something as malleable as water) Or do we develop a positive shift through insight, grace, and words integral to building, not breaking?

The perspective we hold is exclusive to our respective experiences, but the question remains: are you on your knees to beg for the universe to look blindly on how you treat others, or are you on your knees as a means of wishful thinking… hoping for the betterment and growth that is being built moment by moment?

I felt as if an entire universe had shifted itself off its axis when I pulled up to the building. Memories of a soul's growth once flooded these four walls, and now I had to say goodbye to them. However, in watching the sun crawl over the trees and houses that lined the street, I realized that so much changed. It was for the better. I spent hours sitting on those

Beautiful Souls

steps, wondering if I could ever have a better life, but I was wishing and praying for the wrong things: it is the people who surround you that make your life amazing. The experiences mold you, but buildings cannot do anything for you. Something incredibly stationary can't shake your world and jolt your existence. Sure, buildings give you perspective and shelter, but for how long?

I couldn't help but feel somber about penning the final chapter in the church, especially like this. No matter how holy a place could seem, it still comes down to what you exude from your heart and soul. It comes down to how you spend each moment, each word, each breath, for at the end of the day, when the sun sets and the colors fade to gray, your world can't be at peace if its clouds are blocking your hopes and dreams from shining through. One day I knew I would look back and smile at these days: maybe not tomorrow, or next week, or next year, but one day.

And on that day the sun will rise over four walls filled with memories, and they'll know that they served their purpose. A shroud will be lifted and the walls will serve another gentle, cracked soul. Then an invisible plaque will hang on the altar that says: this house is not for sale, but this house sold its purpose for growth and prosperity many sunrises ago.

The boxes stood before me, representative of a wall between the man I was and the man I could so desperately become. Overcome with intense emotion, I ran from the church panicked and full of misery. My head was spinning and the last thing I could remember before pushing through the church doors was Morena's voice behind me: a cardboard thud emulated as she screamed, "Scott! Wait!"

I got in my car and drove.

I drove further away until the church became the background of a life remembered.

I pulled up to Francis Lewis Park, where Morena was waiting for me against the wooden fence.

'Not now Morena,' I shouted as I pushed past her in an absolute tizzy.

"Not now Morena," she said mockingly, "Well it's gonna be now!"

She rushed after me as my feet leapt off the wooden steps and into the sand. I fell to the floor and she was sure to follow.

Merciless screams escaped my body as I threw myself close to the water that was ebbing and flowing closer to where we sat. The pressures of waiting for Emma to wake up and leaving the church were mounting, and all I could do was cry over what never will be.

Windows of Opportunity could have had a beautiful home within the walls of that church, but the universe had other plans brewing deep from within the cosmic backdrop of this crazy world.

Now the doors were closing, and it felt like the windows were slamming shut… and to add insult to injury, Emma's words were seething into my skin.

"You're thinking of her too, aren't you," Morena's hair flew backwards as the wind began caressing both of our souls.

She knew. She could read me. Emma's words cut like a knife, and losing the church ripped the wound clear open.

"Every day we stray a little bit further from the light that is inside us because we cannot fathom a world where we are the villain in somebody's story," Morena spoke softly.

'I am not the villain, Morena. There is no villain,' I quipped.

"You are right. You are not," she snapped. "In your story, that is. You don't get to control her narrative. You don't get to tell Emma that your intentions were pure and that she needs to believe that as her truth. You don't know exactly what she thinks is right or wrong. All you know is that you are not in her life anymore."

Tears welled in my eyes as I tried collecting some semblance of words to fight the demons within me. A breathy whine escaped my mouth, 'But Morena, I loved her, why doesn't she love me?'

The tears fell from my eyes and splashed onto my cupped hands. Morena bent beside me and whispered, almost in the manner that some fairy godmother would in a children's fantasy story: "Because you remind her of what she could never feel towards another human being. She needs to learn to love herself before she can love another… and that, my dear, is your crime: you loved the pieces of her that she couldn't comprehend. She couldn't appreciate you because she couldn't appreciate herself."

'Morena,' the setting sun brushed my eyelids open, for I just had to see the sky above and show appreciation to the world around me.

"Love yourself Scott, because at the end of the day, you need to learn to love the one person who will walk with you for life," Morena bent down and leaned against me as we watched the sun fade beyond the New York skyline.

Beautiful Souls

"We all learn eventually," she muttered, "We all learn to."

Once the sun disappeared, I felt the urge to return back to the church. I told Morena that I would see her there, and something within her must have forced her to stall a bit… for I pulled up to the dark church all alone.

As it always had been.

I quietly slipped into the back pew in the darkness. All I felt was the thumping of my chest and the creeping sensation of an oncoming asthma attack.

"Help comes to those who ask for it," I heard in my own voice. It was echoing through the empty sanctuary. It was empty and drenched in the darkness, yet filled with light. A long pause followed by a deep sigh.

'Well here I am…asking for help.'

I knew I still loved her, because four years ago, exactly from that day, I laid on the couch downstairs from that very sanctuary, and asked God about her. I prayed and asked if what I was feeling was real, and who is this girl that I just met. She caught my eye and my soul from day one, and four years later I was sitting upstairs in the sanctuary, maybe for the last time, asking God and the angels for help.

I missed her. I was not ashamed to admit it.

Four years later I'm asking the same question. Who is the girl I met four years ago? Was she the real deal?

As I sat in the darkness, I whispered into the vastness: "I trust you father. I trust the universe and my angels. I also know we are the creators of our own reality."

Maybe this is sad, but I desired the following to be my reality: If there was ever a miracle this is what I prayed for, I didn't only want to have her friendship back in a major way, but I also desired to have these beautiful souls get along with one another and collectively feed my spirit, so that I may accomplish the impossible.

I continued my outwardly prayer: 'Thank you, universe, for all my blessings seen and unseen, and please forgive my sins, and my shortcomings. I'm so sorry that I can't shake this depression and that I can't connect to my inner strength and light again. I want to, but knowing I'm a disappointment is impossible to live with. If I can't make the dreams a reality, what is the point of anything?'

I took a deep breath and turned inward.

'I know you blessed me and I see those blessings.'

A door thudding in the darkness made me realize I truly wasn't alone.

'Thank you. Amen.'

"Scott," Morena beckoned, "we have lessons and long-term light in our life. Sometimes people are clear in their role, other times they are not. I-"

It felt as if a message was flourishing through my soul, and I felt Morena's words fading away.

'Something,' I whispered.

"What?" Morena looked somewhat startled.

'Something is coming.'

We stood in absolute silence as she moved closer and closer.

'Time after time I have taken hit after hit. This one was excruciating, personal, deep, shattering, tormenting, and agonizing torture. How do you hand someone your soul, your inner demons, your thoughts, and most importantly your love, while they just take it and ram it heart first into a concrete wall?

'My soul, heart, mind, and spirit were demolished, and I simply couldn't fathom how someone so close became so far. Sometimes you'll want to disappear because the mask you wore was drenched with so many tears that it corroded. The pain succumbs your whole body and shatters you. You can't pick up the pieces and put them together because they stole most of them and refused to give it back. I was holding countless blank keys in my hand that didn't fit in any lock. I could not get into where I wanted because I was permanently locked out.

'My soul believes she completes me. My heart says she is the only one with the key. My body longs for her touch. My head is filled with conflicting emotions. My world lies in ruined disarray.'

"The timeline is speeding up," Morena muttered under her breath.

'I expect nobody to know what it's like to walk in my shoes, and nobody can. This is the scariest crossroads I have been on, and the one I have to show the bravest face,' I glared at Morena's eyes that were immersed in a pool of pristine white light.

It was time.

It was coming.

I retired to my car and allowed my thoughts to melt into a dreamlike state.

Beautiful Souls

My phone rang and jolted me from any semblance of rest I would have.

It turned out to be a representative from a national television show. For weeks, she promised she would interview me and promote Windows of Opportunity, but when we finally spoke, I was devastated yet again.

She said that I did not really have a story to tell and that Windows of Opportunity would not go far.

A lot of people did not have faith in Windows of Opportunity. I was starting to think they were right.

However, time after time I felt I lost myself because someone else was nurturing me, loving me, or encouraging me. This time, I needed to step up and show up, regardless of circumstances.

There were no more excuses left and no more tears left to cry.

Time and time again, I have taught youth that as long as your religion and your faith give you values and morals, then they shouldn't be filled with trepidation when expressing what they believe in.

I always told the youth in my program that nobody has the right to dictate the parameters and boundaries of how they should live their lives. At the end of the day, we are all surrounded by unconditional love as long as we believe in ourselves.

When I was younger, I was told by the religious figures in my life that I was asking too many questions. The community I was a part of was blind to the abuse my sister and I were dealing with at home.

It was a painstaking experience and I did not want the youth in my programs to be judged by their style, their hair color, their relationship preferences, or just about anything.

Our respective relationships with God and the universe transcend different aspects of our lives. This may happen at different times, but regardless of where we are on our individual journeys, the light still resonates within us.

The beliefs we hold near and dear are there for us, even when we do not outwardly see them.

We must listen carefully to the voice within our souls because when we reject our inner light, it could take a lot longer to realize your own self-worth and purpose.

I wish I had realized all of this earlier in my own timeline, though I am thankful for all of my experiences for they all made me the man I am today.

This House is Not For Sale

∞ ∞ ∞ ∞ ∞ ∞ ∞ ∞

In the midst of my departure from the life I once knew, I was thankful for the support from my son. At this point in time, Bryan was a part of over half of my life and got a chance to see my growth.

Though Bryan was holistically unaware of my experiences in Texas, he saw what his mother and I did in order to take care of him.

The two of us went to see a movie and as we walked out of the theatre, he put his hand on my shoulder and said, "Pop, I'm proud of you."

It meant everything.

Words carry so much weight to them and can make or break someone. It is phenomenal to see that my growth and progress transcended into my son's actions. The two of us walked down the street to our respective cars, since he was rushing home to his longtime girlfriend.

My son is my world and I wanted nothing other than for him to live a fulfilling life.

I was so happy that he found someone who understands his soul and who makes him genuinely smile.

True love is such a rare treasure and it is a blessing that he was gifted with an exquisite relationship of his own.

The second I got into my car I fell sound asleep.

I dreamt that Morena and I were eating at a diner. The two of us sat there discussing Washington, D.C. and the curriculums.

"You know," Morena started. "With all of your ideas, you should become the next president."

I almost spit my coffee from my mouth.

'The next president? Are you crazy?'

She looked up at me with a smirk plastered on her face.

"Maybe a little, but when you dare to dream is passion truly insanity?"

Before she could say anything else, Eve walked over to us and began screaming at me. She sat down and was trying to explain some sort of story, but it was interlaced with harsh quips and not-so-subtle judgments.

Morena moved next to me and placed her open palm on my shoulder.

"Hey," she whispered. "Did you catch that one? I guess some things never change."

I clenched my fist and Morena wrapped her fingers around my hand.

Beautiful Souls

"Don't let her get to you."

'What should I do?' I turned to Morena. 'Should I go back?'

"Hear her out," Morena motioned to Eve as she continued to ramble. I began to calm down and breathe deeply.

"Maybe what you are searching for, isn't what you are looking for…" Morena's words faded into the recesses of my mind.

When I woke up, I realized it was just a strange dream.

After spending the day with Bryan, I did not understand why my mind suddenly shifted to Eve's presence.

The windshield was fogged over and I was utterly confused.

Why did Morena say president?

Did she mean becoming the President of the United States?

Why was she keen on Washington, D.C.?

Why did Eve appear?

What was going on inside my head?

I pressed down on the brake and shifted my car into reverse. I wrapped my hands around the steering wheel and put on the radio.

Bon Jovi's lyrics boomed from the speakers as I shifted the car into drive.

> *"Look what they've done to this house of love*
> *It's too late to turn river to blood*
> *The saviors come and gone, we're all out of time*
> *The devil's in the temple and he ain't no friend of mine*
> *Look what they've done to this house of love."*

I pulled into the staff parking lot at work and shut my eyes. My mind was mottled by shades of black and white, pictures of people who I had not seen in years, and a podium illuminated by a solid white light.

My eyes slammed shut as the music on the radio dissipated.

∞ ∞ ∞ ∞ ∞ ∞ ∞ ∞

I stood looking down at the people below.

What separated us was a solitary, yet sturdy, glass pane dividing us from ever getting too close and personal. I wonder what it would be like not to have glass divide us.

What would it be like to reach out and touch someone directly in front of you?

To extend your arm and someone be within reach?

Being 48 floors up, I realize it would be humanly impossible to touch another person from behind the window. Yet somehow, I don't think I meant physically touching them in those moments.

What would life be like if we didn't have glass windows that divided us from touching another's soul?

What if we could reach out and hold the ones we love dearly… to actually hold them and not just some superficial meaning of the term hold.

To touch someone and be touched.

To have another human being fully wrap their soul around yours.

Is it possible to fathom someone who was your equal?

Someone who you could be miles apart from, yet feel their every move and twist.

Someone whose very breath would shatter the ground beneath you, then restructure it as they inhale your beauty, then exhale their fears and inhibitions.

I wonder if soulmates or this concept of twin flames are a real thing, or was it made up to justify human nature's inability to compute loneliness?

I extended my hand to touch the glass.

A single fingerprint left its trace on the window, reminding someone that pensive thoughts were developed here. My pain is beauty and tragedy mixed up in one hopeful breath.

Do you see me?

Can you see me?

Would you ever understand me?

Are you out there somewhere in the universe? In the abyss?

I could go on forever asking questions about love and how souls just naturally, or unnaturally, click… but what for? What if I am just doomed to walk this Earth imprinting love and joy on others, but have no one fully grasp each and every fiber of my being… and just understand me.

Is anyone listening?

Can anyone hear me, or am I self-absorbed in the universe's soul?

Can everyone hear me deep inside, but have the inability to understand the words I am saying?

I am but a singular fingerprint on a glass pane: slightly noticeable, constant and unwavering, yet latent until you move closer and acknowledge my existence.

I will forever be your fingerprint, whomever you are out there: a solitary mark on your heart that flows within your blood. A phantom of the love you yearn to have for me, though you do not know I exist... and as your blood circulates through your system, you exhale my soul and I inhale every ounce of you I can.

You have chosen your own path in this lifetime, one without me, one with shortcuts and back alleyways.

Maybe you are out there somewhere rockin this universe.

You didn't try to cling to even an iota of my soul in this time and space reality.

Is that true?

Have you marched on without even an acknowledgement of my presence, or do you whisper for me every night when your head hits the pillow.

Do you know I am here and will we find one another again?

I can either live with that for the rest of my history, or I can move on, or have an undying faith that maybe... just maybe...

Though how could you move forward once your soul knows it has been engulfed in another's flame? A flame that burned strongly from another place and time? There is no remorse or regenerative soul who could see from my eyes, from behind this glass pane on the 48th floor. Yet I so wish there was... Could there ever be another me? Another lost soul rolling around in rubbish, waiting for someone like me. It is a hopeful sense of doubt. You aren't waiting anywhere for me, are you?

You don't exist, yet you do in my mind.

Are you there, universe? It's me, the one you rescued.

Or does life not work that way?

I guess it doesn't.

If you did hear me, you would acknowledge my prayer.

I am closer to you on the 48th floor. I am right near a window.

Can you see me now? Are you listening?

I am rambling now, that is just it. No one knows this is even happening in the outside world. My facial expression is too shallow to comprehend, and with everything going on, I just fade like a shadow into the abyss.

As always, I am the clicking pen or foot tapping that serves as background noise until someone focuses in on me. Maybe I am just a dream. Maybe I can push this glass forward and just step out into thin air. Maybe I am a figment of someone else's imagination moving through the darkness, pulled in the direction of lost souls or beating hearts.

Where do I go from here?

Is there anywhere to go?

Is there anyone out there?

My soul so yearns to find you.

A murmur derailed my train of thought: some children laughing in the distant corner and crayons rolling down the hall with a reverberating echo.

The vibration touched my soul.

The room spun abruptly and caught my attention.

Where had the glass gone?

I reached out and placed too much of my body weight on trust and faith. Tumbling out of the window, I felt my inhibitions screaming and fading fast.

With my head as a torpedo, aiming directly for the ground, I found my target.

Come find me.

Please...

My eyes jolted awake and the roof of the car met my startled head.

CHAPTER 7

Carpe Diem

"Dear my love, haven't you wanted to be with me? Haven't you longed to be free? I can't keep pretending that I don't even know you...Take my hand. We're leaving here tonight. There's no need to tell anyone. They'd only hold us down... All I want is to give my life only to you. I've dreamt so long I cannot dream anymore. Let's run away, I'll take you there."

- Amy Lee, American singer, songwriter, pianist, Riverside, California

I started to think that maybe the answers to my soul's discomfort were not people. I figured maybe the answers were on a plane that I did not discover or establish yet.

The answers to life's quintessential challenges may not be readily accessible or available at first, but that is what makes the journey through life so fulfilling. Spending time weighing your heart down with the misnomers and false images of another apparition only brings heartache.

It was time to release the pain.

Instinctively, I called up Morena and told her to meet me at Alley Pond Park. Though it was mildly cold outside, I knew that she would still walk with me. It occurred to me that through thick and thin, Morena would always be standing beside me. She may have her quirks and odd tendencies, but she has a genuinely kindred soul.

Though she acted as my spiritual guidance in times of trouble, I knew that she held more empowerment deep within her.

She had a gift, as did I, but both of us were years away from actualizing all of that potential in the universe.

As I pulled up to Alley Pond Park, I saw Morena sitting at the rustic picnic table where I last saw my Aunt Barbara. When Morena turned around to meet my gaze, I could have sworn that the smile adorned across her face belonged to the woman who gave me so much hope.

Aunt Barbara helped to shape the man I am today.

She instilled in me the fortitude I needed to keep my soul intact.

For her, and for the rest of the people in my Circle of Angels, I am grateful. I will forever harbor a sense of gratitude for those who perished and watch over me, and a sense of respect for those who are my earth angels.

"What's going on, kiddo?" Morena pulled her sleeves over her hands and shifted her body so that we were parallel one another.

'Can we go for a walk?'

"Sure," she reached for my hand and stood up.

Both of us began walking up the path and through the slightly blooming trees that appeared to bend towards us.

The two of us walked in silence until she suddenly looked up at me.

'What is it?'

She paused for a moment and looked at the trail ahead.

"Why did we come here?"
'I just needed to breathe some fresh air.'
The pain in my lower back was getting worse, but I kept pushing forward.
Maybe that was my real fatal mistake: not listening to my body.
"Okay," Morena smiled as the two of us continued walking.
'I think it's time.'
"What time?"
'I am fully giving my soul to the universe.'
Morena chuckled, "Your soul is a part of the universe, silly."
'No,' I started. 'I mean truly letting go and letting God handle everything.'
"The universe has looked very kindly on you, Scott."
'I know, I know.'
"Do you know?" Morena stopped and I halted as well.
'I think so... I mean, I thought so for the longest time. Then-'
She stopped me and wrapped her chilled fingers around my arm, which covered the infinity symbol tattoo on my forearm.
"Do not give into another soul, Scott. Find your own soul."
I looked at her quizzically. 'I know,' I said. 'I just said I am letting go and letting God-'
She started to talk over me as if she was discharging a prophecy from her lips: "In the mountains, through the prairies, through the oceans white with foam. God blessed America, and has also blessed you. You have a gift. You have a light. Do not obscure it. Let it shine and those who don't want to bask in its glow can seek solace elsewhere. Their loss. Your gain. You physically are in another realm; emotionally, mentally, spiritually... you are elsewhere. They are here, in a land they do not yet understand or grasp."
I looked over at her, as the sun seemed to cut directly through the trees in search of her.
'Who are *they*, Morena?'
She spoke softly, "Give it time, for the sun will shine."
The two of us stopped as we reached the steep part of the path. In this part of the park, it always seemed like this crackling paved set of steps was our humanistic way of immersing man-made creations in nature. I had a hard time breathing and quickly began to hyperventilate.

'I can't do this,' I leaned against the wooden fence that lined the path.
"You can't do what?"
'I can't keep going on like this.'
Morena sat down in the dirt and began to run her fingers through the earth. "What is it you always say," she began. "Keep the faith?"
She looked up at me and smiled.
'How do I release this pain burdening my chest?' I pounded my fist against the center of my rib cage a few times as tears began streaming from my eyes.
"Music always speaks to your soul, correct?"
I stopped crying for a moment, 'What does that have to do with anything?'
Morena began to hum a familiar tune as she closed her eyes. The wind picked up and whisked her hair in front of her face. My own hair fluttered in the sudden breeze as I lifted my head towards the sky.
Her voice became more angelic and took on a spiritual tone.

"We've got to hold on, to what we've got,"

She paused and tilted her head to the sky.

"Does it really make a difference if we make it or not?"

She sounded like she was singing Bon Jovi's "Livin' on a Prayer," but it came across as if she was chanting a prayer.

"We've got each other, and that's a lot."

'Morena-'
She continued as the trees began to sway:

"We'll give it a shot."

My eyes dropped to where she was sitting, and suddenly I didn't feel like crying anymore.

Carpe Diem

"Ooooh, we're halfway there.
Ooooh, we're living on a prayer..."

She extended her hand and opened her eyes. Morena's irises appeared to glow in the bursts of sunlight that were cutting through the trees.

Although it seemed that she was physically in front of me, it appeared that Morena was translucent. She was not a part of a linear timeline; rather she was a manifestation of exponential opportunities in this universe.

Her voice faded back in again:

"Take my hand, we'll make it, I swear."

The two of us in unison sang,

'Whoa, living on a prayer.'

In those moments, it felt like everything made sense. It seemed as if all of my hardships and turmoil were supposed to be a part of my soul's experience. It appeared to me that my definitions of divine love and being a power couple were taking on an entirely new meaning.

The soul who I was most compatible with would have to be as spiritual and as sincere as I was. The other half of my power couple would need to be insightful, diligent, and able to transcend any challenge with grace and poise.

Until that moment arrived, I would not settle for less.

I would not settle for someone who did not match my vision and values. Although I was steadfast when it came to my ambitions, I was not going to completely shut out someone who was complimentary to the positive energy I planned on immersing myself in.

I knew there were people out there who also had a fire burning deep within their respective souls, I just needed help finding them. The journey I was on had to intersect with others who were finding or found themselves. It was becoming clearer and clearer.

Morena and I continued walking the path and talking about different concepts for education reform. It was almost like I was looking into a mirror: she understood me on a spiritual level that made it appear she was a figment of my imagination.

Beautiful Souls

For all intents and purposes, Morena was a different version of myself, and my soul.

The wind had simmered down and it was just the two of us walking around at this point. We wandered past the pond, a group of children laughing and kicking a soccer ball around, and a quaint shack that served as a storage area for the park.

Morena darted into the playground area and leapt onto the swings. The creaking metal winced at her every whim.

As she moved like a pendulum back and forth, I instinctively watched her.

'What are you doing?'

"Well, what does it look like I am doing?"

'I don't know, Morena.'

She paused and smiled for a moment, "I'm living."

Morena threw her head towards the swing and I jumped on.

The two of us swung in unison with the Earth's gravitational pull. We were giggling as if we were like little children again.

Finally, after what felt like half an hour, I turned to Morena and watched her hair whip in front of her jubilant face.

'Hey,' I spoke softly, yet loud enough for her to hear.

"Hey!"

The two of us looked at each other for a moment again while basking in the sounds of nature.

"How do you feel?"

'Alive,' I shouted. 'But I feel alone.'

"Hey Scott," she placed her feet on the ground and I stopped swinging. She looked over at me as a gentle breeze caught her hair.

"You are never alone. No one ever truly is, you know that."

'Do I, now?'

"And besides," Morena started. Her voice became more sing-songy:

> *"I see everything you can be*
> *I see the beauty that you can't see*
> *On the nights you feel outnumbered*
> *Baby, I'll be out there somewhere."*

"That is breathtakingly beautiful, did you write that?"

She stood up from the swing and started walking to the gate. I watched her take a deep breath as she basked in the glory of the fresh air.

"Dermot Kennedy sings it, its called 'Outnumbered' and I heard it on the way here."

'It's beautiful.'

She whipped her head in my direction to watch the words register in my soul.

'You know,' I walked over to her. 'I hadn't been on the swings since I was a kid.'

Morena laced her fingers in the chain-link fence.

"You didn't exactly have a childhood."

'No,' I placed my finger between the chain-link fence as well. 'But I accept that my childhood wasn't easy.'

"Neither was Rebecca's"

'No,' I ran my left hand along the black paint. 'Not at all.'

"When she calls you, answer it."

'What?'

"There will come a time when she calls you," she said. "Be there for her."

'I will,' I assured. At the time, I was holistically unaware of what was about to happen to my family.

I had been so far removed from my parents and my sisters' lives, that when Rebecca called days later to tell me what was going on with my mother and father, part of me needed to register the words she was saying.

The two of us chatted for a while about what was going on in our respective lives, until Rebecca suddenly adorned a solemn tone.

"Scott, dad is really sick."

With a tinge of concern in my voice, I asked 'How sick is he?'

"Well," she began. "Not as bad as mom is."

'What's wrong with mom?'

It had really been years since I had an in-depth conversation with my parents. Though I knew my parents divorced and my father started a family with his new wife, I always had the feeling my parents were not too enthralled with my organization and my life. Bryan maintained a relationship with his grandparents and my parents and I were cordial to one another when we were together, but we very rarely spoke.

"Uh," Rebecca cleared her throat. "Mom has Alzheimer's. She doesn't really remember too much anymore."

I felt terrible for my mother, for I knew deep down inside she was a tortured soul who needed to be understood. However, in this irreversible state, my mother didn't remember what she did to my sister or me in our youth.

It was like she pushed the reset button, though our scars still remained.

With nowhere to live and my sister in need of help, I moved in with my mother and slept on her couch for quite some time.

Our relationship transcended into a different light, for she was so far removed from the woman she was in my childhood.

The first time I walked up the stairs and back into the house where I was thrown out of, my mother greeted me at the door jovially.

"Scott," she gleamed with excitement. "I'm glad you're home. Did you bring the milk?"

'Uh,' I didn't even know she wanted me to bring milk. 'No, mom, I forgot.'

My mother looked at me with a sense of wonder. "Forgot what?"

Rebecca appeared from behind her and shrugged as she smiled.

"Mom," she put her hands on our mother's shoulders, "Go back inside and sit down."

"Okay," my mother said. This was the first time I didn't see her stubborn demeanor emerge from nowhere. She retreated into the dismal living room adorned with old family photos.

'What's wrong with mom?'

Rebecca whispered, "Like I said, her memory is practically gone."

'I didn't think you meant *gone* gone.'

Our mother plopped down in the cocoa-colored recliner and glared at the static image on the television screen.

"This is my favorite part," she shouted as she pointed at the screen.

'Oh,' I remarked. 'That's great, ma.'

I turned around to look at my sister who was clearly holding back tears.

Rebecca and I sat at the table and talked for a bit until she had to go off to work. I brought a bag of my clean clothes in from the car and placed them on the floor next to my mother's couch.

It was a faded sunflower-colored sofa that seemed to have been there for well over a decade.

The sofa, and all of the other furniture in the room, appeared to be as weathered and tattered as my mother was.

She kept rocking on the recliner and humming various unrecognizable tunes to herself. I looked on in amazement, for the two of us were able to be in the same room despite our horrid past.

I guess it helped that only one of us remembered what life used to be.

Her clothes were baggy and desolate. Though she was clean and her hair was neatly tied back, her sweatpants and large t-shirt were not a sight I was accustomed to. Although she was not stylish in the sense of models strutting on a runway, my mother was always well kempt.

Whenever we went to temple, she wore neatly pressed clothes that embodied the matriarch image she put forth. In her current state however, she appeared to be completely unwound.

It was almost as if the ribbons of time she once clasped firmly in her hands were tangled and in ruins on the floor.

As I watched her peacefully rock back and forth in the chair, I discovered that her entire life was now removed from her recollection.

She turned and caught my glance as small tears began to run down the edges of my cheeks.

"Oh hello," she said with a grin. "Are you comfortable there?"

'Yes,' I replied. 'I am, thank you.'

I turned and looked up at the pictures hanging on the wall. She spun her head around to see what caught my eye.

"Oh," she pointed to the picture of me in my scouting uniform. "Are you looking at my son?"

'What?'

"My son." She pointed up at the picture and smiled, "He's such a good boy; he should be home any minute now."

I looked on at her in amazement.

She didn't know who I was.

It was almost as if years and years of my abuse and maltreatment faded into the sunset because she could not remember what happened. There I sat, in the house where I was destroyed as a child, watching my mother's soul finally exist within inhibitions.

It seemed the woman I knew was gone forever.

My mother rambled on about various different things and would often stare off into the distance. It was disheartening and it was something difficult to swallow.

Seeing her mind deteriorate was painstaking, yet my soul just wanted to weep openly for the memories that trickled from my mind.

The abuse was harsh and painful, yet here I was, sitting perpendicular to the woman who tried to destroy me. Although I hoped that I would eventually hear my mother say precisely why she did what she chose to do to me, the moments were fleeting.

Even if I did confront my mother regarding how she treated me, she would not have understood what was going on. Her life was dramatically different from the woman who raised my sisters and me. My mother's thoughts were compiled of what she could manifest based on her current perceptions.

She looked at me with innocence in her eyes, for she saw me as a man who was helping her, not the one she belittled and bruised in the spiritual sense.

I had to excuse myself after a while and I told her I was going out to get some air.

I hopped in the car and rested my head on the steering wheel.

That night's anxiety attack was the worst I had ever experienced. Usually I can talk myself out of it, but I knew the moment I left the house that it would be a matter of minutes until I just snapped.

I wasn't wrong.

I felt the pangs of pain shooting up my spine. I felt my core fill with magma just before I erupted. The lava flowed through my veins with rigor and persistence. I was gone.

I had been gone for a long time.

I let go and I kept moving forward.

The car and I were out of sync, but I kept driving.

Something inside of me said, "Don't stop, you can make it. You can fight through this." And so, I did.

I was on fire.

I was beyond the point of no return.

I opened my mouth but instead of screams, there was just silence. Even my voice couldn't muster up any comprehension of what was going

Carpe Diem

on. I went into lockout mode with the door swung wide open. Pieces of my shattered existence crumbled before my eyes, and I was picking up my own pieces while more kept crashing down.

Tears gushing from my eyes reminded me I was still alive. I could still feel. Not everything broke down.

There is that Elton John song, "Someone Save My Life Tonight" or something like that… and I didn't need someone… I needed myself.

I pushed myself into the anxiety attack, and I mustered all the strength within to pull myself out.

My mother was not the person who she once was. She was a shell of the person who helped create me.

It dawned on me that if she was able to release the negative energy she once harbored, even though it was due to her deteriorating mental state, and live, then I could do the same.

It was a debilitating and liberating epiphany all at once.

I crashed and rose up all at once.

I shattered and put pieces together instantaneously.

I was my own worst enemy and my hero between heartbeats.

I was prouder of myself than anything or any accomplishment in my life, for I truly saved myself.

I did.

Shattered pieces and all, I was still a hero. I picked myself up and dusted myself off while momentarily dragging myself through the dirt. I had not been okay for a while, but somehow beauty rose out of ashes.

Resiliency was my first name, followed by Not Today and Get Back Up, You're not KO'ed yet.

The angels helped guide me home, whispering all along the way. They sat up above making sure I lived to see tomorrow. And when I walked in the door and caught my glance in the mirror, I did not see faded tears and flushed cheeks. I saw a warrior. I saw a cracked halo. I saw who I was and who I could be. I saw that clinging by a thread meant I was still holding on and tight.

The fight didn't end when my tears started. The river was just flowing in such an uninhibited manner at that point. Yet, I refused to drown. I refused to succumb to the water seeping into the cracks of this boat. I didn't need a life preserver because I can float on my own.

Beautiful Souls

I knew in my heart I would need to stand my ground. I was more powerful than ever. My dreams were just beyond my hand's grasp. And come hell or high water or sleet or rain or ashes… I knew I would not falter.

I was anxiety manifested into hope, and I was not ashamed to step into the light anymore.

I closed my eyes and whispered what I knew the universe was compelling me to say: 'Look out world, for here. I. Come.'

∞ ∞ ∞ ∞ ∞ ∞ ∞ ∞

It was a strange sensation: I wasn't homeless anymore, but I was living with the woman who re-shaped who I could have been if I did not have such a traumatic childhood.

The universe seemed to be working its magic: here I was, back in the house I was thrown out of decades ago, yet the same woman who led to my homelessness is now embodying another consciousness. In this odd twist of events, she was now welcoming me into her home.

It was almost as if my experiences were an infinite loop: every moment would eventually come full circle.

Morena and I continued to build Windows of Opportunity, and she would consistently check in on my mother and me while we worked out of the basement of the house.

My mother would offer snacks while Morena and I were sitting at the table working. It was almost like she was reverting back to my childhood, most likely assuming that I was on a playdate, although the two of us were in the process of changing the world at a dingy kitchen table in College Point.

One day Morena and I heard a knock at the front door. A large letter came in the mail for me and I was unsure of what to think of it.

Morena smiled and prompted me to open it right away.

The letter was addressed to me and had Lincoln Memorial High School's name on it as well.

Upon opening it, I came to the realization that an anonymous person wrote a recommendation letter for the Social Worker of the Year Award for the entire school system.

And by some chance, I won the award.

Carpe Diem

'How could this happen?' I looked over at Morena partially stunned.

"I don't know," she replied. "Maybe someone saw all of your philanthropic work with youth at Lincoln, and realized that you deserve this."

She winked at me and I had a feeling that somehow she was behind it. Morena never did confess it was her, but deep down inside my soul knew the truth.

'I don't deserve it, Morena.' I dropped the envelope down. 'What have I really done?'

"Maybe it's not all about what you have done, but what the kids created."

'What?'

"I can't tell you how many kids you have saved because of your programs. You may not see it, but deep within you I know it is clear."

I dropped the pen I was holding onto the table in a dramatic fashion.

'What is clear? What did I even do?'

Morena's tone grew more solemn. "You created a literal window of opportunity for these kids: programs, friendships, experiences. Without you, where would they even be?"

I looked up at her. 'I don't even know.'

She glanced at me and smiled. "Think of your dreams," Morena motioned to everything on the table. "What do you want your legacy to be?"

I smiled and thought of my dreams: to find divine love, to expand Windows of Opportunity, to reform educational experiences, to create leaders… the list could have gone on and on.

'There's a lot I want to do.'

Morena placed her fingertips on the envelope and slid it closer to me.

"This is *your* window of opportunity. Take it."

∞ ∞ ∞ ∞ ∞ ∞ ∞ ∞

Within two weeks' time, I was standing outside a banquet hall in the middle of Brooklyn. I brought Morena with me, though she made it clear that this was my night to shine.

The two of us stood outside of the building glancing at cars passing by. I wore a midnight blue button-down shirt and sleek dress pants. I

Beautiful Souls

was not sure what the night would entail, but I figured that I needed to dress classy for the event.

Morena could tell I was shaking as we walked closer and closer to the door.

I continued to run my fingers down the front of my hair until she finally pulled me aside.

"Stop," she held her hand in front of me.

'What?' I started fidgeting with my shirt slightly.

"You have to confess something." She motioned for me to stand in front of the mirror.

'I don't understand.'

"Do you ever?"

'No,' I chuckled.

"What do you have to say to yourself?" She pushed me in front of the glass panes surrounding the building and motioned to my reflection.

'Nothing?'

"No," she boomed. "You are earning Social Worker of the Year for a reason. Everyone else can see why, but why can't you?"

'I'm not worthy of it.'

"You preach self-worth like it is gospel, yet when it comes to you, you are silent." She motioned to my reflection again.

'Morena, I-' I turned to her as she placed the palms of her hands towards the sky.

"Place your hands face down and shut your eyes, don't ask questions."

I looked at her and raised an eyebrow, but there was no time to ask questions since the event would be starting soon.

When I slapped my hands on top of hers, it felt like we were transported to another place. A hallowed ringing circulated around in my ears and I suddenly felt at peace. It felt like a pristine white light was glistening overhead.

"Now listen," Morena spoke softly. "What does your soul say?"

I paused a moment, but all I could discern was the resolute silence.

'I don't hear anything.'

"No," she said again. "You aren't listening. What does your soul say?"

I tried to clear my mind, but images of heartbreak and pain flooded my mind. As I started to shake, Morena grabbed my hands tighter.

Carpe Diem

"Breathe deeper, then say something... anything."

As her words trailed off, I opened my mouth and words finally came out:

'All along, I had been trying to fill in the cracks of my soul with people who were endlessly suspended in hollow emotions. I had hoped they would heal me because I had no idea how to heal myself. I developed a learned helplessness from someone else's instruction manual, because I was too afraid to find my own voice.

'The more I read into another person's set of standards, I realized I didn't fit. I was never going to fit. I could roll through countless sheets and mattresses, over tables and torn couches, but I knew I would never be able to rest until I found the one who I could spend the rest of my life loving and caring for. I needed a sign that there was an ounce of hope left in the world, as long as I could see that what I was searching for isn't always what I was looking for.

'I was searching for the answers to my struggle and hardships in the sunken eyes of broken hearts, and I was always willing to destroy myself and hand the shattered pieces of my heart to someone else so they could pick and choose from my broken pieces... so they could mend themselves while I deteriorated. Not a single person accepted all of me for who I was and who I could be, and I had always settled for less than what I ever deserved.

'There is a certain sensation of loneliness you get when you realized that you've been mistreating the one you've loved all along. The one person you are always with, always thinking about, and the one person you should always do what is best for: that person is yourself.

'In hindsight, I see that so much of what I have done may have been hurting other people, but most of all I was damaging my soul. At many points in my life, I gave up on myself. I looked to other people and said, "Heal me, fix me, fill in the loneliness." Only I was never alone, because I was there for myself.

'I saw the good and the bad times. I saw the suffering and the innate pleasures. I watched pain try to swallow me whole, but I always stood with my soul firmly rooted in the ground. As a tall oak tree towers over the rest, I too have seen the rain, the heartache, and the catastrophe try to burden me. Only I knew deep down inside that nothing could move me or shake me.

'I will always grow from the pain and fight the good fight: not with my fists, but with my words and my soul that has been to and through hell and back.

'Still, I am the tree.

'Still, I have and will overcome adversity.

'And as long as I live and breathe that is my mission: to share my positivity and light with the world… no matter how many try to extinguish my flame.

'I was the answer all along; I was just asking the wrong questions. I am the who, the what, the when, the why, and I believed that those women were my "how." All along, I was the answer to my own soul's questions.

'It just took me years to realize that I had the light within me all along.'

A stale pause filled the air as I waited to see what would happen now that I exposed my soul, my true soul. I shifted my gaze to meet Morena's eyes, which were overflowing with tears. I could see the weight of twenty years fall off her shoulders and crash to the floor. I wrapped my arm around her shoulders and pulled her closer to me. Morena's hands floated to my chest as she rested her forehead above my heart. We were completely parallel to one another, and our hearts and emotions were aligned in that moment.

As her tears dripped cautiously, a calm smirk grew on my face as she wept.

'You do understand,' I began. 'That my soul is finally shedding deep-rooted pain. I am growing.'

She began sobbing even more, and despite her intense tears she did not wince once.

'Why are you crying,' I asked.

"Because after all this time, you woke up."

The last particle of sand in the hourglass dropped at the exact moment her last tear fell. Years of ambitions, hopes, and dreams flowed through my mind. The answers were within me; I just had to listen.

We started walking into the building. Our hands swayed like a pendulum keeping perfect time with the universe. For once, I felt true and honest relief. The world became balanced perfectly under my feet. This was an innate love that superseded Elyza, Gemma, Emma, Faith, Olga, and all of the other souls in between. This was true love, and I could finally admit that the relationship was between me, myself, and I. It's true, they were all beautiful souls in their own way: they helped me piece together the puzzle of who I really became, and they brought me along their own paths before dropping me in a sea of loneliness and forcing me to swim to the safest parcel of land. Each time, I was cast back out into the ocean again, only to have someone else hoist me above water before I grew tired and drowned. Then the cycle would repeat over and over again...

Until now.

Once we walked up to the doors, we were thrust into a large crowd that seemed to have hundreds of people gathered around to see the man of honor enter the room. For once, that man was me.

A shorter man in a crisp black tuxedo zoomed to my side, tugging me down a spiral staircase and into a sea of jovial faces. A cacophony of voices filled the air as I was getting rushed from person to person by some man I had never met. Morena faded somewhere into the background as I lost sight of where she was being relocated to. I could not grab her hand and pull her back in.

"Scott," a mysterious man shouted, "Congratulations! I am so proud of all you accomplished." A symphony of formally dressed men and women were patting me on the back and uttering some form of "Congratulations" as I made my way through the room. I felt heavily underdressed.

As people flew up to me, all I could do was smile and pray that everything would be okay. At one point during my confusion and acceptance congratulatory comments, Morena appeared in front of me, almost masquerading as a stranger for a moment, to pat me on the shoulder and murmur, "This is your moment, go!"

She grinned from ear to ear as I walked past her.

As I went up to accept the award, I turned to Morena who was beaming with pride and purpose. She was standing in the shadows of the bright chandeliers suspended from the ceiling.

Her gaze was unlike anything I had seen before.

Later on, I realized that Morena's stare was not new; rather, I was a renewed soul.

I was finally able to see things through a different set of eyes. My new perspective and I received the award and stepped off stage. Others

Beautiful Souls

gathered to obtain their respective awards, so I moved towards the back of the room to find Morena. It was no surprise at all that she seemed to have just disappeared out of thin air.

Though I lingered there for a while to socialize, the questions filling my head were of a higher philosophical nature for a change.

I always considered my thoughts to be insightful and rather bold, but my ambitions were sounding more attainable: education reform was possible, finding my other half was possible, and remaining positive would prove beneficial for Windows of Opportunity.

Despite being in such a jovial state, my lower back continued to throb rapidly.

In hindsight, I realized that this moment must have been my final warning.

In due time I left the banquet hall and found myself resting complacently on the bench outside. My reflection even took on a new persona as I smiled at myself.

When I bowed my head to give thanks to the universe and all of the positive forces brewing within me, I started to murmur to myself:

'God, say your prayers for the lost and lonely. Say your prayers for those battling a war within themselves, yet fighting each day. Say your prayers for those who remain speechless, though there is much left unsaid. Say your prayers for those dying, for those who are deceased. Say a prayer for all of those about to be at peace.'

When I reopened my eyes, Morena was standing directly in front of me. She held out her hand and pulled me off of the bench.

"Congratulations, Mr. Social Worker of the Year," she smiled.

'Thanks,' I replied. As I straightened out my back, I felt the throbbing pain radiate up my spine. My hand instinctively felt out the pain.

"Maybe you should go to a doctor for that?"

'No,' I assured her. 'No, no, I am fine.'

She glanced at me and tilted her head sideways. "Okay then."

'Come on,' I led us down the street. 'Let's go to the diner and talk about future plans.'

The two of us wandered to my car and as I got into the driver's seat, the one question in my mind was: 'What's next?'

Carpe Diem

Morena picked up my award and ran her fingers along the edge of the wooden plaque.

As she admired it, I felt that she was the one who helped me see what I could manifest and create.

She looked over at me and remarked, "You're going to have to put this in a real important place."

We both laughed for a moment and I felt that both of our souls were suddenly elevated. Although Morena seemed like she was not real, and at times appeared to be a figment of my imagination with regard to how quickly she vanished into the shadows, like tonight, I accepted that some of life's mysteries are just meant to be that way.

∞ ∞ ∞ ∞ ∞ ∞ ∞ ∞

After a night of walking by the Brooklyn Bridge and grabbing a bite to eat, I didn't remember precisely how I got home.

When I woke up, I saw Morena in my mother's kitchen making both of us breakfast. The sheet clung to my body as the warmth of the sun slid through the window.

'What happened last night,' I looked at Morena quizzically. I reached for the teacup and sipped gently.

"You finally woke up," she remarked.

Tea shot from my mouth as a smile formed on her exhausted face. A breathy chuckle and sigh escaped her mouth.

Morena looked like she was holding something back. Something huge.

'What are you thinking, Mo?'

"It's nothing important," she broke her steady gaze as her eyes darted to the window.

'Seriously. What?'

"I said it was nothing."

'Mo-'

We paused and she twisted her body towards mine. A sentence fluttered through her teeth and slammed me right in the chest: "What do you want Scott? What do you really, really want?"

We sat parallel to each other on the couch, mirroring a semblance of urgency and compassion.

Every waking thought led to this moment. To this second. To this ounce of hope dwindling in the shadows. Maybe my dreams were foreshadowing something major. Maybe all of these years of questions and ambitions were leading to something completely outrageous and exciting.

"What?" Morena tilted her head and stirred her cup of hot cocoa that was sitting on the table.

'Mo,' I remarked. 'I want to be president.'

"That's a pretty bold statement, Scott." She did not sound surprised.

'I know, but we have so many thoughts about leadership, why not take it to the next level?'

The two of us began to talk about the leadership concepts Windows of Opportunity has been preaching for years. Our insight was our gospel and leadership was our religion.

It is clear that children show us the dysfunction of America. They are the next generation of leaders and revolutionary thinkers who could truly set a new standard for themselves and the universe.

We are doing revolutionary, missionary work. We are the ones we are waiting for. We are the frontlines and the ones who are going to determine what our nation will become. We have to have the hard conversations that may cause plenty of debates, but our words are necessary in order to create monumental changes within our society.

'I need our community to have my back so I can have theirs,' I told Morena.

"Well," she started. "Let's fight for a higher cause and the universe will work itself out. Speak about truth to power."

I reached over to my bag and started to pull out our curriculums and empty notebooks.

'It is time to fight for our planet. To fight back for it. We must fight for our lives. Our individual lives so we can find our individual light. Life loves us. The Universe loves us. So many souls love us. In that exchange of love, we can love the planet back.

Love must be reciprocated.'

Every breath we take, every smidge of food we put into our bodies, enables an infinite amount of opportunities for ourselves and for our planet to thrive. Mutual energy that creates an existence that propels a connection that supports growth, peace, love, and harmony. Together that love storm can accomplish anything, can fight anything, and can transform that energy into everything in this universe.

When you dream of a flame you hope to manifest in the universe, it is possible to make a political vision come true. It could transform the planet.

We are here.

From the birth of this vision, an exponential development of positivity and light will emulate throughout the world.

People do not understand the special vision that exists in society until they live it themselves. They must experience the power deep within them, although there could be moments where they can be brought to their knees.

However, our lives are composed of moments: some beautiful and some that need to be flushed out.

Make every moment count.

Make every second matter.

Every solitary instance is a chance to live.

Frederick Douglass said, *"Education makes you unfit to be a slave."* Currently, we are slaves to the economy, slaves due to a lack of spiritualism, and slaves to a complex world.

We must rise above and build: the pipeline from education to leadership is here. Upon soul-searching and discovering what exists within you, you can find your empowerment as well.

"The time to stand for a higher consciousness is now," Morena's words cut through my train of thought.

'We must close the gap of negative attitudes,' I replied.

My mother wandered through the kitchen and sat down in front of the newspaper.

"Scott," she clamored. "Did you eat breakfast? I made breakfast!"

I was reminded of her mental state and how fragile our souls innately are. Her experience created negative manifestations in my life, but that did not mean I was going to deny myself a beautiful life to be lived.

At that moment, I realized we are all living proof that it is not just another day. Today, every day, is the day to become something or someone positive: individually, we are beautiful creations, and together we can all become a force to be reckoned with.

We must rise up.

Social emotional learning was just a concept, but it is inherent in our souls. We all have it brewing inside us, and we must tap into that energy.

It is not just about education reform, it is about transforming the world.

All of us have potential to learn.

Teachers do not *teach* a subject for a living, they *teach* children.

We can all be teachers of society.

We need curriculums that speak directly to youth; the curriculum has to connect to youth in living color. Their life must be in the heart of the issue. They must see themselves in the work they do. It must be culturally competent and relevant.

Learning must be relevant and responsive to our youth.

Youth are brilliant, but they need the environment to thrive. You need credibility to connect to youth. You must earn it. It doesn't come with a title. You must engage. You must be real. You must bring equity to your classroom and into your life.

You must meet people where they are.

You meet them where they are and pour your soul into their moment, then they will evolve: they will peel back their layers of pain as they realize they are extraordinary. They are impacted by society and situations.

How do we blame them for that? Adults are the same.

We have to close the gap between empowerment and hopelessness; that's how youth, and ultimately society, achieve greatness and excellence.

At this point, Morena and I had all of our papers across the table and were mapping out our framework for education.

It's not about the test grades, it's about whether youth want "it" or not. That "it" can be absolutely anything. The passion burning inside of us for what we wish to create and manifest; that's where the change happens for all of us.

It's in the desire, not the actual grades, it happens as a by-product of soul connections and wanting to enact change.

Live these ideas and the data will come.

"Let's build this framework and it will happen," Morena remarked.

Get excited about connection and learning, and if it means something to you, then you will see change.

Carpe Diem

With excitement brewing in my veins, I gleefully shouted: 'We must be excited for the future in order for transformation to happen now.'

She folded her left leg under her body and leaned closer to the papers as she said, "We must stand on the shoulders of real history. We have to carry the greatness of our country and educators, within schools and within society; they must have the will to be amazing at their craft. It must be about the vision."

Are you a superstar?

Do you want to be a superstar?

You have to be the best version of yourself every single day, second to none.

It's not an ego trip; rather it is a mindset.

The world becomes better because of how we lead.

What mission do you have in life?

What is your mission statement?

This isn't a job. It's not a career.

This is a spiritual mission.

How are you responding to the universe?

What is your role in it?

Do you realize that you matter? For you truly, truly do.

We all do and we are all here.

We have a responsibility to lift one another up, now and always.

Staring off into the distance, you'll see the path in the darkness. You'll see whatever and whoever you need to be or see in that moment.

God gives you whatever you could handle and people don't get that. They think: Why can't I win something nice for once or have something nice for once? You can't get it because you are so much better than that.

You are given what you can handle.

Why can't I have something once that says here: you can handle it? It won't be what you truly deserve… it is like a scrap drawing versus the Mona Lisa or something.

Get what you deserve. Earn it.

While flushing all of this out with Morena, she remarked, "I know you wish you had something decent, someone decent, but it is not a competition."

I had to start truly transcending the man I was. I had to strengthen the bond I had with those who helped me develop.

Beautiful Souls

Naturally, I called Faith and asked her if she would meet up with me as friends.

∞ ∞ ∞ ∞ ∞ ∞ ∞ ∞

The two of us met at a restaurant close to where I worked for a quick bite to eat. Faith seemed genuinely happy to meet me, and we discussed our spiritual friendship.
"The bond we have as friends is truly unique," Faith smiled.
'It's higher consciousness,' I remarked.
"Higher consciousness," she repeated. "I like it."
We had a fulfilling conversation about her new relationships, her children, and all of her plans for her blossoming cleaning business.
'I am so proud that you have been able to grow so much in such a short time.'
"Short time? It's been years and years."
We both grinned at each other sincerely.
'It has been, and we have respectively grown so much over the years.'
"I agree," Faith seemed as if a weight was lifted off of her shoulders, "I agree."
As we walked down the bustling city street, my eye caught a glimpse of curtains rustling in the wind. Faith's words began fading at that point and I felt a tinge of the past over my shoulder. The burden of a past love clung to my spine with such a strong gravitational force.
A scene was materializing over my shoulders: four years ago flooded my mind as I watched the ghosts of a misplaced love echo through the wind. Memories melted into reality as I distanced myself from Faith. I was captured by the naturalistic sway of the billowing curtains.
Two pristine drapes whipped around the French doors of a bar: a scene so familiar to a former version of the man I could have become. Breaking away from Faith, I saw an empty table along the back of a bar. A solitary photograph etched in time reminded me of an era when Emma and I were at that very table. The landscape painted itself before me: her co-workers mingling and moving along while we sat engulfed in each other's exquisite beauty. Her smile and laughter were almost a solid reality, yet I knew that in this present timeline, she was gone.

Carpe Diem

She was a mere apparition clinging to what is left of my shattered feelings towards her. My heart sunk as I saw our scene play out before me... her twirling her hair and leaning into my every whim. The scene was a magical reminder of who she once was and who she never could become.

In a sense, this was her living funeral: the empty table in the present-day image before me was a solemn reminder that she put the nail in her own coffin. Miraculously, she even buried herself: she was that stern in her rejection of our love ever manifesting into more than just a six-month speck on the saga that would be her life.

She meant so much more to me than I did to her. Yet in realizing all of this, the stinging loneliness that once filled my heart when I saw a place where we once stood became enriched with utter hope and devout blessings: it is night and day compared to where my soul now rests its head.

Faith's words grew louder as I re-entered this atmosphere.

"And so I said that all you need to do is just try harder..." her words carried no merit to the expansion of my soul at that moment.

Her words, like dust, settled somewhere in the vacant recess of my mind. I could not process Faith's ramblings while engaging in such a powerful memory. Though in some juxtaposed revelation, it was me who chose Faith over Emma, then decided to go back to Emma, then ran to the arms of Faith and found a stern friendship... and here I am again on this merry-go-round of fleeting adoration: I find myself trapped in the memory of mine and Emma's first passionate evening together...

But that is just what it is: a memory casting its shadows four years too late. That is when I realized saying goodbye was okay.

Saying adios y vaya con dios to Faith would not be in vain. Saying it is just another day would fade into the gossamer corners of my mind. Today would not be just another day.

Today would be the day: the day I discovered that like our love, like the empty table in the bar, memories would fade into the sunset or dance majestically into the wind. Memories would sink into a realm where we could say, "We were here, we made these memories."

And all at once, a rush washed over me: the closure I deserved wrapped itself around my once heaving frame.

The tears dried. The sullen sensation no longer weighed heavy on my soul.

Beautiful Souls

"And what is the deal with lotion anyway, I mean, how many different bottles can advertise silky smooth skin..." Faith's words knocked at my mind, but I would not let them in.

'It is okay,' I whispered just beyond comprehension.

Glaring into the bar I could see Emma's frame fade away. I could sense the past versions of our souls pulling apart and being just that: the past.

The present is now; the future is coming.

There would be no more pain or tears of prevalent sadness flooding my eyes due to a sense of departed longing.

No.

I had everything and anything I needed before me. My eyes finally had the appropriate lens to visualize all I had all along: the strength and love within.

I had the greatest love of all before me. I had the passion, ambition, and stamina at my fingertips.

In that epiphany laced moment, I came to a revelation that-

"Are you even listening, Scott?" Faith tapped her foot in a manner that snapped me back into reality.

"Scott," she quipped, "What is with you?"

A waitress dragged her cloth along the empty table in the bar. The wind died down and dropped the curtains to their resting place.

'What,' I was confused where the last 10 minutes went.

"Scott, you need to listen and pay attention more."

Faith marched forward in her driven state of mind. She ignored my momentary pause outside the bar, for she did not know what reality had just materialized before her...

I was a growing soul with the same respect as the lives that graced my presence.

I walked us back to the car as the street faded to a distant sunset caught in the balance of yesterday and tomorrow.

∞ ∞ ∞ ∞ ∞ ∞ ∞ ∞

Morena and I continued to work in the fading hours of the day. We were working tirelessly on building the framework that we often worked past the moments when dew would form just outside the window.

Carpe Diem

I continued to feel my lower back pain get worse, but I figured that I had to take care of the framework and the future before whatever was ailing me.

The two of us began talking about my past.

We looked at all of my experiences in terms of moments of growth.

'I still believe in divine love,' I told Morena.

"Oh yeah," she smirked. "Well, what is love anyway?"

I turned to her and felt a wave of insight wash over me:

'Love is a drastically dangerous weapon. One moment you think you are enamored by the soul before you, dripping passion and beauty in its most raw form. The next moment, that love you feel stabs you in the back through silent pangs of sunlight that creeps over the daybreak.'

"How insightful," she remarked.

'It is a sinking, devastating feeling... but somehow you lurch forward and try your hardest to keep loving despite having a broken heart. Then you meet another soul you truly connect with. You find someone whose eyes beckon you to bridge the gap between everything you have been through and what you realize you had to deal with in order to get here. You find home within their very soul and comfort in their tender arms. Then it happens again: fate rears its head and twists your soul into a wrought pit of desolation: the love leaves you. Once again, you are homeless.'

Morena dropped the papers in front of her and appeared to be moved by my words.

'You are saddened by the love you thought you had, but lost. Everything and anything seems impossible because the one you thought you adored was a fallacy of epic proportions. You walk the streets alone and seemingly hopeless until you prepare yourself to repeat the cycle again: find love, fall in love... and crash. Crash and burn so deeply and so violently at the feet of someone you thought you loved dearly... and you adorn a mask once again, teardrops straining to inch from your eyelids between moments of desperation: Does anyone love me? Am I ever going to be enough for anyone? Then you look up into the eyes of something or someone who you think could be your home... knowing full and well that you are just steps away from the night crawling into your skin and sucking your heart dry. It is painstaking agony, the act of love. Then one day the mask finally shatters on the floor and you have to face your own reflection in the raindrops before you... what do you do? Well, what... tell me.'

Morena glared into my tear-filled eyes: "You move, and you make a new home. Your real home eventually shows itself in how it genuinely puts your mind at ease. You don't have to run anymore... because you succumb to the comforts of a true soul."

'When,' I shouted at her, 'When does that happen!'

"You'll know," she whispered, "You will know."

We continued to shuffle through papers, until she found something about a peace conference within her pile.

"Hey," she held up the flier. "What's this?"

'Oh,' I looked up and snatched the paper from her hand. 'It's some conference they run every year.'

She looked intrigued. "Who are they?"

'The professional meditation organization I worked with years ago. They were there when I started looking into financial grants for Windows of Opportunity years ago.'

"We should go," Morena said nonchalantly.

'Go? It's always at some rather out-there place.'

"Well, let me look it up," she opened up her computer. "Where is it this year?"

'Who knows, we have work to do.' I continued to shuffle through papers.

She squinted at the screen. "It's on Martha's Vineyard."

'Where's that?'

"Massachusetts," she quipped back. "It is beautiful there."

'Great,' I replied. 'We have work to do. What would we even do at a peace conference?'

"It is a different perspective that we may need for our programs," she paused for a moment to wait for my response. "Come on, Scott. It's a few weeks away and we can talk about the framework there!"

'I don't know, Morena, how do we even get to Martha's Vineyard.'?

She shifted the computer and already had a map in front of us.

"We can take a train and a few buses and a ferry-"

I cut her off. 'Great, we go on some grand amalgamation transportation journey.'

"Ha. That rhymes," she chuckled. "Or we drive up."

'Drive? Why are you so keen on going?'

She seemed to look for a reason. "Because."

'Oh, because, that's a great reason!'

"Just," she seemed frustrated. "Let's go."

Since she was so steadfast in having us go to the conference, I told her that we could go as long as we brought the framework with us. Morena agreed with a devious smile and I squinted at the sight of her sudden jubilation.

'What's that look?'

"Nothing," she spoke nonchalantly. "Absolutely nothing."

Little did I know, Morena must have known what was waiting for me at the conference.

∞ ∞ ∞ ∞ ∞ ∞ ∞ ∞

Days passed and before I could even blink, we were five hours into a road trip to the state of Massachusetts.

Morena sat quietly on the way up, glaring out the window at the lush greenery on the highway. Spring was in full effect and she did not seem to want to miss a moment of its beauty.

We talked about the framework here and there, but she appeared to want to just bask in the glory that was nature. After all, nature is a stunning part of our lives. We must appreciate and give our thanks to what the universe has bestowed upon this planet, for it was created without our afflictions and long before humans materialized on the planet.

The ferry to Martha's Vineyard required that we store the car at a commuter lot in Woods Hole, Massachusetts. It was a quaint town that boasted its oceanic center and delicious food.

On the ferry over, Morena disappeared into the crowd on the boat. I figured that she was enjoying the wind rushing through her hair on the top deck of the boat.

I sat with my arms leaning on the railing, gazing out into the Atlantic Ocean.

The chapter that was the church slammed shut, and all that remained was the hope that the peace conference I would be attending in just a few days on Martha's Vineyard would provide some semblance of transformational guidance.

Things just had to go up from here.

They have to.

When we arrived on the island of Martha's Vineyard, the building where the peace conference was seemed a lot closer than I imagined it would be. It was a beautiful building with ornate architecture and such a breathtaking view.

People were walking around and socializing, and before we all knew it, leaders from around the globe managed to find each other on this stunning island.

Hours were passing before us, but time stood still in the room where peaceful meditative activities were transcending the hearts, minds, and souls of the people there.

As we all spoke in small groups, I looked across the room at someone who seemed captivated by my presence.

Her whimsical nature captured every last crevice of my soul. A sense of belonging filled every broken piece of me in a manner I never truly fathomed before this moment. Her hair swayed rhythmically to every passing heartbeat that radiated through my core. She had a smile that only angels could concoct with their harmonious ways. She was not real. She could not be.

This angelic figure had to be yet another figment of my imagination manifesting before my very weary eyes.

The figure glanced at me and my heart melted. My soul erupted in a melodic sigh of "at last," for I realized that this beauty before me was real.

She existed.

She was not a figment of any imagination or any realm: she was grace, poise, and elegance wrapped up in a solitary human being.

She was what I had been looking for, not searching for.

My mind was confused beyond any comprehensible notion, for her energy could never be duplicated or felt the same, synergistic way ever again. With the curling motion of her pointer finger, I shot across the room as if I were on a string, tied mercilessly to her heartstrings.

"I have been trying to get you close to me all day," she spoke in breathy, hushed tones.

Carpe Diem

I sat motionless. I could feel the presence of the universe around me, smiling: her resolute grin... reminding me that I had a life left to live. Her aura escalated and permeated the room.

"I'm Layne, and you are?" A sense of anticipation hung on her lips as she leaned in closer to my gravitational energy.

'Scott,' a smile crept along my face, 'I'm Scott.'

My life would never be the same.

CHAPTER 8

You Gave Me Her

"Take your time, don't live too fast. Troubles will come and they will pass. You'll find a woman and you'll find love. And don't forget that there is a someone up above… All that you need now is in your soul… Don't you worry. You'll find yourself. Follow your heart. And nothing else. And be a simple kind of man. Be something you love and understand."

- Lynyrd Skynyrd, Southern Rock Band, Jacksonville, Florida

Beautiful Souls

Within an instant, our souls collided.

When I looked into her jade eyes, it was as if the entire universe grabbed me by the shoulders and said, "Stop searching, because she is the one."

No one else mattered.

Nothing else mattered.

The years upon years of misery and impatience were symbols that someone greater than I could have ever imagined would walk into my life. Her presence was strong enough to entice me from across a crowded room of people. It was an energy and a vibrancy that no other human being had ever provided me.

In an instant, everything suddenly made sense. I finally had an answer to all of the questions that were once lingering in my soul. I had a finite sense that there are people out in the world whose souls can burn just as bright and in tandem with yours. The sun's bright potential would not shine with nearly enough fortitude now, for her undying beauty and brilliance eclipses utterly anything that could be produced in the universe.

Every solitary question that once flooded my head manifested into a sign. Her aura was not one to be trifled with or touched, for it was the penultimate experience to compliment a soul who was in the process of developing the most optimal form of higher consciousness.

Each breath that flowed from her mouth was significant; for it meant that she was bound to move a step closer to breathing life into the world's consummate healing aura. As the two of us spoke for the first physical time in this realm, it seemed as if we had met a thousand times before. The passion and energy from both of us combined was reminiscent of lifetimes of budding, building, and blooming into the most decadent roses to grace this universe.

When we looked at each other, it seemed like the two of us were rekindling an old flame that existed throughout the permeable course of history. In this lifetime, however, it just took a little bit longer for the two of us to find each other. Still, we were the chosen ones. We were expected to converge upon each other at a specific point in time: the moment when both of our souls were undeniably ready to enact change in this universe.

The progressive, passionate, and monumental changes were about to grace this world with the necessary amount of energy to substantiate comprehensible action within the universe.

Combined, we would light up the world.

Together, we could construct previously unimaginable enlightenment for ourselves, and the respective souls in this universe.

For years upon years, I was asking all of the questions that would lead me to her.

Days would pass in my own world; my soul would wallow in enough agony and challenges that would shape the man I would become. Everything in the world had to be just right. Everything had to be just perfect so that once the two of us rightfully found one another, we would be able to spark the revolutionary shifts needed to elevate our planet.

We had to respectively evolve before the two of us could revolutionize the universe cosmically manifesting before us. Individually, we had to align our souls so that once our respective souls met again, this time we would get it right. This time we would take the innate experiences from centuries of walking this Earth in order to create. Moments that would develop our pioneering sensibilities had to come before us, so that we could utilize the aftermath to grow this universe.

It was a matter of finding the appropriate sensations: two people needed to endure and overcome aspects of their respective journeys, so that the world would be able to heal.

We healed so that we could harbor the strength to inspire positivity and purpose.

Although my soul was suddenly soothed in her presence, it burned with the fervor to comprehend that I finally found the one.

I finally found her.

"You have a story to tell, I am sure of it," Layne spoke in a manner that enticed me. I always stood behind the philosophy that everyone has a story behind their story, and here she was: asking me about who I was.

I wanted to hear about her story. I wanted to know each and every aspect of who she was: Where did she come from? How did she find me at the right moment? Why did it take her so long to discover me?

I guess the last question is, in a sense, a moot point. She was traveling on her own journey so that once the timing was right; we would know that we found each other.

And we should never let go.

My mind faded back into the conversation.

'My story? What about yours?'

Picturesque memories of her life seemed to flash before my eyes. She began to tell me bits and pieces of who she was and what she was building.

"I am a writer," she pulled a notebook from her bag and dropped it on the table. "It's always been my dream to get published, but I haven't gone anywhere."

'Why not?'

Layne shrugged, "I think I have good ideas, but I have a feeling it isn't my time yet. I came here today to meet my favorite author, he was supposed to be here at this conference, but he cancelled at the last minute. That's just my luck."

My heart was palpitating, but it was not out of panic: it was a sense of sheer admiration. She would be the window of opportunity that beckoned my soul to reach its utmost level of higher love.

"Where do you come from?"

'New York.'

"That's exciting," she leaned towards me and grabbed my hand. "I have always wanted to see New York. Tell me, is it as wonderful as they say it is?"

I looked down at our adjoined hands, which tingled with promise. 'It's magical.'

As I glanced up at her, we locked eyes and practically said, "I know you," but without our words.

Our souls were speaking to one another in a manner that transcended all of the idle chatter dancing about the room.

The energy between us beckoned me to dig deeper into the seemingly instant connection we appeared to have.

"I am from Martha's Vineyard."

'That's exciting.'

"That's exciting? It's a rather small place."

'It is beautiful,' we locked eyes again. I paused. 'The island.'

"We are a few hundred miles from New York, you know."

'Oh yeah, the drive up here was beautiful.'

"I am sure of it. I heard the foliage along the highway is gorgeous."

Though it seemed like we were engaging in somewhat nonchalant chitchat, every word she spoke carried a purpose. She did not waste her breath on anything that did not carry the weight of her passion.

'This author that you were following here, is he someone I may know of?'

"I don't think so. He was a local here on Martha's Vineyard for years until his books became incredibly popular. I was hoping that I could talk to him and see how he managed to get his writing out there for the world to see."

'That's exciting.'

A breathy laugh escaped her lips. "Do you think everything I say is exciting?"

Instinctively, my soul responded: 'Yes.'

We both chuckled and leaned closer to each other. Eyes around the room seemed to be entranced by our energy.

"I hope I am not being too forward in saying this, but it feels like I have known you forever, Scott Matheson."

'It feels like I have known you forever too, Layne-' I struggled to search my mind for her last name.

"Don't worry," she smiled. "We didn't exchange last names, I read your name badge."

'Oh,' I laughed. 'I wasn't worrying.'

"I know." A pause allowed us to collect our respective thoughts before we dove deeper into who we were.

Individually, the two of us were attempting to restructure systems; she aimed to write about shifting systems and what the world was truly about below the surface. I shared I was working on education while she explained she wanted to overhaul every system imaginable through her words and insight.

"Surprisingly, I did not consider the education system," she began. "I am largely self-taught. I needed to get a full-time job to support my father and my younger sister. I would buy old textbooks from college bookstores and teach myself. I would sit and rewrite the pages for days in between serving tables at an Italian restaurant."

'You are self-taught? That does not surprise me.'

We smiled again. Being innately happy was not difficult to do around her. Actually, it was an invigorating feeling. She was indifferent to the past I endured. Rather, she made an effort to learn about my experiences.

"I want to know all about you."

'What's there to know?'
"Everything."
'Everything?'

The two of us were tasked with presenting our thoughts about peacefulness. The activity required that we write out our ideas on a massive piece of chart paper and talk about it with other people in the room.

As the two of us discussed our insight, all eyes were on us.

The flow of energy between us took on a synergistic light: it was almost as if we always collaborated on projects together.

Once the two of us moved off to the side of the room, I felt my cell phone vibrate in my pocket.

'I don't know how much time you have.'
"Time is irrelevant when you create a soul connection."

She felt it too.

My cell phone vibrated in my pocket again.

I was trying to stay consumed by her energy, but the third phone call piqued my interest.

Rebecca was calling and needed me to come home. Our mother was throwing a tantrum and she didn't know what to do.

For some reason, the universe was pulling me away from Layne for a temporary interlude. However, our intricate melody had just begun.

I found myself missing her presence the moment we physically stepped away from each other.

"Until we meet again, Scott Matheson."

Her eyes clung to me until I left the room.

I walked outside and found Morena alone with her thoughts.

'What are you doing?'
She looked up. "What?"
'You missed her!'
"Her who?"
'Layne.'
"Is she the woman who was watching you from across the room practically all day?"
'You saw her looking at me? Why didn't you say anything?'
"I don't know. I didn't want to interfere."
'With what?'

She quipped back, "What?"

'Why are you so weird?'

"It is who I am." She extended her arms and plopped down on the curb next to a stunning patch of sunflowers.

I bent down next to her and told her about my mother and how we reluctantly had to leave.

The two of us walked back to the dock to catch the ferry.

A familiar voice cut through the crowd.

"Scott!"

I pivoted to see Layne dashing up the path.

'Hey stranger, I haven't seen you in so long.'

She chuckled and put her hand on my shoulder as she adjusted her high heels.

'I want you to meet-' I turned around to introduce Morena, but she had vanished.

How typical.

"Meet who?" She looked past my shoulder at the apparition of the woman who managed to be more mysterious than the woman before me.

'Nevermind, I guess.'

"Okay," she looked up at me. "Sorry to chase after you. I didn't give you my business card."

It was a stunning picture of her with her information plastered along the edges of the card. I handed her my card in return.

'It's a bit lackluster, but you can't really compete with such a perfect picture.'

She giggled. "You're too kind."

We parted ways and I heard her heels click as she receded from the wooden planks of the dock.

I found Morena sitting against the railing of the boat looking out into the water.

'Why do you keep disappearing like that?'

"Some things are better unseen than seen."

I rolled my eyes as the ferry's horn sounded in anticipation of our departure.

Once we made it back to the car, we had a grueling five-hour car ride back to New York. The entire time, I could not stop thinking of

Layne. Something drew my soul to hers, and I was destined to find out what it was.

∞ ∞ ∞ ∞ ∞ ∞ ∞ ∞

Walking out of the car, I felt a finite sense of peace. I think it was peace of mind, yet when I crawled onto the couch and shut my eyes, all I could see was a silhouette of her figure laying next to mine.

Was she really there?

Did she exist?

I reached out to grasp her but realized her image was a farce.

She faded into the darkness like she did hours earlier. I could not make sense of Layne, even in the slightest bit.

With my mother out cold for the time being, I got dressed again and left.

I started driving around as thoughts of the past weekend pounded through my mind. I needed to think. I was utterly confused and conflicted and I did not know which way to turn.

I drove aimlessly as questions flooded my mind. Global leadership, the planet, purpose, and profit were on the forefront of my every move.

My car squealed as it approached Francis Lewis Park. I had to get some clarity since I was fearful of falling back into the same dreaded routine. This time, I did not want my heart shattered to pieces. After all, it was already decimated more times than I could count.

The bridge was illuminated in its sparkling blue, yellow, and red lights. A calming sensation washed over my body as I perched myself upon the dimly lit benches. As I inhaled and exhaled repeatedly, I began to whisper my gratitude into the universe. Everything and anything I could be grateful for escaped my pursed lips.

I was not sure exactly what happened, but I needed to just talk.

My connection with the universe appeared to have brought me to the conference and welcomed Layne into my life at a quintessential moment.

When I actually sat down and thought about it, it was a combination of the universe and Morena who brought me to that conference. She was the one who pushed for us to go there.

It is yet another example of why she seemed too good to be real. Morena is number one on my gratitude list; without her unconditional and insane compassion for who I am, I doubt I would have made it this far in life.

"Some things are better unseen than seen;" Morena's words rang throughout my head.

There is power in alignment. There is a certain intrigue in seeing someone from across a crowded room and suddenly recognizing their soul.

The lyrics to Bayside's "Landing Feet First" began making sense to me:

> *"I hope you weren't waiting long*
> *I hope this night makes up for time lost*
> *Feels like I met you years ago*
> *And we're picking up right where we left off."*

The sensation was truly uncanny.

We made each other laugh in a manner that was both infectious and made my soul smile. Parts of me wanted to write to her and say:

"From the moment I laid eyes on you, I haven't stopped thinking about you. Your face, your eyes, your beautiful heart. You inspired a light to shine within me, when I didn't think it was ever possible to see that light shine again. Only it isn't just shining… it is gleaming. It is beaming. It is brighter than I had ever imagined. It is all because of you.

When our eyes met, my soul's prayers were finally answered. With every word that flowed out of my mouth, you became the rhyme and the reason. My entire world was in alignment for the first time in my entire life. I had gone through fire and fury just to find you. I would survive through all of my struggles and sacrifices an infinite number of times if it just meant to see you smile at the end of my journey through it all.

You came in just when I was losing hope and faith. You are a miracle embodied in perfect harmony… yet you are miles away."

I deleted the message from my phone upon reading it over again. After the intense pain I went through with Emma, I could not fathom feeling such desolation again.

I had to wait.

Out of necessity, I needed to ensure my soul would not be smashed to bits once again. Adversely, her soul could not be harmed either.

Beautiful Souls

She is too precious of a beautiful being to endure absolutely anything I experienced. Then again, I didn't fully know her past at that point: she could have been living a similar timeline to mine, and as a result, we found each other.

I thanked the Circle of Angels for the blessings bestowed upon me and stood up. My drive home to College Point was oddly soothing, and by the time I made it into the house, the sunrise painted the sky with vivid and monochromatic hues.

A new day had come, literally.

∞ ∞ ∞ ∞ ∞ ∞ ∞ ∞

I must have passed out on the couch, for although it seemed like I blinked, I imagined Morena was driving along a cobblestone-paved road somewhere in Massachusetts.

Angels were circling our car, singing something while floating around us. Morena stopped for a moment and opened the window. An angel reached in and grabbed my face, and told Morena to drive.

It started raining and Layne got into the car. We had to go find someone and bring them somewhere. We drove for a while talking about random things, until Layne turned to Morena and said, "Does he know?"

I responded, "Does he know what?" I glanced at Morena and then looked into Layne's eyes.

She whispered, "Your secret is safe with me" and winked.

I didn't know what she meant by that. The radio came on and the angels started circling the car faster. They kept saying, "wake up, wake up, wake up."

So, I did.

∞ ∞ ∞ ∞ ∞ ∞ ∞ ∞

The moment Rebecca came in from work, I rushed to Alley Pond Park.

For a while I sat with my back against the fence glaring out into the lush greenery in front of me. I tried imagining what life would have been if my aunt hadn't left me.

How do you go from being on top of the world to being cut down within a simultaneous swoop?

It is painstaking. It is agonizing to lose someone… yet it is virtually healing. Through loss, an angel is gained. Through sacrifice comes unwavering liberation. Between the pangs of our rapidly beating hearts, there is peace.

There is a moment to begin again - a split second to reflect on the air you consume and the negativity you dispel.

It is a feeling far beyond gratitude: you are built up and broken so you may grow again.

Glow sticks are merely chemical-filled tubes until they are snapped and shaken. Once broken, they are not destroyed, for rather they are given the opportunity to provide a soft light. The neon coloration fills the air with hope and promise that you, too, can be broken and shine even brighter than anyone could imagine. That is the beauty of pain: as we rebound, we develop our renewed foundation.

We lay the bricks and reconstruct our souls.

We have the power to shift the universe based on how we lose and how we enhance each other's spiritual journey.

After all, the beauty of life can be found in the darkest corners of the world: it is just a matter of creating your own light to obscure the past and illuminate the present.

Morena appeared at the picnic bench in the blink of an eye. I didn't even see her arrive or walk over.

"Why are you sitting on the ground, Scott?"

'I don't know.'

"You are deep in thought; you are downloading some sort of message… I see it. I feel it."

'I don't know how to tap into this part of my soul,' I told her. 'All I know is a layer has been ripped wide open; exposing my awareness to a realm of my soul I wasn't aware existed. The alignment, the energy, the connection, was beyond real.'

Morena looked at me and rolled her eyes.

'What?'

"I despise that the limited words of our English language cannot capture the right sensation."

'I guess you're right,' I stood up and leaned against the fence. 'It was magical, compassionate, synergistic. It was like two lost souls found each other and instantly went back to work together.'

"From what you are saying, it seems like she echoed that sentiment."

'You know,' the two of us started walking up the path. 'I trust the universe. It brought me her.'

I could not help but wonder if my mind was playing tricks on me:

Did I imagine all of this?

What was I missing?

I felt lost.

It seemed like I was on the verge of feeling love again, but how was it possible to find such a rare soul like the one I found in Layne?

This was not an accident.

It felt good to be genuinely and holistically happy for a change. Though I was in the process of growing my soul, and I knew that a person alone does not make you happy, something about her was mesmerizing.

In the days that followed, Layne did not text me. She appeared to have been too busy creating something powerful, which, in hindsight, was phenomenal.

When Layne puts her mind to something, her soul and heart follow in such an exponentially groundbreaking way.

Morena and I ruminated on the connection I had with Layne.

"I see it, I saw her. She acknowledges your soul," Morena spoke as if she was speaking a prophecy.

'Have you ever traveled somewhere and never wanted to return? That is what life feels without her now.'

Morena tilted her head and chuckled.

'What?'

"Patience, dearie. Have patience."

As the dull, mundane normalcy seeped into my day, it appeared that life without Layne was beckoning me to re-think my daily habits.

I would go to work, help the youth develop insight into the world around them, then retreat to my mother's house where Morena and I would collaborate on shifting the education system.

Each night I would dream of the woman who resurrected parts of me that I never knew existed.

In this dream, I sat in the car next to Bryan. He was trying to say something to me, but I abruptly silenced him. I knew the two of us should have sped away from the scene, but a storm was encircling us.

It was too intense and visceral not to watch it.

We were right in its path.

As a cyclone crept inches closer to my car, I turned to see if we could outrun it. It was a total loss.

The storm ripped through the car and I could feel my entire body convulsing. The vibrations were beautiful, yet tragic at the same time.

I wondered what was happening to my body, both in the physical and emotional senses.

I woke suddenly from the nightmare, only to realize that I was suspended in time. The night air hung my soul out to dry, and I wasn't able to process what had just happened, what I felt, and what was real.

Looking to my right, I saw the wallpaper peeling as it always does. To my left, a faint ghost of who I was merely 10 days ago.

Everything seemed so raw.

My lips were arid and stiff.

I grasped at the water on the table and toppled it over in my nauseated state. The clinking noises startled me and I jumped up.

The neon glow from the clock burst forward 3:15 A.M.

One more hour of sleep... would it be sleep?

Would I just toss and turn while thinking of her?

This loss could be the end.

Yeah, I get it; I was being dramatic.

I was not speaking about the death of me; I mean the death of my soul. She was extremely close and she was right there.

How do you go from lost to found to lost again?

How did she manage, like water, to slip through my fingers?

Maybe she is just as fluid as I am: having to constantly change with the ebb and flow of the tide.

Maybe she, like Morena, is just a ghost of a manifestation of my hopes, dreams, and fear wrapped up in one. Yet, Morena said she saw her... do ghosts see ghosts?

Layne is real, and I didn't know how or why, but I was drawn to her existence. She was the Massachusetts version of me.

Beautiful Souls

At the time I wondered: Does she remember I exist?

Does she lay awake at 3:15 A.M. thinking of me, too?

"Once changed, never the same," rattles around in my head, bouncing between my eyes like a basketball… and the weight feels just as severe.

I prayed to the universe: 'Layne, if you can feel this vibration reverberating through your body, hear my prayer: Come home. Come back to me.'

My eyes drooped again and my head hit the pillow with a resounding thud.

There is a theory that each and every fiber that exists on this planet is a manifestation of stardust. We are inherently magic creatures, built with the intention of spreading our light into the hearts of others who we encounter.

Sometimes, the combination of two souls creates a supernova: a star that suddenly increases in its brightness because it has been impacted by an explosion of some sort.

What was once dark becomes illuminated by the creation of something majestic in nature. We have the inherent power to create that magic and have it radiate into the souls of billions of people on this planet.

Our vision can develop the space necessary to shine brighter than anything anyone could have ever imagined.

We can provide clarity to the blind ambitions that exist out in this world, and could help these ambitions become quintessential stars that ignite a passion bright enough to light up the sky.

I wondered: How can I unsee what I have now seen? How can I unknow what I now know is the truth within my soul?

∞ ∞ ∞ ∞ ∞ ∞ ∞ ∞

Later that evening, I sat on the bench in Alley Pond Park for a while. I kept looking at my watch. I sat tapping my fingers nervously on my knee. I convinced myself she had to show up. She had to. I shut my eyes for a moment and she appeared.

"Hello Scott," broke the still silence in the park.

'I didn't know if you would get the message,' I said, looking deep into her eyes. They were a soft hazel. She smiled and extended her hand.

"You want to talk, let's talk." Aunt Barbara held my hand and hoisted me up.

We walked down the trails in the rainy weather, leaves crunching beneath our feet.

"Now is not the time to take life for granted," she said wistfully.

'I know,' I responded, 'I need your help.'

She smiled and laughed a little. "You, of all people, need my help. That is why you called me?"

'I need all of the angels, please, please please,' my cries became more desperate.

She patted my back and we kept walking. "You will be okay, my son."

I denied that to an extent and she laughed.

We kept walking on the path.

I asked why I was going through so much confusion, and she responded, "Because this is your experience."

A man stood there, in the park, looking at me with tears in his eyes. I didn't know who he was. He put his arm around me in unison with Aunt Barbara.

He explained that I didn't know him, but he knew me well. He said that I was an investment and quite a tough cookie to convince.

We spoke for a while longer, and he told me that he needed me to stay strong and listen to the universe.

Aunt Barbara nodded in agreement.

Then she said, "How is she?"

'She who,' I responded.

"Judy, how is my baby sister?"

I thought that she was older than my aunt, but I guess not. I responded that she had her good days and bad days, but I think she is okay.

Aunt Barbara smiled.

We spoke a while longer about what I can do to keep the people I cared about safe.

She told me, "Go the distance and go to a doctor before it is too late."

'Too late for what?'

"Goodbye my sweet boy."

I shouted after her as she began receding: 'Too late for what?'

When I turned around, my backpack was on my shoulder and a bicycle was resting next to me. As I put my hands on it, I looked up and saw a sign: Route 118.

Though I was confused, I seemed more exhausted and delirious.

I didn't really know where I was going, but I was trying to find my way home. I rode the bicycle until I came to a dirt road that led towards the woods. It was not picturesque. However, the dirt was solid enough to walk on.

As I looked down the road, someone ran into me and stole my bicycle, my backpack, and for some odd reason, my passport. It seemed like I was in the middle of England.

I walked back out of the trail towards the main road. The people walking around appeared to be robotic and unnatural.

Then my parents suddenly appeared.

'Mom? Dad?'

"We came to rescue you," my father said. My mother was clutching his arm anxiously.

"We were concerned about you, darling," my mother reached out to touch my cheek.

'I'm fine, I don't need you.' I pushed past them and tried moving forward.

"Son," my father rushed after me. "You have to protect yourself."

'I'll be fine.'

"You're going to die if you don't take care of yourself," my mother shouted.

'Leave me alone!'

When I turned around, they were gone. I didn't understand what my mother was talking about.

'This is just a bad dream, it has to be,' I spun around and saw Morena standing by a coursing river.

As I approached her, she turned and handed me her notebook.

'Why are you giving this to me now? What else is in it?' I took it from her cautiously.

She looked me in the eyes and hugged me tight. Morena whispered in my ear: "Keep the faith, Scott."

When I pulled away from her, I was alone again.

I didn't want to lose my backpack, my identity, then end up lost in the woods in a foreign land.

I didn't want my parents to come rescue me.

'I'm not ready,' I told myself.

My eyes jolted open and I felt like I had to go to the bathroom. As I watched the blood pool in the toilet, I knew that something was terribly wrong.

When I told Morena what happened, she appeared to hold back tears.

'I am going to go to the doctor in a few hours,' my tone was solemn and I couldn't ascertain what she was thinking.

"Here," she passed me her notebook from her bag. "Read this when you are settled in the waiting room."

When I arrived at the doctor in the afternoon, I was not sure what to say. My mind was racing and I felt like my heart was about to burst from my chest. It was not normal to urinate blood, but then again, my life was never normal.

I crossed my ankles and put the clipboard filled with medical forms on the chair next to me.

Morena bookmarked a spot towards the middle of the book, which read:

"We have the power to create the life we want to live: it all comes down to the opportunities we choose to align ourselves with. There will always be obstacles thrust in our path and there will always be distractions. We will consistently feel as if life is flying by and we are too busy to accomplish everything we would like to in a time frame that would be ideal for us.

However, do not assume that you have no time for something or someone: it is just a matter of realigning your priorities. What is most important to you? If you can logically define what you want or need then stop stalling and go get it. Stop waiting around for the day for things to just appear in front of you. Surround yourself with people who will help get you closer to your dreams.

You can fantasize about what you want, but if you just keep thinking about it and refuse to do anything to get it, then that is your loss.

Yoda says, "Do or do not, there is no try." Either you give it your all, or you allow yourself to fall. Hard work and unwavering dedication are necessary in order to achieve. Hold firm to your values and beliefs.

Once the path begins to get treacherous and more difficult, then you know you have something worth pursuing, something worth fighting for.

Do not lose sight of your mission, your vision, and your overall goal.

Never settle for something second rate or minor, when you know you are born to make a major shift in this universe.

Exude positivity and actually practice what you preach.

Life is most difficult for those who can handle clinging tightly to their hopes and dreams. Go for it, you do not know what will happen until you take a chance.

What are you waiting for?"

I shut the book just as my name was called to see the doctor.

∞ ∞ ∞ ∞ ∞ ∞ ∞ ∞

"So, what did the doctor say?" Morena looked up from her lasagna, but she kept dragging her fork along the plate.

'He told me that I would get the blood test results in a few days.

"Oh," she dropped her eyes towards the plate. "Okay."

'Hey, your entry was really powerful. I didn't read anything else, but what else am I allowed to read?'

She took the notebook from me and shuffled through it for a bit.

"Here," she passed it back to me. "Read page 88. I wrote it from your perspective. It is what I sense you feel about Layne."

I took it from her and squinted to read her words:

'*Unconditional love is the most exhilarating feeling in the world. To have someone look at you and see the real you is a blessing. I can't describe it, but a weight is lifted off my shoulders. I float; I fly. You are my wings. No matter what, those moments elevate me. Excite me. Your glances remind me why I do what I do... most of the time it is because that look in your eyes makes me melt.*'

I looked up at Morena, who was sitting on her folded legs to get a better glimpse at how far down I was reading.

I continued to read:

'Your warmth and my frigid exterior make me breathe again. It is a balance. I could never replace that feeling. It is beautiful in every sense of the word. No matter what, I know you see the real me for who I am. You see more of me than anyone. For that I am truly grateful. I love you for when you speak about your past and future, because you show how much you have grown. You show me life's greatest blessings. You make me a better person. Romance novels and movies are drastic exaggerations of love, but you my dear are real. Real in every fiber of everything you do.

'You are more than an angel. People are intimidated by what they don't know. You know me and yet you are drawn in closer.

How?

Why?

What makes you remove all bias and see a tattered, crushed soul?

'Sometimes, when you aren't looking, I glance at you to take in the breathtaking wonder that is your energy. I respect that energy. I respect your will, your tenacity, and your idealism. I love every inch of every part of you. You are destined for greatness.

'You are the sun, the stars, the whole galaxy and universe in one. You light up the darkness and I light up yours, and I am grateful we shine bright together.

'Nothing can replace the way I feel when I cross your mind. I feel you thinking about me. I yearn to be a thought in your existence.'

Morena cleared her throat and read the final line, which was further down on the page than the rest of her writing:

"I am but a mere shadow in the glory that is you, for my light shines so you can see the way."

I wiped the tears from my eyes.

'Wow Morena, that's breathtaking.'

She took the notebook from my hands. "Thank you."

Morena sat back down and tucked her coy smile into her right shoulder.

This was the first year I prayed with the intent to manifest holistic positivity.

Beautiful Souls

I prayed that there is no pain; I prayed that there is peace. I prayed that there is wisdom and I prayed there is faith. I prayed that there is hope and joy and laughter everywhere.

I prayed for a better present, for each day is a gift. I prayed we would find solutions to the world's concerns.

I prayed to empower. I prayed to encourage leaders. I prayed to become a better person. I prayed I could overcome anything. I prayed I could become stronger. I prayed for the beauty that is family. I prayed to create a world where our children could be proud of the strides we make as a nation each day.

I prayed for justice. I prayed for peace. I prayed for humanity, civility, honor, light, stamina, resiliency, and beyond.

I prayed that the world would heal. I prayed. I prayed not in a church or a temple or a mosque, but I prayed in a school, out of a school, and someday, we will pray together as one.

Amen.

On living and loving, there are so many thoughts that came to mind. Love is not defined by words; it is defined by actions. I have all too often heard someone say, "love you," in passing to someone, but it seems that "love you" has just become a superficial utterance that people toss around like a ball during recess: people don't really use it to show devotion to one another, and then they reminisce about the "good ol' days" at recess when they used to run around.

Recess is a beautiful thing, sure, but you always have to go back into school.

In hindsight, are kids thinking about whether or not they utilized every moment from recess to the best of their abilities? I doubt it, because self-reflection is something that is developed over the course of a lifetime… and not just in the elementary school years. I think about recess in the context of love: did I cherish every moment of it? Did I really take it all in: every smile, every laugh, every movement and sensation? Or did I, too, take it for granted, like recess?

I wondered if I could go back in time, would I change everything… I say I wouldn't, because I see myself now and genuinely smile at everything I have become. Sometimes, I can't help but look back at all the different someone's I have become: a mask here, a mask there, a glimmer of the real me shining through for a moment. I chose this path, regardless. There is no one to blame but myself, in all honesty. We love in every language as we go throughout life, and that echoes what I wrote long ago: "If you love in every language, at some point your music will be loud enough for someone to hear."

But did I hear it? Now I do.

I realize that the person that has come in second place is myself. Everyone else has heard my love first and foremost. People have experienced my love and my life, as I have over the years, but I think, while I am sitting alone in someone else's living room, that I need to love myself way more.

I am older now. I am here now. I am committing my love to fighting for the greater good. Unwavering. This moment on. That's it. I love myself through helping others. So what if I am in second place?

I think of all of the seconds that brought me to this moment: the moment I shed my second skin and just flow into myself. Face the music. Face the facts. Face everything as I always have, but face it with another's hand in mine.

About 7 hours remained on that day.

I stood there, about to shed a layer.

I knew this is what I must do and had to do for the betterment of my life. There was no turning back, for everything is "if it is meant to be, it will be."

And so it goes… and so it will be…

And I'm not alone.

Never. Again.

∞ ∞ ∞ ∞ ∞ ∞ ∞ ∞

My perspective on life changed after I left the church, and before then I wasn't counting my blessings, though I began to start appreciating them. All of them. Every ounce of me and within every second that passed, I began cherishing life. It was another chance, another opportunity, and another mark on the timeline to become a stronger person.

Strength has no limits, but tolerance for negativity does.

Beautiful Souls

We have been given a beautiful gift: 365 new days, with 365 new chances to blossom, to pursue our ambitions, and to create opportunities from the ashes of fireworks that light up the sky. In times of celebration, fireworks dust the sky with their aura of beauty. Thousands of chemicals are compounded into tubes, and forced to burst miles above where they were placed. Under pressure and in absolute duress, the fireworks created a magical glimmer that brought joy and hope to billions of people across the globe. With the forthcoming 365 days, it is possible to carry on the light that you saw when the 365 days started.

Manifest that light within your own soul.

Convert the thousands of chemicals that burst in the sky and reflected in your eyes into love, passion, beauty, empathy, hope... and transform it into whatever you needed to be or hear this past year. Grow. Blossom. Burst and let your energy seep into the eyes of those around you. Let them gaze upon your inner power and your beauty. Fireworks are built to explode once and drift away, but you are different. Be the magical, beautiful, out of the box soul that you are. Be passionate about what sets your soul aflame.

Seize the day and seize every single opportunity that brings you to the next level. Shine daily with the warmth and compassion that radiates from you. You have to let your positive vibes grace this world.

No matter what obstacles you face, no matter what setbacks may fall in front of you, allow passion to be the center of everything you do. Let every window of opportunity become wide open... and let it stay that way.

Delve deep into the recesses of your mind. Find peace and devout bliss in the seconds that pass. There is much to overcome and disavow. You must pull all the strength from within you. Find your balance. Seek solace in who you are and your experiences. you have the cloak of protection, yes, but there needs to be something else: a mental protection or a calming of sorts.

My train of thought halted abruptly when the phone rang. The results came back from my doctor, and they needed to bring me in to do a series of tests and scans.

Something was not right in my system.

In order to bring my soul some solace and tranquility, I decided that I was just going to watch a movie.

My mother had fallen asleep for the night and the lumpy couch was calling my name. After rattling the remote around in my hand for a while, I stopped on a documentary-type filmed based on the United States government. *Vice* was a film I wanted to see for quite some time, and it just so happened that on the night rambunctious thoughts were rumbling through my head, the movie appeared before me.

Two hours flashed before my eyes, filling my head with grandeurs of sly actions and deceiving notions.

I sat there frozen, gazing at the credits as they rolled past the top of the screen. I did not know precisely what to feel or think, but my aunt's image came to the forefront of my mind.

Purpose filled my soul.

The movie itself covered the story of Former Vice President Dick Cheney, but it detailed the underlying message that crime penetrated the very foundation of our nation.

I felt the weight of society's wrongs and a broken promise that burdened America's soul: it was revealed that we went to war on false premises and pretenses.

This prolonged my devotion to pursue a higher vision: leadership is all about exemplifying passion. Leadership requires that someone stand for strong morals and a progressive vision. If someone does not stick to the ethical and moral code that is sworn upon, then what does that one person genuinely stand for?

We cannot turn our heads from the truth.

We each harbor a respective responsibility to our souls.

We must be vigilant when it comes to being grounded in our ethics and morals.

The world looked and felt different after seeing that documentary. I was angry. I was hurt. I was disgusted.

I vowed to be a voice for those who could not defend themselves, for those who perished long before their time, for all of the souls who passed on or related to September 11, 2001.

For my aunt.

All of this was on my mind as I returned to the hospital days later to discover what was happening with my body.

The doctor called and said I needed to meet him immediately.

I sat in the hospital waiting room with my thoughts consuming the energy in my core.

Glaring at the painting across from me, I realized how I had never actually seen it before. I sat across it many times: with each child I had to escort to this hospital, here was where I sat: across from the nature scene. The painting echoed my inner feelings at once: the dead tree drawing attention to the forefront of the painting, my soul dead and desolated from years of presupposed divine love that just was not what it seemed to be.

Yet now, that dead tree was more alive than ever. The brown embers cascaded along the tree as gently as a simple waterfall on brisk April morning in the park. The painting gave its full display of nature and showed how nurturing passion could bring about such genuine beauty in the world.

I was the painting, and the painting was me.

The lush greenery behind the rich chocolate tree was brighter than ever. I could feel the moss brushing through my fingers. I could taste the early dew that formed on the grass. The mountains majestically beckoned me to join them in the tranquil scenery.

Tears streamed from the edges of my soul as I took in each breath appreciating this hospital's choice of scenery. The immense joy it brought me, despite my pain, reminded me that each and every gift on this planet was part of the present: a glorious reminder that starting over and beginning again were peaceful acts: I would heal. I would be okay.

As the sun rose over those pristine forest mountains, I too would rise again. I too would sing from the top of those mountains, just as beautifully as the birds that graced the branches of the tree.

Life was beginning for the hundredth time in my life, yet this time was vastly different than I could have imagined. I was within the painting and within the boundaries of my newborn soul simultaneously.

I was alive. I am alive. All the pieces of the puzzle make sense now: despite strife and struggle, the consequence was being born again in the context of an old soul in a new perspective.

No matter what, and no matter who graced my presence, nothing could alter my perspective of the once deceased tree that was resurrected from the charity and clarity of my glance. Now, I was that painting. I had to carry on the elegance of the painting, and let others see the conviction that was being torn and tattered, yet strikingly gorgeous all at once.

When I went and spoke to the doctor, he told me what I desperately feared:

I had Stage 1 Bladder Cancer.

The doctor's demeanor shifted from professional to utterly grotesque in nature. I felt like I was being examined like a laboratory specimen: in his eyes, it appeared that I was devoid of human emotions.

"You'll die if you don't handle this," hung on his lips.

In order to potentially salvage what was left of my bladder, he said we needed to operate immediately and there were no guarantees I would ever be the same.

A tinge of numbness crept up my spine.

Tears streamed from my eyes without remorse, for it felt like this was the last chance I had to cry before succumbing to whatever news he would bestow upon me next.

I just found Layne. I was only at the cusp of understanding what sort of energy we had growing between us.

The doctor's words bled through my ears: his thoughts were fluid, but my mind could not compute the very implications he was making.

"That's life, kid, what could I tell you," the syllables from his words dripped from his mouth without repentance.

It appeared that this was going to be my final confession: I was apparently dying, and fast.

In shock and without a clear thought in my mind, Morena left a message on my phone:

"You'll be okay. You'll thrive and live and survive like you always dreamed. This is just a mere obstacle that is hindering you from moving physically, but that does not mean you cannot move emotionally, spiritually, and mindfully. Your body is healing, your soul is aflame, you're going to embark on a journey and most of all, you will be okay. Choose positivity over strife, and choose living over just a life.

Please be patient. Trust the process. Soon you'll be okay.

Soon is just a few moments away.

Please, please believe that."

Beautiful Souls

Something was wrapped around me, but only in the metaphorical sense. I felt a tinge of sadness flood throughout the inner crevices of my soul.

The phone rang and shattered my thought bubble. Morena's voice was a sullen, yet stern reminder of life happening outside these four walls. Her words were burning into my brain as she tenderly tried to reassure me that I would get better.

Deep down inside, I knew I would.

The surgery I would need to have would take place within a few days.

I could hear her searching for words. Trying to find a sliver of positivity to tell me something that would make me happy or better. She could not piece anything together and the noise in the background pinged for her to return. There was sorrow in her voice, yet she was still trying to masquerade as being energetic and positive.

I could only hope she understood what was going on within my soul. Yeah, only hope.

As the phone call ended fear consumed my soul, but I was trying to raise my state of consciousness. This was my final shot: all of the warning signs must have been there for years, but I was not listening.

The negativity, the pain, and the detrimental habits I had would prove to be my downfall… that is, if I gave into them.

It was time to live the fullest life possible.

It was time I rose up and owned who I was as both a leader and a human being.

My health had to be most important. The rest, including personal love, sex, laughter, fun, money, and incredible living, were all just additional benefits I could thank the universe for. They were blessings in their own respect, but they were no longer priorities.

∞ ∞ ∞ ∞ ∞ ∞ ∞ ∞

Relationships had always been such a crux in my life's story. I am a father, a lover, a spiritual friend, part of soul connections, and take on so many roles in my life. When I really sit down and think about it, my life consists of countless connections I have made. However, when it comes down to it, the strongest bond and connection that needs to be made is the one with yourself.

I had a hard time understanding that.

It was difficult to even see this while enduring such agony from dealing with the cancer diagnosis.

Then Layne finally texted me.

She apologized that she had been so distant, especially since our connection at the conference.

I felt an overwhelming sense of healing flourish over me.

Positive, inspirational videos that she sent ushered me into my doctor's appointment later that day. Nervousness and anxiety were clinging to my body, for the unknown aspects of my diagnosis were abundant.

"Barbara," the medical assistant popped her head from behind the desk. I looked around and saw someone stand up and walk across the room.

"It is a sign that everything will be okay, Scott."

'Morena?'

She smiled at me, "Do you think I would not be here for you?"

'No, I just-' I grinned. 'Thank you.'

Her presence was usually sporadic and spontaneous, and somehow, she knew just when to appear.

"Come on," she handed me her notebook. "Read a little something in there."

I flipped through the pages, yet nothing caught my eye at the moment. I just wanted to talk. I wanted to be present to my soul's growth and the negativity that would soon leave my body.

A mesh, tan tarp rose and fell from the top of the roof and draped over the office window. As it drooped down, the sun would beam directly through it and appear to burst as the tarp and sunlight met.

It was a sign from the universe that even when barricades try to obscure our path, the light still shines through.

The doctor explained that the surgery would require that he operate cautiously. He said that there are different layers in the bladder, which consist of tissues and muscle.

The procedure would take place the next morning.

The first surgery I had was to remove an orange-sized tumor. By some miracle, the cancer did not reach the muscle. I was told I had a 40% chance that the tumor could come back, and that the next few weeks would involve more surgeries to inspect my bladder.

Not to get too technical, but the tumor I had within my body appeared to be calcified and did not spread far into my system; it enveloped the tumor and prevented it from spreading into the more vital part of the organ. We spoke about treatments, other options, and what my life would look like, but it all seemed incredibly overwhelming.

As I woke up from the surgery, I discovered that a catheter was placed inside my body. The clear, dense plastic bag clung to my leg by Velcro straps in order to ensure that I could retain my mobility and prevent incontinence.

The doctor assured me that the surgery was a success, and that I would be moving around later that night.

However, my intuition was screaming at me.

Despite the doctor's seemingly encouraging words, I was in tremendous pain.

Two days later he removed the catheter prematurely, which began the spiraling nightmare my life would become over the course of the following weeks.

While staying at my mom's three days after my first surgery, I had to rush to the Emergency Room at 1:30 in the morning. The immense pain overpowered my body.

Death appeared to be knocking at my door, but I refused to answer it.

Shame and embarrassment would wash over me, as I had to explain to nurses that I had kidney issues and bladder cancer.

In my spiritual solitude, I watched the fluorescent lighting and lime green walls slightly fade to black as a catheter had to be jammed into my private parts.

Though there was immediate relief once the nurses did that, nothing stopped me from feeling wholeheartedly defeated.

Texas embarrassment all of a sudden flooded my memories.

A piercing sound reverberated in my mind.

Not a single person was here to fill the loneliness deep within me.

While caught between a battle encompassing my physical and emotional well being, questions began to consume my every whim: Where was Morena when I needed her most? Why does she appear at certain poignant moments, yet as I lay in a hospital bed, she is nowhere to be found?

My hand hovered over her number in my cell phone before my eyes flickered shut and I drifted into a hazy dream-like state.

A woman's presence lingered next to me.

"Don't show them what you are made of, show them it is their loss that they will never get to fathom what you are made of," were the words whispered in my ear when I opened my eyes.

I laid relaxed on the floor and started counting the ceiling tiles above me. 44. I wonder how they got all of them so high up; I guess somebody had a really big ladder.

Resting my body against the linoleum, I felt peace. She stood over me, looking down at my peaceful demeanor despite everything going on.

"Do you have any questions?... Why you are here, perhaps?" her voice was trailing off a bit. "Answer me," was on the cusp of her lips.

'No,' came flowing from my mouth, a smile forming peacefully.

"No? No... you are content with not knowing where you are," she started walking across the room, almost floating. The fluorescent lights were dimming.

A wider grin was growing across my face. Her presence was fading.

'I forgive you for what you did,' sprung from my mouth with absolute purpose. She was glancing nervously in the direction of the door.

"You can't forgive me. I don't accept your apology," though crossing her arms, she kept moving steadily towards the door.

'I am not apologizing for your behavior or how you have treated me. No, I am merely saying that I forgive you for harboring hatred and jealousy throughout your body: from the crevices of your fingers to the depths of your soul. It is time you forgive yourself for what you have done,' sitting up, I could see the tears welling in her eyes.

"You don't..." her voice was breaking, "you don't know me. You can't judge me." She was starting to crumble.

'I am not judging you,' I spoke calmly, 'I am freeing myself from your grasp. You don't dictate my worth. I am the manifestation of positive energy, you must find yourself.'

She was drifting closer to the door, and was hanging in the doorway for a moment.

"Why are you freeing me," she was whimpering.

Glaring at her as the light from the doorway consumed her, I was genuinely smiling, 'don't mistake my kindness for weakness,' I was standing now, inching closer to her, 'Forgiveness is about liberating my own soul. It is time you tried to do the same, or you could fall forever.'

It was the remnants of my mother's memory planted somewhere in the recesses of my mind.

A series of cries echoed as she was falling down the long tunnel from the doorway. I didn't hear her hit the bottom, so I knew there was still hope for her to find peace... she may have buried herself exponentially, but she still could save the sliver of her that existed between the darkest hours of the night.

At some point during the night, I returned home to my mother's couch and passed out. The catheter was still hanging on my body, wrapped around my leg, obscured by my denim jeans.

I woke up when I heard the alarm clock gently reminding me of the job I had to do. I had a mission to pursue.

I returned to Lincoln Memorial High School masking the deep-rooted pain I was feeling both in the spiritual and physical senses.

As I was about to walk into the building, I was trying so desperately to capture my emotions.

I was not in a good headspace, but I showed up to work anyway.

I meditated, I prayed, and I felt that I was in alignment with the universe.

Though negative energy seemed to be around me, I tried to dispel it.

As the day continued, I had the overwhelming sense that I did not have the strength to go to work that day.

My body was crying out for rest, but I refused to listen.

After dragging my body to the car and dropping onto the driver's seat, I began to weep openly. Everything that I endured during the day manifested into the merciless tears that dripped from my eyes.

I did not want anyone to know the true desolate pain I was in.

Then, as if the universe willed her to reach out at that very moment, Layne decided to call me.

She was positive and spiritually engaging, although she had no idea what was just going through my mind.

Layne, though she just began to talk with me about her projects and what she was creating, began to speak to me about our respective personal lives.

"Will you be able to come back to Martha's Vineyard soon," she sounded very anticipatory.

Without flinching, I was drawn to my soul's every whim.

My soul was steadfast in wanting to be closer to her.

Although the words 'I have cancer' were on the tip of my tongue, I feared that if I told her the truth, she would have told me not to come.

I took a deep breath and felt my tongue dance behind my teeth.

'I can come see you next weekend,' a sigh of relief expelled from my system. I was going to get a chance to be in her presence.

"Really," she exclaimed.

'Really,' I confirmed.

Her genuine smile could be felt through the phone.

The rest of our conversation consisted of deep diving our respective worlds and thoughts. It was oddly refreshing and a soulfully stimulating experience.

No matter what, I was going to do whatever it took to get to her.

However, the universe had other plans.

It turns out my dances through the Emergency Room would be to the tune of a horrific lullaby: my soul was dormant in the midst of my emotional turmoil.

Just before I was about to drive up to Massachusetts, I was rushed to the Emergency Room twice in one night.

During my first trip there, another catheter was attached to me. I was determined to pull through and be strong. After leaving the hospital, I texted her and said I would see her soon.

As I sat and watched television, a solid feeling inundated my core. I discovered I could not urinate and the burning sensation within me remained constant.

Nothing was filtering into the bag, and it turns out the catheter burst within my body. Though the pain was excruciating, I held onto the sliver of hope dangling on a thread: there was still the possibility I would see Layne in a matter of hours.

Beautiful Souls

When I returned to the Emergency Room, the nurses and doctors worked tediously to irrigate my bladder. Crimson clots flooded a bucket as I cried in immense pain.

My soul craved to be in the same physical space with her energy. Between the fear and agony, I was asking if I could travel to Martha's Vineyard.

I remained hopeful.

'Could I get on a train?'

"You would have to wear a bag," the doctor told me. "You are urinating blood clots."

'Yeah,' I told him. 'But I could, like, travel to Massachusetts, right?'

The doctor cast his eyes downward at me, "Sir, you have cancer."

Still, the universe was keeping us apart a little bit longer.

Depressed and devastated, I called Layne and told her I had bladder cancer. As she listened to the whole story and I apologized profusely, all she wanted to do was comfort me.

"Go within," Layne told me. "Talk to your body, meditate, and visualize your soul taking care of your well being."

Something within me awakened while I spoke with her. Each conversation drew me closer to her. Our connection was indescribable and an experience I wanted to explore. I was unsure what drew me to her almost instantaneously, but it was something.

My soul had an innate longing towards hers.

My soul needed to be understood, and she appeared to be the one who could translate the depths of my every waking thoughts.

I knew I had to heal, for I just had to get to her.

She sounded concerned, more than I figured she would be actually.

This is when Layne genuinely blew me away: she began to ask about the treatment options I had and started to look into holistic remedies for me.

I did not tell her the extent of my spirituality or how I was trying to find myself, as of yet, however she seemed to be so compatible with my views.

It was breathtakingly soothing.

Hours later I made it to my car to return to my mother's house.

Pensively, I sat glaring at the streaks on the windshield. Focusing on the glare only proves that you can look at something in front of you, something that is dirty and disgusting, and be blinded by fixating on it.

Yet, if you look beyond the mess, there is a whole world outside that window.

There are cars, trees, people, traffic lights, thoughts, hopes, emotions, and dreams. So much life exists at the edge of our fingertips, and so much light grows within us. Our light manifests itself within our soul, our skin, the little dip above our lips: the light shines in all of us... the question is, I asked myself, are you willing to focus on the dirt on the windshield, or the life behind it?

∞ ∞ ∞ ∞ ∞ ∞ ∞ ∞

I would say I was speechless, but there were so many words flooding through my mind, not even the alphabet could compose itself in an articulate manner.

I was torn between trying to expand my soul, pursue whatever insight Layne could provide, and manage the immense pain emulating from my bladder.

My eyes crept open on my mother's couch and stared at the brightly lit numbers that shined from my cell phone: 10:18 in the morning. I really overslept, but I knew I really deserved it. There were a few emails, but they primarily consisted of bill statements and spam messages.

Though I did not really tell anyone about my plight, no one was accustomed to checking in with me. No one was mindful of my well being minus my son, Morena, and this mysterious new individual in my life, Layne.

I worried so much about the feelings of others but it was easy to tell who cares about me. In the end though, I would always care about them, though in my heart I knew it was not always reciprocated.

I knew I honestly didn't have time to let things like that bother me at all. Life is way too short and I was getting a taste of that fear. I knew I was going to beat this diagnosis and probably become healthier than I had even been... as long as I focused. I could tell the universe was speaking to me; it was warning me about how it could be. If I didn't awaken my soul and appreciate the small blessings, such as the people who love me and go way above and beyond for me, then I could lose it all within seconds.

Instinctively, I found myself wandering to my car to get away from the emotional burden of being in my mother's house.

My car guided me to the Whitestone Bridge, where I would find some peace in Francis Lewis Park.

I got out of my car to stretch and feel the air caress my body. It was raining and the pellets on my skin felt like shots piercing my memories.

Each time it rained that heavily, something drastic happened in my life: my best friend Stacey's funeral, my grandfather's funeral, my aunt's funeral, Emma admitting that Greg wanted to propose, and Paul's death. I wondered what was next.

I could almost hear the angels surrounding me and saying:

"Do you get the lessons? Do you realize your potential? Are you hearing our messages? Keep going within. We are speaking. You must listen but even after you hear, it is your free will to adhere or fumble. Regardless we are always here to love you."

I think my story is really about love, but more specifically about the role of gratitude in loving ourselves, others, and any moment you find yourself in. Someone could be angry or ignoring you, but within that moment you have a choice: You can reciprocate that anger and lash out, which many people do, or you can breathe into the moment and say to yourself 'What do I love about this person? What am I grateful for? What can I learn from this? How can I make this moment an opportunity to be grateful?' Then whatever those answers are for you, you can love the feeling of knowing you rose above and made any situation special. That goes for family, partners, friendships, people you dislike in general, or random strangers, even the news.

This is higher consciousness. This is what matters to our souls. This is what we should be practicing. This is practicing "life." The same goes for any situation that isn't negative either, like sitting at the side of a lake and thinking about who you are. As you see the sunset on the horizon, breathe into its beauty, becoming mindful of just that moment.

There is beauty like that, and moments around us constantly to breathe into - to allow our souls to expand and gravitate towards… and what's great about this appreciation is the more you experience it from a state of awareness, the more beautiful opportunities like that will come to you. This is love. This is gratitude. This is higher consciousness. This is the message from God and the universe that I have been waiting for all along. This is my story.

I was almost certain that the pounding in my chest was a heartbeat, but at times I forgot it even existed…

My heart, that is.

Looking into the depths of a chunk filled bucket, I found peace knowing I woke up today. A chill crept up my spine, a reminder that I could feel whatever I please and react however I could.

The taste of stale antibiotics crept back up my esophagus again. It was going to be a long day, yet it would be as long of a day as I truly wanted.

It was all a matter of perception.

I knew I was sick, but with a smile and a soothing voice, I could conquer anything. Illness or not, I have a job to do… no, wait, forget I said that. It is a mission I need to fulfill. A dream I have to uphold. A vision I need to establish: a half-full bucket that needed to be emptied to make room for bigger and better things… chunk free.

The first doctor I was going to did not appear to bestow much tranquility upon my soul. Upon speaking about him with my boss and principal, Shirley, she referred me to another doctor who she highly recommended.

The new doctor, Dr. V, was considerate, compassionate, and seemed to have the same passion for medicine that I had for changing the world. Dr. V recommended that I have a second surgery, so that he could ensure that the cancer was truly decimated.

I was beyond nervous before my second surgery, but time was moving so rapidly that it became rather insignificant.

The potential for my dreams to collapse before they could even be built was more than I could bear. I could feel the possibility of embarking on some sort of collaboration with Layne though that was not fully clear yet, just a feeling. Morena and I were on the verge of developing strong leadership programs, and I was challenging youth to find their true voice at work.

How would any of these dreams be fulfilled if I were dying?

Why would I meet someone who I had such a fluid connection with just on the cusp of tragic news?

Would I ever witness the dawn of a brand-new day?

I wondered how life was ever going to be considered fair if everything would be built then taken away from me all at once.

Being in the same physical space to explore the connection I was strengthening with Layne was a priority.

Sleeping became irrelevant.

Work was filled with plenty of events to deter me from getting anxious about the cancer, but each day I would have to contend with my inner demons while leading youth. It was a crass juxtaposition that highlighted my need for balancing what I was passionate about and what my soul needed to attend to.

Remaining positive was on the forefront of my mind, but I was masking the panic stirring in my soul.

While meditating before the second surgery, I thought I could feel an angel trying to push through the permeable barrier between my soul and my mind, but the message was ensnared in my anxiety.

It gave me some peace of mind that they were encircling me.

I was hoping to awaken from the anesthetic and hear some amazing news from the doctor. The sharp pains in my stomach were forcing me into a fragile state of mind: my intestines, my bladder, my nerves, and a combination of all of the above were forcing me to spiral.

Going within to quell the voices in my body were ultimately necessary.

Adorned with a thin hospital gown and a crisp white bed sheet, I was wheeled into the operating room.

Before I felt the anesthesia consume my mind, Washington D.C. flashed before my eyes. Morena's notebook was on my mind, as well as the long talks and walks we engaged in by the bridge and at Alley Pond Park. Layne's text messages and phone conversations penetrated my soul quickly; they were a huge part of why I wanted to heal faster, for I knew I needed to see her.

I felt deeply sorry for any and all pain I caused others, as well as the wrongdoings I brought into my life and the lives of those I affected. My human ways were not always meticulous or righteous, though my intent was always considered to be for the good of others. I am far from truth and perfection, though I was learning and still am to this day.

Learning from the experiences I endured changed me forever. I asked the universe and God to allow me to heal completely and rise above.

I knew in my soul the blessings I had been a part of could make a difference. Everything has a purpose. Everything has-

My final thoughts before falling under the anesthesia drifted into another realm.

∞ ∞ ∞ ∞ ∞ ∞ ∞ ∞

Anesthesia can play tricks on your mind and body, though my soul was steadfast in acknowledging all that I deemed to be holy.

While under the anesthesia, I envisioned standing on The Great Lawn at the White House in Washington, D.C.; it was a mystical experience.

Under the condition I was in, thoughts of courage and leadership flurried around my brain. In my mind, I appeared to be wearing a carefully prepared suit with a bold, sky blue tie adorned around my neck.

My fist was resting upright on the podium as I spoke to a group of people:

'Our small moments and discussions carry so much weight in this country. Those who came before us carried the torch so that we could ignite the souls of this nation to pursue their dreams. The liberties we are accustomed to did not come without great sacrifices, and for those sacrifices I am truly grateful.'

Morena and Layne were standing side by side. Morena was in a black suit with her red blouse prominently displaying her presence on such a bright, sunny day. Layne was in a stunning black dress that featured her voluminous curves. Every inch of Layne's stance and appearance were genuine perfection.

It did not surprise me that either of them was with me, but the connection I felt with Layne was apparent even in my hallucinations.

My voice cut through the crowd: 'Where are our ideals? Where is our courage? What example do we set for one another and those who will be the future of our great nation?'

Layne wrapped her right hand around Morena's arm and rubbed Morena's shoulder with her left hand. They seemed to be close in their own right and respect.

Again, I continued to speak.

Beautiful Souls

'The time to dig deep and find courage to move forward is now. We must create necessary change. It may be lonely at the top, as some say, and with bravery comes those who are critics. To face adversity and follow your own vision is vital. We must make our individualism and sense of community synthesize in order to grow as a cohesive country. We all have a voice. We all have the capacity to listen to one another. We all have the ability to lead. "Han" is a Korean word that has no literal English translation, however it is a state of mind. In actuality, it is a state of soul. It is a devout sadness so deep that no tears will come, and yet there is still a sense of hope. The state of our nation rests in the word "han." We all need to take a minute and measure the value of our own words.'

Everyone was glaring directly at me, staring in silence.

'What you say to someone today can impact their life tomorrow. It can impact all of our lives. We must be mindful of the words we feed our children and ourselves. For the youth are looking to us to learn how to lead. It is time for true respect for all.'

The audience began to clap as they dashed over to Morena and Layne.

"Everyone deserves a window of opportunity," Morena stated. "Every child, every soul, every being."

A man who appeared to be a reporter was writing down everything she was saying.

Layne was standing with a group of people who looked like dignitaries from other countries as she spoke.

"We have to create a system that emphasizes character building on all levels. It is about building passion and purpose within all of our souls, not just the few. It is about globalization. It is about growth. It is about humanity," Layne was being very professional and was clearly on a mission.

I found myself traveling to another part of Washington D.C. with Layne, Morena, and some other people I did not seem to recognize.

Upon standing on the steps of the Lincoln Memorial, gazing out at the reflection of the Washington Monument in the waters of the National Mall, I felt it.

I felt the sense that I was being watched. That it had taken me so long to get to DC because it just had to be the right moment. The right time. The manifestation of all of my experiences perching themselves atop the monument, and the overcast skies reminding me that I am, indeed, the light that could guide the way for millions.

It made sense. It all made sense: the trials, the triumphs, the days I wanted to crawl into a hole and never come out, the heartache, the pain. It was all to prepare me for a higher purpose.

Glaring into the stone eyes of President Abraham Lincoln, I knew just what I had to do…

Prepare to carry the torch.

The shadows crept along the wall with such fervor, as if they were pointing to something: My phone. I woke up from the anesthetic to a dimly lit room.

A sliver of light cut between the air and the still dust that lay suspended in time. The glow from the sun was a constant reminder that if it could rise, then I might as well try to.

It had been a while since I last heard from Layne, and I was beginning to think she, like all the others, had vanished into the ornate fabric of my life: caught between the threshold of when and how long. Trapped in the abysmal weaving of my complicated mind.

And I had hoped that in my absence, she would still remember I existed. For after all, she could never disappear from my memory… and I would never try to replace the feeling I get when I stare at her face: half excited, but half scared that she will never look at me the same way.

To all the angels, to all the powers that be in this universe, I pray she remembers me.

∞ ∞ ∞ ∞ ∞ ∞ ∞ ∞

The week consumed me with thoughts of trepidation and the possibility of spiritual enlightenment.

I kept the faith.

I had to.

The universe was on the verge of experiencing all that I had to offer, and something within me said to keep going.

The angels were on my side, Morena was whispering positivity and faith into my ears, and I was receiving soul-quelling insight from Layne.

Between the affirmations and meditation information she bestowed upon me, I was feeling incredibly grateful for her support.

Those who were promoting positivity and tranquility were helping me heal, and for them I will be forever thankful.

Everything within me hoped that all of this turmoil would soon be behind me.

The moment the phone rang I felt my heart palpitate within my chest: these next few moments would shift the balance within my soul forever. I knew deep down inside that no matter the diagnosis, I would fervently push forward and do what I had to do for the greater good of the universe, but just how difficult would my journey be?

I answered the phone and took a deep breath.

'Hello,' I am sure he could sense the nervousness in my voice.

"Hey Scott, it is Dr. V, how are you?" His voice seemed chipper.

'I don't know, how am I doc?' I let a smile seep from the edge of my mouth.

"Well," he said with a breathy chuckle, "good news, man."

I held my breath. The pause was what stung my soul. What was good? Why did this pause seem so painstakingly long?

"Scott," he began, with a tinge of hope in his voice.

"You are cancer free."

Silence blossomed in the air as I heaved a sigh of relief. His words drowned in the flood of emotions that filled my mind.

I was given another chance.

I was free.

Though I went through such a dramatic series of surgeries and moments, with more visits to the emergency room that no one will truly ever realize or fathom, I chose not to be a victim of circumstance. I chose to pursue my purpose with an even more devout sense of growth stirring within me.

It was a momentary resurgence of my faith manifesting into growth. It was proof that negative situations and refusing to listen to your inner voice could cause such horrid turmoil.

Though the cancer was not akin to literally hitting a concrete wall as I did decades ago, the cancer provided yet another metaphorical crash in order to guide me on my path.

You Gave Me Her

Our experiences reveal the innate magic we contain within our souls.

Sometimes, we discover our gifts and growth on our own terms, other times the universe reminds us of what we can overcome.

To this day, I am not sure where the noise came from, but music was playing: Paul Simon's "You Can Call Me Al."

My aunt's memory and the last time we laughed and smiled flooded my soul.

∞ ∞ ∞ ∞ ∞ ∞ ∞ ∞

Morena was thrilled upon hearing that I got the all clear. She jovially hugged me when she saw me.

"What is your first order of business now that you are a *free* man?"

I looked over at her and made a promise: 'I'm going to truly live in the realm of a higher consciousness. I am going to eat healthy, feed my soul positivity, and keep moving forward.'

"I am proud of you," she grinned.

'I have to video call Layne, there is something I need to do.'

Upon pulling my phone from my pocket, my body shivered with excitement.

Layne answered immediately and was ecstatic. She appeared to want to see me just as much as I wanted to be in her presence.

If I could freeze a moment in time, I would have etched her genuine smile in my mind for the rest of eternity. I would infinitely drown in an ocean of my own emotions, if I knew that her love would be the life preserver waiting to catch me if I drifted too far or too deep.

Her inconsummate soul wrapped itself around me and poured itself into the shattered pieces of my deepest darkest dreams. Her heart and stamina were what sealed the pieces of my loneliness back together. If only the darkness inside her would conceal itself beneath the light she emulated regularly, she would then feel just how unequivocally blessed I am for her presence to be a constant gift in my life.

Without her glow as a persistent reminder of the light manifesting within me, I am not sure how my life would have been. It is just so poignant: two separate broken souls were almost able to fully mend each other, and simply by collaborating through trial and triumph; blood,

Beautiful Souls

sweat, and countless tears. Each drop an echoic memory of how far we have come…

And just how high we could fly with our souls intertwined and our hands interlocked, rising above the dust and crowds to proclaim, "Every child deserves a window of opportunity."

∞ ∞ ∞ ∞ ∞ ∞ ∞ ∞

That night, I had another weird dream:

Standing in the doorway, I could see a solitary white wolf inching closer and closer to where I was standing. It shifted its stern legs around a few times while maintaining eye contact with me.

We stood parallel for a little bit until it opened its mouth and formulated actual words. A deep voice inundated with soulfulness erupted from the animal.

"Do you know why you have been brought here?" Its pure fur shook in unison with its firm body.

I watched the white wolf in amazement. It spoke. The first time it spoke.

"You'll have time to rest later, Follow me," it spoke as it retreated from the light. "We have much to discuss."

As the wolf raced down the long corridor, I followed it with sheer curiosity.

'Why now? Why speak now?'

In the depths of my soul, I could feel something shifting. Something was not right. This was a warning of some kind. The earth below began to shake. The wolf caught my stunned expression.

"Are you waking up yet, peaceful warrior?" The wolf stopped in its tracks. It shifted its weight and moved closer and closer to me. I could feel the energy growing stronger between us.

It nudged its head for me to get closer to it. I leaned down, holding my body up by my bent knee and vicariously placed hand.

"It is time you woke up and faced the music. Run towards the light, my child," at once, the wolf leaned its head into my leg, and the energy shift was complete. A circle manifested itself above us as it morphed into an infinity sign. Lights flickered. Wind whisked around us and I held the wolf as if I were preserving it from the fierce wind.

"See you soon, my love," it started softly, "You know, in your soul, what you must do. Keep her safe."

I awoke in a darkened apartment. Sky blue walls cohesively circled beige furniture and a wooden coffee table. I did not recognize the room. A sole light crept between the doorframe and the neighboring wall: the entrance to a white bathroom.

'Where am I?' flew from my dehydrated lips.

I arose from the padded couch and headed towards the illuminated room. The door creaked slightly.

The wolf was sitting in the middle of the floor. It almost perfectly blended into the white tile floor, though its midnight eyes were a reminder that it was distinctly unique from its surroundings. It swung its head, motioning me closer once again.

Small whispers escaped its mouth, "Wake up."

Puzzled and very exhausted, I let a small sigh creep out: 'But I am awake.'

"Not yet," it peeped gently.

"Not yet. Give it time, Scott. You are almost there."

I jolted awake to find my phone buzzing with glee. Layne was calling to check up on me and ask when I would be returning to Martha's Vineyard. I checked my schedule and told her that I would be there this weekend.

"This weekend, really?" Her voice was illuminated with glee.

'Yes,' I replied instinctively. 'I am coming up there.'

"That is wonderful," she proclaimed. "But you do not have to come so soon after your surgery. You have to recover!"

'Telling me not to see you,' I began, 'is like telling the sun not to rise in the morning.'

I packed my bag and eagerly awaited the end of the week.

The calendar crept closer and closer to her presence becoming a devout reality in my life. I stood patiently at the edge of the curb, gazing up at the skyscrapers and wishing she were here.

We had so much to talk about. So much to catch up on and share. Pieces of a flourishing soul would collide to balance a universal shift. It was just a day away.

Sitting on the bench in the teacher's lot that Friday afternoon, I rolled my keys around in a circular motion - the jingling became music to my ears. Birds fluttered up above. Faint laughter from children and the murmurs of park goers swirled in the air: all poignant reminders of life diversifying the environment we have been so accustomed to. No one single conversation is the same.

My countdown from a day prior rang in my head: 17 hours, 52 minutes, and 36 seconds… 35 seconds… 34 seconds.

As I drove up to Massachusetts, anticipation mounted in the colorful kaleidoscope of memories that flooded my mind as her name and sweet nothings were on my lips.

The advantageous hope lingered in the placated pieces of my soul. Her aroma, though faint, was apparent. A gentle breeze ushered my longing to see her into clear view.

As I boarded the ferry to Martha's Vineyard and sailed closer and closer, time became irrelevant to the fact that she was coming nearer. Suddenly, the mundaneness of each fleeting moment became crass and almost turbulent.

The dock was nearing closer as the ferry rocked; it was a shift in the universe perhaps.

She arrived. Layne was here.

CHAPTER 9
Home

"Take me now. The world's such a crazy place. When the walls come down, you'll know I'm here to stay. There's nothing I would change. Knowing that together everything that's in our way. We're better than alright. Walking between the raindrops. Riding the aftershock beside you. Off into the sunset. Living like there's nothing left to lose. Chasing after gold mines. Crossing the fine lines we knew. Hold on and take a breath. I'll be here every step. Walking between the raindrops with you."

- **Lifehouse, American Rock Band, Los Angeles, California**

Beautiful Souls

As she stood on the dock staring out at the ferry, it was almost as if she were a lighthouse. Her bright light appeared to beckon this tattered, worn soul to the shore: her soul was summoning me home.

I never knew what I wanted in life. In terms of love, professionalism, spirituality, I never knew. Yet something in her eyes told me that I was about to find out. I was about to dig myself into a deeper hole than I could have ever imagined...

And I just hoped that somewhere, deep within, she felt the passion burning between both of us.

She was captivating in the sense that she was driven by her heart. Layne's beauty was breathtaking, though it was her inner voice that made her spiritually enriching.

As I approached her on the dock, she was standing in a perfectly fitting trench coat that fanned out by her waist. The cotton black dress she wore hugged every curve of her body in a manner that summoned all eyes to adore her.

It is truly amazing how the universe works. Months ago, the two of us were physically strangers on this planet. Neither of us realized the other existed; yet the moment we met it was almost like our souls were destined to be together.

The light emulating from within us glowed just enough to illuminate the path before us. Both of us appeared to be on the same page when it came to energy and stamina, yet I was entranced by her passion.

Layne had a burning desire to pursue her dreams; she yearned to write a book to highlight the innate potential hiding deep within the world's souls.

Life grants you moments and situations that you never knew you needed. Speaking with her was an utter delight, as she harbored just the right amount of tenacity to inspire both herself and those who met her to move forward. I wondered if she was cognizant of just how empowering she was: in being such a strong icon of classic internal beauty, could she fathom the opportunities she could create within her own life?

Writing a book takes determination and stamina. I sensed she had the power within her, but I was not sure what was holding her back.

I wondered if she recognized the same diligence within herself that she appeared to discover in others.

Either way, I prayed that she would trust her heart to know what was true would come to fruition.

All beautiful things and dreams are worth the wait.

Fear of the future or pain from the past could ensnare you within a never-ending trap of "what ifs," "could," "should," and "would," though ultimately what matters is the passion in your heart, the strength within your mind, the words you feed to your body, and the voice that comes from deep within your soul.

At this point, it was clear to me that everything in this universe aligns at just the right moment: when things are supposed to happen, they will happen. When words are supposed to flow from deep within you, they will find a way to articulate themselves within the depths of your soul.

Everything has a purpose and nothing truly ever ceases to flow unless you make it so.

Above all, intuition may manifest itself when something seems to be blossoming. We must add water to the soil churning in our core, so that the flowers we develop can grow into whatever we hope our respective lives could become.

I was not sure what sort of connection Layne and I had, but I hoped to find out.

"Hi," her voice was like crushed velvet. It was pleasing to grace her presence.

'Hey,' I cheerfully replied. 'How are you?'

"I'm doing great," she pulled her hands from her pockets. "I'm doing great." She sounded excited, yet slightly anxious.

'I'm glad,' I smiled back at her.

The two of us stood in silence for a moment gazing out at the water.

"It's beautiful, right?"

'Yeah,' I turned to look at her admiring the waves. 'It really is.'

"There is a lot I want to show you," she began. "Martha's Vineyard is a gorgeous place, and I want to make sure you enjoy every moment of this island."

The two of us made our way out of the ferry terminal and onto the main road. The midnight blue sign above the terminal read "Oak Bluffs" in crisp white lettering.

'Oak Bluffs,' I pointed at the sign. 'I thought this was Martha's Vineyard.'

"It is silly, but there are different parts of the island. Most of the time it's a summer vacation spot for celebrities and rich people, but to the locals, it is just home."

'Just home,' lingered in my mouth as I repeated her.

She paused and looked up at me for a moment.

"Do not take this the wrong way, but your New York accent is so thick. The locals around here are going to know you are a visitor."

We laughed and a genuine grin grew across my face.

'I *do* take it the *wrong way*,' I replied sarcastically. 'I guess you'll just have to give me a full tour.'

"I guess so," she grabbed my hand and pulled me out towards the street. "This is Seaview Avenue."

'Seaview Avenue,' I murmured. 'How original.'

The two of us continued laughing as she pulled me towards her white sedan.

'I don't remember seeing too many cars last time I was here.'

"Oh," she remarked. "The island is not some quaint little vacation community. There is a lot of life on this beautiful treasure."

As the two of us got into her car, she began to list the places she wanted to take me to. While she gleefully spoke about introducing me to her version of the Vineyards, I gazed out the window at the picturesque houses that lined the streets.

I could only imagine what sort of higher conscious thinking she was manifesting on the island. It was the kind of place that you could only dream of. Every single building in town looked as if it would belong on a postcard. Every fiber within me wondered what was taking her so long to write, considering she had such a beautiful environment to manifest her creation.

Her voice trailed into my train of thought: "There's a gorgeous place called the Aquinnah Cliffs Overlook that is utterly breathtaking, and I guess the lighthouse there is a little small compared to the ones you would probably see in New York. I've heard about Long Island here and there..."

'I want to see everything,' I told her.

She gripped the steering wheel and looked over at me.

Home

"Well, you are only here for less than two days, so I'll try jamming in as much as possible."

The intense energy between us was radiating off of our minds. It was such a joy to experience such a high vibrational conversation, and even though I felt like a tourist who was just sightseeing on the quaint little island, Layne made me feel like I was not a foreign entity.

In New York, I constantly felt like an outcast or someone terribly different, yet while wandering around with Layne, I felt a sense of peace.

The two of us drove to a place called Lighthouse Beach and she parked her car on one of the side streets. I was starting to lose my sense of direction, for she was glowing as she spoke about all of the different places I had to see.

"We are going to start with my favorite spot, but it isn't on this island."

'*This* island,' I was confused. 'I thought there was only one Martha's Vineyard.'

"Oh, there is," she grabbed my hand and started to dart down side streets. "But there's also Chappaquiddick Island."

'Chap of who?'

She giggled, "Chappaquiddick."

We continued to laugh as I repeatedly struggled, trying to pronounce Chappaquiddick properly.

A building adorned with faded shingles was eclipsed by an aquamarine and gold-lettered sign that read "Gallery."

'What's that?' I pointed to the building.

"That's the art gallery here. Sometimes I go there to get inspiration, but there are other beautiful places you need to see."

The two of us boarded another ferryboat. As it set sail, we could practically see the other island, as the sky was so incredibly pure.

'Aw,' I remarked. 'This is adorable. It is the Chappy Ferry!'

"What," she nudged me playfully. "They don't have cute names for things in New York?"

'I mean,' I stopped to think for a moment. 'There is a sign on the highway that says, "fuggedaboutit," which is kind of cool.'

"Huh," she started to laugh again. "Is that a town down there?"

'No, I think it is like a saying from one of the boroughs, either Brooklyn or Queens or the Bronx.'

"Oh, okay," she rubbed my shoulder with her open palm. "You need to teach me all about New York since I am telling you all about my home."

'Deal.' I shook her hand and before I could even blink, we were on Chappaquiddick Island.

The two of us rode these brightly colored scooters down the street. At first, I admit that I was nervous as I teetered on this oddly shaped vehicle, but Layne's reassuring nod reminded me that I could balance just about anything.

We drove down to a series of dirt roads and came across a pine-green sign adorned with bold white letters: "Welcome to Mytoi."

'What's this?' We parked and walked up to the sign.

"It is a Japanese-style garden that was manifested in the 1950s," Layne put her open hand on my shoulder.

'Did you get that from the sign?' I tilted my head diagonally towards her.

"No," she nudged me playfully once again. "I come here to think. This is one of my special writing spots."

'It-' I glanced at the ornate and stimulating greenery around us. Had I known where we were going, I think I would have prepared my thoughts in a more cohesive manner. In those moments upon seeing the natural beauty surrounding us, I felt a sincere sense of peace washing over my body. 'It's beautiful.'

"It's called the Mytoi Japanese Garden. I have always enjoyed being outdoors and walking through nature's most illustrious creations."

'It's breathtaking.'

"Come on," she grabbed my hand. "I'll show you around."

The two of us walked around gazing at the diverse colors wrapped in the leaves and flowers.

We paused in front of a small, thinly leafed tree that seemed like the centerpiece of the garden. Layne caressed the leaves with such purpose. Her fingers brushed through them so gently, as to not disturb their structural integrity.

"It's a Japanese Maple Tree," she glanced at it as if it were a young child. "I always wanted to have one of these in my own front yard, but I would be mortified if anything were to ever happen to it."

'Why do you say that?'

Home

"I'm not exactly the best plant mother in the world. I used to forget to water the plants at the Italian restaurant."

'Nonsense,' I told her. 'I feel like I know you, though I don't know too much about you other than the fact that you exude naturalistic vibrations.'

"Vibrations," she responded matter-of-factly. "I like the sound of that."

We continued on through dirt paths and talked about our lives. Something compelled me to tell her about everything: my car accident, my aunt, and even my son. I was not afraid to be vulnerable with her, for she seemed like she was whispering, "I'm a safe person to talk to" with each and every tilt of her head.

The intense energy continued throughout the day as we traveled around Martha's Vineyard. It was quite thrilling to be a visitor on this heavenly island, almost to the point where I felt that Martha's Vineyard was a refreshing home away from home.

The two of us wandered for a while and found ourselves walking past a quaint church near the water.

She grabbed my hand and began dragging me towards the door.

"Come with me," Layne walked in and we were met with a flurry of faces drifting towards us. Formal services were not occurring, but there were many souls sitting on the pews with their eyes cast downward.

We approached a series of red candles resting dormant on a wooden table. Small glass jars were holding the candles in place, as if their presence was paramount in supporting the intentions behind the candles' purpose.

Layne brushed past me and reached for a long, solitary match.

As she whisked it towards a candle that was already lit, I could see the miniscule flame reflecting in her eyes. The glow from the match seemingly evaporated as the flame graced the candle.

"Since the moment you told me about your aunt," she spoke softly. "I have wanted to do something to honor her influence in your life."

I nodded silently, unsure of what to think next.

"I am lighting this candle in memory of your Aunt Barbara."

Layne waved the match in a zigzag pattern momentarily, until a trail of smoke leapt from the stick. The smoke drifted between us as we grinned at one another.

Her compassion and her unwavering dedication to honoring my aunt moved me in a way I never knew I could feel.

From then on, I knew that moment would cling to my soul for all eternity.

As night fell upon us, the two of us went back to the cozy bed and breakfast I was staying at and ate dinner on the porch.

There were ostentatious wooden rocking chairs situated at the far corner of the porch where we sat removed from the rest of the patrons staying there.

We felt comfort in knowing that the two of us were connecting so deeply and in such a breathtaking place.

"Seriously, between what you are working on and what I am working on," she eagerly rocked forward on her chair. "Something incredible is going to be born from all of this."

'I see how this can connect in a really powerful way to my larger vision of educational reform for the country and ultimately the world,' I replied.

"You talk a lot about education reform."

'It's a part of the very fabric of my life.'

We watched people walking down the street, their shadows growing taller as they disappeared towards the sunset.

"Us idealists have to stick together," she placed her hand over mine as we swayed in unison. The chairs were in perfect balance with the Earth's rotation.

'We will change this planet for the better in ways nobody can imagine at all.'

As the two of us were moving in tandem, it seemed like we were partners from another lifetime. I did not know how to label the sort of spiritual relationship we had, but it was riveting. While I thought about our sudden connection in more detail, she outright said what I was thinking:

"You know," she leaned over. "I think we are like twin flames."

'What's that?'

"There are different types of twin flames and spiritual relationships in this universe, but it feels like we have been working together for eternity."

'I guess we are the ones we have been waiting for,' I nudged her playfully.

"We are the ones the *world* has been waiting for."

The two of us continued to talk about the work we were creating. It was exciting to see how enthralled she was by the words coming out of my mouth.

Home

"Thank you," she locked eyes with me and smiled.

'Why are you thanking me?' I leaned back in the chair and interlocked my fingers.

"I admire your tenacity for your vision. It makes me feel like my work matters, too."

'Why do you think your work wouldn't matter?'

She sighed and rested her elbow on the armrest. Her chin flopped into her hand.

"Who would ever listen to a waitress?"

'You are still a waitress?'

Layne sat up. "You sound disappointed."

'No,' I assured her. 'I just wonder why no one knows about your insight yet.'

"Family is incredibly important to me. The diner gives me a paycheck and the chance to meet fascinating characters. Writing is a hobby."

'Stuff that sets your soul on fire should not just be a hobby, Layne.'

"I know," she started. "I hear you."

'I hope that you truly do.'

"I share some of my ideas with the regular customers at this diner I work at, but that's about it." She smoothed out her pants. "The midnight crowd at the diner is relatively attentive… considering most of them are lonely or drunk."

The two of us laughed.

'One day you'll make it out of the diner, I get that sense.'

"It's not that I don't *want* to be a waitress. I am thankful for my job," she looked out at the people passing by again. "I just want more; more for this planet. I want my writing to inspire the world."

'I hear you,' I smiled at her. 'Have you ever heard of Paulo Coehlo?'

"Of course, the author of *The Alchemist*, who hasn't?"

'It took him years to get discovered. He writes masterpieces, but it was his second book that made his insight known globally.'

Layne caught my eye again and swallowed nervously.

"Anyway," she stood up. "I am sorry to do this to you, but I am going to have to call this an early night. I could not get off from work this weekend, and I am working the midnight shift."

'Oh,' I shuddered. I desperately wanted to spend more time with her. 'Do you want me to walk you to work?'

"That would be great, thanks."

We joined the patrons whose shadows were growing in the sunset. It was a short walk from my bed and breakfast to where she worked, which was refreshing. I had only been to Martha's Vineyard once before, and it would be easy to find my way back to where I was staying.

After I dropped her off, Layne darted into the diner and grabbed her apron. She seamlessly tied it around her waist as if she were preparing for a performance.

I wondered what she thought of me.

On my walk back to the bed and breakfast, I admired the stars more fondly. In New York City, there is usually so much light pollution that the sky is inundated with bright lights.

You can rarely see all of the bright stars shining up above.

I called Morena and the two of us started to talk about my thoughts. For some reason, I felt odd dropping Layne off at work and walking away from her.

"Why is that?" Morena asked when I told her about my feelings.

'It consumes me, not in an obsessive way, but in a manner like when you go to church and your spirits are uplifted.'

"What consumes you?"

'Layne's spirit… her energy,' I responded quickly. 'It is like sitting down and having tea with God. Not like I know what tea with God is really like… does that make sense?'

Morena chuckled, "With you, does anything ever make sense?"

Upon re-entering the bed and breakfast, I went straight into my room and started to wander around.

"You just need to go with the flow, Scott," Morena was trying to allay my nerves.

'I guess you are right, Mo.' I stood up and started to pace between the windows.

"I don't know," Morena said. "Maybe she is your missing puzzle piece."

'Do you think?' I threw myself onto the bed and heard the springs creak below me.

"The way you talk about her," she started. "It sounds like you are finally happy."

'*Finally*,' I scoffed. 'I don't know what happiness is anymore.'

"Give it time," she remarked. "You'll know when you know."

'I hope so,' I looked out the window at the night sky. 'I hope so.'

My voice trailed off and suddenly I felt more connected to whatever was out there in the universe. There was a sensation, some sort of feeling that for once everything would work out. Everything that was meant to be in this world would eventually be.

It was just a matter of time.

∞ ∞ ∞ ∞ ∞ ∞ ∞ ∞

As the sun rose and beamed through the windows, the light rested its energy just above the headboard of the bed. I rolled over and let the patterned quilt slip slightly off of my back. I folded my hands underneath my head and shut my eyes again.

A few moments later, and with a breathy sigh escaping my mouth; I threw the blanket off of me and leapt up. My toes curled over the hardwood floors below me.

Though my hair was askew and I was in need of a shower, I made it my duty to get ready in time to meet Layne at the diner. Something told me that I had to be the first person she saw in the morning after her long night at work.

I made my way down the street and pushed open the glass doors as fast as I could move my feet.

Layne had her hair tied neatly in a bun; her apron was covered in food stains that loosely resembled mashed potatoes and some form of cake. It looked like she had a really busy night.

"Scott," she looked up and appeared surprised. "Good morning!"

'Good morning, how are you doing?'

"Good, good," she wiped her hands on her apron. "Better now. You're up relatively early."

'I wanted to come see you.'

Layne tucked her notepad into her apron. "It's so nice of you. Are you hungry?"

'Starving, yeah.'

Layne grabbed two menus and plopped them on a table. The plastic clacked against the table as she motioned to the booth.

"Sit down, I'll treat you to breakfast."

She untied the apron and draped it over a nearby chair.

The two of us looked through the menus for a moment. I peeked over mine to see her squinting at the words.

'Are you okay with eating where you work?' I lowered the menu.

"Of course," she dropped the menu on the table. "I love it here. Who wouldn't want to sit on bright red foam with a cruddy plastic table in front of them?"

The two of us laughed again. Layne's laughter was infectious and uplifting.

Since I was leaving later that day, I wanted to make sure that the two of us could spend as much time together as possible. Our deep conversation took on new heights, as I continuously felt a weight being lifted from my soul as she spoke.

Without any trepidation, I pulled the makings of the educational reform framework that Morena and I were working on and slid it across the table.

"This Morena you work with, what is she like?" Layne started to flip through the pages of the binder.

'Honestly, I don't even know if she is real,' I chuckled.

Layne looked up and her face dropped. "Really? Then what is she?"

'If I said an angel, would you think I was crazy?'

We paused for a moment and I looked up at her. Layne's eyes seemed to be searching for something to say.

"No, because insanity means doing the same thing over and over again and expecting change," she reached across the table. "You are reinventing what it means to live."

'I am trying to come up with a holistic education system.'

She continued to read and flip through the pages. "Holistic," she paused. "I like that word a lot."

She pulled out a notebook that looked oddly similar to Morena's.

'What's that?'

"It's my journal," she replied as she scribbled furiously in the book. "I jot all of my ideas and words in here. Sometimes I doodle, but mainly it's for productive writings."

Before either of us realized it, over eight hours flew by. The two of us were consumed with asking questions about each other's plans and ideas. Layne yawned and I knew that my ferry would be leaving within the hour.

'I'm so sorry I need to leave now,' I swiveled the binder towards me.

"It's okay," she collected her papers. "I know we will be jamming together again soon."

'I sense *real* soon.'

Layne took the clip from her hair and shook out the bun. She placed a red baseball cap on her head and held the brim with her pointer finger and thumb before nodding in another waiter's direction.

We stepped out into the receding daylight and began to walk towards her car. Layne insisted that although she was up for over a day at this point, she just *had* to drive me to the ferry.

As I stepped out onto the street, I didn't even think to walk to the corner.

"Why am I not surprised," Layne laughed. "Of course, the New Yorker jaywalks."

'Jaywalking? That's what you think New Yorkers do.' I spun around to watch her run out into the street after me. 'We walk with *style*.'

I took the cap off of her and placed it backwards on her head. 'Live a little bit, Layne!'

She looked utterly ridiculous, but she had an adorable way about her.

"Real cute," she wrinkled her nose.

'Yes, you are.'

Layne nudged me playfully as she seemed to enjoy doing. It was one of those small actions that seem insignificant, but add such gravity to the soul-connecting relationships manifested in this universe.

When she dropped me back at the ferry terminal, the two of us peered into the darkness. I could hear the Atlantic Ocean calling me back to the mainland.

The two of us silently looked at one another as I pulled her closer for a hug. We embraced each other in a manner that spoke a thousand words without either of us opening our mouths.

As I released her from my hold, she gazed up at me. Her eyes appeared to be an olive color in the moonlight.

'Thank you,' I whispered.

"For what?"

'I admire your tenacity for your vision. It makes me feel like my work matters.'

"Hey," her smile took up her entire face. "You can't steal my lines."

'It's not stealing, I am just in awe of you.'

I saw her swallow hard. "I am also in awe of you."

There was another silence between us until the ferry's horn flooded the air.

'I'm sorry. I have to go.'

"I know," she held my hand for a moment. "I understand."

'I hope you do. I really, *really* hope that you do.'

As I turned to walk over to the ferry, her presence and aura sent a warm sensation throughout my body. Everything within me told me to turn and stay, but I did not listen to the voice within my soul.

While boarding the ferry I glanced on the dock to see her hair drifting in the wind. Layne waved slightly before she sauntered away and out of sight.

She seemed like the perfect woman in every way, and I could not help but realize that part of me was enamored by her. With my head resting against the window on the ferry, I watched the dock move further and further away.

My phone vibrated in my pocket and disrupted my train of thought: it was Layne.

'Hello?'

"Hey," I could tell that Layne was sobbing.

'What's wrong?'

"I am so sorry I am calling you, but I bumped the curb with my car and flattened my tire. I am just waiting for the repairman and I wanted to call you."

'Me,' I asked her. 'Why me?'

"Why not you?" She appeared to sound happier.

'I don't know. Are you safe?'

"Yeah," she replied. "Yeah, I-" she cleared her throat.

'Are you okay?'

"I was nervous and I wasn't paying attention, and I hit the curb."

'Well, you are also tired. Why were you nervous?'

"Why do you ask so many questions?" Layne laughed.

'I am sorry, I am just curious.'

"You don't have to be sorry," she started. "I enjoy your curiosity."

We both paused for a bit too long.

"I enjoy your company."

The two of us talked about feeling a shift in the universe and how something major was building in the world and between us.

A horn honked in the background and she hurried to cover the phone for a moment.

"Scott," she sounded rushed. "I am sorry, the repairman is here."

'That's okay,' I assured her. 'I am just about at Woods Hole. Text me when you get home and get some rest.'

"Thanks, I am grateful for you."

'And I am grateful for you too.'

Staring out at the darkness beyond the window, I came to a startling epiphany: we were both looking up at the same sky; the same full moon… yet neither of us was whole without the other.

∞ ∞ ∞ ∞ ∞ ∞ ∞ ∞

As I drove back down to New York, I felt a distinct longing. I just met Layne not long ago, but her compassion and intelligence shook my core. Something deep within her made me want to learn more. Her thoughts and insight were reminiscent of a wise philosopher, though her cave was set in a diner and she was cognizant beyond Plato's wildest dreams.

When I finally made it back to the couch, a lot happened while I was dreaming. The imagery in my head bombarded my soul. The same words were chanted over and over again in my mind: chakras, energy, and flow.

My soul was trying desperately to translate what it meant.

The next morning, I realized that work felt mundane again. I wanted to be back in Martha's Vineyard with Layne.

Instinctively, I texted her to see how she was doing. Though I did not hear from her all day, Morena assured me that everything was going to be okay.

"Just breathe into the moment," Morena told me. "When the time is right, the connections in your life will fall into place. Unplug. Rest. Meditate."

'I wonder what she truly thinks of me,' my thoughts wandered into the abyss.

"You are too focused on what other people think of you and not what you should be. Breathe. You are tired and it is hard to communicate with you when you are like this."

'Like what?'

Her voice grew solemn, "You're disconnected."

I could not disagree with her. There was a shift happening deep within me and I could not fathom what it meant.

The path I once walked alone finally felt whole, and it was due to Layne's presence.

"Be brave," Morena spoke with the utmost confidence. "Be patient and be cognizant that you can choose whatever you wish to feel. Breathe positivity into your life."

At night, vivid dreams of Layne flooded my head. This time I was standing alone in a bar for a moment, I swished my finger around the rim of the cup while humming to the beat of a heartbeat that was not my own. I felt it reverberating through my core. A curious man cast his eyes down at a notebook; the green and gold pages peering back menacingly.

As I picked my hair up over my shoulder, I spoke to a shadow standing nearby, 'What are you writing, beautiful?'

Layne's voice faded "The next amazing spiritual masterpiece."

When I woke up, I realized I fell into a deep sleep.

It was a challenge to focus on anyone or anything else but Layne in those moments.

As I went to work begrudgingly, the smell of marijuana filled the streets. It is a smell that had my skin crawling, for it broke my concentration. In all honesty it is hypocritical for me to have that opinion due to my past. I think the term "opinion" was the operative word here.

I looked at acceptance in society.

No one bats an eye if there is a distinct marijuana smell lingering in the air. I was hopeful that if a society could accept the lingering scent, then people could accept higher consciousness as a genuine state of mind.

Who are any of us to truly judge?

Home

We create our own versions of right and wrong and try to live by these standards. Society taught us that we must have rules; otherwise we are not inherently "good" people.

We manifest something to measure who we are in order for us to create value systems. Whether we consciously do it or not, the standards we put in place are developed by a somewhat forced ideology within our world.

What if we are all here to learn, evolve, and expand our souls?

What if this is just all experiential?

What if clearing the mind, as taught in meditation, clears the way to better communicate with your soul?

Burning questions ushered me into the next day of work. The questions continued to stand out in my mind as Layne's messages popped up on the screen.

She profusely apologized as she told me what she had been up to the past day or so.

Though Layne was constantly working at the diner, she used her free time to develop her ideas. Her insight was impeccable by any standard, and our conversations soon became a quintessential part of my day.

Each time I read anything that she wrote, I was blown away by the miraculous words that spilled onto her journal's pages.

As the two of us spoke, she seemed to shy away from any sweet comments I would make about her and her work.

It dawned on me that maybe I am not supposed to marry the greatest woman on the face of the planet. I thought that maybe the issue was that I kept finding amazing women who were slightly out of my reach.

The big dreams I had were always inundating my personal life. The love I had for the woman in my life matched my dreams, which tended to push them away.

I know that now.

Elyza helped plant the seeds that I was destined for bigger plans in this universe, though I developed a stronger sense of who I was upon being apart from Elyza.

My life has been filled with challenges, but is doused in quintessential blessings.

Each night, I continued to wake up at 3:14 in the morning. I looked up the implications the number has, and it apparently means that it is time to take action when it comes to your dreams. When I told Layne about this, she was stunned.

She explained to me that she kept seeing 315 wherever she went.

The two of us engaged in such a powerful conversation about spirituality. There is a war brewing within souls in this universe. We are all pawns in the game of ego versus ego, yet we are laced with manifestations of the deepest spirituality. We must be mindful of the voice within our respective souls.

We must rise above.

How do you guide righteousness and plant the seeds of faith and hope?

This is a leadership conundrum of the greatest kind. The stakes are only just building. Many factors play into this storyline and it leaves me concerned.

I wonder what lessons will play out in this world.

Even those who are viewed as the greatest leaders in society; there are deep wounds that bleed through.

Again, more questions flooded my mind about Layne. I was starting to feel deeply about her, and it became a reality that I needed to listen to the voice within me.

Do I play the game or push through the lesson from higher consciousness?

Do I be selfish or do I come from a place of self-love?

Who is the "self" in this scenario?

My heart remained heavy in not knowing the answers. These words remind me that there is so much beauty around that we don't recognize and that we are blinded by.

There is so much more than the little stories we allow to consume our lives.

This is all experiential, but we put so much pressure on ourselves to make this our all, and the answer to it all.

There is a bigger picture.

∞ ∞ ∞ ∞ ∞ ∞ ∞ ∞

I awoke in the morning before work, dreading another day not being by Layne's side. Something told me not to tempt fate and stop sweltering under the mounting pressure of my emotional selfishness.

Home

Maybe I did not need to be near Layne.

Maybe I had to let go of any physical tethers that would conflict with my visions.

I wondered if divine love still mattered. My mind wanted to comprehend what my soul wanted, though I was wholeheartedly concerned with my future.

Layne seemed perfect, but I wondered if she was a distraction from the dreams I had.

The spiritual lessons I have received are to love unconditionally. It is not to let someone's actions or excitement for their perspective on success, inhibit personal truth and goals.

My emotions were selfish because I knew I desired this grander vision.

I knew I had so much I wanted to accomplish. Still, the resources handed to me through angelic stretches seemed to compete against or outdo the path before me.

I feared I would look like I was the follower.

There was a conscious feeling that slipped through my mind. A sense of knowing that something, somewhere was happening. A light and airy feeling perhaps, but one that I have yet to be able to put words to. A sign, a signal, a cardinal, a flash…

A flash of light that tells me something else is coming. A burning. A rising…

And the sensation that so many things in this universe and this planet are manifesting before our very eyes, whether we seek it or see it.

A soul, charred and damp, glaring blissfully out the window at the remnants of a broken restaurant. A shed of wood towering in the adorous distance.

An American flag. Waiting patiently. To represent a world and an entity so close to the spiritual world…

That the Earth's axis is placed back into its rightful, honorable location.

Spinning, waving… the crimson and blue shades wrapping rapidly in the air.

Only to wade and wave methodically as time spins over and over in the abysmal yard. Yet the flag is so much more than that. The whipping and whistling of the trees are calling.

Take the lantern, light the way, and answer the call.

Beautiful Souls

It is ringing.

One moment, one step, one second, that's all it takes to make a change. That is all it takes to make a choice.

All the intricacies of the world: different systems, how they interconnect, how they can be improved, who makes those decisions, what team do I need, how do I comprehend history, how has it led to where we are, and how I have to steer the ship we call the United States of America was consuming my daily thoughts.

What do I want here on this planet?

What does my soul want to experience?

At that point I lived through a serious car accident, a bout with alcoholism, battled a drug addiction, dealt with unhealthy relationships, had cancer, and nursed a broken heart.

However, this is not a story of victimization. This is a journey of self-awareness, creation, and ultimate love in its different forms.

This is about living, experiencing, and expanding.

The words of this journey are inundated with spirituality and awakening.

Appearances are not what they seem, for our souls are a combination of energy and higher consciousness. It all comes down to our respective perceptions of reality. We are bigger than the nuances and drama of everyday life.

Everywhere I go, every step I take, and every person I see has a story behind the story. I hoped that I would be able to learn Layne's story behind the story.

I wondered what I could do to improve her life and the lives of others.

The decisions we make in our daily life, though some are crazy and irresponsible, are the fabric of our respective lives. Each of our quilts is composed of patchwork: squares of varying color and length but are the essence of humanity at large. We all have the ability to establish our patch on another's quilt, but our actions and words have the power to either keep others warm or leave them frigid.

On some level that may be a metaphorical perspective, but there is much more at stake here: the search for love.

We are on a continuous journey to find ourselves, and others in this lifetime. It is the natural human way. As we live our lives, we have the capacity to understand soulful love on a devout level.

Home

If we could establish leadership roles that harness that desire for love, we have the potential to transform our planet. Sure, we would have our fair share of challenges, but we can make a drastic shift in the trivial negativity that plagues our lives.

When you think about it, it is clear that a higher love exists within our universe. It may be deep within the stars that cascade across the night sky, or locked away in a heart that beats in honor of the mantra, "The best is yet to come."

It is best we all look introspectively at ourselves in order to deter the pessimism that lurks in the shadows.

Fairness and light always win if we give power to those types of actions and words.

A higher love is present; it is just a matter of time before we unlock our souls to see what this world could become.

Acceptance and love are key goals, with the path to resolution being communication, respect, and listening. We should support one another, not fight each other, for often the battle within us is more consequential than the fighting around us.

Let's put down our fists.

Let's stop degrading one another due to the color of someone's skin or sexual orientation.

There is beauty in life.

Beauty exists within the connections we create, the communication between souls, and moments that take our breath away. Though sometimes they are few and far between, the blessings are apparent within our lives. Sometimes, it takes a moment of silence to comprehend what the voices within us are saying. Therefore, we must actively try to listen to our souls.

Though I was conflicted when it came to Layne, some sort of sensation was brewing deep within. My soul felt challenged by how devoted it was to speaking to and being in the presence of Layne.

I did not want my heart to be broken again, but then again, I did not know if what I was feeling for Layne was, indeed, love.

As our daily texts and insightful conversations continued, I was not sure exactly what direction we were going in. All I knew was that we were both moving towards something greater than ourselves.

I could feel it.

Beautiful Souls

I chose to give into the voice within my soul and do what I felt was right: within weeks of finally seeing Layne, I decided I would go back to Martha's Vineyard to explore the connection between us.

For as long as I could remember, I was trying to save the souls on this planet. Many people blame human nature for their soul's detriment, but the truth is that humanity is not unkind.

It is learned behavior for when our souls are misunderstood.

We must make up our minds, for we have our whole lives to decide what is true. When we look up at the stars, we are not just wishing for love to blaze through our lives. Even when the night is over and it seems like our souls are drifting away from our true intentions.

I know I will still be here, stargazing.

∞ ∞ ∞ ∞ ∞ ∞ ∞ ∞

On the drive up to Massachusetts, I began gazing out at the lush trees that were in full bloom.

Morena and I spoke on the phone for a while to quell my nerves.

"I don't even know why you are nervous," She remarked.

'I don't know either,' I tapped on the steering wheel. 'I just have a feeling.'

"About what?"

I rubbed my neck with my open palm. 'I don't know, it's like… you know when you find something you have *really* been looking for? It's like that.'

"Okay, we are getting somewhere," she sounded relieved. "She is the one you have been looking for."

'Is that a question, Morena, or-'

"Oh," she sounded slightly startled. "Yeah, it was a question."

It was odd: Morena sounded like she knew what was going to happen regarding Layne. It was almost as if she had a premonition that life would be drastically different upon my arrival in Martha's Vineyard during this trip.

Her words were prophetic at times, and had I known what I would be walking into, I think I would have prepared myself a lot better.

At that point I had a challenging time being myself, for I was constantly evolving. I was still working through a lot, though I chose not to outwardly admit it to the world.

Home

I was a transformative soul in progress and Layne's presence would soon be the tipping point.

When I parked at the terminal and boarded the ferry, I continued to remain in this weird reflective space. Now, don't get me wrong, it is not a negative place to be.

The universe just seemed to be speaking to me in a manner that was a lot stronger than usual.

For all intents and purposes, it seemed that the Circle of Angels was shining down upon me from the sunlight up above. The birds chirping and flying close to the boat were echoic of the messages from the Circle of Angels.

I closed my eyes and let the sea air inundate my body. Whispers to my community grew from deep within my soul. I was thankful for the courage bestowed upon me from the stars that are both seen and unseen. Before so many of the angels physically left this earth, they granted me so many life lessons.

Light carries on endlessly despite death.

The infinite remains despite the seemingly momentary presence each of my angels brought to my life.

It is so rare and beautiful to even exist within another soul's timeline; so much that in those moments I was grateful for Layne's impact on my life so far.

Upon reaching the dock, Layne cheerfully waved at the boat. I could see her beaming smile as we disembarked from the ferry.

"Hey," she rushed right over and threw her arms around me. "I missed you!"

The affection she granted me made it seem as if we had not been physically apart for a few weeks.

Layne and I chatted about my drive up from New York as we walked to her car. The white sedan had a small scuff on the passenger side, which was seemingly from the incident with her tire the last time I left town.

I was hoping she would not be nervous this time around.

As the two of us drove towards the bed and breakfast, it became clear that she had another side to her. In actuality she has several sides to her, but regardless of whatever side is present for the given moment, the two of us seem to connect and understand one another so well.

"I really hope you don't mind," she said as we got out of the car. "Tonight is my friend's birthday party and we were invited to the party."

'*We?*' I hoped I did not come off as uninterested.

"Yeah, is it okay with you that we go?"

I chuckled. 'Of course, I am just glad I am here with you. I am surprised I got an invitation, honestly.'

"Surprised," she touched my shoulder and her energy reverberated through my body. "My friends adore you."

'They don't even know me.'

"Don't worry, I told them everything there is to know."

'Oh,' I gulped. 'Great.'

"Don't worry! I explained how you are interested in education reform and they were all intrigued. Don't be surprised if you get asked a lot of questions tonight.'

'I am not worried,' I nudged her. 'I am with you.'

We gazed at each other until I came up with something to break the silence.

'Um,' I cleared my throat. 'Is your boyfriend or anyone else coming with us?'

She smiled endearingly. "I don't have a boyfriend *or anyone else.*"

'Oh,' I adjusted my collar. 'I didn't mean anything by that.'

"Okay." She walked past me and turned around. "I know."

Layne let out an exasperated sigh.

'What's wrong?'

"There-" she swallowed hard. "There is something you should know about me."

'Okay,' I leaned against the roof of the car for a moment. 'I am listening.'

Layne sighed again as she slammed the door. The two of us walked in silence to the front of the bed and breakfast. We took a seat on the rocking chairs on the porch.

She continued to explain to me why she did not have a boyfriend for quite some time. It appeared that years ago, she had a best friend who she did everything with. The two girls were practically inseparable.

Once Layne found a boyfriend, her best friend secretly grew jealous.

Through tears, she held my hand and let the words flow from her, "It got to the point where I left work early one day, and I came home

Home

and found both of them in bed together. I moved out of the house my boyfriend and I were living in that night."

'Layne, I am so sorry.'

"Don't be," she wiped her eyes. "I am thankful we didn't get married… and he said he loved me."

'Love is a special gift; he shouldn't have played with your heart like that'

"Thanks," she gripped my hand harder. "Thank you for saying that."

The two of us shifted to a more positive topic.

We spoke for hours about her plans and dreams. She hoped to do something powerful within this world, and she had such an abundance of ideas, but Layne claimed to need a catalyst to move forward.

I wondered what she meant by it, but I tried not to read into it.

As the night fell upon us, the two of us wandered into a rustic looking bar. Colored seashells and lights tucked into mason jars lined the wall. It appeared to be a secret paradise of sorts where her friends regularly convened.

Her friends greeted me jovially, and it was clear that they started to drink a lot earlier than expected. Layne worked the crowd with ease. She conversed with people she did not seem to know as if she belonged in their respective lives.

Still, the energy did not seem as strong as the connection the two of us had.

At one point as my lack of dancing skills consumed my body, a man cut in and tried to grab her hand. Though he was a stranger, she did not dismiss him in a nasty manner.

Layne gently took a step back.

"I am not interested, thank you though," she bowed out of respect and placed her hand back in mine.

As the man stepped away, the light bounced off of her eyes and cut directly into me. It was almost as if she was warning me: be careful with what you do.

Her friends were very cordial to me and did not leave me out of any conversation whatsoever. The whole situation reminded me that people are not always strangers. Upon having open and honest conversations, the universe continues to move in a symbiotic manner.

The next day, Layne was off from work and offered to show me another tour of Martha's Vineyard.

She took me to a place called the Aquinnah Cliffs Overlook, where the view of the ocean was utterly breathtaking. A quaint sepia-toned lighthouse sat precariously near the end of a long series of greenery.

The rushing water was the quintessential background noise to our discussion about changing the world.

With the sunlight beaming down upon her, the two of us started to move closer and closer to one another. I still did not have a clear read on her or her feelings towards me, but basking in her energy felt amazing.

Layne took me towards a secluded part of the overlook and motioned for me to sit. She took her place next to me and the energy between us took on the momentum of a firestone. With a single spark between us, we seemed to be able to light up the world.

It felt like I had known her for all eternity.

Her hair draped over my arm almost in an angelic manner as she fell into my arms. It was almost as if we were a majestic puzzle whose pieces were once scattered, yet now they were interconnected appropriately. My gentle kisses caressed her forehead in our everlasting symbiosis. Her cosmic energy mingled with every fiber of my heart's longing, yet we inherently knew that our conjoining would exacerbate a force to be reckoned with.

More than a shift, but a soulful awakening: a spiritual diaspora of the negativity we once harnessed melting into the infinite worlds we now expanded upon.

A cathartic sigh of "at last" in a once-concealed force field burdened by the scars of past pain that obscured all the goodness longing to be released into the world.

In that very moment, I felt unburdened by the shackles of expectations. I felt inner peace and frivolity for the first time in forever. I felt the weight of circumstance lift itself from my soul and ascend to its next mission: a means to establish my growth.

I had it within me all along. I had it. I knew I did. I just never realized that I could be the one to bring it out. I have a mind, body, and soul to nurture. I had a heart that still fervently beats as the band marches on.

It is transcendental. It is awe-inspiring. It is growth and freedom and an abundance of life.

It is a rebirth.

A solitary moment became lost in the fabric of time, simply because of the intertwining of two hands and two souls. Interlocking fingers signaling the conjunction of the timeline threading itself in our lives.

A soul connection could never be divided or severed. It could not be broken, though at times it could be bent in the cosmic whip that stands between the sky, the stars, and our human entities. The energy emitted into the air pollutes our minds, but without the negative connotation that comes with pollution existing in the atmosphere.

Love is intoxicating and love takes many forms. Love is its own monstrous being: merging with two respective souls within the blink of an eye or the erection of a smile.

Everything has reason and everything has purpose, it all just comes down to one question: how badly do you want the connection to strengthen?

Now find it within your own soul... then seek the goodness in other souls.

∞ ∞ ∞ ∞ ∞ ∞ ∞ ∞

I planted a gentle kiss on Layne's forehead before I left.

"Thank you for this weekend," she hugged me. "Your expressions and realness are a breath of fresh air. I appreciate you so much, beyond words."

A tinge of weirdness caused me to shudder at her touch.

'I am sorry,' I whispered to her.

"For what?"

'I just want us to stay in a state of symbiosis.'

"We always will be," she grinned majestically. "The universe has already determined it."

Notions of God, spirituality, and higher consciousness flooded my soul. I just knew I had to come back to her again as soon as possible. I was hoping that with the summer coming up, I would be able to make more trips up to Martha's Vineyard and hoped she might potentially visit New York soon enough.

New days were upon us to signify our advancement forward. We had to keep expanding, we had to keep growing; we had to continue to be grateful and inspirational.

Excitement was building with regard to all that was yet to be built. The journey forward was going to be of a soulful and more spiritual one.

It was a profound shift in the universe.

Before I boarded the ferry, she grasped my arms with her tender fingertips. I wanted to kiss her intensely, but I was not sure if the energy I was feeling towards her was truly mutual.

Again, I was fearful of making the same mistakes over and over.

The drive down to New York was filled with fond memories of dancing with her and holding her in my arms.

'What am I doing?' I wondered desperately.

There was a certain thickness in the energy that encircled me.

I felt alone though I should have been so elated after coming back from such an intense and magical weekend. Still, I felt scared and alone.

The cars were parked the same on my mother's street.

My daily routine was still the same.

The damp New York drizzle stemming from the trees ushered in its casual emotions.

My heart was on the verge of sensing a huge lesson here. I felt immersed in a movie scene; wherein the main character was about to have a spiritual awakening that arrives at a pivotal moment.

After everything I experienced, I wondered if I could, yet again, be at the crux of another earth-shattering moment.

I did not think that words could materialize on my lips, yet the letters were able to flow freely from my pen.

This was an atypical combination of energy and vibration that the universe seemed to orchestrate. I figured that above all, Layne needed to breathe into this new role we were both stepping into.

Much uncertainty lingered in what all of this meant and who we were to each other, but I was sure that we would soon find out.

I made it my mission to go back up to see her again.

To my soul, it was an inconsequential longing to be next to her. A bigger picture was forming before us, and we seemed like the ones who would be stepping into the light together.

I was still in the process of emotionally healing from the cancer and past wounds, but the scars were beginning to fade away rapidly.

Home

It appeared that I found my way to Martha's Vineyard for one reason and one reason alone: Layne.

At the time, I wondered what that even meant.

Thinking about it in such complex terms left me somewhat paralyzed, yet I was struck by the numb sensation of feeling her fingers wrapped between mine.

It was not a pestilent numbness, but rather it was a sensation that my frozen soul was beginning to thaw.

As the New York clouds cleared, I realized that I really was not the same anymore. This time however, I could truly feel it.

"You are the best I have ever come across, Scott, I am so sold on you it's not even funny," Layne assured me as we spoke on the phone before I walked into work.

'You truly are the light on the darkest of days,' I assured her.

A breathy laugh trailed into a sigh, which left me slightly confused.

Her thoughts must have been running rampant.

As I walked throughout the building, nothing fazed me, not even Emma.

Standing in the eye of the storm, I felt a sudden rush of peace pass over my body. Her ghosts no longer haunted me. Her aroma did not linger on the forefront of my memory; rather she was an image of a past life.

Caught betwixt the balance of the swirling winds and torrential rain, I realized I had become a byproduct of all of the chaos and calamity that I had endured; yet I was not the chaos. I was not the turmoil. I was me. I was every fundamental aspect of growth and frivolity that had been masked by circumstance. In the eye, I was myself again.

The clarity gave me a rejuvenating feeling. The clarity wholeheartedly renewed and restored my faith. I was underneath the rubble all along.

The desolate destruction could no longer bear the weight of my soul.

Like a phoenix, I rise from the ashes and unburden myself from the stinging sensation of pain.

I rise.

And as I rise above... I realized something utterly earth shattering: I am not in the eye of the storm.

I am not in the eye of the storm... because the storm has passed...

Beautiful Souls

And here I am. A bold new soul standing at the edge of the rocks... glaring out at the new opportunities ahead in the water. A green light holds steady on the buoy in the water: a reminder that I too could live.

I too can shine.

This old soul may have been down, but it is not out. I was buried; then I was planted...

Now it is time to grow.

∞ ∞ ∞ ∞ ∞ ∞ ∞ ∞

I became consumed and lost in the summer nights. Layne's crystalline eyes left me utterly speechless. Despite the darkness that once existed in my soul, I realized that nothing else mattered but her presence.

As I drove up to Martha's Vineyard for the third time in less than a few weeks, it dawned upon me: I would never let her go.

Exhausted and slightly fragmented, I fell onto the seat on the ferry.

There are so many souls in pain on the planet, yet despite the seeming agony we manage to make other souls happy.

It's priceless.

We are the ones who create our own reality. We attract what we desire in order to learn the lessons that excavate the broken bits of our respective souls.

The people we surround ourselves with are a testament to the ambitions we pursue in life. If we inherently want to go the distance, leaders must remember who stands beside them even when all seems chaotic and unclear.

Morena stood beside me for so long.

Best friend is a label that would slight her wholeheartedly; angel seems more fitting of a label for her, but definitely not a human angel. She is someone from some sort of different universe or realm.

Layne seemed to be the next person who I wanted on my team. The energy she emitted from her soul is genuine and spiritually enlightening. Everything within me screamed, "Whatever happens, don't screw this one up. She is the real deal."

In the past, I was too demanding, too pressuring, and attempted to fit people into a storyline that just did not add up. I was forcing love, rather than giving it the space to breathe.

Home

I instilled fear in those I loved, which forced them to run.

Now I found myself in the midst of another test: was the love I felt for Layne real or one-sided?

A resounding thud followed by the boat lurching forward slightly meant that I was back at Martha's Vineyard. Layne was happy to see me once again, and even took off from work so we could spend the entire weekend flushing out ideas.

The overcast Friday afternoon did not put a damper on Layne's spirits, for rather she lit up the sky with the sunlight beaming from her soul.

The moment I got there, I could feel the energy burning through her skin. It almost grasped me and shook me to my core, but I had to reserve my emotions for a few moments.

Did she feel the same about me as I did for her?

The two of us walked down the street for a while until we came to a luscious gathering of trees.

"Scott, come on, I want you to see something," Layne grasped my hand and pulled me off of the concrete path. We whisked through trees and shrubs that were scattered for what looked like miles around. We were inherently alone together, an event that I longed for from the moment she grasped my hand that fateful day. From our first touch, I knew that my search had to be over: she was my destiny.

We pushed through the branches together, stumbling comically through the woods as if we were on a mission to dance in the solitude of the lush greenery forever: just the two of us. It felt as if we were creating our new home far away from civilization, yet we would develop our own society. Our souls would speak to each other in a manner only we knew and our hearts would open up a realm of their own. Just one kiss… and the connection would forever be bound together.

"This is my other spot. I come here to think and write. I wanted to share it with you." A smile crept up her cheeks as she pulled me towards the dirt.

We sat on the ground against a log with a stream rippling in front of us: it was a picturesque scene that would never leave my mind for as long as I live. We were immersed in nature where we both felt an instant connection to the universe. Outside this beautiful hidden cove was a concrete jungle… but hidden in here was just me and her. It was a safe spot to delve into this love story that seems like years in the making. Though in some juxtaposed, elaborate trepidation, we were a romance that blossomed centuries before our time. Our souls were intertwined long before our fingers met in this very moment.

As our bodies wrapped around one another in that fateful moment, Layne's face was merely an inch from my lips. She closed her eyes ambitiously, yet something was preventing us from sealing our combined fates in that moment.

"This scares me," Layne blurted out in a lucid whisper.

'Me too,' I responded.

"If we were together, we would get nothing accomplished because we would be doing…" Layne paused and collected some courage from within, "other things all the time."

I leaned in towards her and our mouths were mere seconds from each other.

Layne paused and placed her fingers on my lips. "Wait."

'What's wrong?'

"Before anything happens, I need you to know that I am afraid."

'Okay, let's talk about this,' I paused. 'I mean, if you would like to.'

"I honestly, I am still working through repairing my emotions. Nothing really replaced the love I felt for my boyfriend."

I placed my hand on top of hers. 'F. Scott Fitzgerald wrote, *"There are all kinds of love in this world, but never the same love twice."*'

She grinned and locked eyes with me. "Scott, I just don't trust myself."

'I promise I won't do anything you do not feel you are ready for.'

"Thanks."

We went back and forth, playing with the danger of what the universe provided us. Both of us fully knowing and admitting to each other that this love we felt for one another was real, but it couldn't go any further. Neither of us wanted to entirely admit it just yet, for we were immersed in the habitual beauty of the moment.

An "I Love NY" keychain dangled in between my fingertips, glowing in the great presence of her unfathomable eloquence. It took 15 hours to get to her after a five-hour drive to Massachusetts turned into a traffic nightmare. It took all of the strength within me from breaking down and melting into an abysmal depression due to what seemed like the

Home

universe pulling us apart. I explained to her that she needed to have the keychain, for I always keep an "I Love Martha's Vineyard" keychain in my pocket. Though it took all the energy I had to get to her, it was worth it. Gazing into her eyes that day, I knew it was worth every second of agony I dealt with.

As she gazed at me longingly, I pulled ants off of her shoulder as they crept along our bodies. Neither of us was phased in the moment. As she spoke about her hopes and dreams in more detail, I pulled blades of grass from near the log. Our arms were wrapped tighter around one another and I drew her closer to my chest to rub a yellow powdery substance from her nose. The sunlight shone brighter on her face as she glared into my eyes. If she were not there to hold onto, I would have melted in that very moment.

My eyes adored every inch of her supple skin pressed against mine. Her mouth was busy forming words that angels whisper to lovers in the night. Layne inhaled deeply and shot daggers through my soul: "Today can't go further than this… I need to feel safe…"

'What,' flowed out of my mouth in absolute shock. We were just getting comfortable holding one another, even in innocence.

"I don't trust myself…. this is a love on a higher level I don't quite comprehend…" Layne continued to speak, but I was deafened by the pain emulating from deep within me.

Each word slammed into me with the intensity of an atomic bomb. My soul was desolated between each breath she took. Our love rotted and morphed into a cataclysmic event: a war between the heart, mind, and soul: how could I just release this beautiful energy between us back into the world without savoring one more moment of her tender grasp? I was just getting accustomed to feeling like someone she loved.

It all came crashing down in minutes.

She pushed against my chest in a seeming fit of silent rage, "I need you to protect me Scott. I need to feel safe." Her voice shattered just as my soul was crackling at that very moment, "I need you to make sure this doesn't go further because I do not trust myself around you." I nodded rhythmically.

I sat in silence, glaring down at the river metaphorically rinsing my pain away.

'Layne, I-' as I began to speak, I could see her mounting another one-sided argument against my soul. I continued processing.

"This isn't good because you bring me so much joy. You confuse me. You blur the lines and I'm scared." My heart felt heavy and guilty. I wanted to grab her face tenderly, kiss her lips passionately, and tell her that my love for her was unyielding and unwavering. I wanted her to realize that I was the one. Me. I was her true soulmate and hers. All of me. Every last piece of my once shattered existence was hers to adore.

She needed to be loved. She needed to be seen and felt in ways that only exist in a state of higher consciousness... and that is exactly what this relationship had to be: higher consciousness. Nothing more; nothing far less than that.

'Layne, listen for a moment,' I adjusted my body so we were now face to face. I placed her shaking hands in mine and held them tightly.

'I will never hurt you. I promise that no matter what happens, I will love you to fill the cracks that permeate your gentle soul. We never have to have a physical connection between us. It is an honor and ultimately a blessing that you are who you are.'

She sat in devout silence and believed my words, though everything in the universe was restraining me from kissing her passionately and never turning back. My role was to love her how she needed to be loved. If that is not higher consciousness... then I do not know what is. To love someone deeply, yet always be at an arm's length, is one of the most soulfully challenging moments to endure. In a blink of an eye, she was mine and the universe's in one fatal swoop.

Layne fell into my arms and cuddled into my chest. I planted a solitary, slow kiss on her forehead and ran my fingers through her peaceful hair.

"I have wanted to touch you from the moment you arrived," Layne whispered. Our meeting in the midst of this universal shift was mind boggling, and in a matter of a few hours I would be back in another world again.

We sat there in the silence of each other's company as the universe filled our hearts with memories distinctly found in other lifetimes and other universes. I now know what a twin flame and true soulmate are. Those are exquisite lines that are reserved for her: the true light of my life and devout beauty eternally trapped in my mind.

Home

"I never knew you would show up," Layne glared at me in a reaction laced with exquisite horror and fascination.

I chuckled for a moment. Emma spoke those very soul-shattering words just a few years ago. And now here we are again. Full circle. Yet this was so different. Layne was the real deal, while Emma had so much potential brewing in her bones. One day Emma will get there, hopefully soon, and I hope she has the courage to tell me how far she has come and how much she has grown. Layne however is already there. Layne is the energetic heartline that illuminates a true soul-to-soul connection. This is why things never worked with Emma: Layne was looking for our profound connection to materialize before our very eyes, but somehow our love was lost in translation.

We were both deeply in love with one another, Layne and I, and said it in the most alluring way imaginable. Being with Layne heightened my soul, for she is the perfect melody that exists between my drastic sense of who I was and who I started becoming. I needed her and she needed me…

But being together in such a spiritual sense of the term "together" always comes with its challenges.

"Scott," she looked up at the raindrops caressing her face from up above, "We should get going." As the rain kissed her skin in places I could now only dream of, neither of us moved from that spot. We longed to savor that memory. We were present to the moment we defined our very spiritual love.

As the rain washed over our bodies, I sensed we would always be intertwined… maybe not in the physical sense, but always in the spiritual sense.

'We can overcome anything together, Layne,' were the last words I whispered in her ear before we emerged into the seascape jungle once again. Our moment of intermingled solitude would never dissipate.

So much weight clenched the heartstrings I was desperately trying to keep elevated. I did not want to start ranting about hopeful messages of love, for this was not what this was about.

Honestly, I didn't know what this was about.

I just had to let go and merely go with the flow.

I believed Layne was here to stay and so much uncertainty lingered with regards to what that meant to the whole vision.

However, all I knew was that her creations and soul were remarkable.

That night, I dreamt that Morena, Layne, and I were hosting some sort of conference together. It was a retreat of sorts with global leaders from such diverse countries.

It felt very real.

It felt very different.

It felt like a memory.

We were hosting, we were not the ones attending the conference. We had global attention that previously felt unprecedented.

It was coming.

It was *all* coming.

∞ ∞ ∞ ∞ ∞ ∞ ∞ ∞

Leaving her utterly broke me. Sitting on a small ferry that's taking me back to the mainland left me with a heavy heart, yet I upheld this heavy heart that had never been happier. The phrases we uttered to one another in distinct silence lingered throughout my head.

Standing at the edge of two worlds, I felt the pressure mounting at the base of my skull. A flood of emotion rushed throughout my body as the gravity of the situation hit me… hard: the answer was finally before me. Layne was the answer to every hardship I endured. Layne was the final chapter. Layne was the missing puzzle piece that my heart finally found. My twin flame was standing before me, just an arm's length away, yet we would never be able to burn together. Still, neither of us was willing to face that fact yet. We both stood with our souls barely touching one another, hoping that the other person would tip the balance of the universe so we could crash into each other passionately. Our love was the manifestation of something that would be in a perfect movie scene: boy meets girl, girl loves boy, boy loves girl.

How do I return to what I once was after the sensation has already crept through my veins? How do I step back from the edge when I was always meant to jump and freefall into her arms?

Being on the ferry felt absolutely heavenly. The atmosphere around the boat was similar to the air we breathed into each other's souls that day. I was with Layne for only eight hours, but it felt like fifteen minutes.

Home

When I look back though, it took fifteen hours to drive to her. Layne was utterly blown away.

This was the most incredibly loving hurt I had ever experienced in my life. It hurt, but I couldn't let it be painful. I had to feel the magnitude of the blessing and role I was upholding in her life. I don't know how to explain that day eloquently.

Yet as words fell short and my mind wandered to our intimate meeting, the ferry approached Woods Hole. I should leave what happened at the stream, at the rocks that are simply atoms moving so rapidly that it appears to feel solid and stationary, but our love permeates this universe with enough power to illuminate billions of souls. How could we hide our love? How could we resist the temptations that exist between us? No, we must. I must.

'We can overcome anything,' I whispered in her ear. 'Let me be the one who provides you the emotional strength,' I said.

Layne responded, "Please do." Her laughter is contagious. We connected on an entirely different level. I could't believe what had happened since the moment I laid eyes on that beautiful, powerful soul.

The boat slammed against the metal dock. That was fast.

Supposedly, and technically, I am going "home"...but I just left home at the water that reverently rippled through the rocks. Layne resting against my chest and embracing my lightened frame, a moment that made time as us humans know it stand still, was the true embodiment of home.

That's my home: her arms... our bodies cuddled as one. I finally found it.

I came to the stark realization that was already brewing within... I am homeless again.

While exiting the ferry it hit me, and it hit me hard: I think the reason I went through all this pain and anguish with Emma was to learn a lesson. "She has a purpose" echoed through my mind. The real reason I lost Emma was because I played my cards wrong. I was too demanding, too pressuring, and tried to get her to fit into the storyline I wanted. Emma needed to grow spiritually before we would be on the same level: our souls were disconnected the moment we met. I was forcing it and not giving her the space to figure things out and breathe. I scared her and she ran. I now found myself in a similar complicated storyline with someone I care about and could not make the same mistake. I must learn from past experiences and had to make sure I swim "in this delicious ice cream", as Layne put so eloquently, and not destroy our relationship. I needed to just enjoy the moments and let it be.

∞ ∞ ∞ ∞ ∞ ∞ ∞ ∞

Being apart from her felt awkward, though being with her meant trying to mask how deeply in love I was with her.

During the work week, I was a patron of Lincoln Memorial High School's atmosphere. Though I enjoyed my job and working with the teachers and the students, being with Layne made my soul sing.

Our regular phone conversations continued nightly to the tune of our hearts beating in tandem.

It became increasingly difficult to catch my breath.

I wondered why the universe was trying to keep me away from her. It was a simple reminder that I waited a lifetime to reconnect with Layne, so that we could finally fulfill our soul contract.

Another few hours before speaking to her on the phone again after each workday seemed like nothing.

I knew nothing would keep me away from her.

Anticipation flowed through my veins: she felt like home. It amazed me that a person could truly carry the sentiments of my heart, my soul, and my every thought.

God built us to love. We can love more than one person. We can be attracted to different things.

Society teaches that there are limitations to love, but that doesn't make sense. Love is the process of the soul expanding. Love is an abundance of appreciation. Love is everything and exists in everything.

Love is in these moments and in the pages of this book.

Love is in the connections, the alignments, the smiles, and in the tears. Fear is the manifestation of not loving your true self. Fear is not stepping into who you truly are. Fear is being asleep, not being awake.

We are all one and the one is split into an infinite amount of souls. Our limitations see this as separate entities, but in reality, we are not truly apart.

This was all making sense.

Our souls are genuinely infinite so that we may learn to develop our oneness. Separation and trepidation are mere illusions.

My heart became inundated with tears of joy.

I came to the conclusion that I was not falling in love; it was rather the opposite. Falling implies losing control, entering dangerous territory, and spiraling in a downward motion. I sense that this phrase came from a metaphorical notion that falling represented freedom and replicated an exciting rush.

However, those are fantastical fallacies we tell ourselves to make sense of the confusion we might be feeling.

Being in love with Layne provided me with an elevated state of mind and being. Love was lifting me up.

The sensation of love was empowering me to discover who I truly was. Any reality and experience I could think of had the potential to become a part of my timeline.

When you truly connect to the energy of love, souls are attracted to one another because we are one in the same.

Our souls desired to connect.

"I want to come see you," Layne whispered into the night.

'So, come to New York.'

"But if I do" she started, "Then I want to drive around and see things and talk about your Framework and our vision on the open road."

'Well, you are welcome to drive my car.'

"Really," she sounded stunned. "You would let me do that?"

'Yeah,' I replied matter-of-factly. 'Why wouldn't I?'

"Aren't guys really protective over their cars?"

'You'll be safe,' I assured her. 'I know you.'

I could hear her grin through the phone.

The two of us agreed that she would take a combination of buses to get to a certain point in Manhattan, and that I would pick her up from wherever the last bus would stop.

Layne was thrilled and by the following weekend, she was roaming the streets of New York City with me.

The two of us strolled in unison, our hands linked together perfectly. It was almost as if our fingers were created to fit between one another's.

Beautiful Souls

With her coming to New York, it was a date marked in the infamy of our worlds colliding for a second. Our gravitational forces were compelled to crash into one another wholeheartedly and without remorse, yet there was something forcing us apart. Though the universe brought us together in a rather cataclysmic way in a matter of moments, it pulled us apart with such fury, as if it were beckoning the words, "No, you can't have her. She is not yours to keep." She is to be idolized and revered, like the statues placed on pedestals in museums. She is to be kept pristine and unmarked by the tainted words that shatter upon her skin upon their fateful release. She is to be regarded to the highest standard and with the most respect and sincerity.

She is to be admired by all, feared in her sense of power, and in accordance with the contract she signed with the universe long, long ago...

And she would be mine, regardless of what the universe said.

For her, I would twist the balance of fate and destiny... for she was what I yearned for all along.

And she would not escape my purview. I did not trek this path to not be in her presence, and as the universe as my witness, nothing physical or emotional would stop me from having her in my arms.

The two of us stopped for ice cream at some quaint shop in the city. As the two of us sauntered down the street, arm in arm, eating ice cream, something told me that this was how life was meant to be: innocent and simplistic.

As Layne walked ahead of me, I snapped a picture of her so I could savor the moment forever.

She shouted back to me: "Why do you do that?"

'Do what?'

"You take pictures of me sometimes when you think I don't notice. I notice."

We laughed for a moment and she seemed to drop the subject.

Little did she know, the faded pictures in my phone were frozen in the ripples of time. Each face she made consisted of smiling and laughing; she was forgetting for one moment that anything else was happening. Each expression's demeanor whittled away pain and accepted a snapshot of "Yes, my life is great," even for a split second between flashes.

The expressions faded once the camera marked its territory, but the photograph acts as a stark reminder that someone cared enough to clasp the moment and preserve it forever.

Home

Photographs are windows to the soul. Pictures are persistent reminders that we were all once frozen in a different state of mind.

We develop, we bend, we break, we shape each other, we mold, and we transfer our energy into different avenues as the passing wind chimes reverberate. The leaves pick up and lift all of us onto another realm. We rise. We look at our pictures and smile at our reflections.

We gaze at ourselves and see our past, present, and future in one swoop. All at once, we are the whole parts of what we have left behind and what we intend to create.

And the beauty of it all? It is frozen in time, captured in a photograph… a treasured keepsake we hold dear forever.

The two of us meandered towards Bryant Park. Layne glared up at the two stone lions that guarded the New York Public Library; she seemed to be in amazement of their permanent beauty.

The lions, like the photographs, were perfectly frozen in time.

We found a quiet spot on the steps of the library where no one seemed to notice that two people were embarking on a spiritual journey of a symbiotic nature.

"I just want to make one thing very clear," Layne said.

'You have cleared up a lot in my life, but go ahead.'

"I would never cheat on you," she gripped my hands. "I don't want to hurt you, ever."

'Cheating implies secrecy,' I assured her. I gazed out at the faces of people passing by. 'We don't have that type of love.'

I spoke as if I knew this truth was coming from deep within my soul. There was no fear about losing her or any potential for her to cheat.

This was an eternal bond of a much deeper than human experience.

It wasn't about fear or loss; it was about a pure love that exceeded the humanistic way of life.

Layne was proof that the universe welcomes love openly, it is just a matter of finding your soul's voice.

Her exquisite soul's beauty, intellect, and poise were worth every single moment I endured throughout my lifetime.

I would live everything over again if I knew that I would find her again. She is worth it.

Beautiful Souls

Layne was what humanity secretly prayed for. She is what I almost gave up searching for.

We both found our home and we had so much to learn before we could accept that fact. One thing was for certain though: we would travel this road together.

As the night fell upon us in Manhattan, Layne asked if we could head back towards Queens. I happily obliged and the two of us listened to music in my Dodge Charger as we sat in traffic on the Long Island Expressway.

The green road signs lined with white borders reflected in the sunroof of my car. The sunset was in the not-so-distant past, but it felt like we had been together for days at this point.

It was a refreshingly satisfying feeling.

As we pulled up to the hotel she was staying at, she asked if I would wait downstairs for a few moments while she freshened up.

Happily, I told her to take her time, for I knew that I could call Morena and fill her in on everything happening.

After about fifteen minutes of talking to her, I exhaled a sigh of relief.

"You really love, Layne, don't you?" Morena said.

'Yeah,' I tilted my head up to the stars above, 'Yes, I do.'

"I am glad your soul recognized her love."

'She is truly amazing,' I assured her.

"You don't have to tell me twice."

Our conversation ended as Layne jumped back in the car. She was wearing a tight black dress that hugged every single one of her curves. We agreed that we were going to go to a bar in Queens, so that she could experience New York's nightlife scene.

She watched my eyes drag along every inch of her body, "Are you okay?"

'Always.'

"Oh, the dress," she smoothed it out with her fingertips. "Sorry, I just figured this is what typical New Yorkers wear on a night out. I wanted you to see this side of me."

Layne fiddled with the radio for a moment until Eric Clapton's "Wonderful Tonight" materialized on the radio:

Home

> *"I feel wonderful because I see*
> *The love light in your eyes*
> *And the wonder of it all*
> *Is that you just don't realize how much I love you."*

We glanced at one another and she placed her head on my shoulder.

"Thank you for all that you do," Layne grabbed my hand as I started to sing the lyrics to her.

We drove out of the lot as she asked if we could go to a place in Astoria, which was about twenty minutes from where she was staying in Bayside, Queens.

Although I am a native New Yorker, her directions were confusing me.

My eyes darted towards the passenger seat as I still tried to focus on the road.

'Are you just giving me random directions?'

"No," the glow from her phone screen illuminated her fingers. "Just drive."

At this point, it looked like we went south instead of west towards Astoria. The two of us pulled onto a dark street in what appeared to be a ritzy neighborhood.

I parked the car and tried to reach for her phone to see the map.

Layne shut the screen off on her phone, changed the radio station again, and pushed the seat back.

> *"We don't need no education*
> *We don't need no thought control*
> *No dark sarcasm in the classroom*
> *Teachers leave them kids alone*
> *Hey, teachers, leave them kids alone*
> *All in all it's just another brick in the wall*
> *All in all you're just another brick in the wall."*

The background noise of Pink Floyd's "Another Brick in the Wall" made it seem like we were in a dramatic movie scene.

Layne sat up and leaned on her left elbow for a moment.

"I'm dangerous, Scott," she moved closer to me and ran her fingers through my hair.

Unsure of what else to do, I ran my fingers through her chestnut-brown hair. As my fingers reached the bottom, her hair fell back to her shoulders with such grace.

As she leaned into me, seemingly in slow motion, my heart began to race.

My hands instinctively brushed against her shoulders as I swayed towards her neck. My lips searched out her neck and moved gently towards her ear.

Layne's soft moans grew slightly louder.

I whispered in her ear, 'Are you okay with this?'

"Yes."

'What are you thinking?'

She locked eyes with me for a moment, "Nothing."

'That's good.'

I continued to kiss her delicately until our mouths moved closer and closer.

Layne pulled away slightly and I stopped.

Her eyelids shut in such a sultry manner before drifting open once again. The two of us gazed at one another as the streetlight and moonlight beckoned down upon us.

I let my hand explore her outer leg for a few minutes. Her pupils dilated as she moved her right hand up the side of my face. I could sense her brushing the stubble growing on my face as I shut my eyes.

My fingers dropped between her thighs as I realized how wet she was getting. As my mind made a desperate attempt to comprehend what was happening, our lips collided.

Layne's teeth gripped my bottom lip as I let out a breathy grunt.

We kissed without remorse as I hoisted her on top of my lap. With her legs straddled around me as I sat in the driver's seat, her thigh rode up and down across my lap.

Our furious kisses grew more passionate as she wrapped her hands around the base of my neck.

My hands were all over her body, leaving a trail of my fingerprints in a fervid path along her skin.

I thought that I was dreaming.

As I felt her reaching such a deep level of passionate intensity, she stopped and began to tear up.

'Don't go inside your head,' I whispered to her.

She tossed her head back and pushed it forward again.

Layne left a solitary kiss on my cheek and moved back into the passenger seat.

"This can't happen."

My chest was throbbing as my heart crashed in the pit of my core.

Unsure of what to do, I decided to keep driving into the night. We sat in silence and let the static of the radio fill the empty space between us.

When the two of us finally reached a random bar, she got out of the car and glanced up at me.

"I'm sorry."

I shut the door and walked to her side of the car, 'Why are you sorry?' "I wanted to know what it was like to be with you."

'Were you disappointed?'

"No," she gripped my fingers. "Not at all. I crave the way you touch me, but I don't want to get hurt again."

'Okay,' I dropped my hands as she released my grasp.

The two of us walked into the bar and did not talk about what had just happened. My anxiety kicked in, but I tried not to make it obvious.

She was likely processing what just happened, but masked her emotions in the alcohol she was putting in her body.

After about an hour, I brought her back to her hotel and told her to have a great night. She flashed a smile at me and shut the car door.

Layne did not text me that night, although I thought she might.

I wondered if she was feeling guilty or if she just drifted off to sleep.

As I wallowed in my own emotions, I could not help but be consumed with the current that flowed throughout our bodies only a few hours ago. How can one even describe the transcendence of that kiss?

A kiss is not just a physical expression between two individuals; rather it is a moment where the cosmic essence of emotion collides all at once.

When a kiss is truly devout, human emotion flourishes to another realm. The sensation of kissing someone who innately matches every fiber of your being is one that awakens a sense of home. Home can mean so many different things within the human world, and above all, home is a sense of belonging.

The most perfect kiss can feel like home; it can be flawless, authentic, breathtaking, electrifying, heart pounding, and conscious-raising intoxication, which could only be duplicated when two souls physically meet with that special kiss. It is not just about the sensual affection of a moment; it is an everlasting and supernatural transformation of awareness. Greatness is breathed into the human form.

This is the type of kiss that is the first kiss of the rest of your life; a million lifetimes are echoed into remembrance by the collision of intensified energy.

It becomes a resurrection: the continuation of a fire from past lives fanning the embers of a timeless passion. It is a kiss that confirms that the universe is aligned; the world's greatest resource is love.

Vulnerability is a challenge for humans to expose themselves to, yet as her enticing lips elevated me into the heavens, it was clear that lifetimes of doubts and pain dissipated as Layne's head rested on the safety of my gentle torso earlier this evening.

Falling helplessly into a moment's bliss manifested the uncovering of truth within our souls.

Dreams that existed for thousands of years crashed onto a devout rarity that is love finding its way. Once again, captivating lips yearned for mine and it became as if she, alone, was responsible for every sunrise, sunset, and all of the moments inside and outside of the boundaries of light.

Powerful kisses seep into each of our souls as if saying, "You are protected, you are loved, and you are evolving exponentially." A peaceful silence washed over me each moment her lips met mine, and those pleasant memories are sealed into my soul for all of eternity. For some time, the noise around me seemed to fade beneath the sounds of our souls colliding.

The gravity of infinite love seems weightless and grounding all at once. "Hold me darling, just a little while," echoed throughout this last "first kiss," as I knew I found the love I would miss. When love exists on a devout soul level, it becomes a different energy entirely: undeniable and eternal; it is a deep, intimate experience that provides proof of how life on earth should be.

As my fantastical thoughts of this evening came back to earth, I realized that I was petrified for whatever tomorrow could bring.
I desperately did not want to hurt her, yet I thought I might have destroyed her. My usual line of questions infiltrated my head:
How could I betray her trust?
Did she actually want to be with me?
What did I do?
I let the slew of questions usher me to sleep for the night as I passed out on my mother's couch, unsure of what tomorrow would consist of. To my surprise, when I awoke in the morning to her phone call, she did not seem upset at all.

"Are you ready to find some special writing places today?" Her voice sounded chipper and overjoyed.

I assumed that it would be just another day, but I was very, very wrong.

∞ ∞ ∞ ∞ ∞ ∞ ∞ ∞

When my aunt passed away, we buried her in the pouring rain. Each time someone died in my life, it rained, whether it was my grandfather, Paul, or Stacey. Rain had become synonymous with pain and fear for years.

That all changed with Layne.

Because of her, rain became a sign of healing and a symbol of spiritual growth.

The rain spoke to me in a way that is truly indescribable. I wondered if I misheard the original messages from the rain: Be sad now, but bliss is coming. Just have faith, and you will be protected.

Layne and I drove to Francis Lewis Park so I could show her where I went to connect to my soul.

As we walked down towards the Whitestone Bridge, the two of us were clearly basking in the sound of the water's ebb and flow.

Though we were laughing and talking about our respective projects, I could not help but think about the night before.

Layne's profound words burst my train of thought: "You don't have to go anywhere to teach me the courage of stars, that light carries on endlessly, how infinity works, and how rare and beautiful it is to exist. All of that I'm learning through your life. Your life holds the pathway of my education, Scott. And it will for all of eternity."

I glanced over at her as the wind picked up her hair and swirled it around.

'You have no idea how much that means to me,' I smiled.

She looked me in the eyes and grinned, "I love you too. So much."

Layne's illustrious words crept into my soul:

"My heart is glowing, Scott. The way you reach inside my soul with the beauty of your expression is truly a blessed and divine experience. Every cell within me has bonded to every cell within you. Thank you for sharing your light. I honor you for just… being. I don't want to see a world without you in it."

Home

It struck me that her love was wholeheartedly present, though her past was obscuring her physical expression of that love...

And I was totally okay with that.

Just having her in my life was a beautiful experience.

The overcast weather hinted that we should go inside and work at a coffee shop, so we did.

Hours upon hours later, it looked like her journal was filled with such beautiful writings. She would not let me read it, but she would occasionally shoot me a coy look from over the edges of the journal.

As the night fell upon us once again, we noticed the downpour pushing at car windshields and billowing umbrellas.

"Come on," she picked up her journal and tucked it into her bag. I followed suit with my papers. "Let's go."

As we dashed out onto the sidewalk, the rain began to drip impatiently from the overhanging trees. The pristine beauty of the damp leaves drew us further away from the music of the coffee shop. Our ears were becoming less enchanted by the melody of the repetitive conversations, and more engrossed in the distilled silence that hung between our bodies in the brisk nightfall around us.

As droplets of rain began caressing her face, I snatched her hand and tried pulling her down the winding roads and to the car. Her soul was caught in the balance of the light from the streetlights above and the lingering sensation that grew more passionate from within her.

Every fiber of her being longed for a night like this: to be exquisitely free.

She yearned to be woken from the frail imbalances within her, which startled her once she was finally immersed in the delicious taste of the drizzle cascading down her now moistened lips.

The grin on her face became more sincere and apparent.

Anyone walking down the street could feel her positive energy bursting forth from once deep within her soul.

Her fingers linked firmly between mine as we started to frolic in the manifesting rainstorm. Our thoughts melted away, and in those innocent, exquisite moments, our once youthful existence sprung forth. Our hair was drenched, but we were not drowning in the mediocre day-to-day troubles that wore us down once before.

Our souls were in a state of infinite youthfulness.

She released her hand from mine and darted into the gutter: she took a running jump and collided with a puddle, which sent water every which way.

Though she was totally engulfed in water from head to toe now, her sweet demeanor said the words she could not materialize just yet.

In those childlike moments, we knew we were far from toy trucks and dolls, for this was far from what our imaginations could develop regardless of how mature we were.

This was paradise and this was solace, for we both knew we took a rainstorm and created a playground of our own.

As she leapt back onto the sidewalk and we trotted down the street giggling, something was brewing inside me. In that moment, with the rain rolling down our skin and the stars disappearing behind the clouds, her face glowed far brighter than the moon ever could.

The picturesque scene evaporated into a quaint, pleasant moment between our two bodies.

In one swift motion, I swung Layne around and swiveled her body so the two of us were swaying peacefully in the torrential downpour. Her head rested on my chest as if it was always a part of me, and we succumbed to the rhythmic motions of the Earth's gravitational pull.

Our hearts synced and beat in time to the harmonious whispers that vibrated from somewhere within my chest: I was genuinely happy.

Our joyous adventure in the rain took precedence over any classic cinematic moment, for it was an experience that surpassed all human expectations: its elegance and beauty were unmatched in the most wholesome of ways... as the outline of our dancing bodies became etched in the stars.

I glared into her eyes and said the first thing that came to mind, 'Layne... I-'

She stopped me mid-sentence, wrapped her arm around mine, and whispered, "I know, Scott. I know."

Layne leaned into my chest and I held her tight. The street was getting dark as the skies opened up.

The Spider-Man poster from my office at my first high school came to mind. The word "Sacrifice" flashed in front of my eyes.

Home

It reminded me to never give up and to do what I could to find answers in life.

The answer was dancing with me slowly in the rain.

Our movements quickly turned into a soft, elongated kiss that whispered passion into our souls.

She wanted me to protect her from herself, yet this was the only way I knew how: to let her go to the spaces where she was conflicted in order to comprehend her soul's wishes.

The rain shattered upon the sidewalk and I sensed people drifting by, but nothing affected us: this was our moment in time.

Rain, pedestrians, our respective pasts, nothing would stop us.

Sometimes when you try to find the right words to tell a specific story, it would taint the purity or meaning of those moments.

It was a moment that was not supposed to happen, though as I tried pulling away from her to respect her space, she kept wrapping her fingers around my neck and drawing me closer.

We inched towards the car and leapt in.

Droplets of water fell along the leather seats as the two of us continued to kiss.

As the two of us undressed one another and let the wet clothes plop on the floor of the car, our hands sought comfort along each other's skin.

The windows began to fog up as our lips crashed upon one another's.

Rain cascaded along the windows as the two of us brushed along the surface of each other's souls. The careful whispers and gentle strokes we placed upon our skin were reflective of the devout connection we had with one another.

"Please don't stop," Layne begged impetuously.

After Bryan, I always used a condom and always had the willpower to stop what I was doing. I would never not use a condom unless I was sure of two things: I was definitely, truly, and deeply in love and I wanted to be a parent with that person. I knew that they would be both incredibly rare to find and if I was ever in that scenario, I knew it would have to be the ultimate, truthful love.

I knew I would just feel it.

When it came to Layne, I finally felt it.

I was sure of it. I was sure of everything.

The two of us continued our passionate twists and turns until a shadow appeared at the edge of my windshield.

A police officer was writing a parking ticket for a long-expired parking slip.

We remained still, slightly panicked that he would see us through the fogged and tinted windows.

It was the most peaceful sensation I had ever felt despite almost getting caught.

After the officer walked away, Layne readjusted herself so we were cuddled into one another. She fit perfectly in my arms and life was perfect.

There were no other words to say.

As the two of us went back to her hotel room for the night, she embraced me in the doorway.

"I never thought I would find a love like yours," she kissed me on the lips and wrapped her fingers around my collar.

As Layne dragged me into the room, I sensed the night was far from over. I texted my sister and asked if she would be okay with me staying out late.

Without hesitation, she agreed, and my night with Layne continued into the effervescent dawn.

There is an indescribable feeling of peace that washes over me while watching Layne sleep against my shoulder.

I felt that the world stopped spinning on its axis for the time being, just so I could embrace the tenderness of her touch against my slightly rising chest. Layne's body moves gently to the ebb and flow of her soul.

For a moment in time, between her heart's synchronous beats, there was such a remarkable stillness that hung in the air.

It was the entanglement of our fingers that drew me into her beauty the most.

The essence of her soul lingered deep within me. It had since the moment I met her, but this was different.

I looked down at the photo of her that I snapped on my phone.

The way she looked at me and genuinely saw me was breathtaking.

Her glance was a key that unlocked my heart. For years, I did not realize it was in a cage. Layne's presence clung to my skin in a manner that rivaled moisture from last night's rain.

We were interconnected and in a state of synthesis.

It was as if I could somehow hear the thoughts of her soul.

Our bodies had become one. Our energy ensnared our souls onto a level of higher frequency.

I must have fallen asleep at some point, for when my eyes fluttered open and I saw her silhouette moving in tandem with my heartbeat, every fiber of my soul sighed peacefully.

As I watched her resting eloquently on the bed, I dashed out to grab some breakfast for her. I wanted to make sure that when she woke up, Layne would have everything she needed: food, love, and my shoulder to rest her head upon.

Just as I softly shut the door behind me and brought our breakfast in, Layne stretched and I could hear her nails tap against the headboard.

Her eyes lit up when she gazed over at me.

"Hey," her sultry voice touched my soul.

'Hey.' I smiled at her as she sat up in bed.

"What's that?"

I held up the bag, 'Breakfast.'

The two of us cuddled up to one another between the sheets.

As she ate breakfast and caressed my arm with her tender fingerprints, I watched her expression turn sour.

'What's wrong babe?'

"It's nothing," she shrugged.

'Something is wrong.'

"I don't know," she started. "Last night, this whole trip, you." Layne moved her hand towards my chest.

'What about it?'

"It has been nothing but magical. Scott, this is so hard. I know what my heart and soul are saying about you."

My fingers searched for her skin. As my hand ran up and down her back, she shifted her head towards mine and planted a gentle kiss on my lips.

Gazing deep into my eyes, she whispered, "I wanted to experience you. I wanted to have last night. I want all of this, but I am scared."

She gulped and I held her tight.

"I don't know what to do. I think..." she moved away from me. "I know this cannot go on. We have to stop and just keep this as a beautiful memory."

'I hear you,' I began to tear up. The wave of powerful, spiritual emotions washed over me. 'I want what is best for you.'

"I don't want to hurt you. You don't deserve to carry my pain with you."

'You could never hurt me,' my pointer finger brushed along the side of her head.

"I am scared, but I love you so much." She paused. "Please promise me this will not be painful."

Without hesitation, I assured her that I would not be hurt by her.

"I want you to stay in my life. I want to explore the book I'm writing and the framework, but sleeping together and connecting on such a high level clouds everything."

We both paused for a moment.

'Layne, I love you, I honor you, I respect you… and I understand.'

"Promise me you will not be in pain."

I forced the tears to remain within my eyes. 'I promise.'

She swallowed. "Thank you."

An impatient silence hung between us.

"We are here," she began. "And I don't want this fleeting moment to disappear forever."

'I'll never let this moment go, Layne.'

She placed our food on the table beside her and pressed her body against mine. As she inched closer and closer onto my chest, our lips crashed into each other's in such a passionate manner.

I felt each sway of her body rock against me sensually.

Her reflection from the mirror was erotic beyond my wildest imagination. My eyes wandered to the daylight creeping through the windows and back to the mirror where I caught the shadow of her body thrusting against mine.

I was lost in her ecstasy.

The two of us were fully immersed in what seemed like our last moment together. Our fingers intertwined as she kissed my neck softly.

I craved her soul.

The next few moments faded into the recesses of my mind as I etched our experience into my memory forever.

Home

I barely remember taking her back to the bus terminal, for my body was so exhausted from our spiritual rendezvous.

"I love you," escaped her lips as she kissed me.

'I love you, too.'

"We will figure this out."

Layne held me tight before releasing my soul from her gentle grasp. As she walked away and boarded the bus, a trail of her spirit lingered with me.

When she left New York, I still felt her throughout the day: a soul connection like ours feels like home.

As I returned to my mother's house and shut my eyes, I felt her heartbeat. I could taste her sultry lips and sense her breathing. It was not just a replay of the intense, physical love we shared.

It was something I never felt before.

This was a new magnitude of spirituality shaking my core.

A sensation woke from within me and I did not even know it was there. Every fiber of my being wanted to get back to her instantly.

I did not want to just stay with her; I wanted to swim in the beautiful flow of what we created.

Part of me knew she could feel our mutual energy simmering within our souls.

If the concept of twin flames does exist, we surely found one another in this lifetime, and for eternity we would find each other again and again.

∞ ∞ ∞ ∞ ∞ ∞ ∞ ∞

After Layne went back up to Martha's Vineyard, the air in New York was stale and unforgiving. Morena sat complacently in my car, dangling a bag of food before me as I leapt into the driver's seat.

Recounting all of this seemed to be somewhat cathartic, but nothing could detract from the longing I had to hold Layne in my arms again. Morena was in deep thought and rather silent. The only time she spoke was thirty minutes into our car ride as I approached a red light. She glared into my eyes and spoke chilling words that I never thought were humanely conceivable or possible: "Scott, you have a phone call."

I glanced down at my black phone screen for a moment. Nothing. Then almost instantaneously Layne's name appeared on my screen.

"Scott, are you okay?" Layne seemed eager to hear my voice.

I paused for a moment, looking into Morena's eyes searching for what to say. She motioned towards the phone and mouthed something like, "Speak to her."

'Hey,' I paused, retraining from letting the tears cascade down my face, 'Hey Layne.'

"Scott, why do you sound so sad?"

'Nothing. Nothing, it...' I choked back tears, 'It was a long day.'

"You promised, Scott!" Her voice boomed through the phone.

'What are you talking about?' I began to panic as Morena gripped my hand tightly.

Morena mouthed me the words "Go within."

"You promised you were not in pain!" Layne's voice cracked.

'Layne, I-" She cut me off and began to berate me with her unfiltered passion.

"You told me you loved me, and you told me that you were okay with how you would love me, yet I hear it. I hear it in your voice, Scott. You love me more than you realize. You crave me, you crave me in a devastatingly drastic way that drowns your soul in an ocean of our everlasting love..." Her tears and heaving were more apparent as she went on. "And I crave you too, Scott. I really, wholeheartedly desire you. I can't explain it; I just really can't find the words to express how I feel right now. I am struggling with processing our love, because I know it is real, but I don't want to be the cause of your hurt. Scott, I just need time."

Morena and I gazed up at each other and back down at the phone.

Layne and I had a higher consciousness love that could never shatter the physical boundaries on this earthly realm. She seemed to agree with me, and her anxiety dissipated. We spoke amicably for a few moments and she thanked me profusely for doing what no other person ever did for her.

As our call ended, Morena looked up at me. She seemed distant and I was worried about her. Maybe she really isn't real. People are not usually too spiritually connected, so when there is even a tinge of low vibration in the world or low frequency conversations, she disappears.

That needs to be rectified.

Home

Angels are not supposed to get hurt, but I suppose they do.

My head started spinning and Morena gazed up at me with shallow eyes.

"Don't even think about going low vibrational, Scott." I could feel the energy building from her soul.

Once the conversation ended and the phone clicked, it hit me: I was in love with Layne and when the time came, I would not know how to say goodbye. I knew at that very moment… this will break me, AND I refused to leave her.

I drove over to the Throgs Neck Bridge and parked the car as close to the rocks as possible. I desperately needed a change of scenery.

After walking around aimlessly for an hour, I was about to call it a night when Layne called.

I was deep in thought.

Everyone has their own lives and I can't expect everything to stop because of me. Still, I embarked on this walk hoping to hear a certain someone's voice, to share, to bounce things off of, yet when I saw the flag waving in the sunset, I knew she would call.

I wondered if there would ever come a time when I don't have to be alone with my thoughts.

Layne's exquisite wisdom rang through my soul. She understands people and she just understands me. I understand her, the real her, not just the waitress who busts her butt at a diner day in and day out.

The two of us found ourselves in the midst of a deep conversation about life, the soul, and existing in general.

We spoke about how "I think I will live today" are the most painstaking words that are ever spoken. After a certain point, when it gets incredibly difficult to move forward or see the bright side of a situation, the difficulty of managing a mass of negativity, or however you chose to describe it, it burns. It burns in an unfathomable way. It burns so deeply that only those privy to the burden genuinely sense it.

When it seems as if every ounce of hope is overshadowed by the plague of darkness, cling.

Hold on.

I tried to think of the goodness from deep within. I tried to extend the light within to those around me. Yet the definition of "goodness" was askew in the public eye. Though good means helpful, honest, fair, unbiased, impartial, appropriate, professional, compassionate, caring, considerate, and being an overall caring person in one respect, the whole world does not always speak your language.

My perspective and my insight into the word "good" are just that… mine. Not everyone is willing to open their hearts to the world. Not everyone is understanding of the higher vibrations and sincere intentions of others.

Though this may seem judgmental, there is no ill will in these words.

I wish everyone in the world could see themselves through pristine, unfiltered eyes. I wish everyone could feel they are wanted, loved, and needed in this universe. When the burden of judgment presses too heavily on your chest, remember to breathe.

It can be hard to breathe. It can be hard to stand up once you feel you have been buried. Change the narrative. Rewrite the script. Do not give into the clutches of hatred that may seem to pull you down.

Keep going.

I stood with my feet in the sand, firmly planted in the belief that I could move forward. I repeatedly affirmed, "I can. I can. I can." You may ask: "Why do I feel ensnared in a trap, desperately trying to claw my way out of the depths of purgatory? Why do I feel the sins of foul words ripping apart the fundamental pieces of my soul?"

Seek for the epiphany within your soul: see the sign that is your soul being uplifted.

You are your own energy source. Dig deep, deep within… allow the wave of acceptance to flood your intricate soul. Turn your pain into power. Turn the misunderstood parts of you into higher consciousness.

Pray deeply and honestly for the lost and lonely. Pray for a better moment. Pray for the weak and the struggling for there are moments where we are all there: in the balance of what to do and how to do it.

The challenges we face may be mounting and tough, but we will face them head on. We will face them and we will survive.

"We will do more than just survive, my dear, we will overcome," Layne's words cemented into my soul.

So, after it all: the sharp words that sting so effervescently, the shock of having to swim while you conceive the notion that your feet may be sinking, the phrases and monikers gifted to you by those who misunderstand…

Home

They will be heard but they will not hurt. They are apparitions of projections underdeveloped souls feel so rooted in their bones. They will grow, as will you, and pray for them. Pray they will awaken to a better tomorrow and a brighter path. Pray they see their innate beauty.

Tomorrow is unknown in the present moment, but live for today. Continue to live. Continue to shine and grow. Fill the emptiness with the angelic wisdom that shines from above and beyond.

Then mutter those words that sever the confusion in your soul: "I think I will live today."

For even angels need to learn how to fly.

We yearn for what we cannot materialize. We grasp at the chances that roll before us, while we mingle exquisitely in the factions that exist before us. We are spirituality and soul wrapped in flesh entities. We are inherently guided by a moral compass that can become askew depending on what we individually recognize as due north. We hastily give in to our human emotions, for we fall short enough from perfection that we tend to fall into realms that materialize in the form of desires. We look not into the light before us. We look not into the areas of growth that lay between the colors painted on the horizon.

We are angelic, though we do not uphold halos. We are spiritual, yet we do not always obtain the lens to visualize all we can become. We manifest a sense that we must comply with the rules of society, for we assume that these are the standards that must dictate our lives.

What about us?

What about soul?

What about divine love and sincere connections?

Why do we tend to trip off of the path while running for our futures? We could speculate for years and get caught up in the horror that is delving into the whys and longing questions of the human world, yet we fall short in the sense that we ruminate too long on the logic. Give in to the spirit. Give in to patience and understanding. Forgive. Forgive others for they are still developing. Forgive yourself for you are still growing.

Wish genuine sincerity upon those still finding their light, for we are all harmonizing on different levels and with different frequencies. It is about time we try diligently to vibrate higher.

Beautiful Souls

Challenge the status quo and remind yourself you were crafted in the hands of the legacies that existed far before your human form was a conceptual thought.

Live and believe in the sense that you can overcome challenges and grow… for life may seem like a dark room, but you, too, can develop from the negatives and illustrate a glorious landscape that is your soul's growth and divine intentions.

∞ ∞ ∞ ∞ ∞ ∞ ∞ ∞

Like magnets, Layne and I found our way back to each other within a weekend.

I travelled up to Martha's Vineyard again, so that she did not have to take off of work. Although she loved the sights and sounds of New York, and she said it inspired her to write, Layne did need to stay close to her father and sister in Massachusetts.

Layne helped me realize that I learned the value of truly savoring little moments, for it is the little moments that string together so eloquently to manifest a genuine sensation that just cannot be disrupted.

Once you begin to place value on those little moments, time becomes insignificant. Time becomes just a social construct that fades into the background, but those moments stay on the forefront of our hearts, minds, and spirits forever.

We have an innate power beholden in our souls: we can choose where to place our energy. We decide who owns our passion, for we are the ones who signed a contract with the universe years ago.

Our respective destinies were aligned to fit a purpose, and we had to extend our souls onto a level of higher consciousness in order to discover this prophecy developed in our honor long ago.

On our respective journeys, we may sometimes feel like an outsider.

We may sometimes think we are consumed by the cataclysmic culture of hate and negativity that is around us… yet we must remember to look in each other's eyes.

Look into the eyes of those around you.

What do you see?

You can see a story behind the story.

Home

You can see the patterned specks of stardust lingering in their eyes.

You can feel the emotion reverberating through their bodies and transmitting messages out for the world to see.

It is when we stop and look into the eyes of another that we find their souls and we see ourselves.

Layne's eyes held such a beautiful experience that etched into my soul with just a touch of the experience that is her.

This double intensity ferments a growing need within us: we yearn to be understood and we yearn to be in another's arms, but it is rather difficult to find a place to call home as you try to find yourself.

Yet we as human beings make it happen: we find our home in the arms of another, and not just in the explicit definition of four walls and a roof.

We find our way through the consummation of ideas and the thorough processing of information. We create our own realities and we develop on a vertical continuum: we seek out our purpose and redefine who we are once we unlock key pieces of our own puzzles. Integration and togetherness then becomes a key.

Just let your soul flower into something bigger or brighter than you could ever imagine.

Embrace the moments as you would embrace another, seep compassion into this world through your positivity and your light, and uncover bits of your path through the proceeding moments before you.

It does not matter who you are in this world, your experience is part of a greater and overarching cohesive whole: our society. We create the fabric of society through the moments we weave together in the cosmic essence of space and this universe.

As the moments melt into the fabric of our lives, I can't help but smile knowing that I am a part of so many little moments in this universe.

My only wish for each soul on this earth is that they realize how fundamental they are to who I have become. Souls grow into their own because of the pleasantries bestowed upon them from other beautiful souls. Shine your light upon another's soul, and see just how magical this world can become.

We may live in juxtaposed worlds or different mandates in society, but at the end of the day, if we all take a moment to gaze up at the stars, odds are we are glaring into another soul's journey... and we will always be able to see a clearer picture of the hearts and minds of those near and dear to us.

Distance is just a matter of being moments away, for we always have the little moments and memories to usher us into the next chapter.

We always have the rose-colored images of our kindled flames plastered in the walls of our memory... and all in all we are not just another brick in another person's wall... we are souls etched in the prophetical tapestries of each other's paths... and that is how it always shall be.

Always.

Layne recognized that and welcomed me with open arms the moment I stepped off of the ferry.

Her soul is a wild, yet reserved and exquisite life force.

Layne tries so hard to restrain herself, but when she sets her mind on something, she will stop at nothing until she gets what she yearns for.

Our pasts paralleled one another: we had both been afflicted by love, but we did not let love of a clearly higher power, hinder our present.

The past became the past.

My love for her stemmed from a place of purity and soul.

Within moments of getting to Martha's Vineyard, we were kissing passionately in her white sedan. The engine revved when she accidentally stepped on the gas pedal, though fortunately we were still in park.

After a short ride to the bed and breakfast, we found ourselves tangled in the sheets together.

Our love stemmed from a place of purity, innocence, and insanity in the most wholesome of ways.

I brushed Layne's hair behind her ear as she cuddled into my chest. My fingers rubbed her shoulder as she wrapped her hand around my torso.

"I love you Scott. My heart has never felt so full," she whispered.

I kissed her forehead tenderly.

'My soul craves yours.'

Both of us laughed gently as she picked up her head.

Layne's eyes pierced my soul as we managed to communicate without uttering a single word. Our lips met again in another spiritually uplifting exchange.

"You are very dangerous, Scott," as the words left her lips, each syllable wrapped itself around my skin.

'Why?'

"If you were here all of the time, you would end up having all of me."

'Then I should move here,' I grinned.

Layne did not respond. There was no doubt that we loved one another.

'I love you.' The way those three words hung off of my lips as I softly kissed her made me never want to leave her side.

Our souls were tethered to one another in a way that whispered, "I know you."

The two of us rose and agreed to physically part from one another for a few hours. I promised that I would take Layne on a date and she agreed. My mind raced as I tried to figure out how to make her happy without overwhelming her.

I didn't want to take a shower simply because I aspired to swim in her scent.

The acceptance and comprehension of two souls can be a complicated process, especially when the energy exchange is heightened past the limits of human normalcy.

This place, each passing second, and this experience are all parts of where I have never been before. It is not a bad thing, but I had to process what this all meant to me.

Life's moments are precious gifts from the universe that are always to be treasured. Everything is a beautiful message or lesson.

It is a blessing for me to stand witness to a soul's full expansion and expression. Layne's passionate experiences are a gift from heaven, from the physical to the emotional aspects of her being.

The universe manifested Layne and created our love.

Layne picked me up as the two of us drove to the Manuel F. Correllus State Forest.

As we got out of the car, I managed to wrestle a picnic basket from the backseat of the sedan.

"What are you doing?" She giggled.

'I wanted to take you on a romantic date that you deserve.' I picked up the basket. 'It is a good thing there was a general store within walking distance of the bed and breakfast.'

We basked in another oasis of hers. I soaked in the moments that danced in my soul; at a point in time, she walked the paths of this land by her lonesome. Odds are, she was processing the emotional pain she harbored from her ex-boyfriend and ex-best friend.

The possibilities of her life were endless.

While walking in her space, I injected myself into her aura, her safety, and her sanctuary.

I disturbed it and filled it with my energy.

Together, our presence elevated the space to an entirely new level.

As we got to an open field in the forest, I dropped the picnic basket on the grass. The weather was more perfect than I had ever felt.

While she unravelled the contents of the basket, something compelled me to put on music. "Blaze of Glory" by Bon Jovi was the first thing to play from my phone.

"You ask about my conscience
And I offer you my soul
You ask if I'll grow to be a wise man
Well I ask if I'll grow old."

I do not know why I chose that song, but something told me I needed to expose Layne to the music of my soul.

The notes, the rhythm, and the lyrics were delicately moving throughout the air in a way I never felt them before. It was akin to a musical high.

In moments when we delve deeper into our soul's layers, we understand how deeply and devoutly the universe speaks to us. Our words materialize as a means of finding who we truly are, and as a way to touch other souls that are on their respective paths.

We intersect, even for a split second, and succumb to the sensations and emotions that can be perceived as overwhelming, but on another level could be the most beautiful incredible experience of your eternal existence.

Fight the fear; expel the darkness and confusion.

Light the way knowing full and well that we are encountering a new level of growth that was previously unfathomable and thought unattainable.

In these moments the universe is providing a magical gift that is an infinite blessing.

Home

We are not at the top of the mountain yet, we have merely reached the plateau, and are about to continue our ascent... in due time. There is no rush when you have these eternal reunions and realizations. There is no doubt about it, that as the universe speaks to us in ways that are beyond incredible, and if you truly listen, she will shake you to your core.

Do not give up because times seem confusing or tough. The clouds clear. The universe speaks truth.

Breathe deeply and inhale the positivity that is all around you, for the universe is so powerful.

When you position your soul to be open to receive truth it will align the most beautiful gifts for you. Everything will be okay. The feelings and energy can be heightened to a level never felt before. It can be awesome and scary all at once, but it will be okay.

The universe looks kindly on those with pure hearts, and Layne had one of the purest hearts I had ever encountered.

As I closed my eyes to process these emotions, I knew I was surrounded and shrouded with those who are sent to protect me.

The universe cheers us on.

In our metamorphic process, we can transform from a solemn, enclosed entity to something greater and larger than we ever could imagine. Our wings are hidden and unfathomable, then one day we discover we can fly.

One day, after all this soul work, you will see energy, sometimes colliding in a way you never thought possible, and the future will look more clearer to you than ever before... and yes, that's scary because we were never prepared for that type of realization. Being in this type of a moment is so exciting and at the same time incredibly scary.

We discovered we could run.

We can soar.

We can push forth as far as we so wish to go.

We are invincible in the eyes of the universe, yet we are trained to be limited by societal norms and our human conditions.

We are fluttering in the sky and flickering in the beckoning wind.

We are drawn to the elements from which our souls once stemmed from, and we feel peace and solace in knowing how close we are to the earth and the water, yet we inject our human emotions into every situation.

If only we stepped back for a moment. If only we thought soulfully from a place of love consciousness instead of in such a human fear-based emotionally driven way, which words would hold more value?

Which words would seep into our soul and seek out the light from within?

Which words would draw upon our inner voice and true purpose?

Would we then realize the weight of the world was just a matter of soul over heart over mind, rather than the other way around?

How do we internalize happiness and genuine love or genuine truth?

Is it all "too good to be true," or if we quiet the mind do you hear the clear and coherent whisper in our souls?

In living in a world of "if only," "should," "could," "would," and any other doubt-fueled words, are we merely hindering our souls from their devout possibilities?

The universe loves us and has our backs and it's important to let go and trust, but these questions plague my soul in a deeper way than I have ever gone.

I am listening. I am trusting. I am scared at times… fleeting moments but there is fear there.

Hope, but fear.

On the other hand, I truly do believe.

I feel.

I know.

I live in between the breaths of words Layne spoke into existence…. for our words are manifesting a true shift on this planet that will last more than seven generations.

For only when words of partially unrequited love are spoken to the universe, will you realize that what you tell yourself, and what you choose to hear, will be your words of wisdom.

Hear clearer.

Hear your kindness.

Speak your passion and let your heart soar; know you are protected by the highest of angels and the entire universe.

Most of all continue to follow your beautiful passionate soul as you speak unto others as you always should speak to yourself.

Choose light over darkness and decide upon your voice… then allow it to manifest.

As my mind wandered to all of these different places, I looked up at Layne who was nibbling on some fruit.

My thoughts quieted long enough to say: 'You are amazing beyond words.'

She moved closer to me and kissed my cheek. "I love you, and I am going to tell you ten more times so that you never forget."

As she recited, "I love you" in my ear very slowly, tears streamed down my face.

It was the making of a true love story.

Layne moved backwards and glanced at me. The sunlight reflected in her eyes and were literally windows to the soul. I see the whole universe when I look into them.

I see Source.

I see divine love.

As the sunlight caressed her pristine face, I could not help but feel a sense of innate peace emulating from my core. Her presence was like no other. We could sit in resolute silence for hours, yet her words would still seep into my soul with the passion and pressure of the Hoover Dam. I felt that I had to hold back, but I knew, deep down within me, that I needed her.

I longed for her.

I yearned to be woven into the fabric of her life in every possible way.

That is what true love is. That is what a soul connection is: wanting to be a consummate part of another's whole being, while inspiring that person to flourish and reach another level of higher consciousness. Her physical absence was painstaking. It weighed my soul down in unfathomable language.

She is due north, my magnetic pole that I base all soulful, spiritual connections upon. Am I being too crass in saying how tethered I am to her every twist and turn? This I do not know.

Am I assuming too much in hanging on her every word and action? Again, I am unsure.

How do you verbalize a soul connection?

How do you comprehend the most beautiful mind you have ever laid eyes upon?

How do you actualize a relationship forged in the particles of stardust that never appeared before?

Layne is perfection, without a doubt. When you formulate a love as deep as ours, you make room in your soul for the fibers of their being. Your individual broken pieces may be sharp and jagged, but together those pieces appear smooth and connective.

You cannot describe, in words or in actions, the value someone grants to your soul. You cannot, in a concrete shape, align a form to something so beautiful and exquisite.

In searching for myself, I found someone who was lost on her own path.

Then somehow, whether it be divine intervention from the universe or just chance, our souls looked upon one another and said, "I know."

Looking at a stranger and recognizing their soul is refreshing.

In an instant, you just know. You realize why everything did not work out all along. You discover your light is brighter than it seems. You configure how this world could be so cruel and so calming in one swoop; Layne was my reason why.

You recognize your reflection in the eyes of another... and when you truly love someone with all of your heart, mind, body, and soul... you make room.

Priorities and excuses juxtapose themselves more transparently, for you finally realize that the holes in your soul stemmed from the universe in order for both of you to merge spiritually when the time is right.

...And that is the beautiful thing: our love was in the universe's hands now.

The two of us packed up our picnic basket and walked along the trails. As we spoke, she would stop periodically to write down what we were talking about.

Our conversation consisted of the notion that we should all become the source of energy that ignites passion in another's soul.

Yearn to create the fundamental parts that will be integrated into society for years to come. Communicate with respect and dignity to those who are embarking on their respective journeys through their purpose.

When you meet someone who generates unfiltered and unfettered happiness in your soul, hold onto him or her tightly. It is like no other feeling to look into the eyes of another soul who just understands you, and to forge a bond that exists in spiritual and humanistic terms.

To watch someone process a soul connection is riveting.

Home

To see someone speak higher consciousness into existence and translate their own soul into a language we can understand and internalize is passion.

The combination of soulful energies and passions coming together is overwhelming, but beautiful. Individuals who are powerful enough to light their own fire in order to shift themselves are exhilarating.

Those who can collaborate and combine their spiritual energies to shift the world will strengthen the universe for generations to come. If you think you have a soul connection with someone, cherish it.

A soul connection's worth is far more valuable than anything else this world may offer you. Show gratitude to the universe for sending you blessings, and pay attention to what the world does. For when you least expect it, miracles can happen.

The balance of the universe could majestically shift and you will enter a realm of new opportunities. Listen closely to what happens around you, for you never know what will happen... and when those miracles display themselves in your presence, never let that person go.

As we continued on through the town, she would grab my arm and kiss me passionately.

I could feel her heartbeat as she curled into my arms.

The two of us strolled down a sidestreet and she pressed her body firmly against mine. Layne caressed my arm slowly and let her nails run up and down my skin.

Her sensual touch made me melt.

The two of us went back to my room at the bed and breakfast before she had to go to work for the night. While she sat and wrote in her journal, I watched her in utter amazement. Part of me could not believe that the first day we met one another was not too long ago.

Though Layne was clearly reserved in some ways, she loved me wholeheartedly in the words and actions she committed to the universe.

I had visions of holding her in my arms at the Brooklyn Bridge. My dream was to bring her there and kiss her with the landscape of Manhattan behind us. This picturesque scene would be a quintessential moment in my life, for it would mark our respective souls' journey coming full circle.

Between her dreams and writing, and my knowledge and vision, we were a force to be reckoned with.

Layne fell sound asleep on the bed with her journal in hand. She looked like a heavenly human being wrapped in beauty and brilliance.

It made me wonder:

How did I win her love?

How did I turn her angel eyes my way?

Why was my soul so special that it was permitted to be a part of her life?

I feel so alive with her and relish in the sensation that I am the strongest man in the world with her by my side. Her eyes fluttered open for a moment before sealing shut again.

When she looks at me I know she's swimming inside my soul.

Soft music from my phone murmured Bon Jovi's "Save the World,"

> *"It comes down to this*
> *I wouldn't exist*
> *Without you it ain't worth the grind*
> *I'd fight for one kiss*
> *On a night like this*
> *You make me feel I could fly, like*
> *I could save the world*
> *Since the night your love saved me*
> *Maybe I can't save the world*
> *But as long as you believe*
> *Maybe I could save the world."*

The song was always on an infinitesimal loop within my mind, but with Layne in my life the words finally had a meaning.

They had a purpose.

They had a voice.

They had a devout reason.

Everything in the universe seemed possible, for she was the angelic light guiding the way.

Her eyes fluttered open and she watched me gaze at her for a few moments.

"I want you to read this," she pushed her open journal towards me.

I shifted the book towards me to take a peek at what she was creating. Her writing was of a higher love:

Home

"My thoughts on Scott:
I want to thank you from the deepest crevices of my soul for being by my side through all of this. Your words speak to me in such a beautiful manner. My gratitude just cannot fully express how much you move me. Thank you. A zillion times. Thank you.

I wish for you to know that today is a beautiful blessing to every soul on this planet because of the breaths you take. Your breaths endlessly expand the universe and even if it's underneath every person on this planet's awareness - they will have a better day because you are here, existing.

The power of your heart and soul is the rarest gift to all of us, and we get to see our light, because you are the beacon guiding us to see it.

Without you this world would be in darkness. Unaware that we have the strength, power and illumination inside of us to truly go after our destinies in life. Thank you for constantly being my shining light that guides my path and unveils the curtains so I can really see myself.

I see myself in the way you see me... and the way you see me is unlike the way anyone has seen me before.

I want you to know that you can only possibly see me in this way because it is so similar to you. I am your mirror, and I am so proud, honoured and humbled, to be your reflection

Thank you - a zillion times for existing so that this could be my reality.

You make life an undeniably glorious experience. I'm so proud that you are doing the work and paving the path for so many to come after you.

Following your footsteps. I am so proud that you are finishing your framework and completing the first chapter of getting your soul out in its full expression with all of that glory.

Great things are ahead and the energy of this rifle wave we are creating is shattering souls at their core in this moment - even if they have no clue what's coming. When your words reach their ears and what you are creating reaches their eyes - they will know.

Hearts will open, as will eyes and ears.

Chapter two will be started soon - and I am the world's luckiest human to be beside you when the world starts picking up on who you are, what you're about, and what you're here to do.

I love you, Scott Matheson."

Beautiful Souls

Layne stirred and woke softly.

"Are you enjoying my great American novel?" Her groggy voice was obscured by her smile.

'Yes,' I placed it back on the bed. 'You are truly my soul's desire.'

She grinned. "Then come here and kiss this soul."

We leaned closer for a passionate kiss and embrace. Layne propped herself up and brushed her fingers through my blonde hair.

"I need to go to work soon, but there is somewhere I *need* to go with you before I go to work."

The two of us hopped in her car and drove towards an industrial part of town. The stars still glistened with such awe through her windshield.

We lowered the seats and started to kiss again as she caressed my back.

Instinctively, I pulled my shirt down to hide my stomach. Layne placed her hands over mine.

"Babe," she whispered. "You don't have to be afraid. I love you. I love all of you. I love every single part of your body."

Layne moved downwards and began to plant sweet kisses on my skin.

The two of us held one another as the night fully fell upon us.

Within moments, it was so difficult to say goodbye to her for the night as the moon crept over us. As she wandered off to work, I had a sinking feeling emerge in the pit of my stomach.

I wished that I could have slept next to her in the quaint bed and breakfast. It would be our little oasis from the world.

I set my alarm for very early in the morning, so when she got off of work I would be the first loving face she would see.

When my eyes shot open as the sunlight crept in the window, I dashed into the shower and got ready in record timing. Though she was the woman of my dreams, I needed to see her in real life to quench my thirst for her everlasting spirit.

As she looked up while untying her apron for the day, the smile she shot in my direction was a breathtaking way to begin my day.

"Come on," she rushed up to me and grabbed my hand. "We're going on an adventure."

'An adventure?' I was startled. 'But you need to get some rest.'

"I'll rest later. It's time to live, Scott!"

'Okay,' I gleefully followed Layne to her white sedan.

Home

The next few hours were filled with driving through cute towns and winding roads. WIth the windows rolled down and her hair blowing in the wind, I found even more ways to love her. We were blasting music and relishing in the togetherness we shared.

It seemed like the whole world was ours.

Song after song came on over the radio, and with each new tune, Layne's entire body took on a different persona. You could see a shift rising over her soul as she started to sway to the music. Layne felt each vibration in the song as her hands would rise and fall.

Her eyes were on the road, but her heart was transfixed by the rhythm of the music.

Layne's entire soul was alluring, for each and every aspect of her was genuinely beautiful.

It does not matter whether you are within an arm's reach of someone or if you are thousands of miles apart. True compassion and a spiritual connection will always strengthen the soul without the need for a hand to hold or gazing into a person's eyes.

High vibration and acknowledging that there are individuals out there who genuinely care about your well being and personal growth are what matters.

You can be an ocean apart from someone, yet they can still swim through your mind.

Their essence becomes their presence, and that is something that could never be replaced.

A bond between two souls cannot be severed.

There are souls on this planet that remind you to be more than a bird, more than a plane, more than some pretty face beside the train. Superman always looked out for the best interests of Lois Lane, but she was not beside him when he was doing his heroic deeds, nor he beside her when she was putting the puzzle pieces of the world together and inspiring others for a better tomorrow.

We are connected and parallel in the spiritual sense.

At times, we must cherish the souls of those who are closest to us deep in our hearts. We must honor those who we care about by traveling on a journey that may take us far from them for some time, yet we harbor the memory of them in our souls and beckon them to our shores. In rough seas

Beautiful Souls

or on the darkest nights, the ones we truly care about are our lighthouses, ushering us home. We may sail far and wide, but the compass will always point due north towards them. We must remember that for ourselves too.

We must remember to call upon the energy emitted from other souls when we need reassurance of who we are. We must conquer fear, trepidation, and doubt with the love, sincerity, and compassion that our connections bestow upon us.

We should honor our Superman, honor our Lois Lane, and honor the souls of those who are our everyday heroes.

We must honor the hearts and minds of those who progress with us and grow with us despite their distance.

Live in the glorious now that is your own progressive existence, go forth and flourish, fly, and float. Still, in the brightest day or in the blackest night, do not let those who vibrate low hinder your vision or sight.

Everything will be okay even if you think you are alone, for in the souls of those you love, you will always be home.

In those moments in the car, as we sat by the Aquinnah Cliffs on Martha's Vineyard, and in the writings she bestowed upon my soul, it became clearer and clearer that Layne was my home.

The two of us sat in her car for a few moments, overlooking parts of the water.

'Can I play you a song?' I reached for my phone.

"Yes, of course," Layne leaned her shoulder against the driver's seat. "You always talk about how music is the window to your soul. I want to see everything in your world."

I fiddled with my phone for a bit until the song started to play. As we hit the chorus of the song, she looked up at me.

> *"They don't know how long it takes*
> *Waiting for a love like this*
> *Every time we say goodbye*
> *I wish we had one more kiss*
> *I'll wait for you I promise you, I will*
> *I'm lucky I'm in love with my best friend*
> *Lucky to have been where I have been*
> *Lucky to be coming home again."*

Home

"What's this," Layne asked.
'The song is called "Lucky," it's by Jason Mraz,' I responded.
"Who is that?"
'Did you *just* ask me who Jason Mraz was?'
She giggled for a moment, "Yeah, why is that weird."
'A little bit, yeah.'
We both laughed as she nudged me.
"Don't make fun of me," she smiled. "Teach me."

The two of us continued to talk about the impact music creates on our respective lives. As we listened to songs and walked up to the cliffs, I told her all about Bon Jovi and the soul connection that each of his songs manifested within my life.

How rare and beautiful is it to exist in the mere presence of a genuine soul. I could not help but ask for more eloquent memories to grace my mind with each passing day.

For her to express the words she says over and over again would be an exquisite masterpiece.

Layne looked up at me as we spoke and said, "I would try to write down all of the brilliance that flows forth from your lips, but just one pen could not fathom the amount of ink it would cost to express your worth to this world. I would give anything to hear you speak your wisdom each and every day."

'Well,' I replied. 'There would not be enough songs on this planet to express to you my unwavering sense of awe that springs forth from your very essence. Your soul is a universe that was made to be experienced by so many, and is a genuine gift in my eyes.'

"Oh wow," she placed her hand over her chest. "How poetic."

With shortness of breath, I would explain the infinite: how rare and beautiful it truly is that we exist in this very time, in this very epoch, within the crystalline drops of magic and stardust swirling down to these very moments. We are the faceted elements of pristine reality that lay as gemstones of a higher consciousness relationship. We are the equation that all adds up to peace and coexistence in another realm.

Neverland is on a plane that we do not dance upon, for the tinges of always and the glory that is the billowing shrubs at the cliffs, sway in our hearts... just as devoutly as the clouds clear and the sun rises.

We are a flame, short of a fire; in need of intertwining light... we touch and we inspire the changes in this world tonight.

In those moments, I whispered to the universe to pick me up, take me higher, for I realized that there is a war not far from here, doused in the pain and tragedy that plagued both of our lives before these nights together. It made me see that we can dance in desire upon the rings of Saturn, or we could burn in love tonight.

"Scott," Layne wrapped her body in between my arms.

'What is it, love?'

"I know that one day we will make it big, we will go further than these cliffs, but I never want to lose these moments. Promise me that we will come back here together."

She looked up at me with purpose in her eyes.

'I promise.'

The wind picked up our hair and swirled it across our respective faces.

We brought lunch with us to the cliffs and began to eat together. Our conversation trailed to painful stories from our separate pasts. She told me all about her ex-best friend and her ex-boyfriend, and what they did to betray her trust.

I shared about how Emma hurt me deeply.

"They are blessings in disguise," she murmured. "They showed us how we could become better versions of ourselves."

She was right. Layne was wholeheartedly right.

I became a better person due to how I healed.

"You know," she stood up and motioned for us to start walking. "Our true love will be the foundation to our global success."

She is everything I ever hoped for and dreamed of.

When I was wishing upon those stars on lonely nights, I was truly wishing for her to walk into my life.

"Even though I push you away sometimes, you still show up for me constantly." We walked on opposite sides of the car and hopped inside. "I honor your soul."

She leaned over and kissed me.

"Come on," she wiped a tear from her eye. "There is more I want to show you."

We drove off to the tune of a playlist we were building together.

Home

As "Never Say Goodbye" from Bon Jovi played over the radio, my tears could not fight gravity much longer. I felt every single emotion burst from my eyes realizing that things would never be the same again.

"Are you okay?" She placed her hand in mine.

'Yes, I am' I locked eyes with her for a split second. 'I am, because of you.'

Isn't it great when the universe nudges you?

The universe does not always send the messages loud and clear like fireworks that illuminate the sky, rather, the messages could appear in between the silent pangs of your heartbeat.

Tune into your own frequency and hear the language of love manifest peacefully in your soul. The signs may appear miniscule and subtle, though the messages are bountiful and often rather generous.

In tranquility and silence, there is clarity.

We cannot ignore the signs that are downloaded and injected into the roots of who we are and what we are growing into.

Relationships, like the one that Layne and I manifested, stem from this soul and spirit connection. As a result of these revelations, it is clear that a lot of work may need to be done between two souls in order to construct a stable house built upon the foundation of love.

Often, rather than not, relationships will be built upon the premise of unconditional love.

However, unconditional love comes with one condition: an unconditional bond must come with understanding. This understanding means that communication lines must be open, clear, and unabashed: being honest is difficult, but unconditional love means that you and the other person involved will talk things through and openly process each other's emotions.

The universe is with you through every twist and turn of your tongue: the words you emit into this world stem from the precedents you set forth. The precedent could be laced with positivity and higher consciousness: if it is not, what you speak into existence may not be fully realized. What you speak into existence becomes your reality, so live it.

Live your words and stand by what you say.

Being honest with yourself and another person could fill you with fear, for fear manifests out of manners of uncertainty and the conditioned sense that we are not enough. Yet, in saying that you may not be "enough," what are we saying to our souls?

I allowed myself to live in pain for far too long.

Layne made me realize that.

She taught me that we must cherish and preserve the infinite potential within us, and we must display the same kindness to ourselves that we wish to transcend to other souls. When you connect on a deeper level and choose to evolve naturally, you attract who you are in your truest and highest form.

You attract what you need... even if you didn't realize that's what you were asking the universe for.

Your past experiences signify how much growth and beauty you have placed in this universe.

Even a solitary drop in the ocean creates a ripple effect, as do you with your consciousness and existence.

You are able to find more of what you are looking for, as opposed to what you are searching for, once you speak with much poise and sincerity to this universe. No words may even need to be said, for your thoughts can be acknowledged and felt. Your prayers and beliefs can be answered. Honor your existence and honor your soul.

When you release and trust in the process, the universe guides you to an incredible truth. It is so elevated that if you do not trust it fully, it can consume you with fear. The polarity of life has to be navigated carefully and there is such intricate beauty laced within that navigation. The destination is a heightened love that's never been created: the highest version of the expansion of love and its possibilities flow freely in the universe... in your soul and in souls you encounter.

Sometimes your heart knows the truth and it just takes time to admit the epiphanies within you. When there is truth, there is no rush. Time and patience are endless and on a continuum. Love is truly unconditional, and self-love is of a divine consciousness. Listen to your soul and your heart, for your mind will shortly follow. Embrace uncertainty, for in those moments, support may not always be seen or heard.

It lingers in between the pangs of your heartbeat.

Beat on and walk on, for there is a present in the gifts you transcend into this universe's timeline, and one hundred percent of

Home

your inhibitions will melt away the moment you choose what you want and head in that direction. Still, your path will be intertwined with other aspects of sense and sensibility: let your mind guide you to the messages this universe bestows upon you, and never forget to play with the ideas that may bewilder you or stun your spirit: there is always a story behind the story and a lighthouse beckoning you home to the shore: wade in the waters and always anchor yourself to those who make you see your own value.

Always.

As our drive came to a halt, I realized that we were sitting outside of a pristine olive-colored house with mint-colored gutters that outlined the building.

'This is such a cute place,' I remarked.

"Thank you," she waved at a young girl in the window. "This is my home."

We got out of the car and a large, burly man opened the front door. A petite girl who looked like Layne popped out from behind the man.

I began to hyperventilate slightly as the moment consumed me. Her father and sister stood before us grinning sweetly.

"I've heard good things," her father extended his hand. "My name is Raymond."

'I'm Scott,' I grasped his hand as he welcomed me into the house.

The young girl walked over and sat on the couch next to me.

"Hi, I'm Marissa. Layne told me not to embarrass her in front of you."

Layne stood up and yelled, "Marissa!"

Her father laughed and placed his hand on his knee.

The three of them leaned into one another on the cornflower blue sofa. It was blatantly obvious that they were incredibly close and a tight-knit trio. Layne definitely surprised me by coming here.

The three of us spoke for a while about Layne's childhood and their journey to Martha's Vineyard. Raymond explained that the family once lived close to the Grand Canyon in Arizona, where Layne and Marissa would hike with their father.

"I have always been drawn to beautiful places," Layne glanced over at me and flashed a smile.

Her father's eyes grew more nostalgic and peaceful.

"Scott, Layne has told me you have big plans for this world." Raymond leaned towards me.

'I mean, I do-' I looked over at Layne who was beaming with excitement.

"He's being modest, dad. Tell them what you told me, Scott."

'No, I-' I chuckled nervously.

"Come on," Marissa encouraged me. "It's okay. Tell us!"

They were literally sitting at the edge of their seats.

'Okay,' I swallowed. 'My vision is that the world becomes one healthy community through higher consciousness education. Education should promote healthy communication to encourage trust-based relationships, support acceptance of each other and reduce fear, and create an expressed open society. This leads to people connecting to and expanding their souls through a higher love consciousness that helps people live optimal lives and supports others to do so as well. I am building the world's first and most comprehensive education system for raising 21st Century leaders and engineering a society that is going to support them.'

They sat in silence for a moment as Layne rubbed my arm.

"Wow," Raymond said. "You have really thought about this."

'I try to think about what this universe deserves, and I just-'

Layne cut me off, "Create it."

'Precisely.'

The four of us continued to talk for a while until Layne began to yawn.

"Looks like you've been up all day again, Layne," Marissa said.

"Yeah," Layne replied. "But I am still focused."

Layne suggested we go to the next few places she wanted to take me, but she asked if I could drive. Naturally, I obliged.

"Take care of her heart," Raymond said as we both walked out the door.

'I will. I promise, sir.'

We embraced each other for a moment as Marissa tried to hug both of us at the same time. Her family was pure and so incredibly sweet.

The two of us hopped in the car and she instinctively reached for the radio. "Never Tear Us Apart" from INXS blared over the speakers:

"I told you
That we could fly

'Cause we all have wings
But some of us don't know why
I was standing
You were there
Two worlds collided
And they could never ever tear us apart."

We travelled back towards my bed and breakfast as I realized our time together was coming to a close. My ferry would be leaving within a few hours, and I would be thrown back into New York's concrete jungle without Layne by my side.

I was praying and wishing that she would come back to New York again, because I wanted another dose of her. Layne is an elixir of the most ravishing kind.

All I knew at that moment was that she was an addiction of mine.

'Where are we going?' I looked over at her.

"I just wanted to cuddle up next to you, can we go back to your place?"

My place. I had a place on Martha's Vineyard.

As we arrived at the bed and breakfast, she asked if we could just rest for a little while together. I wanted nothing more than to hold her in my arms.

We curled up in the bed next to each other as she slept.

I was laying there with a heaviness in my soul. It was not a tragic heaviness, but it was a consuming one. I didn't want to leave her.

I could not leave her.

Yet, I had to temporarily.

The enriching scent of her hair lingered just below my nose.

As I shut my eyes, I heard the lyrics to Bon Jovi's "Always" reverberate throughout my mind:

"Yeah I, will love you, baby
Always and I'll be there
Forever and a day, always
I'll be there, till the stars don't shine
'Til the heavens burst and the words don't rhyme
I know when I die you'll be on my mind
And I'll love you, always."

Beautiful Souls

Layne's voice cut through the melody playing in my head, "Scott, wake up, you'll miss the ferry!"

My eyes jolted open to see her watching over me in an angelic manner. I leapt out of the bed and started to grab my things. I felt refreshed lying next to her, but I felt incredibly sad knowing that we would need to be physically apart from each other again.

There's a difference between sleeping with someone and sleeping with someone whose soul awakens yours. Even just from laying next to her, I felt our hearts soaring above us.

I glanced up at her and murmured, 'I love you.'

She did not reply, but I could see her starting to tear up. Layne's pain was seeping back into her mind.

We made it to the ferry with some time to spare, so Layne suggested we listen to one last song before I made my trip back to New York.

I knew she was still somewhat reserved with her love for me, so I played her "What Ifs" by Kane Brown and Lauren Alaina:

> *"You say what if I hurt you, what if I leave you*
> *What if I find somebody else and I don't need you*
> *What if this goes south, what if I mess you up*
> *You say what if I break your heart in two then what*
> *Well I hear you girl, I feel you girl but not so fast*
> *Before you make your mind up I gotta ask*
> *What if I was made for you and you were made for me*
> *What if this is it, what if it's meant to be*
> *What if I ain't one of them fools just playin' some game*
> *What if I just pulled you close, what if I leaned in*
> *And the stars line up and it's our last first kiss*
> *What if one of these days baby I'd go and change your name*
> *What if I loved all these what ifs away."*

Layne instantly started to cry.

I put my hand on her shoulder, 'What's wrong?'

"Our souls," she wiped her tears. "They are integrated. They are bonded by the positive vibrations we express."

Her words were beautiful.

Home

"I don't want you to go," she whimpered. "I just don't want to hurt you. I am healing."

'I know,' I reached for her hands, but she pulled away.

"Please. I need time."

'I'm sorry.'

"Here," she reached into her pocket and pulled out a rock. "I want you to have this. It's an aquamarine stone. Whenever you feel like you need me close to you, hold it in the palm of your hand."

As I took it from her, it seemed like the universe was whispering something to me. I was not sure what it was, but I figured I would trust the process.

She loved me; it was clear she loved me.

I boarded the ferry and watched her slowly pivot away from the dock. Something told me I would not hear from her for a while, but thankfully I was wholeheartedly wrong.

Upon docking at Woods Hole and getting back to my car, I put some music on to quell my anxiety. I missed Layne, I needed Layne, I wanted her to be with me forever, and not just in spirit.

The song "Feels Like Home" by Matt Johnson ushered me onto the highway:

"If you knew how lonely my life has been
And how long I've been so alone
If you knew how I wanted someone to come along
And change my life the way you've done
It feels like home to me."

The tears streaming down my cheeks resembled the fluid love Layne and I have been experiencing.

I felt that our souls should never truly be apart.

As I reached my mother's driveway, I pulled the stone from my pocket. I spoke to it with the same passion and reverence that reminded me of Layne.

'I love you,' I said to the stone. I followed it up with nine more expressions of my adoration for her.

Ten 'I love yous' in total filled the air.

When I opened my eyes, it was 3:15 in the morning.

∞ ∞ ∞ ∞ ∞ ∞ ∞ ∞

Beautiful Souls

I only remember myself getting just a few hours of sleep. My skin seemed to congeal to the sofa in the oppressive summer humidity.

I could not help but feel her absence creep up each dip and groove of my spine. The sinking feeling in my chest was only contrasted by the weight of where her hand once was pulling me closer to wherever she was off to.

I was eternally her compass, and she would forever be my own personal due north. In due time, we would find our way back to one another, for she gave my life direction. She, for all intents and purposes, embodies every ounce of spiritual meaning that her aura bestows upon this universe: faith.

Layne called and said that being apart from me was harder than expected. She respected that we had to take care of our responsibilities at home and work, but she could not help the yearning she had for our souls to be together again.

"I've been writing still," Layne said with a tinge of hope in her voice.

'I am sure of it,' I replied. 'I would love to hear what you have been up to.'

She giggled. Her infectious laughter made me melt yet again.

"You are amazing, Scott." Layne's voice started to crack. "I miss you in every way."

Our conversation was short. My heart sank the moment I heard the silent pause when she hung up.

As I took a deep breath, I called Morena and asked her for advice. After explaining the magical moments I had with Layne, Morena's jubilance could be felt through the phone.

"Give her time, Scott," she continued assuring me. "Give her time."

As the Fourth of July rolled around, I realized it should not be enough to just eat hot dogs and barbeque. The day was always synonymous with freedom, but I can't just wave the flag and watch the parade go by.

Yes, I love all of the camaraderie the holiday brings, but I did think about my father who was still ill because of a war in the 60s and 70s. My grandfather who fought in WWII and my great grandfather who fought for England in WWI crossed my mind. I think of all my family members and our forefathers who fought for a higher ideal on our planet.

The Fourth of July was bigger than just a day off from work.

Home

I was present for all of the day's events, but I was surely thinking about more than where it's best to see the fireworks. More so than usual, we need to remember and honor the values our nation celebrates.

The world is at a crossroads, for the values we cherish today should be welcome to all of humanity.

It is easy to wear red, white, and blue, attend a parade, eat apple pie, watch a baseball game with friends, and wave a flag, but after centuries of war and unrest, our entire planet is at risk of dying on so many levels.

This is not a political statement; rather it is a call to awareness, to action, and to love.

The United States of America was built on faith, and we all need an ounce of faith at this time.

We must have ideals that are built on human rights and unconditional love for all.

We celebrate a nation that has these precious concepts built into the Constitution and a Bill of Rights, but we must go beyond physical documents.

It is imperative to discover peace, love, happiness, and oneness, and not just within our country, but within our world, and especially within ourselves.

There are so many souls who I tend to see panicking about their daily lives, but we have the ability to introduce tranquility in our world.

The fundamental human rights live within us along with how we care for others, and ourselves.

We hold these truths to be self-evident: the United States of America is bigger than these times. Truth, courage, love, and respect that we need for humanity are within our souls.

We can stand for and represent our country, and we should stand and represent our souls as well.

Later that night, Layne called me and read me a new entry from her journal. She told me that she thought of our soul connection and began to write:

"This is a roller coaster.
Never in my wildest dreams did I think I would be here: doing this, feeling this, being this.

Some days I am eternally grateful for the best and biggest blessing the universe has ever bestowed on me. I feel like for the first time, I know what true friendship, love, spiritual mutualism and support feels like in a healthy way, and all at the same time from one more than incredible person.

I have hit the jackpot.

Who even needs another person when they have a Scott?

Still, I am pained by my past. My soul was gutted and crushed by those who were close to me.

I am not strong enough yet to act upon our connection.

This would be the ultimate betrayal to my soul's healing process.

This won't go away. This feeling in my chest, my stomach, my being. Knowing that we can go deeper and deeper means that at no point is this going to be a surface game again.

Managing this seems pointless now.

My logical brain succumbs to my heart in each instant and I don't know what my heart can possibly do to keep me safe.

When all it wants are things that spell danger to the souls of others.

At some point something needs to give. The rubber band breaks.

Deep breath... Why would the Universe send me something that is so perfect to my soul while I am still healing?

In a time that is so fragile, you are my ultimate test.

I hate to reduce what we have to that word, but it truly feels like every moment with you is a soul-enriching moment.

Every word that comes out of your mouth.

Every text.

Every phone call.

Every moment.

So it's either you're a test, or a huge sign.

What do you want me to do with this? Give me something.

I fear that no matter what that something is, loss is the flip side to that coin: either my soul connects to your soul and I never heal, or you are gone forever.

I need some time to process. I know I don't want to lose you.

I can't lose you.

I love you."

Home

I sat there for a few moments, utterly speechless.

How was it possible that someone could be so self-reflective and spiritually connected to my soul?

We spoke for a while longer about our soul connection and what our respective growth would look like.

Layne's voice cracked, "How do we make this work, Scott?"

I did not know what to say.

I thought about how I soothed my soul in the past, and what methods helped me.

'Meditation,' I replied stoically.

"What do you recommend we do with meditation?"

'Each day, let's take some time to meditate together. We can talk about what that will look like and where it will take place.'

"So," Layne said inquisitively. "We go within."

'We go within,' I confirmed.

The two of us kept firm with our respective commitments to our souls.

On the first night we meditated together, I took her to the bridge and video called her. Layne was in the middle of getting ready for work. She was putting her earrings in as she spoke to me.

'This is where I usually go to connect to my soul: the Whitestone Bridge.'

She glanced at the screen. "It's beautiful at night."

'There is something so attractive about the bridge.'

I recalled looking through my father's station wagon windows at the bridge as we crossed over from the Bronx to Queens when we moved decades ago.

It was a connection to a new light.

It was symbolic of a new hope.

It would become a metaphor for my entire life's journey.

This particular bridge would prove as a means of comfort for my soul throughout my life. When I was abused as a child, I rode my bicycle to the bridge to find peace and happiness.

I try to process the difficult questions in my life on the pine green benches in front of the sandy beach.

'I could go on and on about bridge stories,' I smiled as the waves crashed close to my feet.

"Thank you," Layne said.

'Why are you thanking me?'

"For being you," she smiled.

We continued on about all of the wonderful places where our respective souls have grown and will continue to flourish.

After a few days of this meditative process, we decided that I should travel to Martha's Vineyard to see her again.

As I drove into Massachusetts, my anxiety seeped in.

Every trip prior has become progressively more intense for us.

If the intensity continued, would we reach our pinnacle? Could we reach our breaking point?

The ferry ride was painstaking as my nerves got the best of me. More tourists were on the boat with me: young children smacking tiny plastic shovels against their empty pails.

The sand in their buckets had yet to arrive, but I feared that mine and Layne's bucket might overflow.

As the boat approached the dock, Layne stood there in a flowing turquoise dress. Her baby pink nail polish and hot white heels were glorious accessories to her beaming smile.

Her entire aura was perfect.

'Hello, my love,' I walked over to her and kissed her cheek.

She coyly responded, "Hi."

Layne adorned a tart expression on her face.

'What's wrong?'

"Um," she cleared her throat. "Could you not say that word?"

'Which word?'

"Love. I'd rather we pick out a different word to say."

'What other word encompasses the peace-inducing soul connection we have?'

She looked down towards her feet for a moment, as she appeared to collect her thoughts. Layne locked eyes with me as the word flew from her mouth, "Namaste."

'I namaste you,' I replied.

"No," she laughed. "Just namaste."

We got in the car and drove towards a marina on the island. There were sailboats floating about the water without a care in the world.

We went back to the Mytoi Japanese Garden and continued to walk the different paths there. Our conversations grew more intense as the night fell upon us.

Two vibrant souls were glowing in the starlight descending on Martha's Vineyard.

As the two of us found our way back to the main part of the island, we both managed to start crying almost in unison.

Layne laughed, "Why are you crying?"

I wiped my eyes. My soul was aching for I sensed that she was about to end our relationship. I was fearful that she was going to walk out of my life forever, and that the soulful connection between us would be severed.

'You are just so beautiful,' was all I could come up with. I could not tell her the truth. I thought she might run.

Her tears flowed more rapidly. "Can you stop being so perfect?"

Layne leaned over and kissed me passionately. She began caressing my arm and chest so sensually, but that is where we paused for the time being.

'I can't do this to you.'

"What?"

'I don't want to hurt you, I don't want to add more pain to your soul.'

She wiped small tears from the edges of her eyes, "I namaste you."

'Why did you pick namaste, Layne?'

"Namaste means that my soul recognizes your soul."

I couldn't help myself. My lips were instinctively drawn to hers as we kissed once again.

Part of me thought that I had to leave, but all of me wanted to fight for her. I had to hold the space for her so she could figure things out.

Layne's soul was integrated with my soul. It was obvious that our energies were intertwined. We truly could not get enough of each other.

The number of days that Earth revolves around the sun does not satisfy the flavor of our souls. The recipe for our love was crafted as a cosmic part of this universe, and our love appeared to have the tenacity of an infinitesimal amount of revolutions around the sun.

This is a love story from another plane.

It may be non-existent in humanistic terms, but it is a realm that all souls should be privy to.

How many people can say they truly met their twin flame?

Just because we cannot see something within our current line of sight, it does not mean that nothing else exists.

Everything and anything beyond our purview is just something we have yet to discover.

Upon discovering Layne, I knew my life would never be the same.

She loves me in a humbling way that eclipses any and all pain. Layne knew that her soul was still healing, but chose to welcome me into her light.

Together, we shine brighter than the darkness embodying the depths of our respective pasts.

As the end of our experience came to a halt, for she had to go to work, I stood outside of the diner and looked up at the neon lettering:

"Twilight Diner."

I never realized how fitting it was.

As the sun set, so did my adventures with Layne.

It reminded me of Don Henley's song by a similar name:

> "You see a lot more meanness in the city
> It's the kind that eats you up inside
> Hard to come away with anything that feels like dignity
> Hard to get home with any pride
> These days a man makes you somethin'
> And you never see his face
> But there is no hiding place.
> Respectable little murders pay
> They get more respectable every day
> Don't worry girl, I'm gonna stick by you
> And someday soon we're gonna get in that car and get outta here."

I yearned to bring Layne away from here. I hoped her writings would be worldwide. I prayed her family would be safe, well, and financially stable when she became a writer.

The lyrics echoed through the catacombs of my mind.

I am here, in her world, watching her life manifest her soul's intentions.

The stained glass orange chandeliers reflected against the windows. I could see Layne's tied back hair flourishing about.

Home

Universe, this is all in your hands, I realized.

You brought her to me, you gave me her, she is the answer to everything.

Why would you introduce her to me only to pull her away?

While Layne was at work overnight, my mother's condition began to deteriorate and I had to return to New York. I ran to see her at the diner before leaving, and she tucked a note into my pocket:

"So much to say…but first…thank you for being and for all of the things that you project on my soul. I recognize and know your sweetness, kindness, loveness, connectedness, openness, intenseness, understanding and aligned soul.

There are no words to articulate the pressure in my own heart and know this: everything you feel, I feel.

Thank you for being the blessing and gift that you are in this life, and to this planet. Standing on the outside of what you have created and have been creating your entire life is breathtaking. I am in awe of who you are, and how you express yourself in this world. I truly have also never met anyone in my life like you. You are powerful beyond measure.

I know that you are the answer as well. Your heart will save this world. I know that, because your heart has saved mine.

There will never be enough to say to you. My story for you is never ending. You open my senses in ways I've never experienced nor expressed. There are no words for what you have given me, done for me, or created within me.

I know you. Deeply. That I AM SURE of.

That's all I can say for now as well. Namaste."

I held the crinkled note in my hand as the ocean breeze blew through my hair.

I loved her, and it was that simple. The polarities of the universe turned the situation into "a this and a that" conversation, but the truth remained between us.

How could we have both scenarios so that I get to spend eternity with her and her soul heals?

Layne loves in so many languages and her intellect is beyond anyone's wildest imagination.

I could take a moment and bring up her writing or ask a philosophical question, and her mind expands and flows with the most impeccable perspective. Whatever her soul is made of is the same material needed to save our planet, I was sure of it.

Our souls combined, mingling in the universe, were beyond magic.

As I touched my forearm, I felt her fingers caressing my soul. I held her aquamarine stone in my hand before planting a gentle kiss on its surface.

I was hoping that wherever Layne was, she would feel my love.

We fit perfectly in every way, shape, and form, including spiritually, mentally, emotionally, soulfully, and physically.

My chest grew tight with trepidation. Again, I was worried I would lose her.

∞ ∞ ∞ ∞ ∞ ∞ ∞ ∞

When I got home, my sister and my mother were sound asleep on the couch. I took a wrinkled magazine off of the brown recliner chair and let my mind wander.

In my dreamlike state, I imagined that Layne and I were getting married.

She was standing before me in a crisp, luxurious white gown that wrapped around her perfectly.

I felt myself tearing up at the sight of her beauty.

When it was time to give my vow to her, I knew exactly what to say:

From day one, I knew you were it. Every second, every moment, every experience: it was you. All of my life's questions were unanswered. I was roaming and rambling through what I thought was a lifetime of confusion, then you answered my prayers. The second I looked at you, all of my worries and issues faded to black, and you were the light. You were a beacon of hope that beckoned me to live. You reminded me to keep the faith and genuinely refuse to sink under the weight of this world.

With your hands intertwined in mine, I know for a fact that every weight, every hardship, every agonizing tear, was shed knowing that you would be waiting for me at the end of the storm.

Home

And when I was at my breaking point, you picked me up and held my hand. You looked into my eyes and spoke the words I never knew I would need to hear.

You are the best thing I never knew I needed. You are the response to every call I made that echoed through the darkness. You are my destiny, my empowering heart, and the divine love that encompasses the phrase, "seize the day."

You are my brand-new day.

I owe my soul to your undying, exquisite beauty. I owe my love to the woman who recognized the twin flame standing across from her. Our love burns brighter than that of a classic love story, because we live our lives beyond the boundaries of society standards, and with this ring, I pledge my loyalty to our bond, our growth, and our coexistence together.

It is a brand-new day, and we are going to live it together. We will live it time after time in each other's arms and with passion. For you are one-hundred percent of the reason why my soul is floating high above the clouds, and I know, for sure, that our love story embodies the notion that the best is yet to come.

All my life, I wanted an ocean view somewhere. As long as I am next to you, I do not care. I want to live our life in an infinite realm of possibilities, for you, my darling, you are truly my home.

Before she could say anything, a beam of light brushed against my face. I could feel the ghost of where her fingers were just a few hours ago. I hoped her touch was not just a dream, I had hoped that last night really happened and that she would long to hold me in her arms once again. She was an angel who was thrust into my life for no apparent reason, though months later I understood that she flew in to show me that there is a fire within me.

And now all I want to do is let it burn.

∞ ∞ ∞ ∞ ∞ ∞ ∞ ∞

When it came to trying to figure out how to love Layne without causing her any unintentional pain, I reverted to my pen to dig deeper into my soul. I wrote for hours in what should have been my framework notes to comprehend what to do with my mind's discontent.

Layne was the one person that could communicate with me and connect with me on a level that I never experienced before.

I promised Layne I would not hurt her, yet I feared that I was pushing too hard against the firm walls she constructed to protect her soul.

Every fiber of my being loved her with all I manifested to that point, but how could I express myself fully while honoring her? I felt the sun setting on my soul, yet she said I was supposed to see the sunrise at those moments.

I convinced myself I had to be stronger and remember the vision.

I knew what I saw in her eyes, I knew what I heard in the timbre of her voice. Her connection to souls and the way our hearts beat in tandem were not misaligned or misguided.

Her mind and soul lit the flame deep within me. Once you've seen something magical, it is not like you can just reset your brain. There are some things that awaken you in a way that reveal the positive vibrations deep within you. As a result, you can't deny what your soul truly desires.

You cannot unseen what you have seen.

When I look in her eyes, tears may be falling from mine, but I see happiness and feel happiness because I see her energy.

Anything can change in a moment. Within the blink of an eye she walked into my life, and I must cherish that.

She managed to resist me quite well, but like I had noticed before, when she caves into her desires, she crashes wholeheartedly. Within the parameters of this human experience, I loved her with all of my heart and soul and I knew she loved me.

I wondered, 'Why does this relationship seem to challenge me so much?'

What were two souls, that love one another and stand for a higher consciousness connection, supposed to do?

I wept openly over my book as Morena came into the room.

She placed a cup of tea on the table next to me, "What is wrong, sunshine?"

'Nothing,' I wiped my eyes and gazed up at her. 'Just nothing.'

"You miss her," Morena sat next to me and folded her hands over each other.

'Yeah,' I picked up the tea and sipped it gently.

"How could you not miss someone so crucial to your soul?"

I looked over at her again. 'You get it.'

"Heh," she laughed. "I see more than you realize. I heard a quote somewhere that said, *'Let the waves of the universe rise and fall as they will. You have nothing to gain or lose. You are the ocean.'*"

'How wise.'

"It is from the Ashtavakra Gita."

'It's like something Layne would know.'

"Maybe she does know it, maybe she just needs to unlock that part of her soul."

'I think it's just time to hand everything to the universe.'

"Stop saying it over and over again, unless you are truly going to start believing it."

'Is that judgment I hear, Morena?'

"Judgment is not my cup of tea, rather," she cleared her throat. "Sometimes you just need to let go of fear."

'Oh,' I coughed for a moment. 'Is that what I am feeling?'

"Maybe," Morena stood up. "Maybe you just need to listen to the voice in your soul."

'I am listening to the voice.'

She smoothed out the creases on her blue dress. "Listen closer."

Morena walked out of the living room and I called after her as I stood up, 'Morena, I-'

When I looked into the kitchen, she was gone. It figures.

I was convinced she was, indeed, an angel of sorts.

As the summer was speeding before me, I went to a conference in Baltimore with Morena to present about the framework. Though I was in my element talking about education, I missed Layne standing beside me.

Baltimore was not far from Washington, D.C., so I chose to go there to surprise Morena. As the signs on the highway flashed by, I watched Morena's eyes light up when the sign for the Arlington Memorial Bridge appeared on the road.

The possibility of real change existed in the streets I was about to enter, with the desire to change the world burned deep inside.

As we walked down the streets of D.C. at night, I envisioned what it must have been like for the presidents who passed through these roads in their motorcades.

Real systemic change was being conjured within my soul, but I feared I was being too histrionic and grandiose for my own good.

The streets were empty and I thought: If New York is the city that never sleeps, why did it appear like D.C. was taking a nap?

Morena turned her eyes to the Washington Monument as we stood on the steps of the Lincoln Memorial. Standing up there gazing out at the Reflecting Pool was majestic.

It solidified my dreams and put it all into perspective. It gave me a path of hope. As I took in every step, I felt the universe guiding me and welcoming me to the next stage.

The White House, much smaller than I thought, felt like home.

It seemed so doable, almost as if I had lived there before.

There was a homeless veteran out at the front of the gates, I wondered if any President spoke with him.

I was told he's been there forever.

Can we invite him into dinner and hear him out? Why is he there? What does his soul search for?

World peace has to be a possibility.

The game has to change.

Standing on the steps of the Lincoln Memorial made me feel as if I was looking up at the gates of heaven. Lincoln and I have a long spiritual relationship, and I have always been amazed by his story.

There is something about a man who brought this country back together while struggling with his own physical illness, depression, and a difficult family is phenomenal.

He struggled with who he was but cared about all others.

He fought a war based on civil rights: the right to be human, to love yourself for who you are, and to have faith.

How is that different from the social emotional work we do daily?

He was a man of heart and true character.

Home

When I think about my relationship with the heavens, I always feel pulled in by the story of Lincoln, just as I felt invited up the stairs of the monument. I felt invited by him tonight as if the angels lined this moment up for me.

I took each step consciously and mindfully felt my feet touch each stone, raising me slowly to the message I was about to hear.

Walking into the temple was as if the universe and angels were calling me into a realization about what my life is all about.

On some spiritual level you can see the words of God and the angels intertwined in the words of his speeches.

We need to go back to that time of conviction, of making this world better for a higher purpose.

We must search our souls and we must become one.

There is still a civil war going on, not just in our country between Democrats and Republicans, but in the world and in our individual souls.

We must bridge the gap, we must soul-search, and we must have peace on earth. It's as if the closer we got to accepting love of same sex marriages, the older child known as civil rights resurfaces in the form of gun violence, systemic racism, wrongful deaths, and police shootings. Like raising a family, we must love and nurture all our children.

If society's issues are our children, we must navigate and communicate in a way we can understand the roots of souls better.

At the end of the day, we can love one another and love thy neighbor.

We must bring the world to gather as one, UNIFIED, as Abraham Lincoln wanted. Staring up into his eyes, I felt like he was passing the torch to me, but he was also with me, putting his hand on my shoulder as I sat in his temple and meditated.

I prayed for guidance and I felt the puzzle pieces come together.

It took me a long time to realize I love my life, I love the world we live in, I love the anticipation of hopes and dreams, and that look in Layne's eyes.

Maybe some things are not meant to be no matter how you look at them, but that night, as I stared into Lincoln's eyes and felt his presence, I knew anything was possible.

Later on in the evening as my legs grew weary I stopped at McDonald's for a Happy Meal. I walked with Morena to the Capitol building at two in the morning enjoying my chicken and my All-American meal.

'Whether Layne is by my side or not,' I told Morena. 'I am moving ahead on this journey as I now realize no matter what path you take, it will lead to the same place.'

"The place you are meant to be," she responded.

Morena and I walked the streets of Washington, D.C. until the sun started to rise. We began to talk about love in its most pure form.

As a kid, there was nothing more romantic than creating a mixtape for a girl you liked. It was the utmost expression of love and just showed creativity. I always believed music was the language of the soul, and going all the way back to the days of being with Robin, I knew the melodies and harmonies created a vibration to lift our consciousness to a new level.

Yet with modern technology, mixtapes have been escalated to playlists of sometimes hundreds of songs.

Layne texted me here and there since my last trip at Martha's Vineyard, but we did not seem to harbor the same soul connection as we did during the first few times we were physically occupying the same space. I wondered if our mutual melody hit its final verse.

Our first kiss, our first physical encounter, the way the vibrations from music make her body sway, it was clear that when love can't be expressed in terms of words, music fills the space between us.

"Sometimes it's about words and music," Morena replied.

'You can't have one without the other most of the time.'

Layne's aural melody was exquisite.

I only wished that love could stand the test of time, just like the music notes that graced my mixtapes and playlists over the years. However, the greatest concierto by far was not one written by Mozart or Beethoven, rather it was composed by Layne's connection to my soul and the way my heartbeat fluttered when she looked at me.

Love is truly the greatest music of all.

∞ ∞ ∞ ∞ ∞ ∞ ∞ ∞

Home

As Morena and I got back to New York, a taxicab was pulling up to my mother's house. Confused and slightly concerned, I got out of the car and placed my right elbow on the roof of the Dodge Charger.

"Surprise," Layne exclaimed so loudly that she almost dropped her suitcase from her hand.

'Layne?'

She rushed over and threw her arms around me.

'How did you get here?'

"I can navigate a bus map, but this city is surely something else," Layne grinned and glared at me lovingly.

We lingered in the moment, waiting for each other to say what we both longed to hear.

'Oh,' I turned. 'Layne there is someone I want you to meet.'

When I went to the passenger side of the car, I noticed that Morena was gone.

"Who, Scott?"

'My,' I hesitated for a moment. 'My mother. Come inside!'

The two of us walked into the house as Layne explained she had to see me after my short stint in Baltimore. We chatted for a few moments until my mother emerged from the living room.

"The men are working on the plumbing again," she muttered.

Layne looked at me quite confused, "What?"

I pointed to my head and Layne got the hint.

'Mom, this is my friend Layne. Layne, this is my mom.'

Layne extended her hand, "Nice to meet you, Ms. Matheson."

"Oh," my mother seemed startled. "Hello dear, it's nice to see you again."

Layne and I moved into the living room and spoke with my mother for a while. As she recounted stories of her teaching days, Layne looked on in amazement. When we left the house later on, I realized why.

The two of us took a walk in Alley Pond Park and spoke about past pain.

"It is fascinating how the human brain works," Layne looked over at me. "Your mother doesn't remember anything she did to you when you were younger?"

'No, not at all.'

"Fascinating," she looked ahead on the trail. We waited there a little too long again, which made it seem like we were going to ease into another passionate kiss.

Somehow, Layne managed to contain her soul's desire.

As we walked further into the park, she fell into my arms crying hysterically.

'Layne?' I rubbed her shoulder.

"I just didn't realize how hard this was going to be." Her tears pooled on my t-shirt.

'I am here for you no matter what,' my voice softened. 'I am not going anywhere and you call the shots.'

"Thank you," she nestled into my chest.

'I will be whatever you need me to be, even if it means I need to disappear forever in order to soothe your soul.'

"I never want you to disappear," she whipped her head up towards my face. "You are always in my soul."

We walked the park for a little bit longer, until she said she wanted to go back to her hotel to rest. As we drove back, she sat in relative silence while I kept my eyes on the road.

As my car drove into the underground parking lot, static filled the radio. The two of us locked eyes for a moment before we opened the doors.

When the two of us made our way towards the elevator, a whole barrage of rats scurried past our feet. We ran quickly and started to slam the buttons on the elevator. The two of us darted away from the rats and rushed into the stairwell.

While giggling over the sheer chaos that just occurred, I looked over at her.

'They never do this,' I assured her. 'Yeah, I mean, there is that rat who stole a whole slice of pizza, but… that was in the subway.'

"You're adorable," she grabbed her bag from my hand as we walked up the steps. We laughed and made our way up to her room.

It was clear we were ensnared in a cycle of struggle and passion, with hope for the future.

The moment the door shut behind us, she put on some music. The way her body moved to the lyrics was exhilarating, though I had to restrain myself from moving towards her.

Home

I stood there in the doorway as she swayed her hips in the shape of an infinity sign. Layne extended her hand, "Dance with me."

The lyrics called me in.

Ed Sheeran's words to "I See Fire" were perfect in that moment:

> *"Oh, misty eye of the mountain below*
> *Keep careful watch of my brothers' souls*
> *And should the sky be filled with fire and smoke*
> *Keep watching over Durin's sons*
> *If this is to end in fire*
> *Then we should all burn together*
> *Watch the flames climb high into the night."*

When the song ended, she flopped on the bed and curled into the sheets. I saw her sigh heavily as she gazed out at the city's skyline. From Queens, she had the perfect view of Manhattan.

Not lying next to her felt like I was missing something.

My soul felt empty and I could not catch my breath.

"You can lay next to me," Layne motioned for me to sit on the bed. I left space between us so that she did not feel pressured.

'You came all the way to New York, after you relax for a bit, I want to take you to a few places.'

She flipped over in the bed so she was facing me. "Okay."

A smile crept up both of our faces.

'Okay.'

A few hours later, the two of us were walking along the Brooklyn Bridge Promenade. We strolled arm in arm glaring out at the Freedom Tower.

'The Twin Towers once stood there,' I pointed out towards the southern part of Manhattan.

Layne shut her eyes and seemed to feel the energy from my aunt's soul. A few deep breaths later, she opened her eyes and we continued to walk.

I took her to eat at a blues bar in Manhattan. She loved the music, the decor, and the food they had.

"We don't really have anything like this on Martha's Vineyard," she pulled out her journal and started writing.

Beautiful Souls

As the stars rose in the sky, I took her on a driving tour of New York City. The two of us listened to music throughout the entire ride, with her body ebbing and flowing with each elegant note.

"So Alive" from the Goo Goo Dolls appeared to reflect her soul's intentions at those moments:

> *"Open up my heart like a shotgun*
> *Blinded by the light of a new sun*
> *Get up, get up, get out and get done*
> *For the first time I feel like someone*
> *Breaking down the walls in my own mind*
> *Keeping my faith for the bad times*
> *Get up, get up, stand like a champion*
> *Take it to the world*
> *Gonna sing it like an anthem."*

So many people take New York City for granted, especially since the hustle and bustle of commuters regularly fills the atmosphere. Watching Layne breathe in every single element of Manhattan was breathtaking.

After driving uptown, downtown, and across midtown for quite some time, we found ourselves gazing out at the bridge in Astoria Park.

"You have such beautiful bridges in New York," Layne watched the lights twinkle atop Hellgate Bridge.

The water has a certain calming presence over my soul, which has captivated me ever since I was a young boy. Even at the tender age of eight years old, I sensed that I had a higher purpose and a story that transcended even my deepest insecurities.

That was why it was water, her tears that streamed down her alabaster face, which awoke me from the trance-like slumber my heart was in. Though in the midst of facing some of my darkest moments, I couldn't help but hear her tears as an echoic reverberative melody inside of my soul.

The love that emulated from her heart was beyond real. It was powerful. It was magical on an entirely different level.

Coexisting with her is a type of fire that I didn't mind getting burned by, though it is more than that.

Her love and her spirit were cosmically intoxicating.

Home

Her essence was a solitary flame that sparked my inferno. On nights like those, I tended to walk through the cool, crisp night trying to gain my thoughts; I usually caught myself glancing at the stars.

Part of me hoped that wherever in the universe her soul truly was, she was not in pain.

The universe has become brighter since the moment she walked into my life. There was a light coming from her that shined so bright, no shadow could come close to touching her glowing nature. In the moments she whispered to me that she loved me, she missed me, or when she simply grabbed my hand or cuddled into my chest, all of the internal storms brewing within fell to a complete silence.

Her energy crept inside of me in a way that repaired every torn crevice of my soul. She taught me that when we allow ourselves to open our hearts, and in expressing and exploring this higher love consciousness, love will open your mind to new dimensions.

It would expand your soul to the furthest corners of the universe.

Loving her, and receiving her love, is the igniting of potential which unfurls an unimaginable force across the universe. It lifts our spirits vibrationally, and that of every soul in, and not of, this universe. Walking through these streets, looking at these stars, and remembering all of our magical moments uplifts me and blesses me with the ability to see a brighter tomorrow.

There is a silence here.

There is a silence that carries your name in my heart throughout every second of the day, every moment of the week, and every season of the year.

I love Layne this way because my soul knows no other way.

I leaned over to her and whispered: 'You are the path to my dreams, and each cobblestone represents the little moments that led me to your effervescent beauty. It made me see that once you realize the dreams of your heart, anything you face is manageable. Your life takes on an entirely new meaning... and I mean anything I have tried to run away from: my heart, from my truth, and beyond that. The only thing I have discovered is that it is impossible to escape from my heart, no matter how hard I try. Instead, I have now stopped trying to run as fear cascades through me. I sit and listen.'

Layne looked over at me and smiled.

Beautiful Souls

'I listen to my heart and it screams at me passionately. It has much to say. Much of it makes my soul sing. I'm coming to the end of this starry night, and this cool brisk air creeps inside me sending a chill down my spine. It is almost as powerful as the memory of your kisses, your smooth skin, your electrifying touch, and the kindness that emanates off your soul, leaving my soul trembling. Though my mind is racing with questions, the only word that surfaces on my lips is the one that you gave meaning to: "Namaste." And suddenly, the world does not seem like it is succumbing to the dawn and dispersing the illustrious stars above.'

"Rather," Layne spoke. "We are creating an infinite, spiraling path into the sun, and actualizing just what it means to be immersed in the essence of two words that describe our everlasting growth: twin flames. We are twin flames who will burn forever, and no matter what, forever will always be ours to cherish eternally."

We glanced at each other as the next song played over the speakers.

Layne shut her eyes as Amy Lee's voice seeped into the car. Evanescence's "My Immortal" seemed to touch yet another exquisite part of her soul.

I watched the music move through her as she closed her eyes and sang in such an angelic manner:

> *"I'm so tired of being here*
> *Suppressed by all my childish fears*
> *And if you have to leave*
> *I wish that you would just leave*
> *'Cause your presence still lingers here*
> *And it won't leave me alone*
> *These wounds won't seem to heal; this pain is just too real*
> *There's just too much that time cannot erase*
> *When you cried, I'd wipe away all of your tears*
> *When you'd scream, I'd fight away all of your fears*
> *And I held your hand through all of these years..."*

I watched the next few words spring from her mouth with such illustrious purpose. It was almost as if her soul was guiding her lips:

"But you still have..."

Home

She paused for a moment along with the song. I honed in on the energy she emitted while singing the next few words:

"All of me."

Layne opened her eyes and saw my tears rolling down the edges of my eyes. I could not help but cry at the sound of her illustrious beauty, both internal and external.

The two of us sat in silence when the song ended until she asked if I could drop her off at the hotel.

When I walked her up to her room for the night, she kissed me gently on the cheek. The metal door opened as she slid inside. As it slammed shut, I walked down the hall hoping to hear the door open again.

The elevator arrived and the only sound I could hear was the ding reminding me that my soul was in a current state of solitude.

Layne only came in for the weekend, so I had to make Sunday count as best as possible. The two of us had breakfast after I picked her up, and we sat in Francis Lewis Park talking about our relationship.

"We are beyond the 3D aspects of our world," Layne spoke softly.

'What do you mean?' I adjusted my body so I was directly facing her.

"As human beings, we live in a perpetual state of physical consciousness. Our world has concrete, black and white realities: we are born, we are here," she motioned towards both of us. "We die."

I nodded my head and leaned towards her.

"The 3D view mandates relationships have a lower vibrational frequency and are integrated with a lot of fear. Sometimes even that fear is so strong that it constricts us from growing spiritually. Our souls are not respected as a higher power."

'So, it's like a non-spiritual way of being.'

"We are 5D," she said matter-of-factly.

'5D?'

"It is the elevated sense of love. It is the highest and most challenging state of consciousness, yet we live it each day."

Layne stood up and walked over to the iron fence in front of us. She spoke as if she was educating the water before us; I felt the wind tearing through my soul.

"Everything is spiritual, of a higher power, and focuses on the foundation of love in a 5D relationship."

'Love is the life force.'

"Yes," she turned towards me and her hair got caught in the wind. "The heart, the mind, and the soul each have a different language."

'Feelings are more intense and expanded upon.'

"Love is not love, connection is not connection, integration is not integration," her entire face illuminated as if she suddenly became enlightened. Layne ripped her journal from her bag and started to write furiously.

'You live authentically and as a universal, spiritual being.'

"Yes, yes!" She dropped onto the bench and continued writing.

'When you live from your heart and soul, there is an instant connection.'

"And in this 3D world, life is challenging because we struggle to balance the 3D and 5D aspects of our lives."

'It's the vibrations in our soul that make us who we are.'

Her scribbling was more audible, "Vibrations."

'It's unconditional love without any asterisks, without what ifs, and without buts.'

"Yes," Layne slammed the journal shut and smiled at me. "It's an instant connection."

Her eyes began to wander around the park. She glanced over at the bridge, the grass, the children playing on the swings.

The rest of the day flew by, but she seemed to have a renewed sense of who she was. It was almost as if something finally clicked in her brain.

When I dropped her off at the bus stop in Manhattan, she seemed happier than usual.

'Thank you,' I held her tight for a moment.

"I am glad I got to see you, Scott."

We did not let go. It seemed like that was our final goodbye, though I knew that something was shifting within both of us.

It was more of a "hello" situation. We were finally meeting each other without filtered hearts.

Still, as she boarded the bus and it drove off, my heart sank in my chest once again. I needed her desperately and I missed her so much, even though she had just left.

Home

When I returned to my mother's house, I was clearly sulking as I got out of the car.

"What are you doing?" Morena appeared in the shadows as she usually did.

'Nothing,' I wiped the tears from my eyes.

Morena flew in front of me as her dress swooshed past my leg.

"Don't let yourself get like this. She is what you prayed for and you wanted for the longest time. The universe presented you with her."

I tried walking away from her, but she appeared in front of me again.

"You wanted to love yourself, holistically and without remorse, and she brings out that side of you. She is the epitome of happiness and all that genuinely stands for the term holy."

'Morena, I-'

Her voice cut through my thoughts: "She is your happiness and light serendipity, you must understand this on a spiritual level."

The two of us walked into my mother's house and started to review the latest ideas I had about the framework. Every time I paused to turn the page I envisioned Layne sitting across from me, scribbling something down in her journal as she wrote the greatest novel known to humankind.

I shut my eyes for a moment and allowed the breeze from the fan to usher me into a tranquil state of rest.

∞ ∞ ∞ ∞ ∞ ∞ ∞ ∞

As I woke, a smile crept over my face. The image of her faded deep into the recesses of my mind, as I sat up hopeful I would see her again in my dreams tonight.

Something swimming around in my subconscious anchors her to my soul. My undying love for her exists within multiple universes, and it blatantly shows through how she manifests while I sleep. Though she is not really next to me, I find comfort waking up in the morning and seeing her image be projected in the empty space next to me.

Hearts may break, but nothing will break my unwavering dedication to what we once were. I will cherish her memory in my mind, soul, and heart until every ounce of life is drained from me.

Even in whatever afterlife exists, I will still make it my mission to reconnect with her soul. If not in this universe, I will find her in the next.

That is how strong our connection is.

And it always will be. Even if sometimes a little bit of me strays from her light, I know that her shadow stands tall. The remnants of our shadows lay somewhere intertwined, if not in the light, then in the recesses of all visibility where souls have the privilege to connect.

Layne was pushing me away as if doing so would fix everything.

I wondered if she was wrong.

I wondered if pushing me away would be the biggest mistake she would ever make.

What if we don't get the chance to live out the blessing we were handed?

I did not want to do anything without Layne by my side. Everything felt wrong without her there.

Our love may not have a stronger word than love, but it is what we have. It's from somewhere else and we both acknowledged that. We both felt the energy between us.

I knew we had to follow through with this feeling.

Since the second our eyes met, I knew that my life had meaning because of her.

'Please don't leave me' escaped my lips. 'Look in my eyes and tell me you love me.'

As I turned the aquamarine stone over between my fingertips, there was no answer from the universe.

My soul was screaming out to hers, but a dull silence filled the air.

When I stood up, the stuffing from the couch appeared to follow me. Even the internal filling of the couch wanted to rise above, how metaphoric.

Days were flying by and before I knew it, I would be counting down the final days of summer. I wanted to make one last-ditch effort to confess my love to Layne, although she was fully aware we were in love.

The two of us did not have labels, but when it all comes down to the inherent truth, we were each other's twin flame.

Her texts and calls were coming few and far between each sweltering day, and I wanted more than anything to run right up to Martha's Vineyard and whisk her into my arms.

Home

Layne's pain seemed to be overbearing and her soul was still on its path to recovery, and I wanted more than anything to be her hero.

I had the potential to be her savior; every fiber of my soul assumed my love would rescue her from the internal hurt that haunted her each day.

As my march towards going back to work was starting to take place, Layne called me one day in a fit of excitement.

"I'm doing it," she exclaimed.

'Doing what?'

"I am going to head back towards the Grand Canyon where my father, Marissa, and I used to visit."

'That's awesome,' I assured her. 'Why now?'

"I think my book needs that final scene where the Grand Canyon acts as the backdrop. It was the most illustrious place where I used to write as a child, and I need to go there and breathe in the scenery."

'That's cool,' I swallowed hard for a second. 'Do you mind if I come with you?'

She paused for a moment and sighed, "Of course."

Layne was taking a flight from Boston and I was taking one from LaGuardia Airport in New York.

We met at Jackpot Airport at the very top of the state of Nevada. She was able to convince some of her old friends to drive up and pick us up, but my flight somehow managed to come in a bit earlier than hers.

Since she was ensnared in a layover in Chicago, I found myself wandering around all alone.

I was looking at a screen with incoming flights, and was curious about the airport's code: KPT.

My inquisitive mind compelled me to ask a flight attendant why the code was KPT. She shrugged and continued walking by. Sometimes people are so busy, I wonder if they ever stop to notice the little things in life like airport codes.

When Layne finally arrived, her friends and I jumped in a pine green Jeep and headed south towards the Canyon.

We had a great conversation about Layne's book and she began to read some entries to us. I was in awe of how much her writing grew over the past few months.

She nudged me and replied, "I have you to thank."

Beautiful Souls

Her smile was wider and she appeared to be more in tune with my soul's vibrations. I lingered on her compliment for the rest of the car ride.

The sun was setting as the two of us got all the way to the south rim of the Grand Canyon.

"The south rim arguably has the best view," Layne said.

"Oh yeah," her friend remarked. "Hands down."

Layne's friend dropped us off and said she would come pick us up when it started to get really dark.

As we walked closer to the Canyon, I saw the setting sun touch each rock with a pristine softness. The vivid colors drenched the Canyon in a rare vibrancy that I never even knew existed.

'It's,' I took a breath for a moment. 'Beautiful.'

Layne looked over her shoulder at me and extended her hand. "Let's keep walking."

I took her hand and began to follow her through the path. There were multiple places that were not fenced off too well, and a sudden fear of heights seemed to seep into my mind.

Looking down at the huge drop, I must have worn my fear on my face.

"We'll make it, I swear," she laughed and pulled me towards the path again.

I watched Layne sit and write underneath a partially rotten tree for a while. My own mind wandered to a state of peace, for the sounds of the Grand Canyon compel the soul to go deep within the cavernous elements of your own being.

When the sun completed its dissent, we got a ride back to a hotel in town. At the front desk, they revealed that only one room was booked instead of two, so I naturally offered for Layne to stay in my room.

She accepted with a petite grin.

We sat in the hotel room on the sole queen-size bed debriefing what we saw out at the Canyon.

'How long are you staying here?'

"Just a few days, I want to make sure that I get all of the scenery just right."

Layne began to flip through her journal, which appeared to be almost full.

'Wow, you have written a lot.'

"Mhm," she nodded. "Since my last trip to New York, I had a sudden burst of energy. Everything seems to make sense in my soul."

'Everything?'

"Yes," she replied. "Including our relationship."

I swallowed hard, 'Oh?'

"Our love is real, it's intense, and I have so many choices to make."

'Like what?'

"Are you everything I ever wanted? Yes. Are you more than perfect? Yes."

'Do you love me?'

"Is that even a question?"

'Sorry,' I propped my head up against the headboard. 'Continue.'

"Is all of this enough?" She paused. "No."

'No?'

"No, Scott."

We sat in silence for a few moments before lying parallel to one another.

"Higher love consciousness is extremely rare. To lie together and love one another, and speak about why we can't be a couple is beyond rare, but I need to grow. You need to grow."

As tears slowly cascaded from my eyes, I murmured, 'But you need to grow?'

"And you do, too," she extended her hand and touched my forearm.

I sat in desolate silence.

"Based on my life choices, I know I need more time to heal before I fully commit myself to anything or anyone else. I have my book. I have my writing. Who knows where it will go?"

'But what about us?'

"I love you," she began to cry. "I namaste you."

We sat in silence a little while longer, while Layne continued to search for the words stemming from the voice in her soul.

"I can't continue expressing to you what is in my soul, for I know I am still healing." She placed her hand over my heart. "You are still healing."

'I know,' I teared up a bit more.

"I am still healing."

I saw the tattered wallpaper in my peripheral vision. The terra cotta pots sitting on the night table were still and rustic, almost echoic of the way my soul seemed to shrivel up inside.

Beautiful Souls

The rest of the night into the morning consisted of a long, emotional talk about our respective pain and our individualistic journeys.

"We made it here, because we are the souls the world has been waiting for."

Her words struck my soul with the truth. How could I deny I was still relishing in my past pain?

My love for her seemed to consume my soul at times, and I was rejecting any sort of healing energy I could manifest.

All of my energy was going into our relationship, not who I could become.

I needed to step into my own power, as did she, no matter how much it hurt our souls for the time being.

If it were meant to be, then it would be.

Before we fell asleep, the two of us decided we would dance to one last song together.

Layne snatched my phone and started to scroll up and down with her finger. As she squinted at the screen, the faint light from my phone illuminated her eyes.

As the song started playing, she looked at me and said, "I am thankful for you, and I hope you know that this song reminds me so much of your soul."

The melody and lyrics to Vanessa Williams' "Save the Best for Last" echoed throughout the room:

> *"Sometimes the snow comes down in June*
> *Sometimes the sun goes 'round the moon*
> *I see the passion in your eyes*
> *Sometimes it's all a big surprise*
> *'Cause there was a time when all I did was wish*
> *You'd tell me this was love*
> *It's not the way I hoped or how I planned*
> *But somehow it's enough*
> *And now we're standing face to face*
> *Isn't this world a crazy place?*
> *Just when I thought our chance had passed*
> *You go and save the best for last."*

Home

I doubt that either of us remembered falling asleep.

An hour later, I looked over at the clock and panicked. It was four in the morning. I had to run and catch my flight, since I was only there for less than a day. There was no time to shower or waste a moment.

I kneeled down next to her and tousled her hair between my fingers. I planted a solitary kiss on her forehead and whispered into her ear just how much she meant to me.

And I loved her.

I couldn't leave her.

I knew once I did, I could be penning our final goodbye in our chapter.

Layne's eyes crept open in the darkness. The dim light from the bathroom shined bright enough for me to see the outline of her pure facial features.

Her groggy voice lurked out into the dusk: "Are you going?"

'I don't want to, Layne.'

She shifted her body so she could hold me.

"I know."

'I have been trying to leave for ten minutes.'

I could feel her smile as she held me close. Her heart was beating in tandem with mine once again. Our bodies fit perfectly together.

"Don't miss your flight."

'Yes, my love.' I held back the tears.

"Have a good day, Scott."

'I will, babe,' I whispered back.

Neither one of us moved, as there was clearly a deeper message in this embrace.

After what seemed like an hour, we slowly pulled apart. My lips were just as close as they were on that first day we kissed, except this time I honored her request and did not give into what I so passionately wanted to do.

My lips were right there.

I felt her about to cave as well.

For a moment, I ran my fingers through her hair and held her forehead against mine.

'I love you Layne,' I inhaled and exhaled deeply. 'I always will.'

She was silent for a moment and whispered, "Namaste."

435

I softly kissed her forehead and pressed my ear against her chest for a moment. Her beating heart was the last sound I wanted to hear before I fully said goodbye.

As I pulled away, she whispered, "Text me when you land."

'Of course, Layne.'

I wasn't sure if I would.

She rolled over and was consumed by the darkness.

With my heart racing to the tune of what would normally be tears, I glanced over at the pad and pen on the night table.

I lifted the pen with such purpose, and wrote her a quick note:

Layne,

I will love you forever. You are perfect, your story is perfect, you have made my existence perfect, and the world needs you. Don't ever forget that.

Always,
Scott

As the door shut behind me, I took one last look at her fast asleep under the blankets. She looked like an angel.

My angel.

My love.

The door closed behind me as two long, slow teardrops fell from each eye.

I remember that day, for the world shifted back to a sadness I had not experienced in almost a year.

I got to the terminal and through security in what seemed like record time.

KPT is an airport code I will never forget.

It is an airport I will never return to.

It is a memory I never want to revisit, though in usual fashion, even a final goodbye with Layne is extremely breathtaking.

I wondered if she would be sitting in this same airport in a few days' time feeling the stale air of this universe, which I clearly felt at that moment.

Home

Nothing will ever be the same again.

I looked around.

Maybe Morena's essence would guide me through this. I could have used that angelic wisdom at that moment.

I was alone.

Upon arriving in New York, the souls in the airport seemed to have an emptiness to their energy: I could not connect to anyone.

Layne and I talked last night about how we are no different than the other souls on this planet, and how our ability to connect is a responsibility to the planet.

We could feel one another miles away, and we can connect to other souls and show them their possibilities. Just because we see the light doesn't make us better. It's a gift we must pay forward.

We deep dived for hours, just the two of us.

A hotel room, two hearts, two souls, and one vision.

Our conversation was insightful, stoic, and exponentially deep... it had global implications. Her vision, her energy, and her writing could connect souls to their inner power, and ignite their healing process so that they can work to improve our planet. It sounds like a very valuable reason to sacrifice the greatest love story never told.

Her soul was leaps and bounds ahead of our time, and knowing that she would still be out there in the world gave my soul a tranquil feeling.

The darkness behind the large terminal windows mirrored the darkness in my soul. I had to mirror her wisdom and also try to make a change on this planet in a devout manner.

However, my numbness didn't feel like I could do so.

Last night we spoke about how Layne and I need to take the final step into owning our respective power, yet my hypocritical heart didn't believe I could do the same.

There will never be another Layne and Scott. There is never the same love twice; she is proof of this.

Goodbye Layne. Namaste times an eternal infinity.

Your soul will always be my home.

The automatic doors opened and I stepped out into the bustling cityscape once again.

Beautiful Souls

Morena picked me up at the airport. The sun was shining brightly in New York, which was an utter juxtaposition to what my soul was feeling.

"Hey stranger," she was smiling. "Long time no see."

I had only been gone about a day, but Morena was clearly trying to boost my spirits. She knew something happened in the hours prior, she could feel it.

'Hey,' I wiped tears from my eyes again.

She grew more concerned. "What's wrong?"

'Nothing,' I tartly replied.

"Tell me, I know something is up."

When the car door shut behind me, the waterfall enclosed behind my eyelids burst forward.

'I can't even find the words to express it anymore. It is the most amazing and difficult love story, it shakes me to my core and I can't wrap my brain around it. I get it when she says, "my brain explodes." I don't understand it, but I do understand it. I have everything, but selfishly I want more. I just really want more time with her, swimming in that energy. She has all of my heart, and every single day my heart expands even more to the point where I didn't know I had that much love for one person. When I think I am going to plateau, I look into her eyes or hear her and the expansion continues. Our love is infinite like the universe, and that is how much I love her. I know what she means when she says I break her brain, because I feel it too. When you swell up with that much love and energy, the human vessel could only contain so much energy. It turns into a flood. The flood is how I express talking about her: my love for her pours out of my soul. It is overwhelmingly intense and it is the greatest feeling in the world.'

I could see Morena's eyes closing slightly.

'You're not even listening to me,' I quipped at her.

"No," she snapped. "You listen to me. Listen hard and listen good, because I am only going to say this once."

"I don't think you actually know what it feels like to love someone, to genuinely love someone, and watch them look right through you."

We paused for a moment as Morena gripped the steering wheel.

"You have love, you have loved deeply. You know this truth to be evident within your soul, yet you squander away your self-worth because you think *you* are not worth it."

Home

I was speechless. 'Um, Morena, I-'

"Love yourself, Scott. Isn't it about time you recognized your own soul?"

I didn't know how to respond. All I knew was that despite years and years of finding love and letting it go, I knew I had the perfect love right there in Layne, yet I wasn't ready.

I didn't know if I ever would be ready.

Though time and time again, I assured myself through the three words that my soul knew to be the undying truth: "Keep the faith."

I knew I was worth it, for just when I thought that all of the love in my life had passed, I realized that I was the one who saved the best for last.

CHAPTER 10

Beautiful Souls

"I don't want another pretty face. I don't want just anyone to hold. I don't want my love to go to waste. I want you and your beautiful soul. You're the one I want to chase. You're the one I want to hold. I won't let another minute go to waste. I want you and your beautiful soul."

- **Jesse McCartney, American singer, songwriter, actor, Ardsley, New York**

There was a resolute stillness in my soul.

We live in a society that teaches people to deny their own feelings, which leads to denying their own truths.

I wondered how many times I lied to my soul over the years.

Lying on the ratty old couch, I wondered how something so beautiful could be over. How could something universally delivered and so perfect in every way have a defined ending?

Layne's departure and final words seemed prophetic, yet each passing moment felt like a pungent question mark that reverberated through my core. Day by day, I held in my tears to prevent questions from my students and colleagues.

My own family did not even recognize the pain seeping through my eyelids.

That first week without hearing from Layne, I awoke startled by my mother's rantings and ravings. Not long ago, I was staring into the soul of my twin flame and dancing through a painstaking goodbye.

Tears rolled down my cheeks as nothing felt just, though I was sinking through the familiarity of loss.

Actually, I was drowning.

What did I truly have now?

Well, I had wisdom from all of these life experiences. I had the comprehension of human experience. I had the ability to overcome extreme adversity and use hardship as a place of empowerment.

After finding my twin flame and loving her from the deepest truth imaginable, I lost that expression of love in the physical sense.

However, Layne remained in my soul.

She always said that everything has its equal balance, and would give an intellectual sermonistic view of the world.

The greatest love known to humankind therefore becomes the greatest pain known to my soul.

I had to move forward, but I couldn't see through the tears rushing down my face.

The city bustles and roars during its ritualistic 9 to 5 culture, though the inside of my soul was wrought with the deafening sensation of Layne departing from my physical existence.

September came back with a vengeance.

Beautiful Souls

Kids were depending on me to show up fully, and I had to dig deep to do so.

Layne wasn't just another love; she was the pinnacle of a higher love consciousness. To say goodbye to her, to not have Layne in my life, to not have my twin flame continue on this journey with me, it simply felt like a life that no longer made sense.

The two constants in my life were my son, Bryan, and the voice of my inner consciousness, Morena.

I had a big vision and throughout thick and thin, the two of them were there to act as my symbiotic support system. They each provided something exquisite for my soul to continue to grow.

I had a heart and soul filled with love that seemed to go on and on despite hardship, sacrifice, and turmoil.

I kept praying for one of those magical movie endings, where I would walk the Brooklyn Bridge or show up at Francis Lewis Park, and she would be standing there with a changed mind and a changed heart.

The day in believing that fairytales come true never actually happens; rather we learn to rewrite our own endings.

Knowledge becomes an exquisite blessing and a curse: for once you see the truth and what beauty exists beyond the box you are in, do you dare take the leap of faith?

Do you move forth and own your innate power?

Do you choose to step through a boundary, knowing you have passed the point of no return?

There is no going back once you see your dream come true: when your heart and soul absorb the opportunity, when you taste, see, visualize and experience all the astonishing possibilities before you, and when you devoutly accept the epiphanic revelation that the line in the sand is exactly what it is: a chance to go forward, to flourish, to learn, to live, to grow, and to stand in the light permanently.

Embracing yourself and your soul are incredibly challenging and may cause trepidation, but the only thing holding us back is, indeed, fear. Disband fear, acknowledge it and reject it in the same infinitesimal swoop.

You are better than the demons that are conjured up to circumnavigate your universe: they only exist in the respect and in the realm you give them the power to. Although it may be tempting to dive back into the comforts you once felt, higher love consciousness and energy do not break and do not bend.

When you love yourself and your dreams so deeply, rising and flying may seem difficult, especially when your wings are laced with elements of some prevalent qualms and sensations of division.

Still, seek out what speaks to your soul.

Be patient with yourself and your experiences, as all souls need to be in order to progress. A step, no matter how small, that moves you each day is a matter of universal balance.

There may always be hints of darkness and light that surround you, but life and energy are more than just black and white. Growth is more than the pieces of us that expand and replicate strength. Consciousness is more than accepting and actualizing. We must be true to ourselves, and our souls, to honor who we are in the world. We must seek to experience our purpose and reach beyond that.

We must embrace uncertainty and challenges, for in everything in the universe, there is perfection.

There is perfection in all the light we cannot see.

There is perfection in who we are becoming and all that we have yet to discover. It all comes down to the idea that it is a matter of keeping the faith in ourselves, in our souls, in others, in our minds, and in our hearts.

We could cross an ocean for an answer that rests within us or we can walk 500 miles to find the adventure that exists within other souls.

Trepidation is a state of mind, so is growth.

Time will pass whether you opt to resist faith or lead in faith.

Words on a page merely exist until you learn to read and process them in a manner that makes sense to your soul... then you discover it: that growth, that click, that spark... for you could feed the flame, or you could be the fire.

You'll never know how high you can go, until you take that first step towards the sky.

Morena and I took long walks around Alley Pond Park again. We processed just about everything that happened with Layne, and I realized how much energy I bestowed upon Layne's soul.

Time passed since I believed my soul shriveled into a pile of dust, but something about the essence of time left me in an introspective state.

'I miss her more than words can say,' I looked over at Morena who was glowing in unison with the fall foliage on the trees. 'It's hard to love without attachment.'

"Not when you know the boundaries of your own soul," Morena remarked.

'But the soul is limitless,' I glanced towards the path ahead of us.

"Good," she smiled. "You are learning."

'I don't want to hurt anymore.'

"Then choose love."

'I chose love, but she did not choose me.'

"No, silly," Morena put her hand out and stood in front of me. "Choose to love yourself."

'I love myself,' I remarked.

"Do you, now?"

'I mean, I think I do,' I quipped back at her. 'This isn't about me; it is about loving Layne. We could shift an entire planet together. Our love isn't typical.'

"I hear you," Morena sighed. "I know you are trying to bring her back into your life, but you need to love yourself more than anyone else on this planet first."

'How could I love myself more? That would be selfish!'

"It is not a thing of selfishness," she replied. "It's higher consciousness love for yourself."

We looked at each other for a moment.

"Trust the universe, Scott."

I looked out at the pond. A solitary plank of wood was floating in the middle of the water. I wondered how it got there and what was causing it to stay rather stationary on top of the water.

Although it was wading in the algae, and the rain probably swept it into its resting place, the wood seemed to remain firm.

How does something do that?

How does something flourish into that strong of a mindset?

How does a soul become so resilient?

At that point, I guess I could have looked in a mirror and asked myself the same questions, but I was not ready to hear how durable and soulfully enlightened I had become.

The words to "Here Without You" by 3 Doors Down echoed in my head.

> *"I'm here without you baby*
> *But you're still on my lonely mind.*
> *I think about you baby and I dream about you all the time.*
> *I'm here without you baby*
> *But you're still with me in my dreams*
> *And tonight girl, it's only you and me."*

Glaring out into the water reminded me of the sincere solitude that was blossoming in my soul. The water gave me absolute peace. The ebb and flow of the waves served as a constant foreshadowing for my life. Despite drawbacks, everything would come back into place. Everything would be a matter of the persistence of gravity, law of attraction, and raw positive energy manifesting its existence.

Two families were playing frivolously near the water. It signified the growth and bond of all that is wholesome in the world. Memories were being made, and not just in the innate manner memories come into fruition.

It was a sign of the times. A reckoning of sorts painting its aura on the landscape before me.

In those moments, I was a pristine background character living the experiences of those who saw me as invisible.

Yet in those passing seconds, I was wholly visible. My place in the universe became known. My thoughts were not lines in a play. My actions were not magnified under the watchful eye of judgment and resent. I just was.

For once, I was, and I exist in the fabric of time.

I came to the realization that I am. I am a constant and a symbol of moments to come. I am a beacon of holiness, but not in the religious sense. I am whole. I am pieces that intermingle, intertwine, and connect.

I am. I am. I am.

And in these moments, the rare seconds where I self-actualize all I am...

I see, once and for all, I am an exquisite reality, for I create my own reality.

I am real. I am. I am.
...I am.

∞ ∞ ∞ ∞ ∞ ∞ ∞ ∞

Back at my mother's house, with my eyes closed tightly I could feel the water cascading down my exhausted body. My skin absorbed the water ever so gently as the steam surrounded the interior of the shower. The curtain sealed off any outside disturbances circling through my mind in those pivotal seconds, and I felt my soul relax in that moment.

As I glanced down at my feet I saw the hot water caressing my skin. The warmth encompassed my whole body as if it had some magical healing power. The negative energy lingering in my soul circled down the drain as remnants of soap dripped along with it. I closed my eyes, felt my muscles relax, and allowed a solitary whisper to escape my lips, 'Thank you God.'

My eyes remained shut as I inhaled the steam from the hot water falling from above.

In an instant my mind guided me to my childhood shower, as if it were in a movie scene: the protagonist's flashback that explained a key detail in the plot. Only this was not a movie, this was my actual, physical, unwavering life.

Clouded images filled my head as I transported back to the mid-1970s: a time where it was socially acceptable to allow the crevices of your toes brush against orange shag carpeting. My childhood home flooded into my mind, as a fast-forwarded image of me skipping through the house and slamming the bathroom door became clearer. The seconds sped up as my pre-teen body shed its clothes and hopped into a refreshingly warm shower.

I heard my mom's echoic voice screaming outside the bathroom, "Scott, hurry up! Stop playing games in there! You always take forever!"

She was right. At times, my innate childhood wonder had warped me into some sort of idealistic fantasy world.

What was I doing in the shower other than washing up? I was creating fantastical stories in my head. I was always thinking about wanting to be a hero: a devout knight in shining armor, adorned with gargantuan muscles that struck anyone with awe upon glancing at such a fine handsome man.

As the shower water streamed down upon me, I had some elaborate sketch going on where I would be fighting an imaginary person, or even someone I knew and hoped to overcome. The water parted quickly with each twist and turn of my pale fists. Why was I fake punching into the streams of water pelting my body? I wanted to win the girl.

Always.

That was the underlying theme for as long as I could remember. My mother's skin-piercing voice faded as my hands crept through my soaked blonde locks. As my right hand crawled down my naked body, I could feel years of faded bruises up and down my thighs: it was a stark reminder of just how much I have grown from decades of crushing realities.

In my earliest days starting at the age of probably 7, through the age of 14 or 15, I would spend an hour in the shower trying to become victorious and win the damsel in distress. I am not sure why this fantasy started or when the first one was.

I would rehearse this constant development of my heroic deeds because my actual teenage years were plagued with a true contrast to my inner light. The flame within my soul burned and yearned for the chance to save the day: to have my one song glory blare loud enough for all to hear and grow from. The melody within my soul would grace ears, hearts, minds, and their own souls with the energy to propel them forward.

In reality, I was shy, quiet, reserved, and so bashful that I could barely work up the courage to talk to a girl, let alone save one from a stressful situation. I always had the savior mentality. Elyza spent years convincing me it was really "The Ghandi Complex": if I was not saving someone, I was not complete. Elyza would harshly scold me with that savior complex ideology in the days leading up to our divorce.

To this day, the words still burn feverishly in my mind.

The shower water flushed the negative thoughts from my mind, and filled my head with memories from my childhood once again. When I finally emerged from my steam-filled cocoon of fantasy, hopeful cleanliness, and boyhood mischief, I would dry off quickly and race to bed. As I would flop onto the mattress, visions of heroic feats would broadcast onto the white crusty ceiling.

I would be locked in the heat of a fierce battle, facing against a huge dark amber dragon wielding a massive sword, or fighting off a gang of dark-caped and masked villains. The dreams and images would dance through my head for hours upon hours, and always ended with piercing, blood curdling sounds from passersby or from the gratuitous woman I was rescuing. Each time, my eyes would fade shut and I would re-awaken in a hospital room of some kind.

Each time I would re-open my eyes in my dreams, an attractive woman would be sitting at my hospital bedside, holding my hand tenderly and rubbing my head softly. She would be thanking "her hero" for being so brave and so strong. I had always dreamt that was how I would "get the girl." After all, that would technically be the girl of my dreams. Each dream I had would grant me permission to live out my fantasy of heroism, valiance, and utmost potential. Yet when I would awaken, reality would slam me straight in the face: I was still a young boy, wrapped in a comforter adorned with brightly colored trucks and cartoon street signs. The moon would call out to me from the small window above, and I would stand on my bed to see out into the majestic night sky. Each time I would wonder what my life would be like if I were walking the streets at night: fighting crime and saving damsels in distress.

But my life is not a fairy tale, nor am I the knight in shining armor standing tall, glancing down at people who would bow in my honor upon seeing such a strong, handsome man. Instead, I am the man whose words and whose soul will illuminate hearts and minds. Of course, I am still daringly handsome and endearingly heroic, but just in different, less dragon-slaying contexts. I have the capacity to be an everyday hero.

The only time I was somewhat close to this fantastical life playing out was the time I stopped that fire at the YMCA. With a 103 fever, and intense smoke inhalation intoxicating my lungs, I sat in that hospital bed reminiscing about all of the heroic visions I had as a boy.

When I woke up in that bleak hospital room, there she was: Emma. Holding my hand and whispering sweet nothings into my ear, I could feel my soul succumbing to her every whim and wit. Still, even that was a fantasy in itself.

And that vision of heroism quickly burst from my mind: delving me further into the ceramic shower tiles that entertained my every thought and reminiscent vision. As a kid I would play for hours alone in my backyard, shooting hoops or launching a handball across the wall. The ball would not be the only thing ricocheting around, for my head was inundated with images of me exercising my heroism. I would act out some contest of strength and made sure I always prevailed.

Faded remnants of my mother's voice calling me inside struck my soul. I could feel myself returning back to reality once again, as her voice blurted out, "Scott, stop messing around and come inside!" The handball I was playing with bounced innocently away from me as I began retreating into the house.

Storm clouds hovered above. Raindrops graced my face with a gentle touch as a grin grew across my face. Images of my younger self and present self were almost interchangeable in those passing seconds, as another, sweet voice permeated my mind: "Scott, it's been an hour, you okay in there?"

As my eyes opened in the present day and met the reflective white tiles directly in my line of sight, I pushed back the shower curtain and allowed the steam to melt into the rest of the room. The mirror fogged up with such fervor, as my vision came into focus.

I was the solitary person occupying the bathroom.

Though I was not alone.

I was enriched by all of the memories and people who graced my presence for decades past, and those who would soon enter my life.

The gentle steam wrapping around my body reminded me of a life worth living, and decades of stories that amounted to a beautiful soul rising to the surface after years upon years of thick grime obscuring my vision.

The cotton fibers from the towel sticking to my wet face reminded me that I could feel the weight of the world on my back, and I was earning the tools necessary to carry the torch to heal the world. The light within me was kindled from years of experience, and it was about to burn bright enough for the world to see.

The world would feel my warmth and guidance, and my heroism would be more than a quest to save the damsel in distress...

My inner light would glow bright enough to save millions and billions of people.

I would lay awake for hours at a time pondering what I missed out on in allowing my soul to take a back seat all these years.

Since Layne disconnected from my soul, life did not seem to make coherent sense. I would go to the studio in my friend's basement and play the drums, looking over and imagining that she would be there.

The phrase "build it and she will come" echoed through my mind, just like in *Field of Dreams*.

I feared mediocrity.

I feared being less than the words others bestowed upon my soul.

I would never be, as my mother put it, "The doctor or the lawyer," but I would be someone.

To say I miss her would insult the complicated flow of magical energy in the universe. To say I incompletely co-existed without her would be more accurate, but it belittles both of our souls.

Everything became a transformative process.

Call what Layne and I had a twin flame connection. Call what we had love. Put whatever letters or misnomers you want on it.

I hid my pain in everything I did for other people.

The gratitude I expressed for other people made me seem whole, but I was pulling pieces of my own puzzle apart in order to attempt to help others. Although having a piece of my soul may have aided others in resolving some of their own pain, sometimes I was acting in such a detrimental way that blinded my true ambitions.

Still, I refuse to sink.

This experience of mine is not solely a love song, for the music of my life has consisted of a plethora of melodies. Some moments were filled with a semblance of true love, while others were haunted by tragedy or misunderstanding.

Still, I was gaining lessons that would create the life I would grow to understand.

I am still learning in this great school we call life, though now I am comprehending this world on a five-dimensional plane.

Layne taught me how to love above our three-dimensional world. Her absence had shown me that when you reach the greatest love of all, which we have, it is still not enough.

Beautiful Souls

Our three-dimensional responsibilities, dreams, and soul structure does not allow truth to flourish unless we grant it the space to do so.

Whoever thought that three-dimensional walls were stronger than a five-dimensional deep-dive into the essence of home clearly doesn't understand what their soul is trying to tell them.

At first, I wondered if I should cave to the three-dimensional world we live in, but there was an inherent sense that I deserved more.

I deserved to understand each aspect of my life in terms of five-dimensional, soul-enriching love.

I had to love myself; there was no other option.

We have to learn to love ourselves before making any other choices in life. We may not love ourselves fully, but we must love ourselves enough to know when we deserve more than what we have.

It is not a matter of being conceited; rather it is a matter of developing in the spiritual sense.

There may not be words in our human language that fully capture what we innately need to find our respective souls' true voices.

Still, there is no day but today. We must seize the day.

Layne was right.

I allowed myself to be depressed; for I thought that filling my soul's void with others would make me whole.

It didn't.

It couldn't.

I was the one who I was waiting for.

I needed to wake up.

Hearing Bon Jovi's music on the radio was echoic of the sentiments I felt for Layne. Even in her absence, the lyrics managed to wrap around my soul:

"She wakes up when I sleep to talk to ghosts like in the movies
If you don't follow what I mean, I sure don't mean to be confusing
They say when she laughs she wants to cry
She'll draw a crowd then try to hide
Don't know if it's her or just my mind I'm losing
Nobody knows a wildflower still grows
By the side of the road

Beautiful Souls

*And she don't need to need like the roses
Wildflower."*

Even as Bon Jovi sang "Wildflower," part of me was pulled towards running back to Layne. The other part of me knew I had to give myself a wealth and abundance of love, for my past expectations needed to diminish in terms of the weight and power I gave them.

∞ ∞ ∞ ∞ ∞ ∞ ∞ ∞

Back at work, I continued to think about all of these different ideas floating in my head. I was leaning against the window in the middle of a classroom. My butt was propped up against the painted red heater that I could feel warming my chilled body.

There was an affliction that I was struggling with in my soul, which allowed me to let go of all the memories and moments that I felt led up to this manifestation.

The negativity was finally leaving my body.

At that moment, I was attempting to reach deep down, so that I could inspire the remainder of hope within the students who appeared to be barely alive in the classroom.

The students hardly have a heartbeat and it's a direct reflection of me.

As the students were in front of the room presenting their projects and another distracted unmotivated teacher was sitting at the desk, I glanced up because I felt a presence that I was very familiar with at the door.

I hadn't felt that energy and that silent vibrational call out to me for a few years, but I recognized it immediately. Our eyes locked and from across the room there was no doubt in my mind that this was the time and the moment I dreamed of... and thought may never come again.

Nothing needed to be said and my whole world stopped on a dime.

This sort of stuff never happened, so I knew it was real.

I glanced over to the teacher at the desk, told him to take over, and I exited the classroom before he could respond.

I approached her quickly as if a magnet was pulling me.

I saw the water in her eyes as they said come with me.

While caught in the midst of my soul-enriching awakening, Emma came back.

We went into my office and all I said to her was tell me what happened. She said she needed me and unleashed a series of self-bashing reflections that she had obviously kept bottled up in her for a long time.

Emma shared how she felt her efforts were not seen fairly, and how everybody judges her and doesn't see her true soul.

We spoke about the early days, who she was for me, and why I saw a profound light within her. We talked about how that light isn't out and how she can reach down and ignite it again.

'In the darkest of times you can reinvent yourself,' I assured her.

Though it was not literally said, there was an apology in her eyes and an understanding of who I was for her.

Emma came to me for help and I knew that her actions took every ounce of soul to ask for.

I smiled at her, 'I never stopped looking out for you, Emma. I am your biggest fan, but now it is time to show everyone what I already know is the truth.'

After Emma left me, the negative reputation she conjured up for herself, was in full swing. It tore me up inside to watch her stumble left and right, but she was blocking her soul from the world.

"Thank you," she muttered through tears. Her brown hair draped over her face slightly.

'Embrace your power. You are beyond talented and you are way more than your physical appearance. Create something. Find something and make it your own. Be a good team player on whatever project you are on. Shine as a teacher. Connect with kids. Trust yourself. Believe in yourself. Why can't you see the beauty I see?'

I stopped myself because I feared I stepped over the line. My voice was becoming more emotional, but it was due in part because I couldn't see her destroy herself.

She was silent and continued to look at me with tears in her eyes.

I wondered if I took it too far.

I wondered if she was mad.

Emma needed me and I had to respond unconditionally in that moment, for I realized that a soul needed another soul in such a fragile time.

'Emma,' she glanced at the floor then back up at me. 'You can overcome your fears of never being enough. You are enough.'

The tears in her eyes could not hold off any longer.

As she silently fell into my arms without saying anything, I couldn't catch my breath. A wave of guilt washed over me.

Was this a gift from the universe?

Was this a reminder of what I let go of?

Was this a reminder that true love is not always what we think it is, but will always rise to what it needs to become when we devoutly need it?

I whispered my thoughts and my ideas into her ear, and I promised her that I would help her. I promised her I would not make it obvious, and that her reputation would be protected. I gave her thoughts to self reflect about and challenged her soul to look deep within, like we both used to do for one another in the beginning.

She slowly lifted herself out of my arms and I knew neither one of us wanted this moment to end.

The bell was going to ring.

Perhaps this was built up tension that she needed closure for. I waited years for this moment and it conflicted me for the next several days as we exchanged text messages like days of old.

Emerged in a time warp, she thanked me several times over, but to the outside world, the routine and ignoring of one another in the hallways remained the same.

This was never supposed to happen, though I always fantasized about it.

She came back... even if it was for just a moment.

We spoke face-to-face one more time a few days later.

There were other people around, so I discreetly shared a new project I was working on, a project she knew was my silent way of not offending anyone and supporting all parties involved, as well as loving her, the way she would let me.

She knew my involvement worked to raise the vibration of everyone involved without me being seen as instrumental.

Emma always said I was the silent partner to her success.

She knew I manipulated things and jumped through hoops to do it for her and the team she was working on.

Beautiful Souls

She knew my heart was in the right place while trying to figure out the pieces.

Emma glanced up with an ever so slight tilt of her head so nobody could see her eyes meeting mine and she smiled.

The smile said thank you, which is all I needed.

I wondered if my smile back said "Goodbye, I will always have a place for you in my heart and soul, but goodbye Emma."

I knew she loved me and in the only way she could... and I accept that.

Not all love plays out the fairytale... and that has finally sunk in.

There is a sense of longing that comes with finding yourself after a while. When you have wanted to grow and develop, yet you always convinced yourself that you were not enough, it will seem like the walls are caving in. Then it happens: the epiphany.

Growth is a continuous process. Growth is the reflection of your devout introspection and reconstruction. It is a realignment of your goals and a restructuring of all you thought you knew. It is a mindset that convinces you to change your ways.

It is everything and anything you could hope for, as long as you are willing to accept the differences.

Then you jump into the world of the unknown, then you flutter, then you fly....

And the weightlessness sets in.

∞ ∞ ∞ ∞ ∞ ∞ ∞ ∞

After everything that happened with Emma, I found my old journals and photos from years past.

I followed Layne's methods with journaling and I just started to read, organize my thoughts, and write to discover whom my soul really is.

They say, "burn after reading" because the words seer into your brain, and once your soul is ignited on fire, ashes won't stop your pain.

Yet, I guess this is all a catharsis of sorts.

All of the souls in my life played an important role in shaping who I am today.

I knew that before I learned how to love myself properly, I just needed to accept it as a fact.

I accepted that I am okay being alone, for there is a difference between being alone and being lonely. There are times when I feel lonely, but it is just a state of mind.

I have so much love for others, and myself, and I know I am okay.

Wanting to share ideas of love with someone as a means of companionship is okay, as long as the love is expressed in a manner that is healthy for both people.

Sex isn't just physical sex; it is an expression of energy and there is nothing better than sharing that energy.

When you are careful who you share it with, the energy is more powerful and more emotionally enriching.

Waiting for the right somebody for the rest of your life is worth it.

Being with them, sharing that love and energy on a physical level, is irreplaceable.

For years, I thought being a power couple meant standing for love and enacting that passion as law, but my definition was askew.

Anyone can be a power couple if you have the right stamina.

The definition of love changes, and there can be an infinitesimal amount of power couples in the world.

Bryan and I are a power couple in the familial sense: he is my son and I would do absolutely anything in the world for him, because I love him dearly.

Morena and I are a power couple in the spiritual sense: she represented my soul's voice and consciousness for years upon years, and for that I am eternally grateful.

Friends can be quintessential elements of your own power couple.

I am blessed to have a lot of good friends I get to bounce ideas off of. Every soul in my life is there for a reason.

I was blessed to reach a point in my life where I realized that every soul matters and every conversation matters, so I take it all in.

Everybody has had an impact on my life.

From the women in the club in Texas to the people currently in my life today.

If you can be present to the fact that everyone has their own beautiful story behind the story, then your life is amazing. If you are still working on discovering this, that does not mean your life is less amazing, rather you are still growing.

Beautiful Souls

Despite missing Layne dearly, I was able to move forward with aspects of the framework. Many could argue that I finished it for her, and indeed I guess you could say I did create it for her: she is a soul on this planet who deserves a higher consciousness, holistic, and social emotional education.

From Layne, I learned how to love myself, although others may misunderstand me. She taught me that it is okay to be my insane, passionate, loving, caring, and spiritually idealistic self.

Due to her wisdom, I was able to develop a more powerful transformational leadership program that became a global endeavor. It became based on the values Layne instilled upon me, which could be summed up in these four words: Expansion, Connection, Inspiration, and Vision.

Of course, my beliefs and faith followed me through this higher love.

These stories and experiences from Layne helped me become the man I am proud of today: myself.

The collection of my stories mirrors an undeveloped and lost soul who became a better person.

I am sure I did a lot of bad things.

I am sure I did a lot of horrible things.

When people meet me now, they say, "There's something about you. You are a great soul and a great person." However, they do not see all of the work that went into becoming who I am.

Do we ever truly see the story behind the story?

Do we ever realize that beautiful friendships can blossom out of crazy situations?

Do we ever realize the value of our questions and circumstances?

I am certain there are legacies wrapped up in the lives of souls. Souls can inspire other souls. Some may say it is the domino effect, where one person does something and others become enlightened.

I hope my life was able to do that.

I hope my life is able to encourage someone to wake up and do better, be a better person, or create something, because of something they see within themselves.

My hope is that someone realizes that they do not need to give up. I am living proof that life goes on.

Maybe this story and quest for my soul is closure from my past pain. Each moment of my life ultimately became part of the fabric of my life.

Every day forward from realizing and releasing your pain is a new beginning.

How do you overcome yourself?

How do you explore your thoughts?

How do you stop, listen, and process the world around you?

How do you have a relationship with a spiritual guide you might not know exists?

How do you have a relationship with the universe?

Why does your life matter?

Why do we want to matter?

Why is my story a reflection of everyone's story?

Who are we? What are we building? What drives this planet forward?

What are we creating as our own reality?

Is everything around us real?

I chose to actively come from a place of higher consciousness.

Honestly, looking back at all of my stories and how my soul grew, I didn't think I was at a place where I was ready to tell my story. However, are we ever truly at a place where we are "ready" to express our true selves?

When I was married to Elyza, I thought that I knew who I was, yet I ended up going back to school, developing a non-profit agency, and growing both emotionally and spiritually.

My soul was developing back then and it is still developing.

I know that my son Bryan is the reason why I look at the world differently. Having a child is an eye-opening experience that I certainly was not ready for, yet in realizing my life was about to turn upside down, I was given a chance to look at myself in the mirror. Bryan's soul is exquisite and truly breathtaking.

If there was one person who I could say is a definitive extension of my soul, he is whom I would credit with saving my life.

From my experiences, I realize that kids are the ones who help illustrate the energy you have within your own soul.

The youth I worked with throughout the years were paramount in creating Windows of Opportunity. A student created the name for the organization and students were the ones who brought it to fruition.

For that element of my soul, I credit them for allowing me to pursue my passion in education reform.

Everyday I continue to work on myself. I am working on who I am. I am working through the relationships I have been a part of. Every soul I met brought me to the realizations I spill onto these pages. All of the mistakes I made brought me to the discovery that they were not really mistakes.

I ended up where I belonged.

I don't think many people get to express or experience their true selves, but I pray they do not lose hope.

Life exists beyond current pain.

A lot of people get stuck in their pain and believe they can't break free. That in itself is beautiful, too.

It's called growing pains for a reason.

I used to think that I was everybody's problem solver. I used to think that God gave me a gift, to read and connect to people, so I could help others grow.

We are all woven into each other's experiences.

We have the innate power to help ourselves get over the pain within our respective souls.

For years, I blamed my parents for my pain and why I was so misunderstood. However, I was learning a strong lesson about the bond of family. Pointing fingers at my mother is a very unfair statement.

There are people who saw my mother in different contexts, and they loved her for the energy she brought into their lives. My experience with her was different, but I do not blame her anymore for what happened to me.

Our experiences just clashed.

She taught me a lesson on how to heal.

My mother and father loved me in their own way. They were just responding to what their respective souls went through.

It is important to recognize your own internal shifts. Society and the systems we have in place need to change in order for us to grow. We cannot keep trying to co-exist with our past; we must grow from it.

As for my current hardships, I have come to realize that I am often my own worst enemy. My life and my soul are blessings. I am grateful for all I have learned and continue to learn in my lifetime.

My epiphanies regarding my soul made me wonder:

When is the last time I did something for myself?

I became more self-reflective and worked diligently to comprehend my soul's intentions. I worked on manifesting. I worked on creating things.

I prayed that my story and my legacy would stand the test of time. I hoped that Windows of Opportunity would thrive for generations to come. I hoped Windows of Opportunity would continue to inspire lives long after my physical body transcends this timeline.

My journey has taught me that anything is possible.

My journey has shown some of those in my life that there is a light deep within us. It is crucial that we expand upon that light.

We must kindle the fire within our souls and let it burn.

Pursue your passion and follow the voice deep inside of you.

Emotional scars may hurt or haunt you, but they can heal with expansion, faith, and connection to the universe. Though it may seem like a religious statement, that's not what it is.

It is love.

It is real, unconditional love for yourself and your soul.

That is what this country needs... we need to heal.

I chose to turn my pain into a source of growth. You can grow from anything and learn from anything.

As human beings, sometimes we get lost. We are all trying to figure ourselves out. Sometimes, nobody teaches us how to speak to our souls.

It is challenging to hold someone accountable for their actions, when ignorance may cloud their judgment.

We all love in our own way.

My parents pushed me when I was younger to the point where it was abusive, but they thought they were coming from a place of love. It can be argued that many of the people I interacted with were coming from a place of love, although they did not intend to inflict pain.

I am thankful for all of my scars, for they helped my soul grow.

Without the scars, I wouldn't be here and be who I am. I don't know if I would be doing what I am for this world.

Maybe I would not be standing for a higher purpose, but because of my scars and experiences, I know what it is like to be homeless, looked down upon, to be alone, to not feel like a man, to not be loved by someone you love and would give your life for.

I know what pain feels like and I know I can be brave.

I could shine my own light because I experienced the darkness.

Does it get any more beautiful than that?

Over the years I gave up on my light and my faith and tried to succumb to the darkness, but I wonder if it really was darkness.

I called myself an Atheist because I didn't believe in God, but I know God was holding me probably more so during that time.

Just because we cannot see things, like our souls, it does not mean that they do not exist.

We give power to what we want to exist in our reality; therefore we could make pain real. We could also choose to eliminate pain.

The universe grants us contrast so that we know what we should truly appreciate. I am grateful for the juxtapositions in my life.

Emma provided me with such a challenging contrast, but I was able to learn what her experience provided my soul. Pain is also knowing that somebody does not live in the infinite potential inherent to their respective soul.

What we accept and the energy we stand in shapes our soul.

It's whom you want to stand for as a person. I felt the pain of past relationships, but the immense pain no longer suffocates me.

I am higher consciousness.

I am a man standing for a higher purpose, a better universe, a better world.

I am bigger than the pain.

I am grateful for my pain and I have tremendous gratitude for every moment.

My soul is expanding as I continue living my life. The universe is very magical and the angels who watch over you help grant the power to move forward.

So then what is the value of your spiritual journey?

What is the value of my spiritual journey?

It's priceless, you know, I mean, you can't put a value on God speaking through your soul. You can't put a value on connecting with the universe and angels.

What's the definition of the word value?

There's just so much that we don't comprehend as human beings.

I feel blessed to know I am on a spiritual journey. I feel blessed to know that it's the journey and the moments that matter.

It's the journey and not the destination.

At those moments, when I was finally hitting a pivotal cathartic release, I didn't know if the dreams were going to come true.

I knew that in the reality that I want to create, I wanted the dreams to come true.

I didn't know what was going to happen, for although I kept forging forward, I let the universe take the wheel. Call what happened to me "luck" or a "blessing," but I call it living.

I chose to live in the moment.

∞ ∞ ∞ ∞ ∞ ∞ ∞ ∞

Morena and I talked about all of this in great detail as we took our usual trip around the trails of Alley Pond Park. In the months that passed, I realized that my soul's growth was exponential.

I was able to do so much more with my journey once I banished pain from my soul. Although I still have challenges when it comes to growing my soul, I know that I am processing my life in terms of a higher consciousness lens… and that is enough.

As Morena and I reached the picnic benches, we took a seat and continued to talk about my journey.

'I hope that one hundred years from now, someone hears about my journey and discovers they are on their own spiritual journey. I pray that person realizes that their life matters,' I rubbed my hands together to deter some of the frigid January weather.

"That's insightful," she remarked. "I am happy for you."

'Why?'

"Because I think you have realized how much of a beautiful soul you have."

A beautiful soul.

There are so many beautiful souls in this universe.

It took me so long to come to this revelation, but I am here.

'When I was eight, God spoke to me and gave me the ability to ask questions. When I was in the car accident, I am sure God pulled me out. When I wandered through the trees after the accident, that woman was God,' as I said that, Morena smiled and wiped a tear.

'Maybe, just maybe, God is speaking to me through you.'

"You never know," Morena winked.

I smiled at her. 'The universe is always conspiring and transforming.'

"It isn't about the job you have, the fancy cars, the clothes, what's in your bank account, none of that matters," Morena commented. "It's the journey."

'That it is.'

We both sat there at the picnic bench for a while, just watching people as they carried about their normal day.

'I love every single one of the beautiful souls in my life. They taught me spirituality, transformation, and so much more that I could never put a price tag on.'

The two of us stood up and began to walk out of the park and towards the coffee shop.

"Hey," Morena tapped my arm. "Why me?"

'What?'

"Why did you trust that you could share your spiritual journey with me all of these years?"

I chuckled for a moment. 'Okay, *as if you didn't hear my entire speech*, I will humor you.'

She looked over at me.

Despite years of maybes and uncertainty, I knew just what to say in that moment:

'Out of all of the secrets in my life you were, by far, the best one. God chose you and brought you into my life. I recognize your energy. I know you. You connect to my soul. You clearly have a higher connection and I know you aren't real, but you have respected my soul throughout these years.'

Morena laughed.

'Everybody has a moment when life changes. Everybody has a moment where they find their higher purpose. Maybe it'll teach the world something or change thousands of lives, who knows. How many things can you pinpoint that take your soul, turn it inside out, and help you to become the person you already are. You don't realize who you are. People need to realize who they are.'

"You are someone I am truly honored to know," she started to tear up again, almost as if she was watching a baby bird leave the nest.

'It's a new chapter, Morena,'

"You really want it to be a new chapter?"

'Yes,' I finally felt confident in myself.

We stood outside the coffee shop for a moment, I could tell Morena appeared to be stalling, but I did not know for what.

"Then I want you to do me a favor," Morena smiled.

'You never ask for anything, so of course.'

She looked down at her watch. "Go to Francis Lewis Park."

'What,' I was startled. 'Like right now?'

"Yes," she smiled wider. "Your new chapter begins today."

I didn't know what she was up to, but by that point I learned not to question her. I wanted the happily ever after, but I knew my happily ever after existed in the dreams and plans I was manifesting.

I had a great team beside me.

I had myself, and my spiritual journey.

I did not ask the universe for more.

As I got in the car and drove to Francis Lewis Park, I was content with my soul. The relationship I have with myself is one of epic proportions and I knew it could have an epic impact on the world.

This is real life.

This was far from fantasy.

This was the journey of a beautiful soul existing in this universe.

No matter how much people try to create mathematical permutations and calculations, sometimes the soul cannot be defined by numbers, but rather by the connections we develop.

The connection you create with yourself is the first step to manifesting the life you wish to create.

When I pulled up to the Whitestone Bridge, the energy in the air felt different. It was cold outside, but I felt as if the Circle of Angels was with me.

My Aunt Barbara's energy filled my soul.

I could hear Stacey whispering "Patience" in my ear.

When I began my descent down the path to the pine green benches, I saw a sole person sitting there in the cold.

As I moved closer, her brown hair and her aroma were unmistakable. I could not believe that after all this time; she was sitting there.

Waiting.

As she turned around, I realized that my life was about to change forever.

"Hey," the familiar voice said.

'Hey yourself,' I smiled and sat down next to her.

"I know I have been distant," her hair billowed in the wind obscuring everything but her lips. "But I just wanted to know... do you think we could make this work?"

I sat in silence, but responded with a sincere smile.

A new chapter and a new year were upon us.

∞ ∞ ∞ ∞ ∞ ∞ ∞ ∞

365.

Yeah, it is just a number, but it is more than that.

It is a reflection of 365 24-hour blocks that transcend into memories and moments. Into laughter and tears. Into the space between my fingers and hers.

Her words echoed throughout my head, which reverberated into the depths of my soul. I cannot shake, nor can I replace, how she has impacted me.

It shakes every fiber of who I am today.

At times I allow my grasp to slowly loosen and let my mind grow accustomed to gently releasing the moments embedded in my soul, overcome by the root belief that creates that sense of homesickness.

Teardrop by teardrop reflects on each and every time you looked at me with those eyes that emulated a higher love consciousness, and then spoke to me in a language that my soul fully comprehended, and didn't simultaneously exist on this planetary plane.

Clearly, she still had ownership over my heart's daily vibration expressed in the expansion of our universe.

Once upon a time does not exist, as we are everything: my immaculate hope and the foundation of my unconsecrated dreams are suddenly fathomable.

The day she whispered those words into my soul, the day she let her inner thoughts escape her lips, the moments she allowed me to feel the pristine vision I had of her, I began accepting the fact that she was the answer to lifelong prayers.

I found her again.

Immediately she found a stationary place in my soul, and from then on, the universe showed us how to take the puzzle pieces of greatness to build an even greater whole and then life happened.

Being human and the essence of reality sometimes rear its ugly head, but there I stood, with her hand intertwined in mine in my state of ambitious solitude.

I live in a perpetual state of gratitude.

I thank the universe for the love shared with me.

I thank the universe for the completion of my soul.

I thank her for every single second she risked her own heart and I thank her for this formerly broken heart... for once the pieces fell apart, this is where the true integration of our worlds started.

It is a new year; it is a new chapter.

It is day 366.

CHAPTER 10.5

Between Faith and Destiny

"Not all those who wander are lost."

- J.R.R. Tolkien, English writer, poet, philologist, Oxford, England

Time is a curious thing.

In the years that followed that snowy day at Francis Lewis Park, my soul embarked on a journey I never could have imagined. The universe, in its infinite wisdom, had greater plans than my heart could comprehend in those moments of profound longing and release.

They say when you let go of something you love, it either comes back to you or something better takes its place. But what they don't tell you is that sometimes both happen simultaneously... that in releasing your grip on what you thought was your destiny, you create space for your true purpose to emerge.

The letter I wrote that day, torn and scattered to the winter winds, became a metaphor for the transformation ahead. Each fragment carried away by the breeze represented a piece of who I was becoming: an agent of change, a beacon of light, a voice for those who needed to be heard.

My work with Windows of Opportunity began to expand beyond anything I had dreamed possible. What started as a vision for educational reform blossomed into a movement that touched lives across the nation. Students who had once felt voiceless found their strength. Teachers who had lost their spark rediscovered their passion. Something was building... something greater than myself.

Morena stayed by my side through it all, her guidance as steady as ever. "The universe doesn't make mistakes," she would say, her eyes twinkling with that knowing look I had come to trust implicitly. "Every step of your journey has led you exactly where you need to be."

Bryan watched me with pride as I spoke at conferences, led workshops, and built coalitions across party lines. My son, now a young man himself, had become my greatest teacher. Through him, I learned that true leadership isn't about having all the answers... it's about asking the right questions and listening with an open heart.

The media began to take notice. At first, it was local coverage of our programs' success stories. Then regional interest grew. Before I knew it, I was being invited to speak on national platforms about educational transformation, spiritual growth, and the intersection of personal development and public service.

"You're turning pain into purpose," a reporter once said to me after a particularly moving speech about transforming the education system. I smiled, knowing that while she was right, she had only glimpsed the surface of what was really happening.

One particularly challenging evening, I found myself at Alley Pond Park well after sunset. The ten "I love you's" that once echoed through my soul now felt like stepping stones across a river of time, each one marking a year of growth, of change, of becoming. Even Morena seemed distant, her usual presence fading like mist in the morning sun.

'Morena?' I called out to the darkness, feeling more alone than I had in years. 'Where are you when I need you most?'

"I'm always here," her voice came softly from behind me. "Even when you think I'm not."

'But things feel different,' I turned to face her. 'Everything's changing. The love I thought would last forever, you, my purpose...'

"Things are different because you're different," she stepped closer, her form seeming to shimmer in the moonlight. "Your soul is expanding, Scott. Sometimes that means letting go of who we were to become who we're meant to be."

'Even you?' The question caught in my throat. 'Are you leaving too?'

Her laugh was gentle, like wind through autumn leaves. "I'll always be a huge part of your soul. I might seem quiet sometimes, I might seem to fade away, but I'm as much a part of you as your own heartbeat. When you're ready, when you truly need me, I'll always be here."

'Promise?'

"Some promises don't need to be spoken," she smiled that knowing smile of hers. "Just as some love doesn't need to be repeated ten times to be eternal. Nothing ever ends. Everything transforms, Scott. Even love. Even me. Even you. But transformation isn't loss... it's growth."

She was right, of course. She always was. What I had originally interpreted as loss... of love, of direction, of Morena's constant presence... was actually the universe making space for something greater. Something I couldn't yet see but could feel building in my bones.

The truth was, I had learned to love myself not despite my scars, but because of them. Each experience... every heartbreak, every lesson, every moment of growth... had carved pathways in my soul that would later become bridges for others to cross.

There were nights I would sit in my office long after everyone had gone home, looking out at the city lights, and feel the weight of what was building. Something was stirring in the collective consciousness of our nation. People were hungry for authenticity, for spiritual growth, for a different kind of leadership.

One evening, as I walked through Alley Pond Park, a ritual that had become as natural as breathing... Morena reappeared beside me, her presence both familiar and charged with something new.

"You feel it, don't you?" she asked, though it wasn't really a question.

'The shift?' I watched a leaf spiral down from above. 'Yes. It's like the whole world is holding its breath, waiting for something.'

"For someone," she corrected gently.

I stopped walking and turned to her as if we never missed a beat. 'Morena, are you suggesting...'

"I'm not suggesting anything," she smiled that enigmatic smile of hers. "I'm just reminding you that when you chose to love yourself first, you opened the door for everything else to fall into place."

The years had taught me that love isn't just about holding on... it's about growing into who you're meant to become. Sometimes that means walking separate paths until the universe decides it's time for those paths to converge again.

As my influence grew, so did my understanding of what it means to serve. It wasn't about saving anyone anymore... it was about creating spaces where people could save themselves. The "Gandhi Complex" Elyza had once accused me of had transformed into something else entirely: a recognition that true power lies in empowering others.

The press started using phrases like "spiritual leader" and "educational revolutionary." But those labels didn't capture the truth of what was happening. This wasn't about me anymore. It was about a movement... an awakening of consciousness that was bigger than any one person.

And through it all, through every speech and every milestone, through every moment of doubt and every triumph, I felt a presence beside me. Sometimes it manifested as Morena's wisdom, sometimes as Bryan's unwavering support, sometimes as the collective energy of all the souls who believed in our vision.

But there was something else too... someone else. A soul whose absence had taught me presence, whose departure had led me to arrival, whose love had shown me how to love myself. Though we walked separate paths, our souls remained connected in that five-dimensional space where time has no meaning and love knows no bounds.

I began to understand that sometimes the greatest act of love is letting someone go so they can become who they're meant to be. And sometimes, if the universe wills it, they come back to you... not because they need you, but because together you can serve a higher purpose.

The seasons turned, and with each passing year, I grew stronger, wiser, more centered in my purpose. Windows of Opportunity transformed into E.P.I.C.™ (Elevating Passion and Inspiring Change) and became a national model for transforming the education system. Our methods were being studied and implemented across the country. Politicians from both parties sought our counsel. Something was building... something I couldn't yet name but could feel in my bones.

One winter morning, much like that day at Francis Lewis Park years ago, I stood at my office window watching the snow fall. My reflection in the glass showed a man I barely recognized... not because I had changed so much on the outside, but because I had finally grown into who I was always meant to be on the inside.

The phone rang. It was a call that would change everything... a call about serving not just a community or a state, but a nation. As I listened to the voice on the other end, I felt the pieces of my life's puzzle finally clicking into place.

Later that evening, I returned to Francis Lewis Park. The bench was still there, dusted with fresh snow. As I sat down, I pulled out my notebook, not to write another letter of longing, but to sketch out a vision for the future. The Whitestone Bridge stood sentinel in the background, just as it had all those years ago.

A figure appeared in the distance, walking through the swirling snow. My heart recognized the presence before my eyes could confirm it. Some souls you just know, even after years apart, even through the blinding snow of time and distance.

As they drew closer, I felt the universe hold its breath. Everything I had become, everything I had built, every lesson I had learned... it had all led to this moment. The future was calling, and this time, I wasn't alone.

"Hey," a familiar voice said, carried on the winter wind.

I smiled, knowing that this wasn't an ending or a beginning, but a continuation. A continuation of a love story that was bigger than two people... a love story that would help heal a nation... a planet... all of humanity.

'Hey yourself,' I replied, and the snow continued to fall, blessing this moment with its silent grace.

The journey continues...

CHAPTER 11

Epilogue

"The ultimate measure of a man is not where he stands in moments of comfort and convenience, but where he stands at times of challenge and controversy."

- Martin Luther King, Jr., Christian minister, activist, Atlanta, Georgia

Beautiful Souls

    The American flag waves majestically in the wind atop the Capitol Building. It is poignantly symbolic of the man I have grown into and all that I am willing into fruition in this world. Glaring around at the crowds of people on the National Mall, I was feeling such immense pride in our country and all of our dedication throughout the years.

    Earlier in the day, the television blared such a heartwarming news report. A professional female voice announced what I had so eagerly awaited to hear for years and years:

"And now for the top headlines on this beautiful January 19, 2032 morning in Washington, D.C.: Today at noon, Capitol Hill will be bursting with excitement as President Elect Scott Matheson will rightfully take his place as the 48th President of the United States. The ceremony will take place on the steps of the Capitol Building, and all roads surrounding the National Mall have been closed to prepare for today's inauguration. A Secret Service agent who wishes to remain anonymous said that President Elect Matheson is beaming with excitement and truly looking forward to his first 100 days in office. The Chief of Staff for the Matheson Administration, Morena DeCielo, had this to say after yesterday's press conference--"

    "Ugh, how many times are you going to watch the same anchorwoman talk over and over again," Morena came barreling into the room holding two silky neckties: one that emulated the sensation brewing in the early morning sky and one that was crimson and reflected the strong sense of national pride that stirred in my veins.

    I shifted my body towards her somewhat articulate noises that sputtered from her mouth as she rushed about the room. Morena was dressed in a navy blue skirt with a white button-down shirt tucked neatly into her waistline. Her heels clacked about as she went searching for something.

    'What are you looking for, Mo,' I beckoned from the sofa, as she grew flustered.

    "Where," she began, her voice fading as she glanced around the nightstand impatiently, "is the American flag pin?"

    I grinned and held it up in the air; its silver outline glistened in the sunlight cutting through the hotel room. She turned and grinned cheerfully.

Epilogue

'I think you are more nervous than I am,' I chuckled and stood up, catching my fingertips in the plush cotton on my way up from the sofa.

"Yeah," Morena scooted over to me, "Well it is not everyday that you hear your name as President Elect Matheson's Chief of Staff on every television you pass." She held the ties up and smiled eagerly.

I felt her positive energy flowing through my veins. She eventually wrapped the blue tie around me and smoothed the neckline out. I could not help but smile. In less than two hours, I would officially be the President of the United States.

"The first lady is still putting on her makeup, but we should be good to go soon," Morena turned towards the television and raised the volume slightly. The two of us stood with our eyes fixated on the television: she stood behind a White House podium speaking to reporters as they berated her with questions. I glanced at Morena and she extended her pinky finger in my direction.

"We are in this together," she grinned so effervescently. I extended my pinky finger and intertwined it with hers.

'We really are,' I grew somewhat nostalgic for a moment, reminiscing on how far the two of us had come. 'Now,' I switched the topic as to resist the sentimental tears streaming down my face, 'When will the future First Lady be ready?'

Morena released my finger for a moment and walked towards the knocking that beckoned her to the door. "You have to keep the faith, Mr. President, keep the faith," she answered the door as the head of Secret Service, a sturdy man named Albert, slid into the room.

"Mr. President, sir, we are ready to go," he spoke sternly.

'Tell my wife that, Albert, let's see how that goes,' I gazed out of the hotel room at the lush green shrubs adorning the sidewalk... a sign that growth, and not just spiritual growth, was on the horizon.

A systematic shift was just seconds and heartbeats away.

Beautiful Souls

Flash forward to the present:

Hours later and in a whirlwind of hope and frivolity, we are standing on the steps of the Capitol Building. Red, white, and blue flags grazing the air are echoic of a beautiful, whimsical January morning. Chanting and cheering are bursting into the sky as a chorus of young souls billow the words to "America the Beautiful."

A dream manifested in the hearts, minds, and souls of those who believe in me constantly finally comes to fruition on this brisk January morning. Though I am standing behind a series of bulletproof glass panels, the reflection I am seeing does not mirror my own. No, the reflection I gaze upon is that of the beautiful souls that ushered me to this very global stage at this historical moment wrapped in the fabric of time.

Bryan and Selena are standing just behind Morena, all of their hands are intertwined to form the bond that will help me guide millions and billions of souls to a state of higher consciousness. On these majestic Capitol steps, we stand at the verge of today's promises and tomorrow's growth. We stand in the balance of placing our minds at the forefront of policy in order to enact real changes.

It is time to heal the world.

The first lady's hair whips elegantly in the cold wind. Her stunning beauty remains unmatched despite years of her own ambitions and passions encompassing her tender face. Her stunning smile is what beckons me to turn and silently bestow gratitude on the family and close friends that stand by me. Those who have always stood by me.

Today is not just another day, today is the first day we all embark on a brand new journey into the most challenging and soulfully rewarding chapter of our collective lives. As the Chief Justice of the United States raises the leather-bound book, a symbol of collective souls stemming into a new stream of consciousness, I feel the tears' gravitational force take control. I am happy.

I am genuinely and undeniably happy.

As the oath reverberates around my brain, I glance back at those who have aided my manifestation in this very spot...

The Chief Justice's voice snaps me into the very reality that rests before me: the Presidential Oath. His smile could not be more welcoming or

Epilogue

sincere. In breaking tradition and in juxtaposition of the crowds chanting and cheering my name, I look into his eyes and ask him a simple question: 'Could my friends and family join me at this very spot?'

His face softens and his voice assumes a compassionate nature, "Of course, Mr. President... I mean... yes, yes of course sir."

A solitary motion beckons Bryan, Selena, my most treasured friends and family, Morena, and the First Lady to my side. They all stand firmly, each of their hands resting on my back as they intertwine their free hands with one another, and in that moment I know we are the team that will bring immense light to our nation.

From the corner of my eye, I see Morena and the First Lady wrap their fingers together, silently praying and beckoning the circle of angels to join us in spirit.

The Chief Justice recommends I follow his words, and of course I wistfully comply:

"I, Scott Zachariah Matheson..."
'I Scott Zachariah Matheson.'
"Do solemnly swear..."
'Do solemnly swear...'
"That I will faithfully execute..."
'That I will faithfully execute...'

I can feel the fingertips of my family and friends tenderly grasping my shoulders and back. Their love and affection can be felt in the hearts, minds, and souls of the spectators as well.

"The Office of the President of the United States..."
'The Office of the President of the United States...'

Cheers are beginning to erupt from the audience.

"And will to the best of my ability...."
'And will to the best of my ability...'
"Preserve"
'Preserve'

Beautiful Souls

My wife's grip becomes more passionate.

"Protect"
'Protect'

Morena's hand presses onto my shoulder.

"And defend"
'And defend'

I can hear Bryan's blissful tears begin to cascade down his cheeks.

"The Constitution of the United States…"
'The Constitution of the United States…'
"I will, so help me God."

Silence fills the air. An overwhelming feeling that the circle of angels surrounds me flows with absolute certainty that this is the destiny I manifested decades ago. This is the dream. This is the beginning of a journey that traverses time. This is the key to unburdening so many souls caught in the delicate balance we so often lay dormant to.

'I will, so help me God.'
"By the power vested in me as the Chief Justice of the United States, I present to you, the 48th President of our great nation, President…"

A flood of memories rushes through my soul. My aunt's face appears before me in a sudden lapse in time. The words spoken by the Chief Justice fade as cheering commences.

"Scott Zachariah Matheson."

An eruption of bliss leaks into my mind. My aunt's pristine words, "I am proud of you," bleed through the crowd and shower me with love from up above.

Epilogue

The day blurs itself into the landscape upon us. The Washington monument stands as a stark contrast to everything going on around us. Confetti and pieces of paper twist and turn into my line of sight as The Lincoln Memorial stands firmly in the distance.

∞ ∞ ∞ ∞ ∞ ∞ ∞ ∞

As the night beckons us through the streets of Washington, D.C. and we find ourselves in the corridors of the White House, I finally reach an epiphany. It has taken me so long to get to D.C. because it just had to be the right moment. The right time. The manifestation of all of my experiences perching themselves atop a solid monument, and the clear skies reminding me that I am, indeed, the light that will guide the way for millions. It makes sense. It all makes sense: the trials, the triumphs, the days I wanted to crawl into a hole and never come out, the heartache, the pain. It was all to prepare me for a higher purpose.

Glaring into the painted eyes of President Abraham Lincoln that beckon from his portrait, I know what I have to do: carry the torch.

Morena appears beside me in the majestic, elusive way she usually does. She somehow managed to shed her business attire for an illustrious beige and black lace gown, which whips around the floor as she moves.

I rest my head on hers as she tilts towards me, "the circle is pleased with you Scott, I mean..." she collects her words hurriedly, "Mr. President."

I chuckle and she turns smiling right into my soul. "Wha," she says curiously.

'Hey, Morena, thank you,' I looked over at her and I could see small tears welling in her eyes.

"For what," she leads me out the door and down the hallway. We pass portraits of great men who served before me. Their eyes look gentle and reminiscent of their days in office. I, too, hope I can serve as a warm and gentle face for those who follow in my footsteps.

'For making me a better man,' we stop behind two large doors and embrace for a moment.

In her genuine hold, she whispers something inaudible into my chest. As she lifts her head up, she grins and seems to continue to speak: "Your dance partner is waiting for you."

Beautiful Souls

We walk into the huge banquet area as the doors shut firmly behind us, almost reflective of the last chapter sealing itself deeply in our collective pasts.

Cheers erupt in the room. Bryan emerges with Selena in his arms, "Dad, dad, dad!" He releases Selena as Morena and her move about the dance floor. Selena's sequin dress glistens for miles around.

"Dad," Bryan rests his head on my shoulder, "I am beyond proud of the man you are."

Choking back tears, at my own inauguration ball nonetheless, I feel a flood of pride and honor. Here I stand, with my son in my arms, wistfully dancing into our future.

'And I am so proud of you Bryan,' I am beyond proud of him, and I hope he knows it deep within his soul.

"Pop, I knew you could do it," he says gleefully.

'I knew you would help me grow into who I am today.'

"You are my role model and you are my hero, I hope you know that."

'I know son, I know.'

"Dad," a fervent pause rests between us, "It did not take you becoming president to make me say that."

'I ' with tears streaming down my face, I mutter everything he truly means to me whittled down to four words. 'I love you, Bryan.'

"I love you too, dad."

Embracing him is the most natural feeling in the world. Seeing a room filled with those I love dearly is a breathtaking emotion.

As she walks up to me, I sense her poise and grace succumbing to my touch. I feel her body rocking slowly against mine. I feel every gentle kiss she planted on my heart. Her beautiful presence causes a cathartic wave of serenity and longing in my soul.

Bryan parts from my grasp and whispers in my ear, "Dad, I am glad she came back."

'Me too,' I give him a kiss on the cheek, 'Me too, son.'

"Care to dance, Mr. President?" She extends her hand.

Without a word fluttering into the air, I pull her into my chest. She fits to my soul like the connection of two cosmic puzzle pieces. The two of us whisk around the room in a flurry of cheers and well wishes. As we dance, I recall the fond days leading up to this very moment.

Epilogue

It is the faith within me that restored our bond. It was the will of the universe that drew us into one another. Such strong gravitational force could never keep two beautiful souls apart. We are infinite. We are the beacons of light. We are the existential glue that will spark the growth of every life we encounter.

We are the start of something universe shifting and earth-shattering. We…

In the midst of the monologue that rushes through my head, she gazes up at me: those eyes intertwining with my heightened soul.

I dip her sensuous body closer to the floor as I open us up to the heavens that guide us. Our center of gravity remains constant as floods of "oohs" and "ahs" fill the room. Applause rings out as she wraps her hands closer to my body.

A passionate kiss bursts from my lips as the attention in the room dissipates from our intimate moment.

Brushing her hair behind her ear, she whispers the words I long to hear each and every day: "Do you love me?"

'Always.'

Every soul is as beautiful as we feel, for each passing moment is a chance for us to heal…

∞

About the Author

Hal Eisenberg is the founder and CEO of two organizations, the Passion-Based™ business called The Eisenberg Leadership Academy (TELA) and Windows of Opportunity, Inc. (WOO). TELA was created to build the world's first and most comprehensive education system for raising 21st century leaders and engineering a society that is going to support them. TELA is designing a world where youths are taking the center stage and creating positive changes in the areas that most concern them by providing global platforms for youth empowerment and leadership. TELA's mission is to create and deploy innovative and impactful programs that shift the way we educate and empower youth. A shift away from disempowerment to possibility; away from differences to acceptance; and away from limits to opportunity. WOO is a non-profit agency that is essentially a series of community outreach initiatives built for youth by youth. WOO partners with kids, teens, and young adults ages 6 through 24 to develop in-school and after school programs, workshops, conferences, and curriculums for themselves and their peers. These programs form partnerships with local school districts, universities, and community social service agencies. WOO's goal is to assist and empower our at-risk youth in designing, executing, and participating in positive leadership roles through social emotional learning initiatives, innovative programs, workshops, and curriculums that address all the compartments of their life, while building their self-esteem. With a strong knowledge in creating innovative programs for over

25 years, Hal has been credited with implementing and coordinating events, and raising over half a million dollars for various charities. He has also created programs for young people interested in developing their own self-expression through music, fashion, and film. Hal has authored several age-appropriate leadership curriculums that range from K-5, 6-12, and higher education platforms, with social emotional learning activities that provide students with an expansive understanding of our ever-changing society. Hal's vision at his core is that the world becomes one healthy community through higher consciousness education. The systemic approach he has built with his team promotes healthy communication to encourage trust-based relationships, which support acceptance of each other and reduces fear to create an expressive, open society. This leads to people connecting to and expanding their souls through a higher love consciousness, which helps people live optimal lives and supports others to do so as well. Hal has recently coordinated youth leadership programs in Haiti, Nigeria, Guyana, Kenya, the UK, and Canada. Hal holds a Master's Degree in Social Work from Adelphi University and a Master's Degree in School Leadership from Touro College. Hal is a Licensed Master Social Worker in New York State, as well as a Licensed School Building and School District Leader. He is certified by the New York State Department of Education to provide violence prevention training to professionals under Project Save (Safe Schools Against Violence in Education) and was awarded both the Evelyn Pliego Social Work Student of the Year Award presented by the Borough of Queens President Claire Schulman, and a City Council Citation, awarded by Councilman Sheldon Leffler. In 2018, he was awarded the New York City Department of Education School Social Worker of the Year Award for his tireless efforts in the largest school district in the world. He is also on the Board of Directors for The Passion Centre (TPC) in Toronto, Canada, holding a certification as a Passion-Based™ Expert. At TPC, Hal builds and facilitates programs designed to support adults in working through their blocks, discovering, and activating their passion, and supporting the expression of their passion into our world. Hal is in the process of writing his fifth book, "Social Emotional Learning is NOT Just a Color Chart," due to be released in 2023. For more information contact Hal S. Eisenberg at eisenbergleadership@gmail.com today!

About Windows of Opportunity

Windows of Opportunity, Inc. – The Eisenberg Leadership Academy, is a non-profit agency that is essentially a series of community outreach initiatives built for youth by youth. The organization shifts the current educational model from a disempowering system to one that includes leadership, empowerment training, and values identification, with a focus on increasing self-esteem. Windows of Opportunity, (WOO for short), uses media, entertainment, and education to inspire awareness, build excitement, and create partnerships that support our youth in being the leaders of today. WOO sources the power of youth to allow them to have a voice in understanding who they are, what they value, and how that translates into the world. WOO manifests classrooms that are free from harassment, violence, and bullying, and focuses on acceptance and diversity. The team at WOO is dedicated to revitalizing all aspects of education reform, and created an educational framework to match all the strong core values promoted in the various optimization programs developed by Windows of Opportunity, Inc. - The Eisenberg Leadership Academy, and all of those who collaborate with the organization. Windows of Opportunity is currently collaborating extensively with The Passion Centre out of Toronto, Canada, on building the world's first and most comprehensive education system for raising 21st Century leaders and engineering a society that is going to support them. It is their combined vision that the world becomes one healthy community through higher consciousness education. In addition, this vision intends to promote healthy communication to encourage trust-based relationships that support acceptance of each other, reduce fear, and create an expressive, open society. This school of thought will lead people to connecting to and expanding their souls through a higher love consciousness, which helps people live their lives in an optimal manner, and will support others to do so as well. For more information contact Hal S. Eisenberg at **eisenbergleadership@gmail.com** today!

About The Passion Centre

The Passion Centre is a collective of amazing people finding and activating people's passions, building dreams, and creating optimized humans. The Passion Centre acts like a Passion Incubator; we help people from all walks and stages in life understand their PASSION and turn it into ACTION to move the world forward in a positive way. At The Passion Centre, we know that following your Passions and building your dreams aren't easy, but they are ENTIRELY worth every effort you put into it. What The Passion Centre has learned over the years of working with hundreds of people is that Passion is **NOT** an elusive abstract concept that is hard to understand, or one that is based on 'pie-in-the-sky' emotional luxury thinking. It is a very real component of whom we are, how we operate as humans, and if properly understood is a tool to help us live out our most optimal life. The Passion Centre has gathered research from areas in Neuroscience, Psychology, Design Thinking, Orientation and Navigation Training, to Business and more, to reveal the world's most comprehensive way of understanding peoples PASSIONS and identifying ways to put it to good use. The Passion Centre is fundamentally guided by the notion that people's passions are their most sacred value to the world around them.

them. Our Passion to see a better world drives our inspiration and motivation to provide you with a unique opportunity to get the guidance you are looking for to move into the life you were made for. The Passion Centre's programs have been designed to help you answer two of life's most BURNING questions: **What do I REALLY desire?** AND **Where should I be spending my time to get there?** The Passion Centre has built the world's most comprehensive system that will teach you everything you need to know in order to find your passion and make decisions around stepping into your dream and bringing it to the world. You will learn from leading experts who have done exactly what you are thinking of doing, or thinking of thinking of doing, so that you can be given the best formula for success possible. The Passion Centre's proprietary methodology allows all participants to go from absolute confusion, to clarity in just a matter of weeks. And from that point of clarity we take them further into a structured system that step-by-step allows them to unveil the direction that is sure to create excitement! The Passion Centre's method has won the hearts of our clients who have taken our system and have created entirely new Passion Ventures. Passion Ventures are projects that align to their Passions and GIFTs. We have helped people start net new business ventures, foundations, not-for-profits, entirely new careers, post retirement passion projects, books such as the one you just read, and a host more! The Passion Centre caters to those of you who want to experience a live community to work alongside, those that would prefer to experience the program from the comfort of their own home via our webinar trainings, and those that prefer one on one coaching. No matter your goal, objective, or style of learning, The Passion Centre caters to you. As long as you have a deep desire to find that dream that you know is in your heart somewhere, we can take it from there! For more information contact Kira Day at kira.day@thepassioncentre.com today!

Fatima Farrukh – Illustrator bio

Throughout high school, Fatima was the type of young woman who was genuine, sweet, considerate, and all-around kind. Though she was proficient in connecting to oth- er students and school staff mem- bers about spirituality and wisdom beyond her years, Fatima needed to dive deeper to continue expressing her voice. This led her to being unto a rare youth committee to discuss what is needed to transform education with The Mayor of New York City. Not only did we have this in common, but her artwork was reflective of a vision that thinks outside the box. When I discovered Fatima's first painting, the realism blew me away. I sat with her to discuss the vision of this series, and her interpretation of

Beautiful Souls

what I wanted to capture and gift to the world was so aligned to my soul, that I knew that the only masterpiece I wanted representing the cover of this 4-book series would be designed and painted by Fatima's hand.

In bridging the story of *Beautiful Souls* to the universe, it was only natural that Fatima's artwork becomes a bridge to the world's heart and soul

In the words of Fatima herself:
"It all ends in madness they say… As I live amidst the madness that is the overflow of ideas and artist high I feel as a painter, I work towards combating the prevailing stereotype of the starving artist.
Having brought up on the crossroads of two completely differently cultures, I have cultivated my experiences throughout my life and used them as contrivances for ideas when it comes to designing prospective paintings. I revel in the freedom of painting.

I am an admirer of creativity and ingenuity, and it is through my work that I anticipate brining light to the world, and expressing myself in the purest form."

Fatima, I thank you from the bottom of my heart for our endless conversation towards comprehending the universe, as well as the masterpieces you bestowed upon *Beautiful Souls*.

Made in the USA
Columbia, SC
12 January 2025